Passengers and Ships Prior to 1684

Volume 1
of
Penn's Colony

Genealogical and Historical Materials
Relating to the Settlement of Pennsylvania

Walter Lee Sheppard, Jr.

HERITAGE BOOKS
2006

HERITAGE BOOKS
AN IMPRINT OF HERITAGE BOOKS, INC.

Books, CDs, and more—Worldwide

For our listing of thousands of titles see our website
at
www.HeritageBooks.com

Published 2006 by
HERITAGE BOOKS, INC.
Publishing Division
65 East Main Street
Westminster, Maryland 21157-5026

International Standard Book Number: 978-1-55613-664-1

The Welcome Society of Pennsylvania

When the Welcome Society of Pennsylvania was incorporated in 1906, one of its specified purposes was "to collect and preserve historic data relative to the settlement of the State of Pennsylvania and the founding of the City of Philadelphia." This book is offered as Number 1 of the Publications of the Welcome Society of Pennsylvania.

The membership of the Society is composed of persons who descend from passengers on the ship *Welcome* which brought William Penn to America, or from passengers on any other vessel carrying people primarily to Pennsylvania and which arrived between 1 July 1682 and 2 November 1682, inclusive.

PASSENGERS AND SHIPS
PRIOR TO 1684

PENN'S COLONY:

Genealogical and Historical Materials Relating
to the Settlement of Pennsylvania

VOLUME I

PREFACE

Contrary to a common belief, few ship passenger lists of the 17th century for the Middle Atlantic States have survived. Those lists that exist for the 18th century are largely of "foreign" immigrants who were required by law to take the Oath of Abjuration upon their arrival. There are, of course, occasional lists of indentured servants, transported prisoners, or other specialty groups, but in each ship, coming to the colonies, there may also have been paying passengers of whom today we have no record.

Making up or reconstituting passenger lists has been a hobby over the years for a number of persons of varying ability and discrimination, and the results, often of uncertain quality, have been accepted all too uncritically by the self-appointed family historian or genealogist.

Today many of the early lists are coming under the scrutiny of more able and better informed specialists. With careful study it has been possible in many cases to eliminate some names, and to add others, so that by careful revision what may be reasonably acceptable lists are achieved.

We may class the types of evidence used in assembling a ship's list as of roughly three kinds: (1) positive, (2) most probable, and (3) supplemental or circumstantial. As in all things, some evidences fall into the gray areas between definitions, but we will try to classify these as best we can, with primary reference to those evidences used in assembling passenger lists of the 17th century Delaware River.

1. We may consider the following types as indisputable and positive proof that a person under study was a passenger in Ship X.

   (a) He is identified in the ship's log or other ship's document as being aboard.
   (b) He is named in a merchant's papers or in court papers or other similar contemporary document as transported on Ship X.
   (c) He made a will, or other legal document dated aboard Ship X.
   (d) He witnessed a will, deed or other document dated aboard Ship X.
   (e) He kept a diary or wrote letters aboard Ship X.
   (f) He is named as executor of the estate of some one who made his will and died aboard Ship X. (He would have to be present to assume custody of the personal estate.)
   (g) He testified under oath in court that he was aboard Ship X, arriving at such and such a date. (As the period of the testimony becomes more remote from that of the voyage, this evidence may shade into group 2. as the deponent may enter a period of faulty memory or senility.)
   (h) His presence is mentioned in a letter, diary or other instrument written aboard Ship X.
   (i) An object or document known to have been continuously in his possession bears the signature of a passenger aboard Ship X, at a date when the ship was known to be at sea.

(j) Census, list of residents, or other official record, made within five (5) years of his arrival, records his statement that he was aboard Ship X.

(k) A servant's indenture, or similar instrument, showing that he was aboard Ship X.

(l) Deed or grant of land to him later which recites his passage and arrival on Ship X. (As for instance grant of a 50 acre "headright" a certain number of years after arriving as an indentured servant.)

(m) Statement of a passenger on Ship X that the person in question was also aboard with him. (Like item g, this item in later years can shade into group 2.

2. We can consider it <u>probable</u> that a person was a passenger of Ship X when:

(a) A message or letter is addressed to him aboard Ship X.

(b) A message to another passenger aboard includes some news, etc. for him, as being also aboard.

(c) He was named heir to the personal effects of a passenger who wrote his will and died aboard Ship X. (It would be unlikely that a person dying aboard ship would leave clothing and personal objects to a person not present to receive them.)

(d) Letters or testimony, at a somewhat later date, by a person NOT a passenger on Ship X, in which the passenger is stated to have been aboard.

(e) He shipped personal goods aboard Ship X which from type and quantity appear to be personal "trading stock" rather than a merchant's supplies. (The owner would want to be aboard to keep an eye on his property, and prevent it from being stolen.)

3. Evidence that is circumstantial and supporting, but not conclusive in itself would include:

(a) Persons associated in England with the alleged passenger (from same village or very close by) were aboard Ship X.

(b) The person was known to have been in England shortly before the ship sailed and is seen in Pennsylvania shortly after the ship arrives. His presence in America may be demonstrated, for example, by the issuance of a warrant for lands, or by court records. (For this to have real meaning, Ship X must have sailed from a port convenient to the alleged passenger's home.)

(c) An apprentice or servant of a person who was a known passenger on Ship X, which apprentice is seen in England shortly before Ship X sails and in Pennsylvania shortly after Ship X arrives.

(d) A wife or minor child of a passenger on Ship X, seen in America shortly after Ship X arrives. (This is made considerably stronger if the passenger was carrying a removal certificate from an English Friends Meeting to one in Pennsylvania, which certificate is made out to the man and his wife and/or minor child.)

(e) A later statement of the <u>date</u> of his arrival in the colony, which date is within a few days of the arrival of Ship X, and not too close to that of another vessel.

Until fairly recently the value of the British Port Books to the study of passenger lists had not been observed. British law required the maintenance of these records, most of them that are still surviving being in the Public Record Office in London. Marion Balderston (Mrs. John Balderston) was one of the first to use these records to support, correct, or add new names to the tentative passenger lists. Her pioneering analytical work on the tentative list that Mr. Edward Armstrong put together for the ship Welcome was published in November, 1962, in Volume XXVI of the Huntington Library Quarterly and the importance of the article was seen at once by the Editorial Board of the Pennsylvania Genealogical Magazine, which asked her to augment her first article with ones covering the Penn fleet for the years 1682 and 1683, which she did in three excellent articles. The exhaustive biographical and genealogical notes appended to them are largely the work of Hannah Benner Roach (Mrs. F. Spencer Roach), the Editor of that publication.

In this volume the above four articles are reprinted as they appeared with a few corrections made in the text. In addition Mrs. Balderston and I have worked to collect the available data on ships that sailed to the east (New Jersey) bank of the Delaware prior to 1682, and the result of our research is here offered for the first time in print as an additional article. The first part of the book concludes with another previously unpublished paper. Mrs. Balderston discusses the merchandise that accompanied the colonists on their removal to the wilderness of Pennsylvania, and the kinds of goods that the merchants found in demand and shipped as cargo in these vessels.

The value of making this information available in one book with a single index is self-evident, and due to the kindness of the original publishers we are able to include in Part II of the book my article on "John West and the Welcome" which appeared in the New England Historical and Genealogical Register, and Mr. Francis James Dallett's article on "Mrs. Thomas Wynne and her Family," from the Pennsylvania Genealogical Magazine. Two source items known as Books of Arrival for Philadelphia and Bucks Counties have been newly transcribed by Mrs. Roach. These last are actually contemporary records made under the Pennsylvania law of 1684 requiring the registration of all residents. Though they are quite incomplete, the data given in them are of high quality. Mrs. Roach's introduction discusses them fully. As earlier published there were many errors in transcription, and these have been corrected by Mrs. Roach. The reader will find this text more accurate than the articles previously published in the Pennsylvania Magazine (viii, 328 et seq.; ix, 223 et seq.) and in Futhey and Cope's History of Chester County and Battle's History of Bucks County. The log of the Submission is reprinted with permission of the Genealogical Society of Pennsylvania, and this too has been corrected by Mrs. Roach.

Lancour's Ship Passenger Lists (New York Public Library, 1963) lists only three other items for this period: Passengers on the Friends' Adventure, 1682, and on the Endeavor, 1683, in Battle's History of Bucks County, (which appears to be taken from the Book of Arrivals, and which has been abstracted for the reader and added at the end of this volume), Browning's Welsh Settlement of Pennsylvania (which is available in facsimile reprint from the Genealogical Book Company, Baltimore, Md.) and lastly Edward Armstrong's "List of Pilgrims of the Welcome" from volume 1 (1864) pages

467 to 471 of the Memoirs of the Historical Society of Pennsylvania. It was
the errors in this list that caused Mrs. Balderston to write the first article
in this book. Since the entire list is examined in this article it is considered
unnecessary to reprint here the original list.

Also through the kindness of Mrs. Roach we are able to supply the list
of the First Purchasors of Pennsylvania, transcribed by her from the back
of Reed's map. This is the only portion of the known lists that we can be
sure is accurate. The historical background of Penn's Noble Experiment is
carefully considered by Mrs. Roach in this helpful reference, and much of
the material here offered has not previously been in print. Mrs. Roach has
published (1968) in the Pennsylvania Magazine of History and Biography (vol.
92 pp. 3-47, 143-194) a two-part study of the founding of Philadelphia, and in
it discusses sources fully. This is commended to the reader for additional
data about this early period.

We have also supplied a reprint of the map of "Philadelphia as William
Penn knew it, 1684", as prepared by William Wilson Pollack in commemor-
ation of the 250th anniversary of Penn's landing. (Pennsylvania Magazine of
History and Biography, Vol. 59, facing page 59). Finally, included is a reprint from the Pennsylvania Magazine of History and Biography, Vol. 24 pp.
182-186 of an article submitted by Morgan Bunting of abstracts of entries
from the "Darby Township Book", the present whereabouts of which is uncertain. This material apparently first appeared in the Kirk Genealogy, and
some of it was used in the History of Delaware County. A map of "some
part of the county of Chester", drawn in 1683 by Charles Ashcom, surveyor,
illustrates the article. Since the original text is not available for compari-
son the accuracy of the transcription cannot be verified. But so far as can
be determined from other sources the quality appears good and the material
is therefore supplied for the use of those interested.

Walter Lee Sheppard, Jr.
President, The Welcome Society

CONTENTS

PASSENGERS AND SHIPS
PRIOR TO 1684

The Real *Welcome* Passengers

By Marion Balderston

Most of the ships that brought the first adventurers to found English colonies in a hostile new world have had their names preserved and, to a large extent, the names of their passengers. The leaders of the Jamestown expedition to Virginia, for instance, sent detailed reports to the English company that financed the sailing of the first ships, the *Sarah Constant,* the *Goodspeed,* and the *Discovery.*[1] These financial backers, hoping to find gold and quick returns on their investment, would naturally be interested in the behavior of the men whom they had sent over and would probably have to support for years.

Most fully documented of all the early sailings was that of the *Mayflower.* Governor William Bradford, as one of the leaders of that expedition, wrote a detailed account of the 1620 voyage from its inauspicious beginnings, with one leaking ship abandoned and a hundred people crowded into a vessel of less than two hundred tons, to the arrival in New England. Governor Bradford also listed the names of those on the ship and told something about them.[2] Nor was he the only writer in that company.

But there was no one with a sense of history on the *Welcome* when William Penn sailed from England late in the summer of 1682. We have only these facts about the voyage: the ship sailed the end of August, it arrived in the Delaware October 27, and thirty died at sea. We also have the port books for London for 1682, which show who put merchandise on the *Welcome* and what the merchandise was.

These port books are a most important, a most romantic, and, curiously, an almost completely neglected source of information as to who came to Pennsylvania in those first ships, when they came, and what they brought as essential to life in a wilderness. It was necessary at that time to pay a small fee on exports for sale, but not on articles for personal use. Lists of these goods were written in special books

[1]The last two were often called, more appropriately, *Godspeed* and *Discoverer.*

[2]William Bradford, *Of Plymouth Plantation,* ed. Samuel Eliot Morison (New York, 1952).

while the ship was actually loading. In the course of time these books were stored in cellars; many disintegrated or became unreadable from damp or mildew, but several hundred survived. Some of these have remained unread for two hundred and eighty years; occasionally the sand that was used to dry the ink in 1682 falls out of the pages when they are opened today.

The Quakers either chartered their own ships or traveled in independent groups on vessels already in the colonial trade. They had no financing company to which they were responsible; their land had been secured, the Indians had been propitiated, and some white people had already settled in the Delaware valley. They were not sailing into a terrifying unknown. Such letters as exist speak of the good life, the plentiful food, the abundant earth, and (less often than one would expect) their religious meetings.

Nor was Penn ever the figure of a lonely leader; he was not even the first to come. At least fifteen ships preceded his that summer and two others arrived almost the same day. The *Welcome* passengers melted into the other newly arrived groups, anxious to find where their land lay. Everyone was busy getting settled before the winter came, and though letters must have been sent back to England telling of the voyage, none have survived.

One hundred and sixty-nine years later, Edward Armstrong of Philadelphia made the first attempt to compile a list of these *Welcome* passengers. He gave a talk to some members of the Historical Society of Pennsylvania, with no mention of anyone but Penn himself. The next year, however, when Armstrong printed the talk as a pamphlet, he added the names of more than ninety of the hundred people said to have crossed with the great Quaker. He evidently did not regard the list as significant at that time, for the names were printed as footnotes in very small type.[3] He gave such sources as he had consulted: the wills of four men who had died on the voyage, two contemporary but incomplete registries of arrivals, and Isaac Comly's brief "Sketches of the History of Byberry."[4] He also relied on some less dependable material: privately owned papers and "family tradition."

[3]Edward Armstrong, *An Address* (Philadelphia, 1852).

[4]In *Memoirs of the Historical Society of Pennsylvania* (hereafter *MHSP*), II (Philadelphia, 1827), 165-203; original wills in Philadelphia City Hall; registries of arrivals in Historical Society of Pennsylvania, Philadelphia (hereafter HSP).

The last has put on board the *Welcome* enough people to fill a vessel twice its size.

If Armstrong in 1852 did not attach much importance to his list, other historians and particularly genealogists did, accepting the names eagerly and largely without question. The lecture has been forgotten, but the list of names has been copied into hundreds of books and articles written during the last century and has become part of Pennsylvania history. This is unfortunate, since more than half the people Armstrong included could not possibly have traveled on the *Welcome* and did in fact sail on ships from other ports.

Armstrong's biggest mistake was in assuming that seven families (comprising more than thirty people) listed on one Quaker certificate of removal from Settle Monthly Meeting, Yorkshire, came with Penn. For this he naïvely accepted the verbal assurance of a descendant, Robert Waln, who at that time owned the original certificate.

He included the large Oliver family from Chester, citing a manuscript memoir that said their baby was born on October 24 "almost within sight of the Capes of Delaware." The equally large Sharpless family (also from Chester) and some others were added solely on the word of their descendants, who of course had heard of the *Welcome* but not of the other ships.[5]

Edward Armstrong would have been more cautious in accepting these statements if he had considered the geography of England or the difficulty of traveling on seventeenth-century roads. Even the chief highways were badly maintained; other roads were little better than rough tracks. The Settle district is far to the north of England. How could he suppose that these Quaker families would drag their beds, food, tools (one of them took a knocked-down mill along), household goods, and livestock, two hundred and fifty miles south to travel on the *Welcome*, when ships were available after a short haul to Liverpool? Even that was a tedious business, since heavy goods were carried by oxcart in those days and an ox plods along more slowly than a man walks. The journey to London would have been unthinkable.

Moreover, as Quakers they were a marked group. They could be picked up as "vagrants," they were fair game for idlers and local

---

[5]Samuel M. Janney, *Life of William Penn* (Philadelphia, 1852), 213. On December 29, 1682, Penn wrote "a friend," "Blessed be the Lord, that of 23 ships none miscarried."

4

bullies, and they shared the danger common to all who journeyed at that period, the highwaymen who terrorized travelers on country roads.[6]

The Settle certificate, dated June 7, 1682, named the seven families intending to "remove into Pennsylvania." It did not state when the move was to be made, nor on what ship; certificates never did. As the seven families were closely related by blood or marriage, this single testimonial for all of them certainly implied that they intended to go together. Fortunately the Liverpool port books for 1682 still exist, and show that at least four of the seven families took the *Lamb*, which began loading their goods towards the end of June.[7]

As for the Olivers, whose nearest port was Bristol, a search of the port books there shows that they left on the *Bristol Factor*.[8] They reached Pennsylvania the end of October, and would have been within "sight of the Capes of Delaware" by October 24. Oliver's memoir was not at fault, only Armstrong's interpretation.

The lading—to use the seventeenth-century word—of the *Welcome* began on July 7 at London. The first few days were entirely for Daniel Wharley, a rich merchant and a friend of Penn and George Fox. Among the items was iron and a mill worth £53 10s. On the 19th, the ship was laded for Dennis Rochford with iron, haberdashery, window glass, shoes, saddles, dried peas, and flitches of bacon; on the 27th, for Thomas Fitzwater with iron and nails; on the 10th of August, with gunpowder for a Robert Smith; and on the 11th, with tinware and red and white lead valued at £24 10s. for John West, a probable passenger whose name has never appeared. (Evidence for Smith's and West's having traveled on the *Welcome* will be presented at the end of this article.) Penn's agent, the merchant Philip Ford, then put on a variety of wares including shovels, oatmeal, butter, and cheese.

Rochford was lading his goods again on the 15th: candles, copper, felt hats, cottons, serges, more butter and cheese, and pipes—no doubt

[6]Joan Parkes, *Travel in England in the 17th Century* (London, 1925). See also journals of George Fox, Thomas Ellwood, and other eminent Quakers of the period.

[7]The Liverpool port books for 1682, and all others cited here, are in the Public Record Office, London (hereafter P.R.O.); this particular one is E 190/1345/11. Settle Certificate in Comly, *MHSP*, II, 182n. The seven names given are: Cowgill, Chroasdale, Hayhurst, Stackhouse, Walmesley, Waln, and Wrightsworth.

[8]The Bristol port book is E 190/1143/1.

to smoke the Virginia tobacco. Rochford had been a grocer and it seems that he meant to set up as a merchant in the new city. For two days Wharley put his goods on the vessel and was followed by another exporter called John Wilmer. The Free List—things not to be sold for profit—is interesting since Ford laded four hundred pounds of clothing (including twelve dozen "bodices") and a lot of material called fustian. This must have been part of the clothing Penn gave the Indians when treating with them for land.

Shortly after the 21st, the *Welcome* was ready to leave the Thames. Rochford and Fitzwater and their families were on board, and probably West also. Wharley (who later married Gulielma, Penn's half sister), Wilmer, and Ford must have sent people along to act as factors and handle their merchandise in this newest colony; for they did not come, though all were interested in Penn's experiment, and later Wharley and Wilmer were to help him out financially.[9]

Only partially loaded, the *Welcome* sailed around the North Foreland and along the Kent coast to its anchorage in the Downs. This was a quiet roadstead before the ancient towns of Sandwich and Deal, protected on one side by the South Downs and on the other by the Goodwin Sands. As many as two hundred ships had been reported there at one time. Outward-bound merchantmen waited here for late passengers and mail from London, and for a fair wind. It had been a summer of tempests and floods, and many ships attempting to leave the Downs had been blown back into it. But on August 30 the desired east-northeast wind came, and the *Loyal London Mercury* reported that nine ships were able to sail and seven were left, one of which was for Pennsylvania.[10]

This of course was the *Welcome*, with Robert Greenaway as commander, and it had not sailed because William Penn had not arrived. However, according to his friend the biographer John Aubrey, Penn actually embarked at noon on August 30, having, before sailing, time to write at least one letter, and to sign, without reading, two documents presented by Philip Ford, in which Penn acknowledged that he owed that dishonest character a lot of money.[11]

[9]The London port book with the *Welcome* in it is E 190/109/1; see *Pennsylvania Archives* (hereafter *Pa. Arch.*), 2nd Ser., XIX (Harrisburg, 1890), 418, 730 for Wilmer and Wharley.

[10]Sept. 2, 1682 number, quoting a dispatch of August 30, Deal.

[11]John Aubrey, *Brief Lives*, ed. Andrew Clark (Oxford, 1898), II, 134.

The *Welcome*'s displacement was three hundred tons, according to Robert Proud, whose history of Pennsylvania was not published for more than a hundred years after these events.[12] If so, it would not have been a big ship, even for those days; and if it took one hundred passengers, as he said, it was overcrowded. Penn's friend James Claypoole came on the *Concord*, a ship of five hundred tons, and wrote that they would take no more than one hundred and forty people.[13]

The next news of the *Welcome* was from the *London Gazette*. The story was datelined Deal, September 2, and reported that "two days since" three ships had sailed for Pennsylvania, "on board [one] of which was William Penn."[14] It did not name the ships, and the others may have been small cargo boats or two of the many ships for Maryland or Virginia. The geography of the New World was still vague to the news writers of the period, who sometimes referred to Pennsylvania as an island.

The *Welcome*, then, left late on the 30th or the 31st and stopped somewhere along the Channel coast to take on more food and water, perhaps even to pick up more passengers. Penn wrote that it was two weeks before they saw the last of England, six more before they sighted land in America. Eight weeks—always counting from the Downs—was an average time for the crossing against the prevailing westerly winds, although a month later the *Jeffrey* from London took only twenty-nine days.[15] We know nothing of the voyage except that smallpox killed thirty persons, presumably crew as well as passengers.[16]

Armstrong numbered his list and republished it in 1864, by which time he was taking it very seriously indeed. He wrote then that it was "almost perfect."[17]

The names on this list, with Armstrong's own numbering and spelling, are as follows:

[12]Robert Proud, *History of Pennsylvania*, I (Philadelphia, 1797), 204. actually 284 tons.

[13]Letter to James Freeman dated Jan. 13, 1682/3, printed in *Pennsylvania Magazine of History and Biography* (hereafter *PMHB*), X (1886), 273.

[14]*London Gazette* for Sept. 4-7, 1682.

[15]*PMHB*, X (1886), 269.

[16]Richard Townsend's memoir, or "Testimony," in Proud, *History*, I, 228.

[17]*MHSP*, I (1864), App., 467.

John Barber (1), wife, Elizabeth (2), Sussex. He died on the *Welcome*.

William Bradford (3), printer. Authority, Dixon's *History of William Penn*.

William Buckman (4), wife, Mary (5), children, Sarah and Mary (6 and 7). Registry of Arrivals, Bucks Co.

John Carver (8), wife, Mary (9), Hertfordshire. Authority, Isaac Comly.

Benjamin Chambers (10) of Kent. Wrote one of the wills.

Thomas Croasdale (11), wife, Agnes (12), children (13-18). Settle certificate.[18]

Ellen Cowgill (19) and "family." Settle certificate.

John Fisher (20), wife, Margaret (21), son, John (22). Private papers.

Thomas Fitzwater (23), sons, Thomas and George (24-25) completed journey. Wife, Mary, and children, Josiah and Mary (26-28) died on the way over. Registry of Arrivals, Bucks Co.

Thomas Gillett (29) witnessed a will.

Bartholomew Green (30), servant. Registry of Arrivals, HSP.

Nathaniel Harrison (31), servant. Registry of Arrivals, HSP.

Cuthbert Hayhurst (32), his wife(33), and "family." Settle certificate.

Thomas Heriott (34), of Sussex, died on the ship.

John Hey (35), servant. Registry of Arrivals, Bucks Co.

Richard Ingelo (36) witnessed a will.

Isaac Ingram (37), of Gatton, Surrey, died on the ship.

Thomas Jones (38), servant. Registry of Arrivals, HSP.

Giles Knight (39), wife, Mary (40), and son, Joseph (41), of Gloucester. Isaac Comly.

William Lushington (42) witnessed a will.

Jeane Matthews (43), servant. Registry of Arrivals, HSP.

Hannah Mogdridge (44), servant. Registry of Arrivals, Bucks Co.

Joshua Morris (45) witnessed a will.

David Ogden (46) witnessed a will.

Evan Oliver (47), wife, Jean (48), and children, David, Elizabeth, John, Hannah, Mary, Evan, and Seaborn (49-55), from Wales. Seaborn was born at sea. Private papers.

———— Pearson (56), of Chester. Thomas Clarkson, *Memoirs . . . of the Life of William Penn* (London, 1813).

Dennis Rochford (57), wife, Mary (58); children Grace and Mary (59-60) died at sea. Registry of Arrivals, HSP.

John Rowland (61), wife, Priscilla (62), brother, Thomas (63), of Sussex. Registry of Arrivals, Bucks Co.

John Sharples (64), wife, Jane, and children, Phebe, John, James, Caleb, Jane, and Joseph (65-71); Thomas (72) died at sea. Private papers.

William Smith (73), servant. Registry of Arrivals, HSP.

[18]This name is spelled Chroasdale on the Settle certificate. Armstrong omitted the *h*, thus spoiling the alphabetical sequence of the 1852 list; he did not correct it in the 1864 reprint.

John Songhurst (74), of Sussex, friend of Penn, wrote one of the wills.

John Stackhouse (75), wife, Margery (76). Settle certificate.

George Thompson (77) witnessed all four wills—Heriott, Barber, Ingram, and Wade.

Richard Townsend (78), wife, Anne (79); son James (80) born on the *Welcome*, Hannah (81), Richard Townsend's daughter. Townsend's account of trip.

William Wade (82), of Sussex, died on the way over.

Thomas Walmesly (83), wife, Elizabeth (84), sons, Thomas and Henry (85-86), a daughter, and three other children (87-90). Settle certificate.

Nicholas Waln (91), wife, and children (92-95). Settle certificate.

Joseph Woodroofe (96) witnessed a will.

Thomas Wrightsworth (97) and wife (98). Settle certificate.

Thomas Wynne (99), of Wales, witnessed one of the wills.

Bradford's name was questioned soon after the 1852 list appeared, and evidence was produced that the Sharpleses came on another ship. But Armstrong refused to give them up; by 1864 he had become a little stubborn. ("Sharples" is more often spelled with a double *s*.)

Going through his list in greater detail, and with special attention to where these people lived and what ships would be available for them, should help the reader to decide who really came on the *Welcome*.

John Barber and his wife Elizabeth (1 and 2) had been recently married. He was a well-to-do farmer who lived near Billingshurst in Sussex and attended Shipley Meeting, where the Penns also worshipped.[19] Elizabeth was the eldest daughter of the preacher John Songhurst; Penn, in his letters, frequently referred to her as Betty. Unfortunately, Barber died September 20 in mid-ocean, leaving his 2500 acres of unbroken land to "my wife Elizabeth and her child that she is—— and now goodbye." He added a brief paragraph, however, directing his executors to use his estate for the care of the child.[20]

William Bradford (3), originally of Leicester, was apprenticed to the Quaker printer Andrew Sowle of London and later became his son-in-law. Armstrong included him on the word of William Dixon,

[19]MS book of the Men's Meetings, Horsham District, on file at Friends House, London; MS records of the Women's Meetings, Friends Meeting House, Dorking, Surrey.

[20]Original will in Philadelphia City Hall.

whose *History of William Penn* was received with uncritical enthusiasm. He also used Isaiah Thomas' *History of Printing* as an authority. Dixon wrote that Bradford came with Penn, Thomas only that he arrived in 1682 and his wife Elizabeth the following year.[21] They were both wrong. A letter from George Fox written in 1685 introduced the young printer to the Meetings in Pennsylvania, and William and Elizabeth's certificate of removal, dated in London August 12, 1685, was received in Philadelphia the following January.[22] In spite of this evidence, Armstrong kept the name in the 1864 list.

William Buckman, his wife Mary, and his daughters Sarah and Mary (4-7) came on the *Welcome*, as they are included in Phineas Pemberton's "Arrivals" in Bucks County. They also lived near Penn in Sussex (there is still a Buckman's Corners just north of Chiltington) and they attended Shipley Meeting. Edward and Thomas Buckman had bought 500 acres of land from Penn, but it seemed that one of them died, and William took his place on the *Welcome*. Armstrong did not know that the Widow Buckman—of either Edward or Thomas—arrived at the same time. Her sons Edward, Thomas, and William were with her, and her daughter Ruth. They reached Bucks County that fall when William arrived there, and spent the first winter in a cave near Fallsington (not too uncomfortably perhaps, as the widow had brought two thousand pounds of personal luggage with her).[23] It seems unlikely that they would have come on another ship, as closely related families stayed together for mutual help and comfort in those days.

John and Mary Carver (8 and 9) are probable passengers on the *Welcome*. They lived at St. Albans and therefore would have sailed from London, though they had a choice of the *Samuel*, which brought one hundred and eighty people, the *Elizabeth Ann & Catherine*, the *Providence*, or even the fast *Jeffrey*, all of which arrived that fall.

[21]William Hepworth Dixon, *History of William Penn* (London, 1851), p. 226; Isaiah Thomas, *History of Printing* (Albany, 1874), I, 208.

[22]J. Thomas Scharf and Thompson Westcott, *History of Philadelphia* (Philadelphia, 1884), I, 99n. Certificate in Albert Cook Myers, *Quaker Arrivals at Philadelphia, 1682-1750* (Baltimore, 1957), p. 11.

[23]Pemberton's list in *PMHB*, IX (1885), 223 ff., also J. H. Battle, *History of Bucks County* (Philadelphia, 1887), 673 (Buckman's wife listed here as Sarah). Widow Buckman in William W. H. Davis, *History of Bucks County* (Doylestown, 1876), 85. These identical titles hereafter cited as "Battle" and "Davis."

Armstrong's authority was Isaac Comly, who, writing in 1827, put them on the *Welcome* because their daughter was said to have been born October 28, 1682, "in or near Philadelphia." Another story said she was born in a cave four days after Penn landed, and both rely on family tradition and a memorial printed after her death. Carver was a maltster and owned 500 acres of land in the new country. His brothers William, Joseph, and Jacob are supposed to have come with him.[24]

Benjamin Chambers (10) was a *Welcome* passenger, for he helped to write the will of William Wade, who died on the ship. He was a lively character, a turner by trade, who lived near Maidstone in Kent and had bought 1000 acres of land. He settled himself in a large cave dug in the Delaware river bank, which he made so comfortable the authorities had trouble forcing him out. Meantime he was enriching himself buying and selling land.[25]

Thomas Croasdale, his wife Agnes, and their six children were numbered 11 through 18. The Settle certificate is the only authority for believing that this family traveled on the *Welcome*. Since they lived in Yorkshire they would certainly have gone from Liverpool, and surely on the *Lamb* with their other relatives. Thomas had bought 1000 acres of land at the time Hayhurst and Waln made their purchases. He did not live long in the new country, dying in 1684. His sons William and John and his daughter Alice are the only children mentioned in the Bucks County records; ~~it is possible the others died on the way over.~~[26]

"Ellen Cowgill and family" (19) is the way the Settle certificate designated the next name on Armstrong's list. He knew nothing about her, but the Quaker records tell a little. Most probably she came on the *Lamb* with her relatives from Settle Monthly Meeting; she certainly lived in the close group they formed in Bucks County. John Cowgill (probably her son) came on the *Lamb* as indentured

---

[24]Comly, *MHSP*, II, 181; Joseph C. Martindale, *History of . . . Byberry and More-land* (Philadelphia, 1867), 243. Martindale makes no *Welcome* claim, merely gives 1682 as the date.

[25]*Pa. Arch.*, 2nd Ser., XIX, 11, 13, 17, et passim. John Reed, *Explanation of the Map . . . of Philadelphia* (Philadelphia, 1774, reprinted 1870), pp. 2, 20 of last section.

[26]For the various relationships of the Yorkshire–Settle certificate group see "Atkinson Families of Bucks County," *PMHB*, XXXI (1907), 440 ff.

William married Eliz Hayhurst 10-8-1690
John   "   Marah Chapman 28-2-1697
Mary   "   Wm. Smith   20-9-1690
Bridget   "   John Cowgill   16-8-1693
                                   21-11-1693/4

servant to Cuthbert Hayhurst, a relative and fellow passenger. Jane Cowgill shortly married Stephen Sands, another indentured servant on the *Lamb*. These two young men thus saved their passage money and qualified for the fifty acres of land every indentured servant was entitled to claim.[27]

John Fisher, his wife Margaret, and his son John were numbered 20 through 22. Armstrong's authority was "private papers" which may have stated where the family came from; but this information was not included on either the 1852 or the 1864 list. John Fisher was a glazier, and as he came from Lancashire, he would certainly not have been on the *Welcome* from London. He served on the grand jury in Philadelphia in February 1684; either he or a Joseph Fisher had been on the petty jury the previous October. A descendant who owned the original "juror papers" found this good enough evidence to put Fisher on the *Welcome*, and Armstrong accepted it.[28]

Thomas Fitzwater and family (23-28) were from Kingston-on-Thames near London. He is named in the London port book as lading goods on the *Welcome* on July 27 and is also on the Pemberton list as a *Welcome* passenger. He went to Bucks County with his sons Thomas and George, but his wife and two children, Josiah and Mary, died on the voyage. He brought a servant with him whose name was John Ottey, though Pemberton's writing has been read various ways, including the "John Hey" given by Armstrong. Fitzwater married again in 1684, but his second wife created a scandal among the Friends by leaving him; nor could several committees from the Meeting argue her into returning. Fitzwater died in 1699.[29]

Thomas Gillett (29) witnessed John Barber's will. He settled eventually near New Castle.[30]

Bartholomew Green and Nathaniel Harrison (30 and 31) came as

[27]Liverpool port book E 190/1345/11; for Sands, *PMHB*, XVI (1892), 462-463. John, Ralph, Edmund, Jane, and Jennett were apparently Ellen's children. *PMHB*, XXX (1906), 482-483.

[28]*Minutes of the Provincial Council of Pennsylvania* (hereafter *MPC*), I (Philadelphia, 1852), 87, 95. Anna Wharton Smith, *Genealogy of the Fisher Family* (Philadelphia, 1896) accepts the family legend.

[29]Battle, p. 679; "Minutes of the Philadelphia Monthly Meeting for 1696," in *Publications of the Genealogical Society of Pennsylvania* (hereafter *PGS*), IV (Philadelphia, 1909), 209 et passim.

[30]Colonial Society of Pennsylvania, *Records of the Court of New Castle* (Meadville, 1935), II, 69 et passim.

indentured servants to Richard Townsend and were with him on the *Welcome*.

Cuthbert Hayhurst and his wife, Mary, were marked 32 and 33 on the Armstrong list, and the "family" mentioned in the Settle certificate was not counted. They came on the *Lamb*. The Liverpool port book for 1682 shows Cuthbert lading such varied articles as cloth, iron, nails, grindstones, and cheese, on June 26. Hayhurst had been converted to Quakerism thirty years before and some of the earliest meetings took place at his home in the Bolland Forest. He was a minister and had already traveled to Jamaica. He died in March 1683, a few months after reaching Pennsylvania, and his wife followed him soon after. The estate was administered by his son William and his sister Alice Wrightsworth. His name is spelled Hurst as well as Hayhurst in some documents.[31]

Thomas Heriott (34) was a friend of Penn and a purchaser of 5000 acres of land. He died on the *Welcome* September 19, first of the four whose wills we have. It was a nuncupative will (that is, spoken, not written). He left most of his property and his servant "then on board" to his brother-in-law and sister, Dennis and Mary Rochford. He had lived near Hurstpierpoint, a village a little to the east of Shipley Meeting, the great gathering place for Friends.[32]

"John Hey" (35), as mentioned above, was really John Ottey; he was Thomas Fitzwater's servant.

Richard Ingelo (36) witnessed two wills on the *Welcome*, Ingram's and Wade's. Later records referred to him as "Richard Ingels of Philadelphia, gentleman" and the final flourish on his name can be read either way. He was clerk to the Provincial Council.[33]

Isaac Ingram (37) was from Gatton, Surrey, just north of the Sussex border. His is the last of the four wills made on the *Welcome* that we possess; its date is September 26. Unmarried, he left £10 to each of the three children—Adam, Miriam, and Anne—of his deceased sister, Miriam Short. He also left them all the goods he had with him on the *Welcome*. This certainly implied that they were on the ship with him, for what good would household possessions and food in

---

[31]*Pa. Arch.*, 2nd Ser., XIX, 229, 292, 525, 586; Davis, pp. 66, 168; Bucks County wills abstracted in *PGS*, beginning Vol. I.

[32]Original will in Philadelphia City Hall.

[33]*Pa. Arch.*, 2nd Ser., XIX, 380-381; *MPC*, I, 47 et passim.

Pennsylvania be to three young people in England? Miriam was certainly on board the *Welcome*, for she married another passenger, George Thompson, a few months after the ship arrived. Ingram's is the most interesting and the most informative of the four wills. As was usual, he left money to his executors (in this case £10 to John Songhurst and £5 to Thomas Wynne). He also left £2 to David Ogden, one of the witnesses. Even more interesting was his gift of £5 to Jane Batchelor, a young woman of Penn's household in Sussex and herself the owner of 500 acres of land.[34]

Thomas Jones (38) was mentioned as indentured servant to Dennis Rochford. He was probably the "man servant then on board" left to Dennis Rochford in Thomas Heriott's will.[35]

Giles Knight, his wife Mary, and his son Joseph are numbered 39 through 41. Armstrong accepted Comly as his authority and Comly accepted family tradition. They were a Gloucestershire family and their certificate of removal was signed in April 1682 in the Nailsworth Monthly Meeting. The Bristol port book shows that Giles was lading goods on the *Society* on May 2. His brother John and his sister Ann came with him. Ann is included in Pemberton's list as arriving on the *Society* in August 1682.[36]

William Lushington (42) certainly was on the *Welcome*, for he witnessed William Wade's will on September 20, the very day that Barber died. He signed his name in a firm, educated hand and then disappeared from the records. He may have gone to a distant colony, or he could have been an officer in the crew. It is also possible that he, and perhaps a family with him, died of smallpox and were buried at sea. If the dead were listed, the paper has disappeared.

Jeane Matthews (43) was servant to the Rochfords. She may have attended Shipley Meeting, which included several Matthews families.[37]

---

[34] Original will in Philadelphia City Hall, reprinted in part in *Journal of the Friends Historical Society*, IV (1907), 5. For Miriam Short, *Records of the Court of Chester County*, Feb. 1683, Jan. 1685. A good case could be made out for Jane Batchelor on the *Welcome* as part of Penn's "household." She was in Philadelphia the following summer, before the next lot of ships arrived.

[35] *PMHB*, VIII (1884), 334.

[36] Comly, *MHSP*, II, 179; Martindale, *Byberry and Moreland*, p. 299 et passim; Battle, 679; "Abstracts of Wills," MS vol. in HSP; Bristol port book E 190/1143/1.

[37] *PMHB*, VIII (1884), 334.

Hannah Mogdridge, sometimes spelled Moggridge or Muggridge (44), was servant to the Rowlands and a member of Shipley Meeting. The Mogdridges were the problem family of the district, always in debt and in need of work, advice, or money; the records of both the Men's and the Women's Meetings are full of their troubles. Hannah married a Thomas Rogers in Bucks County, but died before her indentured time was out.[38]

Joshua Morris (45) was a tinplate worker. He witnessed Heriott's will on the *Welcome* and died a Keithian in 1696.[39]

David Ogden (46) from London was another witness to Heriott's will. He went to Chester County, married, and fathered nine children. He died in 1705.[40]

Evan Oliver, his wife Jean, and his children David, Elizabeth, John, Hannah, Mary, and Evan, and that seventh child "born within sight of the Capes of Delaware" brought the Armstrong list up to 55. The Olivers lived in central Wales in a village called Glascombe, and it is absurd to imagine him dragging six children and a pregnant wife across England to embark on the *Welcome*, passing Bristol on the way. The port book shows that he was putting goods on the *Bristol Factor* on August 14.

The *Factor* ceased taking on merchandise on August 26. There was, as always, a short time to settle the passengers, followed by a short run down the Bristol Channel before the ship sailed into the open sea, a day or so ahead of the *Welcome*. (According to Penn's letter, the *Welcome* lost sight of England about September 13.) There was no reason why Oliver's seventh child, Seaborn, should not have been born on October 24 "within sight of the Capes." Several ships were converging on the Delaware Bay at that time.

A note in the early records of the Philadelphia Meeting reads, "Evan Oliver R O C F [received on certificate from] Bristol Monthly Meeting, dated 1682-6-26," that is, August 26. This seems confusing at first, for the certificate should properly be signed by the Radnorshire Monthly Meeting, to which the Olivers belonged. How-

[38]MS records of Women's Meetings, Friends Meeting House, Dorking, Surrey; Battle, p. 673; *PMHB*, IX (1885), 225; *Pa. Arch.*, 2nd Ser., XIX, 671, 702.

[39]William Wade Hinshaw, *Encyclopedia of American Quaker Genealogy* (Ann Arbor, 1938), II, 446.

[40]Myers, *Quaker Arrivals*, p. 7; George Smith, *History of Delaware County* (Philadelphia, 1862), 489. Ogden's will in *PMHB*, XV (1891), 192.

ever, the identical wording and date is used for David James's family, who were either close friends or relatives of the Olivers and who lived at Glascombe. But these were temporary certificates, as both the James and the Oliver families had to live in Bristol waiting for their ship to be ready. David James wrote back to Radnor for his certificate soon after he got to Pennsylvania.[41]

————— Pearson (56) is the man responsible for changing the charming name of Upland, Pennsylvania, to the more prosaic one of Chester. Armstrong included him on the "authority" of a casual anecdote in Thomas Clarkson's *Memoirs of the . . . Life of William Penn*, which was published in London in 1813 (I, 332). Clarkson wrote that Penn "turning to his friend Pearson, one of his own society who had accompanied him on the ship *Welcome*" asked him what they should call this place. To which Pearson is supposed to have replied "Chester" from which city he had come. This Pearson has never been identified, though early historians spent a lot of time trying. This is not surprising, since both the anecdote and Pearson the passenger are mythical.

Penn would never have arbitrarily changed an already established name. But many people from Chester had settled at Upland, and they liked to carry familiar names with them. If they had asked Penn to change this Swedish one (pronounced Ooplandt) to Chester he would certainly have done so, as his agent Markham had changed Markus Huuk to Chichester the previous April at the request of the settlers there. If any Pearson existed in connection with this change of name—and there is usually a bit of truth in even the most fantastic legend—it might be the man heading the delegation requesting the name change.[42]

Dennis Rochford came with his wife Mary and two daughters (57-60). We have seen that he laded a variety of goods on the *Welcome* on July 19 and again on August 15. Rochford has been wrongly classed as belonging to the Irish Quakers. He was born in Ireland of English ancestry, but he went to Sussex in 1675, settling down as a grocer in what is now the town of Brighton on the Channel coast. He

[41]Bristol port book E 190/1143/1; MS records Philadelphia Monthly Meeting, ~~condensed~~ certificates in Myers, *Quaker Arrivals*, p. 7; Charles H. Browning, *Welsh Settlement of Pennsylvania* (Philadelphia, 1912), 214, 227; *PMHB*, XXIII (1899), 400.

[42]Samuel Hazard, *Annals of Pennsylvania* (Philadelphia, 1850), 577.

16

first married Patience Life of Reigate, by whom he had a daughter, Grace. Patience soon died and he then married Mary, daughter of John Heriott of Hurstpierpoint, which brought him into the orbit of the Shipley Meeting. Grace was three years old and his daughter by Mary six months old when they left on the *Welcome*; both children died on the voyage.

The Rochfords inherited Thomas Heriott's 5000 acres of land, and after a short stay at Chester, they moved to Bucks County to join their old Sussex neighbors. Rochford must have been a shockingly poor business man, for while others got rich, he grew steadily poorer. One reason was that, owing to a mistake of the land surveyors, most of his land was claimed by Thomas Hudson. When both Rochfords died, the dispute was still on; and the Philadelphia Meeting had to take care of the young American-born children, apprenticing them to kindly and prosperous Friends.[43]

John Rowland, his wife Priscilla, and his brother Thomas (61-63) were on the register of arrivals in Bucks County as having come on the *Welcome*. The Rowlands were farmers in Sussex, members of Shipley Meeting, and neighbors and friends of the Penns. The brothers had bought 2500 acres of land, and Priscilla held another 500. She was still "Priscilla Shepherd of Warminghurst" when she bought it, which meant she either had lived in the minute village of that name, or more likely was part of Penn's household at Warminghurst Place. John and Priscilla were married shortly before the *Welcome* sailed. Their new land touched the proprietor's estate of Pennsbury; Penn's friend and gardener Ralph Smith left Priscilla more land in his will.[44]

John Sharples, his wife Jane, and his children Phoebe, John, James, Caleb, Jane, Joseph, and Thomas, who died at sea (64-72), are named next. This large family lived in Wales, near Chester, and the only authority for including them among the *Welcome* passengers was "private papers." A search of the Liverpool port books shows that Sharples was lading goods May 23 on the *Friendship*, of which the

[43]*MPC*, I, 48 et passim; Albert Cook Myers, *Immigration of the Irish Quakers into Pennsylvania* (Swarthmore, 1902), 278-279; *Pa. Arch.*, 2nd Ser., XIX, 27, 37, 87, 490, et passim; *PMHB*, VIII (1884), 334; Reed, *Explanation*, pp. 3, 10 of last section; London port book E 190/109/1.

[44]MS book of the Men's Meetings, Horsham District, Friends House, London; MS book of the Women's Meetings, Dorking, *Pa. Arch.*, 2nd Ser., XIX, 305, 371, 583, et passim; *PGS*, I (1895), 209; Reed, *Explanation*, pp. 10, 23 of last section.

master was Robert Crossman (the captain praised by Edward Jones in a letter written to his Welsh partner, because Crossman fed his passengers so well). From the letter and the registers of arrivals, we know the *Friendship* (and therefore the Sharpleses) arrived about the middle of August.[45]

William Smith (73) was Penn's personal servant at one time and was with him on the *Welcome*. The unexpired part of his indenture was apparently taken over by Richard Townsend when Penn returned to England. The "Partial List" included him among Townsend's servants, but he applied for his "headland" as indentured to Penn.[46]

John Songhurst (74) was one of the most fascinating characters among the *Welcome* passengers. He was a Quaker preacher, author of two famous pamphlets on the need of love and gentleness in daily life, and a carpenter by trade. His Sussex home has been variously given as Chiltington, Coneyhurst, or Itchingfield, and these three names place him exactly. He evidently lived on the Itchingfield road, at the point where it begins at Coneyhurst Common, which lies in the northern part of Chiltington parish. He could afford to buy only 250 acres of land from Penn. He wrote John Barber's will on the *Welcome*, and his daughter Elizabeth must have been glad of his presence when her bridegroom died.

Armstrong listed him as being alone on the *Welcome*, but two or perhaps three more names could have been added. Songhurst had a wife Mary and another daughter Sarah who were certainly on the ship. He also had a son John (at that time a lad of fourteen) who, however, may not have traveled with his family. Possibly young John came, and returned on some business for his father, for in Songhurst's will (1687) the preacher left his son £200, and made him his executor "if it shall please God he shall live to come from Old England to America." He arrived before his father's death two years later.

A few months after the *Welcome* had arrived, Penn wrote a special letter to his surveyor, directing that Songhurst's land should be laid out just over the city's "liberties," convenient to the town, for his services were needed as builder, minister, and member of the assem-

---

[45]Liverpool port book E 190/1345/11; Scharf and Westcott, *Philadelphia*, I, 100; Smith, *Delaware County*, p. 500; Hazard, *Annals*, p. 604.

[46]For proof that he was Penn's servant see *Pa. Arch.*, 2nd Ser., XIX, 586.

bly. As a kindly gesture, Penn directed that 300 acres should be surveyed for him, though Songhurst had purchased only 250.[47]

Thomas and Margery Stackhouse (75 and 76) were also named in the Settle certificate, so they should have been on the *Lamb* with their relatives from that Yorkshire Meeting. Thomas does not appear in the relevant port book, but he wouldn't if he brought only personal things, and nothing to barter or sell. He had been only recently married to Margery, whose maiden name was Hayhurst (Cuthbert Hayhurst was on the *Lamb*). Margery died the following spring, and unlike most widowers, Stackhouse did not marry again for many years. Two nephews, Thomas and John, are said to have come with him, and certainly the elder and the younger Thomas each owned herds of cows when "cattle-marks" (to identify each animal) were registered in 1684.[48]

George Thompson (74), a grocer, witnessed all four wills made on the *Welcome*. He was not a Friend, but he fell in love with Isaac Ingram's niece Miriam, who probably was. This romance must have flowered on that otherwise grim voyage, for they were married very soon after the *Welcome* arrived. They went to a Swedish priest (who had latinized his name from Lars Karlsson Lock to Laurentius Carolus Lockenius), a fist-swinging, brandy-drinking character who would perform a marriage ceremony at any hour of the day or night and not bother about posting the banns. Hence the marriage was declared against the laws of the province, and bridegroom and priest were haled before the court. Two years later the court called a special meeting "of the inhabitants of Concord, Bethel and Chichester . . . to confer together, how to provide a maintainance for Miriam Thompson and her child." Had her husband deserted her or died?[49]

[47]MS records Horsham District, Friends House, London; MS records Philadelphia Monthly Meeting; *Pa. Arch.*, 2nd Ser., XIX, indexed under both Songhurst and Longhurst; *MPC*, I (1852), 48; *Pa. Arch.*, 8th Ser. (Harrisburg, 1931), I, 43 et passim; Reed, *Explanation*, p. 14 et passim in first section; contemporary copies of early wills in Philadelphia City Hall.

[48]Davis, pp. 77, 169; XXXI (1887), 440-441.

[49]Smith, *Delaware County*, pp. 143, 508; *Records of the Court of Chester County, 1681-1697* (Philadelphia, 1910), Feb. 1683, Jan. 1685. On arrival, Thompson bought 200 acres; see *Pa. Arch.*, 3rd Ser., III, 173. A George Thompson (not necessarily this one) bought half a Philadelphia Bank lot in 1692, sold it next year to his partner at a loss; see *Pa. Arch.*, 2nd Ser., XIX, 130 ff. For Lock see Christopher Ward, *The Dutch and Swedes on the Delaware* (Philadelphia, 1930), pp. 136, 183, 215-219, 265.

Richard Townsend, carpenter, and member of one of the London meetings, came on the *Welcome* with his wife Ann and daughter Hannah. His son James was born during the voyage (78-81). Townsend was a skilled artisan, under contract to the Free Society of Traders in Pennsylvania to work for them for five years at £50 a year. Most of the society's "servants" traveled on that fast ship, the *Jeffrey*, which left in September; but Townsend wrote that he was "moved to go" with his friend Penn. His much-quoted memoir gives us the only account of the voyage, two lines to say that thirty had died, that Penn had been a great comfort to those who were ill, and that they had had many good meetings on board. Not a word as to who "they" were.[50]

William Wade (82) was another passenger who died. He came from a small village called Cold Waltham in Sussex, and must not be confused with the Wades who had left Waltham, Essex, five years before. William Wade made two wills, one on August 24 (a week before he sailed) leaving his 1250 acres in Pennsylvania to his nephew Thomas, on condition that each indentured servant was to have £5 at the end of his time—a most generous gift. The second will was dated September 20 aboard the *Welcome*. Wade left, among other bequests, £250 each to his nephews Thomas and Edmund, and £5 to the poor of Alfriston Meeting in Sussex.[51]

With the inclusion of Thomas Walmesley, his wife Elizabeth, and their six children (83-90), we are back again to the evidence of the Settle certificate; it did not name the children, but the Bucks County records mention a daughter Elizabeth and two sons, Thomas and Henry. Undoubtedly the whole family came on the *Lamb*, and Henry certainly did. Years later the grandsons of Stephen Sands, a *Lamb* passenger, wrote that their grandfather Sands had come over with Henry Walmesley and someone named Wood. The *Lamb* arrived on October 22. Walmesley, Senior, was too ill to go into unsettled country, so they went on up the Delaware to Burlington, where a number of their Yorkshire friends had settled a small town.

[50]Townsend's "Testimony" is quoted in most Pennsylvania histories; see Samuel Smith's unfinished "History of the Province of Pennsylvania," reproduced in Vol. VI of Samuel Hazard, *Register of Pennsylvania* (Philadelphia, 1828-35), 198-199.

[51]Original wills, Philadelphia City Hall; *PMHB*, XXIX (1905), 317-318; Wade had two servants, James Proteus and Eleanor Tain, who may have been with him on the *Welcome* or may have come on an earlier ship; see *Pa. Arch.*, 2nd Ser., XIX, 434.

Two weeks later Walmesley was dead, and it was spring before the widow and her children moved across the Delaware to join their relatives in Bucks County.[52]

Nicholas Waln, with his wife Jane and his children Elizabeth, Nicholas, and William (91-95), was one of the seven listed in the Settle certificate. The Liverpool port book for 1682 records that he put a lot of merchandise on the *Lamb*. The family went at once to Bucks County, where Nicholas had bought 1000 acres of land. He was the only one of that Yorkshire group who did not remain a farmer; he was on the assembly and was active in politics and religious work. He moved into Philadelphia.[53]

Joseph Woodroofe or Woodruff (96), traveled on the *Welcome*; he was a witness to John Barber's will. Probably he went at once to West Jersey, for in Salem there were already several Woodroofes, one of whom was sheriff of the county.[54]

Thomas Wrightsworth and his wife Alice (97-98), who came on the Settle certificate, were on the *Lamb*. The Bristol port books show that, among other items, he exported powder and shot. He made his will a few weeks after he landed, leaving his brothers and sisters five shillings each "if they demand it" and the rest of his property to his wife; she was the sister of Cuthbert Hayhurst. The name in the Bucks County records is variously spelled Wrigglesworth, Wigelsworth, Wrightsworth, and even Wrightstone.[55]

Thomas Wynne (99) traveled on the *Welcome* and was a witness of Heriott's will and one of Ingram's executors. A leading Friend among the Welsh, both preacher and physician, he seems to have lived both in Flintshire and in London. With a fellow Welshman, John ap John, he had purchased 5000 acres of Pennsylvania land. He chose to sail with his friend Penn, but he sent part of his family by the more convenient ship, the *Submission* from Liverpool.

[52]Martindale, *Byberry and Moreland*, 336 et passim; *PMHB*, XXXI (1907), 440-441; for Henry Walmesley see *PMHB*, XVI (1892), 463; for Sands, *PMHB*, IX (1885), 233.

[53]Liverpool port book E 190/1345/11; *MPC*, I (1852), 48; *Pa. Arch.*, 8th Ser., I (1931), 13 et passim; *The Friend*, XXVIII (1855), 364; *PMHB*, XXXI (1907), 440-441.

[54]Samuel Smith, *History of ... New Jersey* (Trenton, 1765, reprinted in 1890), p. 152 of reprint.

[55]Liverpool port book E 190/1345/11; Davis, p. 67; abstracts of this and other wills of the Settle families in the HSP.

The question is, on which ship did his wife sail? Pemberton, who was on the *Submission* and should have known, listed "Jane and Margery Mode, daughters of Thomas Wynne" (they were stepdaughters). Fortunately the passenger list of the *Submission* exists; it lists Rebecca Wynne, aged twenty (Wynne's daughter by his first wife), and Jane and Margery Mode, aged fifteen and eleven. There were only fifty-one on the ship, including servants, and all the names are given. Was Elizabeth Wynne with her husband on the *Welcome*?[56]

Two important people were on the *Welcome*, surprisingly overlooked by Mr. Armstrong.

Zachariah Whitpaine, who witnessed William Wade's will, was one. The name will not be found on the copy of the will in the book kept by Christopher Taylor, first recorder of wills in the infant city, but it is on the original will, still preserved in Philadelphia's City Hall. Zachariah and possibly his older brother John came to look over the new colony and report back to their father Richard, a wealthy London butcher. Later Zachariah married Sarah Songhurst; was this another courtship that began on the long two months voyage?

Zachariah was favorably impressed with Pennsylvania, for during the next year his father began buying land from unadventurous purchasers and soon had 7000 acres and a city lot on the Delaware river bank. Here Zachariah and John erected an enormous brick house, one of the first of that material in the city. Unfortunately the mortar was mixed with ground-up oyster shells which absorbed the damp; and from being a wonder, the house became a menace until it finally collapsed.[57]

The other unnamed passenger was Philip Theodore Lehnman, Penn's secretary, a young man who had bought himself 1000 acres. This unusual use of a middle name puzzled some of the early transcribers of the colony's documents, and, Theodore being shortened

[56]*Pa. Arch.*, 8th Ser., I (1931), 13 et passim; *PGS*, I (1895), "Log of the *Submission*"; *PMHB*, IX (1885), 231; "Abstracts of Wills," MS vol. in HSP; Thomas Glenn, *Merion in the Welsh Tract* (Norristown, 1896), pp. 261 ff.; *The Friend*, XXVII (1854), 228; various notices in minutes of Philadelphia Monthly Meetings. In 1684 both Wynne and his wife returned with Penn but only stayed a short time in England.

[57]*Pa. Arch.*, 2nd Ser., XIX (1893), see index of 23 entries; John F. Watson, *Annals of Philadelphia* (Philadelphia, 1844), I, 428; *MPC*, I (1852), 246; *MHSP*, IX, X, esp. X, 204-205; various references in minutes of Philadelphia Monthly Meeting. Zachariah had not brought his certificate with him; the Meeting wrote the father for permission for the wedding, but he eloped with Sarah before this came.

to Th., his name is often spelled Thelmain. Penn, who wrote a name as he heard it pronounced, made it Lemain.

When Penn unpacked his luggage back at Warminghurst in 1684, preparing to fight Lord ~~Delaware's~~ claim to the three southern counties, the box of vitally necessary papers was missing. Was Lehnman corrupt or merely careless? Penn wrote immediately to Thomas Lloyd in Philadelphia to find and send the papers—a matter of perhaps six months. "Philip Lemain can never while he lives repaire me this wrong" he wrote, and in another letter, "He could not have done me a worse injury if he had had the bribe of £1000." That Penn had some suspicion of Lehnman's honesty is shown in a letter, only a part of which has been published, written a year later to Philadelphia. "Here is a lewd and extravagant bill of P. Lem . . . in his own hand. I have crossed [out] the unusual and extravagant rates; he attests it, if not true let him suffer the law for a forger & if true for an extortioner." Apparently Lehnman had set up a profitable little business for himself, making people pay for several warrants to have their land surveyed, for later in the letter Penn went back to the subject; he was really angry. "It is an abominable thing to have three warrants for one purchase, tis an oppression that my soul loathes. I do hereby require it that P. L. be called to account." Lehnman never returned to England; however, he does not drop out of history on this unpleasant note. When he made his will in 1687 he left his plantation of Broad Creek in Sussex County, below Philadelphia, to his old friend and employer, William Penn.[58]

Thus of the ninety-nine persons Armstrong placed on the *Welcome* only forty-three can be proved to be passengers. Fifty-three, as he counted them, can be proved to have taken other ships, two (the Carvers) are only "probables," and Pearson, as a passenger, never existed. Their names should be listed this way:

ON THE WELCOME		ON OTHER SHIPS	
Barbers	2	Bradford	1
Buckmans	4	Cowgills	1 and family
Chambers	1	Croasdales	8

[58]*Pa. Arch.*, 2nd Ser., XIX (1895), 210 et passim; Reed, *Explanation*, pp. 18, 23 of last section; MS letter from Penn to Lloyd in 1684, Huntington Library; letter from Penn to Lloyd et al. in 1685 quoted in part by Clarkson, *Memoirs*, I, 452-453; "Abstracts of Wills" in the HSP.

ON THE WELCOME		ON OTHER SHIPS	
Fitzwaters	6	Fishers	3
Gillett	1	Hayhursts	2 and family
Heriott	1	Knights	3
Ingelo	1	Olivers	9
Ingram	1	Sharples	9
Lehnman	1	Stackhouse	2 and family
Lushington	1	Walmesleys	8
Morris	1	Walns	5
Ogden	1	Wrightsworths	2
Penn	1		53 or more
Rochfords	4		
Rowlands	3		
Songhursts	3	*Probables on Welcome*	
Thompson	1	Widow Buckman	5
Townsends	4	Songhurst, Jr.	1
Wade	1	Mrs. Wynne	1
Whitpaine	1	J. Whitpaine	1
Woodroofe	1	Shorts	3
Wynne	1	Carvers	2 or 5
Servants	7	John West	1
	48		14 or 17

This list gives the names of forty-eight people known, from various records, to have been on the *Welcome*, with a strong possibility that John West and at least one of the Shorts—Miriam—were also along. It is only legend that put one hundred on the ship. Legend says most of the *Welcome* passengers came from Sussex; on the provable list, there are about twenty-five.

One thing is clear: the Shipley-Chiltington-Warminghurst neighborhood was to be duplicated as nearly as possible in the New World. The Sussex emigrants were to live near their beloved leader, who was also to them the lord of the manor; Pennsbury would take the place of Warminghurst high on its hill. A study of Thomas Holmes' map of Philadelphia and Bucks counties proves this.

The Buckmans and Rowlands, who had nothing to do with governing the new province, went at once to their land near Pennsbury and began to clear it, to be joined later by the Rochfords and others from Shipley Meeting—Shaws, Parsons, and Willards, and by the

Barneses, Songhursts, and Sarah Fuller on the track that led into the city. Penn's intention was that his wife Guli was to be surrounded by friends when she came to live at Pennsbury and that his children would find some of their old playmates.

That Penn was waiting for a special group is shown by a letter he wrote James Harrison in August 1681, saying his friends had not settled their affairs "but when they go, I go." He waited a year and left with those who were ready; he had to get his government started, for, as he wrote, it would not wait until spring. Penn had intimate friends scattered through Yorkshire and Wales as well as those in Dublin and London; but he must have been referring to these Sussex Quakers in his letter.

How did they join the *Welcome*? Rochford, though intimately connected with the Shipley Meeting Friends, was in London seeing his merchandise on the ship. But what of these other Sussex Friends, whose homes lay an average of ten miles from the sea? As they took only personal possessions, they paid no customs, so their names are not included in the surviving port books for Dover, Deal, or the little subport of Shoreham, nor in those for the head ports of Southampton-Portsmouth-Cowes.[59] It is practically certain they did not go to London over fifty to sixty miles of often impassable roads. They certainly did not follow the even longer coast road to Deal, off which the *Welcome* lay. The coast road today is shorter than the old one, for though it serves the same towns and villages, it now follows the sea wall that protects the fertile marshland, where the old road turned inland. Even now with a car, from this bit of Sussex to Deal is the best part of a day's journey. By oxcart over the old roads, it would have taken weeks.

These Shipley Friends were only a little way from the fishing hamlet of Worthing; it is probable they took their luggage there and put it into small boats. These could make the short run eastward to the protected harbor of Meeching (now New Haven) or the longer run west to Cowes, where a ship could anchor in quiet waters by the Isle of Wight. In either place their possessions could be transferred to the *Welcome*. Penn had announced that ships would make special

---

[59]Port books E 190/779/20, E 190/666/14, and E 190/832/3. The entrance to the harbor at Shoreham had silted up and could accommodate only small boats.

stops for thirty or more people—and these were particular friends of his.

It was at Worthing that Penn came ashore two years later. He wrote, in some letters and a fragment of an "Apology"—the beginning of a biography—that the *Endeavor* had put him off just seven miles from his house.[60] (Modern surveying makes the distance from Warminghurst to Worthing a little more.) Whoever transcribed the original manuscript of the "Apology," now at the American Philosophical Society in Philadelphia, misread the name of the village as "Wonder," and so it has been quoted ever since. What Penn actually wrote was "Worden," which would be Worthing as the country folk of Sussex pronounced it then, and indeed, as they pronounce it today.[61]

The British Museum has a small picture of Warminghurst as it looked in Penn's day.[62] It is not true, as has been sometimes stated, that all traces of the house have disappeared. The property was bought from Penn by James Butler, who converted the original house into a barn and built a new house to the east. Of this house, only the foundations can be seen in the meadow; but a great deal of the barn still remains as a reminder of the house where Pennsylvania was planned.

———

This is the case for John West as a *Welcome* passenger:

He was an "inn-holder" at Snow Hill (either the one in Sussex or the one in Surrey), so he would have sailed from London.

He bought 1250 acres of land from Penn sometime before October 1681. *Pa. Arch.*, 1st Ser., I, 39 ff.

He bought £50 of stock in the Free Society of Traders in Pennsylvania. *PMHB*, XI(1887), 175 ff.

[60] *MHSP*, III (Philadelphia, 1836), 235. This was copied from the original in the library of the American Philosophical Society. Penn began with the day he landed from America.

[61] What the early transcriber took for a final downstroke to the letter "n" is really the first part of the next letter, "d." The final letter of the word, however, is quite clearly an "n."

[62] Original map and small sketch, B.M. Add. MS. 37420; this is reproduced in L. V. Hodgkin, *Gulielma, Wife of William Penn* (London, 1947), p. 148.

He put goods for either barter or sale on the *Welcome* in 1682. Port Book E 190/109/1.

He was one of the first to obtain a warrant for his city lot, on June 14, 1683. *Pa. Arch.*, 3rd Ser., III, p. 50. ~~Later he bought the famous Penny Pot tavern at Front and Arch Streets and continued to run it as an inn.~~

Taken separately, none of these facts proves that John West was on the *Welcome*; taken together, they make a convincing case for including him.

Robert Smith's name is listed in the London port book as lading gunpowder on the *Welcome*. Duty had to be paid on gunpowder taken out of the country, whether it was for sale or not. ~~Smith put on too small an amount to suggest he was a merchant.~~ His name does not appear in early Pennsylvania records; however, a Robert Smith applied in 1685 for "headland" of twenty-five acres, and for purchase of seventy-five more, "for importing himself in the year 1682." *Minutes of the Board of Proprietors of the Eastern Division of New Jersey, from 1685 to 1705* (Perth Amboy, N.J., 1949), pp. 87, 263. New Jersey was still making generous offers of land to settlers.

WILLIAM PENN'S TWENTY-THREE SHIPS
With Notes on Some of Their Passengers

By Marion Balderston *

On 29 December 1682, William Penn wrote from Upland (Chester), Pennsylvania, to an unidentified friend, "Blessed be the Lord, that of 23 ships none miscarried. . . ." This is the earliest hint we have as to the number of vessels that brought settlers that year to Pennsylvania. ". . . Only two or three had the small pox," Penn continued, "else healthy and swift passages generally, such as have not been known; some had but twenty-eight days, and few longer than six weeks." He had been in his province exactly two months; so far everything had gone well, and his mood was still jubilant.[1]

The number twenty-three stayed in his mind, for he used it again the following July when he wrote to the Earl of Sunderland, adding that "tradeing [i.e., freighters] 40 great and small since the last summer" had also arrived. Four days earlier he had said they had "had fifty sail of ships and small vessels," and in another letter said "about sixty sail of great and smal shipping" had come up-river since the previous summer of 1682.[2] So we come back to the number twenty-three.

---

* Mrs. Balderston is a native Philadelphian, daughter of the late Albert Rittenhouse Rubincam and his wife Ida May Pike, and is the widow of John Lloyd Balderston, correspondent, teacher, author and distinguished playwright. She is a direct descendant of Johann Philipp Rübenkam and his wife Margaretha Catharina Sartorius who emigrated with her family to Philadelphia in 1726, and of Elizabeth (Griscom) Ross Ashburn Claypoole, more familiarly known as "the flag-maker." With her husband Mrs. Balderston spent many years in England; for her work during World War II she was made a Dame of the British Empire. Currently she is associated with the Henry E. Huntington Library at San Marino, Calif., and has been spending her summers in London abstracting the references to Pennsylvania, 1680-1690, found in the port books in the Public Record Office.

[1] Penn's letter was first printed in part in Robert Proud, *The History of Pennsylvania in North America*. . . . (Philadelphia, 1797), I, 209n, hereinafter cited as Proud, *History*. See also Samuel M. Janney, *The Life of William Penn* (Philadelphia, 1852), 213, hereinafter cited as Janney.

[2] For the letter to Sunderland, dated 28 5m 1683, see Samuel Hazard, *The Register of Pennsylvania*, I (1828), 27, hereinafter cited as Hazard, *Register*. For the reference to 50 ships, in letter to Henry Sidney, 24 5m 1683, see Janney, *op. cit.*, 221; for reference to 60 ships, in letter to Lord Keeper North, same date, see *Memoirs of the Historical Society of Pennsylvania*, I (1864), 440, hereinafter cited as *Memoirs HSP*.

Shipping records were certainly kept in England that year, as customs duties were collected, but apparently they have been lost. However, from two contemporary, partial registers of arrivals in Pennsylvania which have survived, from the English port books, and from letters and newspaper notices, it is possible to piece together a record, at least in part, of the ships and of Penn's "First Adventurers" who arrived in Pennsylvania between December 1681, and December, 1682.

From these assorted records appear the names of twenty-one different ships "with passengers," as Penn described them, and twenty-three voyages; the name of one ship is unknown, and the *Bristol Factor* sailed twice for Pennsylvania. All but one—from New England—were from England or Ireland; they do not include the ships from the West Indies or other British colonies of which we have no accurate record.

The port books are particularly useful. Goods going out of the country and intended for sale in foreign parts were dutiable. Such exports were entered in special volumes with the name of the shipper, who might be a merchant or a passenger, the date, the ship and its master, and the destination. Personal possessions of passengers were not dutiable, even though they might weigh several hundred pounds; they had to pass the customs inspection, but no record of the personal possessions was kept. The captain was paid freightage by the owners for these personal goods, and his boatswain kept a book of records, but the port books do not show these names.

Fortunately, many of the early colonists took with them small quantities of goods for barter or sale on arrival at their destination. In this case the port books list the shipper, the items, the destination and duty, the number of parcels and their weight, the information being entered in several different books.

Although regular merchants also began to send to this new market, it is usually possible to distinguish them from the passengers and intended settlers. Quantities sent by merchants were greater, and their names occur on other similar lists of ships bound for other parts of the world. But since the emigrant with some useful oddments for barter usually took the bundle with him, it seems highly probable the emigrant sailed on the vessel on which his goods are listed.

Of the more than 14,000 port books issued until 1696, when the form was changed, over 1200 exist, many of them large and containing up to 600 folios or 1200 pages each. For 1681 and 1682, the books are fairly complete and fairly legible. Their contents by no means represent passenger lists—permits to leave the country were not required after 1679— for sometimes a ship with as many as 180 people on board, such as the

Samuel from London—an extreme case—listed only half a dozen people who shipped dutiable goods intended for sale in Pennsylvania. But the books do show the names of many persons not known to have come so early; they suggest the parts of England from which the people came, since emigrants naturally sailed from the nearest port, and they correct many errors, both as to people and ships, which have crept from family legend into serious history.

Whether merchant or colonist, the process of putting goods on board a ship was the same. London had seven different customs officials, a small port perhaps four, each of whom had a staff of clerks, weighers, deputies, etc. The owner of merchandise to be shipped had to see them all.

First he took his goods and a bill describing them to the Collector, who totalled the duty to be paid, and passed the owner on to the Controller. He checked the bill of goods previously made out by the owner or shipper, and entered it into his book. From there the owner went to the Surveyor who checked it again, and entered it into his book, and then went on to the Surveyor-General, who did the same thing. These last three officials were primarily interested in the destination of the goods. They usually wrote in the name of the ship, its master, always the shipper's name, and the destination, not necessarily of the ship, but of the particular bale or parcel they were examining.

The shipper next took his bill back to the Collector and paid his customs fee. This official now copied all the details into his book and prepared a warrant. With this "cocket" to show that all goods had been weighed, checked and duty paid, the shipper was free to take his merchandise from the Customs House to have it stowed on the ship. The Searcher now appeared, checked what was going on board, and saw that it was properly stowed. Sometimes he ordered parcels opened and searched, to prevent unlawful exportation. Details of the warrant and the shipper's bill were entered in his book. In the case of the big port of London, additional Searchers were stationed downriver at Gravesend, where another check could be made, using the figures sent down from London.

On the face of it, this would seem to have been a watertight, if cumbersome and time-wasting system. But it was designed to provide a record of the trade of the country, and of the income arising from duties on exports and imports, on which the king's revenue depended. Therefore everything, dutiable or not, had to pass through the customs. The system and its records extended from the small duty laid on goods leaving England to the much larger ones laid on goods coming in, included separate books for wine and wool, and even officials appointed merely to check on other officials.

It was an age of almost universal bribery, and every new system that was introduced immediately developed loopholes. The underpaid officials depended on gratuities. Smugglers flourished, and at one time merchants were forbidden by law to live too near the wharves—too much dutiable merchandise passed over their garden walls on moonless nights!

No figures of exports or imports in this early period can be really reliable, since a great deal more went out and came in than the port books show. But this is a problem for the economic historian; the books themselves are accurate enough for those interested in the people who as emigrants sent goods on the ships, what they sent, and how much.

Special care must be taken, in the case of the larger exporters, to determine whether they accompanied their merchandise, came on another ship, or came at all. Philip Ford, for instance, sent the greatest amount of goods to Pennsylvania, but never came; he was undoubtedly acting as Penn's agent as well as for himself. John Richardson loaded goods on the *Amity* in April, 1682, and again in the *Hopewell* in July, 1683. Did he come on either ship, or was he already here? Again, James Claypoole put hardware and nails on the *Jeffrey* in September, 1682, but did not sail until July, 1683.

Knowing when a warrant to survey land was issued, is useful in determining if and when a colonist came, but not a proof in itself. An agent could get a warrant ahead of time for an employer; Claypoole sent a servant over nearly a year before he came himself, with instructions to build a house. Others sent over relatives or servants to apply for their land. On the other hand, a family might wait in the colony several months before the warrant was issued.

If the colonist was a First Purchaser, having already purchased land to be laid out in Pennsylvania, and if his name appears on a ship's list in the port books, it is fairly certain he came at that time. But there are some exceptions, as with merchants who bought large tracts of land out of friendship for Penn, or as an investment to sell later. Such sales, fortunately, are frequently noted in the minutes of the Board of Property.[3] Dates on certificates of removal from the emigrant's monthly meeting are particularly helpful; a study of them shows that generally they were granted at the meeting which took place just before sailing.

3 First Purchasers (hereinafter F.P.) were those who had purchased in England from Penn, before he sailed for his province in 1682, land to be located and laid out in Pennsylvania. Their names, apparently listed in the order of purchase, with the amount of land each bought, are printed in *Pennsylvania Archives* [1st Series] (Philadelphia, 1852), I, 40-46, and in Samuel Hazard, *Annals of Pennsylvania from the Discovery of the Delaware, 1609-1682* (Philadelphia, 1850), 637-642, hereinafter cited as Hazard, *Annals*. An alphabetical listing of both First Purchasers and later purchasers, compiled by Joseph Reed in 1774, is in *Pennsylvania Archives*, 3rd Series, III, 327-344. For minutes of the Board of Property, see *ibid.*, 2nd Series, XIX (1890), and 3rd Series, I. The "Old Rights," which list alphabetically by county persons to whom warrants for laying out land were issued, and for whom surveys of land were returned into the surveyor general's office, with the dates of such papers, are in *ibid.*, 3rd Series, II, III.

In the port books, for convenience the current day, month and year was written at the head of each page. On the first line was then entered the name of the ship, the master and destination. Then followed each entry, numbered consecutively, of the shipper's name and the bales or parcels of goods which had passed that particular customs official and were loaded on that particular day. In any busy port, just one day's entries, covering a dozen different ships, perhaps, would spread over several pages.

For the purpose of the following record, the individual entries relating to a particular ship have been abstracted, and in some cases condenesd, and arranged chronologically under the single heading of the ship's name. Entries for shippers loading goods on that ship for destinations other than Pennsylvania have not been included.

As the clerks keeping these records used a sort of shorthand in listing the goods loaded, their less familiar abbreviations have been spelled out, and figures for weight or size, given in lower case Roman numerals, have been translated into the more familiar Arabic numbers. Spelling has been modernized. As a result of the vagaries of seventeenth century handwriting, the peculiar method by which quantities were determined, and the physical condition of the pages themselves, the interpretation of many of the entries which follow in the record below, remains open to question.

In the following lists, the ships have been placed in the order, or approximate order, of their arrival in the Delaware River. The surviving port books for London, Bristol and Liverpool, from which the entries have been abstracted, do not give the dates of departure, only the various loading dates. Wind and weather controlled the time of departure and varied each vessel's speed; not all ships made Pennsylvania their first port of call.

The first ship bound for Pennsylvania, the *Bristol Factor*, left Bristol about the middle of October, 1681, and reached New Castle on the Delaware 15 December 1681, according to a letter written from there the following day.[4] A great deal of merchandise intended for Virginia was

---

[4] For the letter, see Ephraim Herman to Capt. Brockholls, 16 Dec. 1681: "Yesterday arryved here a ship from Bristol haueing had 9 weekes passage . . . ," *ibid.*, 2nd Series, VII (1890), 866. In Proud, *History*, I, 193, the date of the ship's arrival is given as 11 December, which may have been the date the ship reached the Capes. Proud claimed, and later writers have perpetuated his statement, that the *Factor* came up as far as Upland, stopped for the night, was frozen in, and obliged to remain there all winter. However, Penn, a better authority, wrote that the winter was "mild, scarce any Ice at all." See "Letter from William Penn to the Committee of the Free Society of Traders, 1683," in Albert Cook Myers, ed., *Narratives of Early Pennsylvania, West New Jersey and Delaware, 1630-1707* (New York, 1912), 226, hereinafter cited as Myers, *Narratives*. The letter is also printed in Hazard, *Register*, I, 433. What the *Factor* actually did was to go from the Delaware around into the Chesapeake to Virginia, from which place it returned to Bristol in the spring of 1682, laden with tobacco.

put on this ship; one port book definitely marks John Bezer's goods for Virginia, the other gives no destination, which in this case implies Virginia, to which colony Bezer had been a regular shipper. Although the ship carried at least sixteen adults and a number of children, the port books show only two entries of dutiable goods destined for Pennsylvania in 1681.[5]

The *Bristol Factor* [1]

Roger Drew, master

28 [September, 1681] THOMAS COBOURNE–NATHANIEL ALLEN & CO: 6 cwt. wrought iron; 5 cwt. nails; 60 lbs. serges; 2 doz. felt hats; 2 cwt. lead shot; 2 cwt. gunpowder; shoes, sugar, wearing apparel, and small items classed together as haberdashery.[6]

6 [October] JOHN BEAZER (Bezer): for Virginia, 5 cwt. wrought iron; 100 lbs. serges; 40 lbs. shoes; 20 goads [goad: 1½ yards] cottons; cwt. gunpowder; 6 doz. woolen hose; 2 cwt. cordage; ½ cwt. soap; cwt. cheese; wearing apparel; 2 firkins [firkin: ¼ barrel] butter; 1 fatt [a large container of varying size] bedding.[7]

---

[5] For the loadings on the *Bristol Factor,* see Bristol port book E 190/1144/2, the Searcher's Book, and E 190/1142/3, the Controller's Book, Public Record Office (PRO), Chancery Lane, London, England. The author is greatly indebted to Mrs. A. M. Millard, researcher in the Public Record Office, for her invaluable assistance in the interpretation of the port books and helpful explanation of the procedure of the customs office.

[6] Companies such as the Cobourne-Allen one, were usually simple partnerships of limited duration. There could have been "silent" partners whose names would not appear on record. THOMAS COBOURN, carpenter of Lambourne Woodlands, Berkshire, and F.P. of 500 acres, his wife Elizabeth and sons William and Joseph, settled in Chester Twp., Chester Co. George Smith, *History of Delaware County, Pennsylvania.* . . . (Philadelphia, 1862), 454, hereinafter cited as Smith, *Delaware County.* A third son Thomas, Jr., arrived much later from Cashel, Ireland; see Albert Cook Myers, *Immigration of the Irish Quakers into Pennsylvania, 1682-1750* (Swarthmore, Pa., 1902), 303, hereinafter cited as Myers, *Immigration.*

NATHANIEL ALLEN, cooper of Bristol, England, and F.P. of 2000 acres, brought his wife Eleanor and children Nehemiah, Lydia and Eleanor; see W. W. H. Davis, *The History of Bucks County, Pennsylvania.* . . . (Doylestown, Pa., 1876), 144, hereinafter cited as Davis, *Bucks County,* wherein the date of arrival is given as 11 December. According to this authority, Samuel Allen, shoemaker of Chew Magna, Somersetshire, and F. P. of 2000 acres, was on the *Bristol Factor,* with his wife Mary and children Priscilla, Martha, Ann, Sarah and Samuel, but see also Note 47 below.

GIDEON GAMBLE, from Devises, Wiltshire, was a passenger; see the transcript, inaccurate in some details, of the Bucks County Register of Arrivals, in *The Pennsylvania Magazine of History and Biography* (*PMHB*), IX (1885), 225, or in J. H. Battle, *History of Bucks County, Pennsylvania.* . . . (Philadelphia, 1887), 672-680, hereinafter cited as Battle, *Bucks County.* The original of the Bucks County Register, in the collections of the Historical Society of Pennsylvania (HSP), was started by Phinehas Pemberton pursuant to a law passed at New Castle 10 3m 1684, requiring the keeping of a registry of all freemen and servants already in or that should come from time to time into the province. Of the two printed versions of the original, noted above, the Battle transcript is more complete in detail, but both leave much to be desired in accuracy of transcription. In cases where the two printed lists are at variance, recourse has been had to the original. Neither follows the order of names found in the original.

In the port books, the "wrought" iron shipped by the emigrants was comparatively soft or malleable iron, and thus more easily hammered or moulded into shapes. Woolen goods were valued by the pound.

[7] JOHN BEZER, maltster of Bishops Canning, Wiltshire, and F.P. of 1000 acres, emigrated with his wife Susanna and children John, Richard, Susanna, Elizabeth and Frances, according to Smith, *Delaware County,* 446, 453. NATHANIEL EVANS, and probably his daughter Elizabeth who later m. John Child, must have been on this ship; both Allen and Evans were jurymen at Upland Court 14 March 1681/2, and no others ships from Bristol came into the Delaware until summer. While Evans may have been the F.P.

Both Nathaniel Allen and John Bezer had been appointed by William Penn commissioners to treat with the Indians about land and conclude a treaty of peace with them. While their ship was loading in Bristol, a small 100-ton ship, the *John & Sarah*, was being loaded in London with additional goods for Pennsylvania. On it two more commissioners, William Haige and William Crispin, planned to sail; their names, however, do not appear in the London port book for 1681. The only hint as to when this ship arrived is found in a letter from Lord Baltimore, dated 11 March 1681/2, complaining about William Haige, who, he said, had come over "this shipping" and had taken observations at the head of Chesapeake Bay.[8]

The *John & Sarah* [2]

Henry Smith, master, from London

26 [September] WALTER MARTIN: 1 small minikin baye [a woolen cloth light enough for clothing]; 25 goads cottons; 2 doz. men's, 3 doz. children's woolen hose; ¾ cwt. lead shot; ½ cwt. gunpowder. [Duty] 8s. 3d.[9]

4 [October] PHILIP FORD: 36 cwt. wrought iron; 24 cwt. nails; 132 lbs. shoes; 11 doz. men's, 14 doz. children's woolen hose; 5 small minikin bayes; 2¼ cwt. wrought brass; 20 cwt. lead shot; ¼ cwt. haberdashery. [Duty] £3 10s. 6½d.[10]

of 500 acres, he bought from John Test an initial 100 acres that same March. See *Record of the Courts of Chester County, Pennsylvania, 1681-1697* (Philadelphia, 1910), 10, hereinafter cited as *Chester Court Records*; also *Pennsylvania Archives*, 2nd Series, XIX, 448.

Bezer brought with him as indentured servants Joseph Cloud and Richard and Mary Farr. *Ibid.*, 361, 411. RICHARD FARR was free by 1686 when he was a juryman at Chester Court, and was constable for Concord Twp. in 1697. *Chester Court Records*, 75, 404. In 1702 he and his wife granted their rights to their headland to JOSEPH CLOUD. He was probably the son of William Cloud, for whom see Note 120 below. Nathaniel Evans brought in as servants "in the y'r 1681" NATHANIEL PARKE and his wife Elizabeth, and their son-in-law (probably stepson) JOHN MARTIN. *Pennsylvania Archives*, 2nd Series, XIX, 482. Parke was free by 7m 1686, when he was named supervisor of highways for Concord. See also Smith, *Delaware County*, 490.

England and her colonies, until Sept. 1752, used the Julian Calendar in computing dates. While the historical year began as now on 1 January, the church, civil and legal year began on 25 March, which Quakers called the first month (1m). Thus between these two dates the system of double-dating was used: 5 11m 1681/2 for 5 January 1682, and 14 1m 1681/2 for 14 March 1682. In this paper, the dates during this three-month period, if not double-dated, are historical dates.

[8] Tonnage of the *John & Sarah* is from a special report on colonial exports in PRO: MS, *Calendar of State Papers*, Dom. Car. II, 418, No. 39. William Crispin signed the ship's charter and presumably began the voyage, but died en route. See M. Jackson Crispin, "Captain William Crispin," *PMHB*, LIII (1929), 127-130. For letters from Lord Baltimore complaining about Haige's activities, see *Archives of Maryland*, V (1887), 348, 375. For the loadings of the *John & Sarah*, see London port book E 190/99/1, PRO.

[9] WALTER MARTIN of Westminster, Middlesex Co., and F.P. of 500 acres, settled on Naaman's Creek in Chester County before the arrival of Penn, according to Smith, *Delaware County*, 483. The earliest record of him in the court records is as a juryman 14 Feb. 1682/3. See *Chester Court Records*, 23.

[10] As a London merchant, Philip Ford's name appears frequently in the London port books as shipper of goods to the West Indies. As Penn's agent, he was active in the early affairs of the province. See William Markham's letter to him listing gifts given to the Indians by Markham "so you [Ford] may know what to send." Albert Cook Myers, ed., *William Penn, His Own Account of the Lenni Lenape or Delaware Indians, 1683* (Moylan, Pa., 1937), 70, hereinafter cited as Myers, *William Penn*.

6 [October] WILLIAM SMITH: ¾ cwt. wrought iron; ½ chalder [chalder: about 36 bushels] grindle [grind] stones. [Duty] 1s. 10d. [At this period, chalder was used when referring to grindstones, chaldron to coal.]

17 [October] JOHN MOORE: 20 goads cottons; 5 doz. men's worsted, 20 doz. men's woolen hose. [Duty] 8s. 6½d.[11]

19 [October] PHILIP FORD: 4 cwt. wrought iron; 2 cwt. nails; 10,000 bricks. [Duty] 4s. 2d.

21 [October] GEORGE COLE: 2 chalders grindle stones; 3 cwt. cheese. [Duty] 2s. 4d.[12]

24 [October] JAMES HAYES: 1 doz. Irish [linen]; 2 doz. men's, 4 doz. children's woolen hose; 1 doz. men's, 1 doz. children's worsted hose [a finer grade]; 3 pieces English linen [piece: up to 30 yards]; 4 lbs. Norwich stuffs [a fine wool]; 15 lbs. serges. [Duty] 5s. 11½d.[13]

The next ship known to have arrived in the Delaware came not from old England, but from New England. Neither the name of the vessel, its master, nor its home port are known, but a surviving record states it arrived in the Delaware 19 May 1682, with at least one passenger.

Ship from New England [3]

RICHARD LUNDY of Axminster, in the County of Devon, son of Sylvester Lundy of the said town, arrived from New England "for this river the 19th of the 3d Mº 1682."[14]

In February, 1682, two ships were being freighted in London with goods destined for the Delaware. One of these was the *Amity* which sailed from the Downs 23 April 1682, and arrived in the Delaware the following 3 August 1682. The oft-repeated statement that the *Amity*, after sailing from London in the fall of 1681, was blown off course to

11 Neither John Moore nor William Smith can be positively identified, although men bearing these names were First Purchasers: John Moore, London merchant; William Smith, yeoman of Bromhamhouse, Wiltshire; William Smith, mariner of Bristol, and William Smith, brass-founder of Bristol.

12 Several Coles, including a George Cole, were London merchants; he, however, was not a First Purchaser.

13 This James Hayes does not appear to have been the man of that name who was servant to Jeremiah Collett of Chester Co. in 1690, as noted in *Chester Court Records*, 109, 195, 206. GABRIEL THOMAS, not listed in the port book, was on the ship *John & Sarah*, according to his own account. See "An Historical and Geographical Account of Pensilvania and of West-New-Jersey," in Myers, *Narratives*, 333. SILAS CRISPIN, son of William Crispin of Kinsale, Ireland, Penn's commissioner, must have been on this ship; he was a juror at Upland with Thomas Coebourne 13 June 1682. See *Chester Court Records*, 15. WILLIAM HAIGE, merchant of London and F.P. of 500 acres, was not only one of Penn's commissioners, but one of the 12 commissioners sent over to organize and set up the operation of the Free Society of Traders in Pennsylvania, the trading company chartered by Penn to initiate commercial and industrial ventures in the province. For its constitution, see Hazard, *Register*, I, 394-397. Haige was also a proprietor of West Jersey.

14 RICHARD LUNDY m. 1st, Elizabeth Bennet, daughter of William, on 26 Aug. 1684, according to Davis, *Bucks County*, 83, and Battle, *Bucks County*, 682, and settled in Falls Twp., Bucks Co. Upon the death of her father, she had become heir to 200 acres. See abstract of William Bennet's will, *Publications of the Genealogical Society of Pennsylvania* (PGSP), I, 204. Richard Lundy m. 2nd, 24 4m 1691, Jane Lyon, who had come in servant to James Harrison. See Note 126 below and *Pennsylvania Archives*, 2nd Series, XIX, 643.

the West Indies, and did not arrive in the Delaware until the spring of 1682, is obviously in error, since the *Amity's* arrival in August, 1682, is amply documented by statements of some of its passengers.[15]

The *Amity* of London [4]

Richard Dymond (Diamond), master, for Pennsylvania

21 [February, 1681/2] THOMAS OGDEN: 500 tiles.

22 [February] GRIFFITH JONES: 15,000 bricks and tiles.[16]

[22 February] JOHN GIBBON (Gibbons): 10 chaldrons coal; 6½ chalders grind stones; 9 lbs. wrought silk [thread ready for weaving].[17]

2 [March] JOSEPH (John?) TAYLOR: 5 tons beer; 1000 bricks; strong board [modern cardboard], paid 19s. 8d.

3 [March] WILLIAM FLEETWOOD: 4 cwt. nails; 6 cwt. cheese; 200 lbs. haberdashery wares; 2 lbs. thrown silk [thread]; 5 doz. candles; ¾ cwt. gunpowder; 2 cwt. lead shot.

24 [March] JAMES BOYDEN: 100 lbs. haberdashery wares; 1 small minikin baye; 1 single baye; 8 cwt. wrought iron; 10 cwt. nails; 5 cwt. lead; 1¾ cwt. gunpowder. From the special Wool Book: 80 lbs. woolen cloth.[18]

[15] The *London Gazette*, Numb. 1715, under dateline of Deal, 23 Apr. 1682, reported that "This Morning the Ships in the Downs, outward bound, Sailed; among them . . . one for Pensilvania." Henry J. Cadbury, "Early References to Pennsylvania in the London Press," *PMHB*, LXXV (1951), 151. For discussion of the *Amity's* sailing, see *ibid.*, LIII, 130; also Oliver Hough, "Captain Thomas Holme, Surveyor-General of Pennsylvania and Provincial Councillor," *ibid.*, XIX (1895), 417, fn. Mr. Hough was in error, however, in attributing Silas Crispin as a passenger on the *Amity*, for reasons noted above. For the ship's arrival date, see Samuel W. Pennypacker, *Pennsylvania Colonial Cases* (Philadelphia, 1892), 110, and Markham's letter, dated 9 Aug. 1682, to Philip Ford in Myers, *William Penn*, 70, cited in Note 10 above: ". . . ye Amity, Richd dymond Mr yt arryved here 3d instant." For the *Amity's* loadings, see London port book E 190/109/1, the Collector's Book; Export of Woolen Cloth (Wool Book) E 190/113/1, PRO.

[16] GRIFFITH JONES, glover of the parish of Mary Magdalen Bermondsey, Surrey, and F.P. of 5000 acres, his 2nd wife Joan, son Joseph Jones, and step-daughter Ann Powell were passengers on the *Amity*. For references to them see *PMHB*, LXXV, 150; also "Notes from Friends Records in England," *PGSP*, III, 227, 228, wherein note is made of Jones' request for certificate of removal for himself and family, and of his servant ELLINOR BARBER, who came with them. Two other servants of Griffith Jones came at this time: JEREMIAH OSBOURNE and ELIZABETH DAY, who married when their time was up. *Pennsylvania Archives*, 2nd Series, XIX, 320, 409.

JOHN OTTER and his wife were probably on the *Amity*, since they requested a certificate from Horslydown Meeting at the same time as Griffith Jones, on 5 2m (April) 1682. Otter could not have been on the *Bristol Factor*, as noted in some of the older histories of Pennsylvania, nor would he have sailed from Bristol, a port more than 100 miles distant. He took up land in Bucks County, but after the death of his wife, moved to Philadelphia and m. Mary Blinston, widow of Isaac, in 1686. See *PGSP*, II, 100, 101. JOHN BUSBY, weaver of Milton in the parish of Shipton, was on the *Amity*; see his deposition in Pennypacker, cited in Note 15 above. His certificate of removal, dated 4 2m 1682, is in Albert Cook Myers, *Quaker Arrivals at Philadelphia, 1682-1750* (Baltimore, 1957), 19, hereinafter cited as Myers, *Quaker Arrivals*. He m. Mary Taylor, daughter of Christopher, in 1690. *PGSP*, II, 162.

[17] JOHN GIBBON, shoemaker of Warminster, Wiltshire, and F.P. of 500 acres, and his wife Margery were settled in Bethel Twp., Chester Co., by 1684. See Smith, *Delaware County*, 464.

[18] William Fleetwood settled in New Jersey; see his indictment in H. Clay Reed and George J. Miller, eds., *The Burlington Court Book* (Washington, D. C., 1944), 70-71, hereinafter cited as *Burlington Court Book*. JAMES BOYDEN was a member of the Assembly from Bucks Co. in March, 1683. See "Votes and Proceedings of the House of Representatives of the Province of Pennsylvania," *Pennsylvania Archives*, 8th Series, I, 13, hereinafter cited as *Votes*.

36

[24 March] ABRAHAM CHITTY: 40 gallons strong waters.

27 [March] FRANCIS COLLINS: 18 cwt. nails; 5 cwt. wrought iron; 2½ doz. castor [beaver] hats; 3¼ doz. felt hats; 50 gal. strong waters at £5 15s.[19]

[27 March] THOMAS HOLME: 6 cwt. lead; 10 cwt. wrought iron; 12 cwt. nails; 6 small, 2 great saddles; 80 lbs. shoes; 1 doz. bridles; ¼ chalder grindle stones; ¼ cwt. gunpowder; 10 horse collars; 10 shod shovels [wood shovels tipped with metal].[20]

30 [March] THOMAS BOWMAN: 6½ chests window glass; 7 cwt. lead.[21]

1 [April] HENRY STACEY (Stacy): 14 small minikin bayes; 9 doz. felt, 2½ doz. castor hats; 12 lbs. shoes; 3 doz. men's worsted, 19 doz. children's woolen, 9 doz. men's woolen hose; 4 cwt. wrought iron; 9 Irish rugs; 2 cwt. ochre; 2 cwt. haberdashery; 15 cwt. lead. The Free List shows he also loaded 260 ells fustians and 100 bodices; the special Wool Book, that he loaded 3 long cloths; 1 penistone frieze [thick wool, the surface brushed or napped, made at Penistone, Yorkshire]; 35 lbs. woolen cloth.[22]

4 [April] JOSEPH RICHARDS: 8 doz. candles; 30 parcels glass; 3 cwt. iron; 3 cwt. nails.[23]

5 [April] THOMAS SEARY: 18 horse collars; 2 cwt. cordage; 100 lbs. shoes; 19 lbs. serges; 4 doz. felt hats; 18 doz. men's, 10 doz. children's woolen hose; 10 goads cottons; cwt. iron; 4 cwt. nails; 2 quarters malt.[24]

---

[19] Francis Collins was a juryman at Burlington Court either before or by August, 1682. *Burlington Court Book*, 11.

[20] THOMAS HOLME, F.P. of 5000 acres and Penn's surveyor general, was on the *Amity*. His sons Michael and Tryall Holme, and two of his daughters, Eleanor who m. Joseph Moss, and Esther who m. Silas Crispin, are said to have been with him. See *PMHB*, XIX, 417, and *ibid.*, XX (1896), 251-252. According to his will, his kinsman JOHN FLETCHER "came over with him," and possibly John Osbourne, whose indentures had not yet expired. EDMUND McVEAGH, who later married Alice Dickinson, who came in servant to Phinehas Pemberton, was another servant. *Pennsylvania Archives*, 2nd Series, XIX, 409; see also Note 126 below. JOHN CLAYPOOLE, eldest son of James, came on the *Amity* as Holme's assistant. See "Extracts from the Letter-Book of James Claypoole," *PMHB*, X (1886), 193, 271; the original of these letters is in HSP.

[21] THOMAS BOWMAN was the son of William Bowman of Wandsworth, Surrey, a glazier and F.P. of 5000 acres. *Pennsylvania Archives*, 2nd Series, XIX, 404. As agent for his father, Thomas sold his father's rights in the Pennsylvania purchase, and appears to have removed to New Jersey. For references to him there, see *Burlington Court Book*, cited in Note 18 above.

[22] Henry Stacy "late of Peeters Alley, Cornhill, London," was a resident of West Jersey; see *ibid.*, 12, and recital in West Jersey Records, Liber B, Part 1, 14: 26 August 1678, Warrant, Edward Billinge *et al.*, to Thomas Ollive *et al.*, abstracted in "Calendar of Records in the Office of the Secretary of State," *New Jersey Archives*, 1st Series, XXI, 397; Liber B, Part 2, 475: 25 Oct. 1690, Samuel Stacy to John Hollinshead, abstracted in *ibid.*, 463; also Revel's Book of Surveys, 37: Return of survey for Henry Stacy, 11 Sept. 1682, abstracted in *ibid.*, 354.

[23] JOSEPH RICHARDS, yeoman of Newgate in Witney, Oxfordshire, a F.P. of 500 acres, was a juryman at Upland Court, 12 Sept. 1682. See *Chester Court Records*, 22. In Smith, *Delaware County*, 496, it is said he and his wife Jane were settled in Chichester Twp., Chester Co., by 1685. See also *Pennsylvania Archives*, 2nd Series, XIX, 357. JOHN and WILLIAM BECKINGHAM came in as servants to the Richards. *Ibid.*, 610. William Buckenham (Buckingham) was involved in a suit at Chester Court with Richards in 1688. See *Chester Court Records*, 129 and Note 57 below. For John "Beekingham," see Smith, *Delaware County*, 544.

[24] THOMAS SEARY (Cerey), farrier of the city of Oxford, and F.P. of 500 acres, took up land in Oxford Twp., Philadelphia Co. The survey was returned into the surveyor general's office 19 6m 1682. He and his widow Sarah who m. William Busby, had children Richard, Miriam who m. Thomas Kenton, and Mary who m. John Hart. *Pennsylvania Archives*, 2nd Series, XIX, 89. It was at Sarah Seary's house that the Friends in Oxford Twp. first met for worship. HENRY WADDY, "millener" of the parish of St. Andrew, Holgate, Middlesex, and F.P. of 750 acres, whose land was laid out near the Seary's, west of Tacony Creek, had entered in the records of the Philadelphia Monthly Meeting that "His Arrivall at Upland in Pennsilvania was the 2d Day of ye 6th mo. 1682." Myers, *Quaker Arrivals*, 17. He apparently brought with him a servant, DANIEL HALL. *Pennsylvania Archives*, 2nd Series, XIX, 26.

11 [April] JOHN RICHARDSON: 4¾ cwt. gunpowder; 2 cwt. lead shot.[25]

[11 April] JOHN BLUNTON: 8 cwt. wrought iron; 6 cwt. nails; 2 cwt. brass; ¼ chalder grindle stones; 2 lbs. serges; 20 lbs. woolen stuffs; 1¼ cwt. books.

12 [April] PHILIP FORD: 15 chests window glass; 9 small minikin bayes; 24 lbs. woolen stuffs; 200 goads cottons; 10 lbs. serges; 12 lbs. linsey woolsey; 2 cwt. wrought iron; 2 cwt. nails; tin wares and colouring value: £15.[26] The special Wool Book shows he also loaded 6 kersies [a coarse ribbed cloth].

15 [April] WILLIAM EVANS: 16 cwt. wrought iron; 10 cwt. nails; 2 cwt. lead shot; 2 doz. felt hats; 50 lbs. serges; ½ cwt. gunpowder; cwt. lead; cwt. cordage; 2 doz. shod shovels; cwt. copper.

[15 April] JOHN SMITH: 2 small minikin bayes; 150 goads cottons; 160 lbs. serges; 5 doz. felt hats; 5 doz. worsted hose; 8 small saddles; 60 lbs. wrought leather; ½ cwt. haberdashery wares; 2 lbs. thrown, 6 lbs. wrought silk; 5 cwt. lead shot.

The next ship to drop anchor in the Delaware was the *Freeman* of Liverpool. It was a fast ship, for the last loading was 7 June, and its arrival date of either 5 or 6 August 1682, is documented by the indenture of William Morton. He was to serve four years in payment for his passage, and would be free 6 August 1686.[27] The term of service invariably began the day of landing or the day after.

The *Freeman* of Liverpool [5]

George Southern, master

24 [May] SAMUEL ELLIS: 2 chests, 2 packs, 1 box qty. [quantity] 70 ells English

[25] This may have been the John Richardson who had a grant of 1200 acres, dated 21 10m 1680, from the court at St. Jones (Kent Co.). See *ibid.*, VII, 199 cited in Note 4 above. He was on the first Provincial Council held 10 1m 1682/3. *Minutes of the Provincial Council of Pennsylvania. . . .* (Philadelphia, 1852), I, 58, hereinafter cited as *Colonial Records*. See also Note 90 below.

[26] In the port books, the term "value" refers only to the preceding item which would be goods not classified in the Book of Rates. The duty to be paid was decided upon between the merchant or shipper and the customs officer. "Value" should not be confused with the duty paid. Other passengers on the *Amity* were JOHN MARTIN, carpenter, and his wife Elizabeth of Edgcott, Buckinghamshire, who got a certificate of removal dated 3 2m 1682, from their monthly meeting. Arriving at Upland on the *Amity*, their personal goods were lost or stolen from the dock. They filed suit against Richard Diamond, master of the ship, as a result of which the jury awarded them £12 and costs. "The Minute Book of the Monthly Meeting of the Society of Friends for the Upperside of Buckinghamshire, 1669-1690," *Records Branch of the Buckinghamshire Archeological Society*, I (1937), 102-104; *Chester Court Records*, 24.

James and William Paxon (Paxson) of March Gibborn, Buckinghamshire, obtained certificates of removal from the same meeting and at the same time as the Martins, they also intending "to transport themselves and families to Pennsylvania." James Paxson brought his wife Jane and children Sarah and William. William Paxson brought his wife Mary and daughter Mary. See Davis, *Bucks County*, 161, 163, 169; also "Account of the Births of Friends Children borne in England given in by their parents," Transcript of Records of Middletown Bucks County Monthly Meeting: Marriages 1684-1780; Removal Certificates 1682-1715; Condemnations 1686-1721; Births 1664-1806; Deaths 1687-1807, 124, 125, Collections of the Genealogical Society of Pennsylvania (GSP), hereinafter cited as Middletown Monthly Meeting Records. For an account of the Paxsons, see Clarence V. Roberts, *Ancestry of Clarence V. Roberts & Frances A. (Walton) Roberts* (Philadelphia, 1940), 209-210, hereinafter cited as *Roberts-Walton Ancestry.*

[27] WILLIAM MORTON came in as a servant to John Brock, bound for four years. See *PMHB*, IX, 224. For the *Freeman's* loadings, see Liverpool port books E 190/1344/1 and E 190/1345/11.

linen; 20 lbs. woolen cloth; 2 doz. woolen stockings for men; 20 lbs. new shoes; 1½ cwt. wrought iron; 1 chest window glass.[28]

[24 May] BARTHOLOMEW COPPOCK: 1 hhd. qty. 60 lbs. woolen cloth; 40 ells English linen; ¼ cwt. wrought iron; 7 lbs. haberdashery.[29]

[24 May] JOSEPH POWELL: 1 chest qty. 20 ells English linen; ½ cwt. wrought iron.[30]

26 [May] JOHN KEELE: packed with other goods [not dutiable], 3 lbs. woolen cloth; ½ pc. [piece] English linen.

[26 May] THOMAS BRASSEY: 6 casks, 2 chests, 1 pann[equin], qty. 60 lbs. woolen cloth; 15 lbs. Norwich stuffs; 60 ells English linen; 6 doz. plain sheep leather gloves; 4 ordinary saddles; 2 cwt. cheese; 6 lbs. leather manufactured [skins dressed and ready for use]; ½ cwt. brass manufactured.[31]

31 [May] THOMAS BRASSEY: per post in foreign bulk,[32] 6 cwt. wrought iron; 3 cwt. nails.

3 [June] THOMAS BRASSEY: 13 piggs [pig: block of lead, 100 lbs. or more], qty. 15 cwt. lead; per post, 5 cwt. lead.

7 [June] THOMAS BRASSEY: 2 mill stones value £5.

The second of the two ships loading goods for Pennsylvania in London in February, 1682, was the *Hester & Hannah.* It dropped anchor at Upland 8 August 1682, after a voyage of twenty weeks. On it was a letter from Philip Ford to William Markham who answered it the next day.[33]

The *Hester & Hannah* [6]

William East, master, for Pennsylvania

1 [February] WILLIAM GUEST: 12 casks, qty. 51 cwt. nails.[34]

---

28 SAMUEL ELLIS obtained warrants for city lots and liberty land 12 5m 1684, "in Right [of] Josia—" probably Josiah Ellis, a F.P. of 1000 acres. *Pennsylvania Archives,* 3rd Series, II, 696.

29 For reference to the two Bartholomew Coppocks in early Chester Co., see Smith, *Delaware County,* 454. One of them, from Cheshire, was a F.P. of 250 acres.

30 JOSEPH POWEL, probably the F.P. of 250 acres, was likely the son of the Thomas Powell who came later in August. *Ibid.,* 493; see also Note 41 below.

31 THOMAS BRASSEY (Bracy) from Wilaston, Cheshire, a F.P. of 5000 acres, was head of the committee of twelve sent over by the Free Society of Traders. He was on the grand jury at Upland 12 Sept. 1682. *Chester Court Records,* 22. For mention of his daughters Rebecca and Mary, who may have come with him, see Smith, *Delaware County,* 448.

32 "Per post in foreign bulk" means the goods had arrived at Liverpool in a foreign vessel, hence might be subject to special or extra duty. Customs officials in the outports, even fairly large ones like Liverpool and Bristol, used a slightly different system from London in keeping their books. The Liverpool books show the actual number of parcels, boxes, etc., such information being considered necessary for the men who packed them in the ship. Men's and children's stockings were mentioned, never women's, in all the port books. It was a way of getting around the customs, which charged more for women's hosiery. This was changed later in the Book of Rates.

33 See Myers, *William Penn,* 70, cited in Note 10, above, for Markham's letter to Ford, dated 9 Aug. 1682, in which Markham said that ". . . ye *hester & hannah* yt arryved here yesterday. . . ." had brought Ford's letter "of 10th mth" (December). The loadings for the *Hester & Hannah* are from London port book, E 190/109/1, the Collector's Book, and Export of Woolen Cloth E 190/113/1, PRO.

34 WILLIAM GUEST took up land in Newcastle Co., now in Delaware, which county he represented in the Assembly held 12 1m 1682/3. See *Pennsylvania Archives,* 2nd Series, VII, 193, and *Votes,* I, 13.

14 [February] WILLIAM GUEST: 6 cwt. wrought iron; cwt. nails; cwt. wrought brass; 5 cwt. lead.

22 [February] CHARLES COLDHAM: 1 box, qty. 50 lbs. wrought silk.

3 [March] PHILIP FORD: 6 cwt. iron; 7 cwt. nails; cwt. cordage; 20 cwt. lead; 26 small gross tobacco pipes; 1 small minikin baye; 10 doz. men's, 8 doz. children's woolen hose; 8 lbs. wrought silk; 80 goads cottons.

4 [March] WILLIAM COX: 1½ cwt. wrought iron; ½ cwt. lead in bars; 2 small minikin bayes; 12 pairs blankets and 2 rugs value £7 17s.

6 [March] WILLIAM EAST: 9 cwt. lead; 5 cwt. iron; 3 cwt. nails; 70 lbs. shoes; 4 cwt. gunpowder; 18 felts, 9 castors [hats].[35]

[6 March] PHILIP FORD: 5 small minikin bayes; 5 cwt. lead. From the Wool Book: 15 kersies.

7 [March] WILLIAM TOESON: 1 box qty. 80 lbs. shoes.

[7 March] SAMUEL SHEPHERD: 40 gallons strong water at £6.

Following the arrival of this last ship, four more came up the Delaware in rapid succession. Of the three that have been dated, the first one brought the first of the Welsh settlers. This was the *Lyon* of Liverpool, a ship of only 90 tons. Four families of the seventeen comprising the Jones-Thomas company of Welsh purchasers, were on this voyage; the whole number of people, including children and servants, came to forty. They are said to have arrived on 13 August 1682, having been "abroad eleaven weeks before we made the land, (it was not for want of art, but contrary winds) and one we were in coming to Upland," as Edward Jones wrote back to his co-purchaser, John ap Thomas.[36]

The *Lyon* of Liverpool [7]

John Compton, master, for Pennsylvania

22 [April] JOHN COMPTON: 8 packs, 1 barrel, 1 hhd., 1 chest, qty. 7 narrow Yorkshire kersies; 3 pcs. English linen; 2 lbs. thrown silk; 9 saddles; 4 cwt. nails; 10 lbs. leather manufactured; 12 yds. frieze; 54 lbs. serges; 26 lbs. Norwich stuffs; 38 yds. flannel; ½ cwt. haberdashery; 14 lbs. silk manufactured; 1 pc. calico; 28 handkerchiefs value 34s. 4d.

---

35 Capt. WILLIAM EAST was still in the province 18 Sept. 1682, when he signed the protest made by Capt. William Lugger, master of the *Mary* of Fowey, before Thomas Revell, "Recorder" of Burlington Court. See "Court Records, Burlington, New Jersey," in John E. Stillwell, *Historical and Genealogical Miscellany* (New York, 1906), II, 5, hereinafter cited as Stillwell, *Miscellany*. This source is not to be confused with the *Burlington Court Book*, cited in Note 18 above. Capt. East was also granted a warrant for a city lot in Philadelphia 17 2m 1683; see *Pennsylvania Archives*, 3rd Series, II, 697.

36 The tonnage of the *Lyon* is given in C. Northcote Parkinson, *Rise of the Port of Liverpool* (Liverpool, 1952), 71. For the letter of Edward Jones, and time of his arrival, see Charles H. Browning, *Welsh Settlement of Pennsylvania* (Philadelphia, 1912), 64-70. The passengers, as noted in this record, included DR. EDWARD JONES, his wife Mary, daughter of Dr. Thomas Wynne, and children Martha and Jonathan Jones; EDWARD AP REES, whose descendants took the name of Price, wife Mably, and children Rees and Catherine; ROBERT AP DAVID, whose descendants took the name Davis, wife Elizabeth and their small child; and WILLIAM AP EDWARD, whose descendants took the name Williams, his 2nd wife Jane, and children Elizabeth and Katherine. For notices of these emigrants, see Browning, 73-74, 81-86. The loadings of the *Lyon* are from Liverpool port book E 190/1345/11, PRO.

The next arrival was also a Liverpool ship, the *Friendship*, which is presumed to have arrived 14 August 1682, this being the date on which John Sharpless, who shipped goods on it, is said to have arrived at Upland.[37]

The Friendship of Liverpool [8]

Robert Crossman, master

22 [May] JOHN SIMCOOTE (Simcock): 3 packs, 4 casks, 1 frayle [large basket] qty. 250 lbs. woolen cloth; 20 doz. woolen stockings for men; 250 ells English linen; 14 cwt. nails; 10 cwt. wrought iron; 30 lbs. Norwich stuffs.[38]

[22 May] WILLIAM TAYLOR: 2 casks qty. 100 ells English linen; 140 lbs. new shoes; ½ cwt. wrought iron; 10 lbs. gunpowder; 14 lbs. cast lead.[39]

23 [May] RANDLE VERNON: 1 fardel [parcel] qty. 30 lbs. woolen cloth; 10 ells English linen; ¼ cwt. wrought iron; 2 doz. woolen stockings for men.[40]

[23 May] JOHN SHARPLES (Sharpless): 1 chest 20 lbs. pewter; 4 lbs. haberdashery; 76 ells English linen; 20 lbs. Norwich stuffs; 2 casks qty. 8 cwt. cheese.[41]

24 [May] JAMES KINERLEY (Kennerly): 1 cask qty. 4 cwt. cheese.[42]

30 [May] JOHN SIMCOCK: 1 bundle, 4 firkins qty. 80 lbs. Norwich stuffs; 1 barrel soap, English making; cwt. wrought iron.

The next ship to arrive was so small it is hard to believe it could have crossed the ocean. This was the *Mary* (called *Marcy* in the Burlington Court Records) of Fowey, an extremely small subport on the south coast of Cornwall, west of Plymouth. Nearby lived the Growdens, father and

[37] See Smith, *Delaware County*, 493, 500, for date of arrival of the ship on which John Sharpless and Thomas Powell are said to have arrived. For the loadings of the *Friendship*, see Liverpool port books E 190/1344/1 and E 190/1345/11, PRO.

[38] JOHN SIMCOCK, from Ridley, Cheshire, F.P. of 2875 acres, and deputy president of the Free Society of Traders, was on the grand jury held at Upland 12 Sept. 1682. *Chester Court Records*, 22. His sons John and Jacob are presumed to have come with him, according to Smith, *Delaware County*, 501.

[39] WILLIAM TAYLOR and his brother PETER TAYLOR, from Sutton in Cheshire, were joint F.P. of 1250 acres. Peter was single at the time of his emigration; William Taylor brought his wife Margaretta, their son Joseph, and two daughters, Elizabeth and Mary. See *ibid.*, 506, and *Pennsylvania Archives*, 2nd Series, XIX, 477, for the marriages of William's daughters to John Powell and Samuel Robinet.

[40] RANDLE VERNON from Sandyway, his brother THOMAS VERNON from Stanthorne, and ROBERT VERNON from Stoke, all in Cheshire, were joint F.P. of 1500 acres. For notices of all three, see Smith, *Delaware County*, 509. For order or warrant for survey, dated 1 7m (Sept.) 1682, for "Thos. Vernon & ors," see *Pennsylvania Archives*, 3rd Series, III, 175. THOMAS MINSHALL, a F.P. of 625 acres, and his wife Margaret, from Stoke in Cheshire, with a daughter who died on shipboard, were probably on this ship. See Smith, *Delaware County*, 485.

[41] JOHN SHARPLESS from Hadderton, Cheshire, a F.P. of 1000 acres, was in error placed on the *Welcome* by an early writer. He came with his wife Jane, children Phebe, John, Thomas who died on the voyage, James, Caleb, Jane and Joseph, according to Smith, *Delaware County*, 500. An order to survey "sundry tracts" for "Jno. Sharpless & Ors." was dated 12 7m 1682. See *Pennsylvania Archives*, 3rd Series, III, 170. THOMAS POWELL, whose presumed son Joseph loaded goods on the *Freeman*, cited in Note 30 above, and son Thomas, Jr., were probably passengers on the *Friendship*. See Smith, *Delaware County*, 493.

[42] JAMES KENNERLY and his brother-in-law HENRY MADDOCK of Loom Hall, Cheshire, were joint F.P. of 1500 acres. Kennerly was a juryman at Upland Court 12 Sept. 1682. *Chester Court Records*, 19; Smith, *Delaware County*, 481.

son, who had purchased 10,000 acres to be laid out in the province; they sent goods on the *Mary* but did not come themselves at this time. Also near them at St. Austell were some of the Pickering family, one of whom, William Pickering, acting as factor for the Growdens, went on the ship. It dropped anchor, probably at Upland, 15 August 1682.[43]

The *Mary* of Fowey [9]
William Lugger, master

19 [May] JOSEPH GROWDEN: Lead and shot 1000 lbs. [Duty 1s.]; 2 packs wrought pewter qty. 5 cwt. [Duty £1 5s. 3d.]. Several sorts iron wares, 48 cwt. 2 qtrs. [Duty £1 4s. 1½d.]; 2 weys [wey: measure for salt, about 40 bushels] Spanish salt, duty paid at importation; 1 hamper shoes qty. cwt. [Duty 4s. 10d.]; 4 cases malt qty. ¾ cwt.; 2 half chests soap qty. 3 cwt., duty paid at importation; 2 packs serges qty. cwt. 3 qtrs. [Duty 19s. 3d. Total: £3 14s. 5½d.].[44]

The exact date of the arrival of the fourth ship, the *Society* of Bristol, is not known. The only reference to it merely says it arrived "in the 6th M° 1682," that is, in August, 1682.[45]

The *Society* of Bristol [10]
Thomas Jordan, master, for Pennsylvania

12 [April] THOMAS PASCHALL: 3 cwt. nails; 4 cwt. wrought iron; ¾ cwt. lead; 2½ cwt. brass manufactured; 5 cwt. wrought pewter; ½ chalder grindle stones; 3 firkins butter; 3 yards paving stones value 3s.[46]

---

[43] See Stillwell, *Miscellany*, 5, cited in Note 35 above, for date of arrival of the *Mary* as given in Capt. William Lugger's protest, dated 18 Sept. 1682. Lugger claimed he had arrived in Pennsylvania "ye 15th August last past," had landed his passengers in three days, and "ye 16th September then following might have sett sayle, But was hindred by Willm Pickering, late of St. Austell, in Cornwall, in England . . . for his building a house, he haueing noe place to secure his goods on Shoare. . . ." The protest was attested by William East of the *Hester & Hannah*, still in the river; by Thomas Wall, presumably of the *Friend's Adventure*; by John Adey of the *Samuel*, and by Edward Read of the *Golden Hinde;* the last three must have just arrived. In addition to these mariners, the other signers included Thomas Phillips who subsequently m. Mercy Jefferson, widow of Edward Jefferson, for whom see Notes 65, 86, below; Philip Michell, William More, and Charles Pickering who shipped goods on the *Friend's Adventure*. The *Mary* got back to Fowey in April, 1683, full of tobacco from "Maryland in Virginia." For the loadings of the *Mary* on its 1682 voyage, see Fowey port book E 190/1046/10, PRO.

[44] Joseph Growden of St. Austell, Cornwall, son of Lawrence Growden of Trevose, Cornwall, each of whom were F.P. of 5000 acres, did not come to Pennsylvania until later. A letter from Penn to Col. Philson Lloyd, dated 24 11m 1683[4], reported "news is brought me of ye Arrival of a ship, at New Castle, & Joseph Growden here, to see me. . . ." Penn went on to say that after "Inquiry of their Voyage & wellfare," he took occasion to talk business with Growden. See *Pennsylvania Archives*, 2nd Series, VII, 4.

[45] For the date of arrival of the *Society*, see *PMHB*, IX, 228, which notes that Ann Knight came on this vessel. The loadings are from Bristol port book E 109/1141/1, the Controller's Book.

[46] THOMAS PASCHALL, pewterer, from Bristol and F.P. of 500 acres, with his wife Joanna and children Thomas, William and Mary, were presumably passengers on this ship. He obtained an order or warrant for the surveying of his land 18 7m (Sept.) 1682, a month after the vessel's arrival. See Howard Williams Lloyd, *Lloyd Manuscripts* (Lancaster, Pa., 1912), 229-232, and *Pennsylvania Archives*, 3rd Series, II, 765. For a letter written by him in February, 1683, to his friend "J. J." of Chippenham in England, see *PMHB*, VI (1882), 323, or Myers, *Narratives*, 247.

[12 April] SAMUEL ALLEN: ½ cwt. wrought pewter; 1 pc. kersey; 220 lbs. shoes and leather manufactured; 6 cwt. nails; 12 cwt. wrought iron; cwt. cheese; 2 small saddles; cwt. cordage; 80 lbs. serges; cwt. lead shot; ½ cwt. brass manufactured; 2 chests window glass; ¼ chalder grindle stones; 4 horse collars; 2 small saddles; 4 Irish rugs; 260 ells English linen; 1 doz. felt hats; 6 parcels wares value £7 13s. 4d.[47]

[12 April] CHARLES PLOMLEY (Plumley): ½ cwt. wrought pewter; 3 cwt. nails; 5 cwt. wrought iron; 3 cwt. lead shot; 50 lbs. shoes; 2 cwt. cheese; 4 bushels pease; 2 pcs. kersey; 50 ells English linen; 5 cwt. English soap; ¼ chalder grindle stones; 6 shod shovels; 1 chest window glass; ¼ cwt. cordage; 10 lbs. serges; 1½ doz. felt hats; 5 parcels of wares value £2 12s. 6d.[48]

[12 April] WALTER REAVE: 50 lbs. brass manufactured; 20 lbs. pewter; 24 lbs. serges; 1 cwt. wrought iron.[49]

22 [April] PHILIP (Thomas?) JORDAN: 40 lbs. shoes; 70 gross tobacco pipes; 7 doz. felt hats; 7 cwt. nails; 8 cwt. wrought iron; 4 pcs. kersey; 24 yds. frieze; 120 goads cottons; 4 doz. children's woolen stockings; 17 doz. woolen and Irish stockings; 80 pairs worsted stockings; 7 ends English fustians; 120 lbs. serges; 1 lb. English thrown silk; 28 lbs. brass manufactured; cwt. haberdashery wares; 30 pairs bodies [bodices]; ½ hhd. aquavita in cases; 3½ cwt. lead shot; 420 ells English linen; 4 parcels wares value £35 3s. 4d.

24 [April] WILLIAM SMITH: 4½ cwt. brass manufactured; ½ cwt. wrought pewter; 12 cwt. wrought iron; 13 cwt. nails; 4 cwt. shot; 70 lbs. serges; 3 pcs. kersey; 2 half pcs. minikin bayes; 20 lbs. linsey woolsey; 3 doz. woolen stockings; 1½ chests window glass; ¼ cwt. lead for windows; ¼ chalder grindle stones; 1 old mill value £2.[50]

26 [April] FRANCIS FINCHER: 1 lb. silk manufactured; 30 lbs. wrought iron; cwt. nails; 6 lbs. haberdashery wares; 8 wheel barrows value £1 5s.[51]

29 [April] THOMAS PASCHALL: 10 doz. woolen stockings; 1 doz. worsted stockings; 80 lbs. shoes; 3 pcs. kersey; 4 half pcs. minikin bayes; 36 yds. frieze; 70 yds. flannel; 40 lbs. serges; 400 ells English linen; 4¼ cwt. brass and copper manufactured; 5½ cwt. wrought pewter; 3 cwt. wrought iron; cwt. nails; 1 doz. felt hats; 1 lb. silk manufactured; 2 doz. plain sheepskin gloves; 5 ends English fustians; 1 chest window

47 While Samuel Allen shipped goods on this vessel, in Davis, *Bucks County*, 144, cited in Note 6 above, it is stated he and his family came on the *Bristol Factor*, arriving in December, 1681. The survey of his 500 acres, laid out for him in Bucks Co., was returned into the surveyor general's office on 4 7m 1682. *Pennsylvania Archives*, 3rd Series, III, 54.

48 Charles Plumley, a joiner by trade, bought land in Bucks Co. from Samuel Allen, but lived in Philadelphia. *Ibid.*, 2nd Series, XIX, 440. When Plumley died in 1708, he left a widow Rose, son Charles, Jr., and a daughter Sarah, both under age. According to his will, he had brothers George, John and James Plumley who predeceased him, and named his brother-in-law Henry Paxson. See Note 65 below. For abstract of the will, see *PMHB*, XII (1888), 373.

49 WALTER REAVE (Reeves) m. 11 Dec. 1682, Ann Howell, and was deceased by 18 June 1698, when Anne Reeves proved his will in Burlington Court. See Stillwell, *Miscellany*, 29, 35, cited in Note 35 above.

50 This WILLIAM SMITH was undoubtedly the brass founder or brazier of Bristol, F.P. of 500 acres. The surveys of his land in Chester Co. were returned 31 Oct. and 10 Nov. 1682. *Pennsylvania Archives*, 3rd Series, III, 167. He may have been the William Smith who was deceased by 15 8m 1692, leaving as heirs, "Clear," William and Mary Smith, and 500 acres in Darby Twp. *Chester Court Records*, 274.

51 Francis Fincher, glover from Worcester and F.P. of 1250 acres, brought a certificate from Worcester dated 14 3m 1683, so that it is not likely he was on this ship. He had three sons, however, Arnall, John and Joshua Fincher, any one of whom might have been sent over with the goods loaded on the Society. Myers, *Quaker Arrivals*, 5, cited in Note 16 above; *Pennsylvania Archives*, 2nd Series, XIX, 351-352.

glass; ¼ cwt. window lead; ½ cwt. nails; 50 lbs. linsey woolsey; 1½ bushels oatmeal; ⅓ hhd. aquavita; 4 small saddles; 2 horse collars; 4 bushels malt; 3 cwt. cheese; ½ cwt. gunpowder; 5 parcels of several wares value £10 5s.

[29 April] JOHN READE: 6 ends fustians; 3 parcels wares value £16 10s. 10d.

[29 April] WILLIAM SMITH: 50 lbs. shoes; 220 ells English-made linen; 6 cwt. cheese; 11 cwt. wrought iron; 4 cwt. nails; 8 lbs. haberdashery wares; 18 felt hats; 30 lbs. wrought pewter; ½ minikin baye; 2 parcels of wares value £2 5s.

2 [May] JOSEPH ENGLISH: 2½ cwt. wrought iron; 2 pcs. English fustians; 10 lbs. tammy [an extra fine quality woolen cloth].[52]

[2 May] KENDALL BRITAIN: 2 cwt. wrought iron; 7 cwt. nails.[53]

[2 May] JOHN SUMMERS (Somers): 5 cwt. wrought iron; ½ cwt. nails; 1 firkin butter; 20 lbs. leather manufactured; ½ cwt. shot; ¼ cwt. gunpowder.[54]

[2 May] JOHN DOLE: ¾ cwt. shot; 6 lbs. gunpowder; cwt. iron; 2 gross tobacco pipes.[55]

[2 May] GILES KNIGHT: 3 cwt. wrought iron.[56]

[2 May] NATHANIEL RICHARDS: cwt. nails; 2 cwt. wrought iron; 1 Spanish cloth; 6 ells English linen.[57]

[2 May] THOMAS BRADFORD: cwt. wrought iron; cwt. nails; 1½ cwt. lead.[58]

---

[52] There were two men named Joseph English in Pennsylvania at this time. The elder Joseph English as a widower, m. Joan Comly, widow of Henry Comly, on 26 2m 1685 "at John Otter's." Battle, *Bucks County*, 682. The younger Joseph English had m. a daughter of Samuel Clift who, then of Burlington, had obtained a grant of land from Sir Edmund Andros in 1680. When Clift wrote his will, dated 23 9m 1682, he devised to his son-in-law Joseph English 30 acres of land in Bucks County "where he [Joseph] has begun to build his house." For abstract of Clift's will, see *PGSP*, I, 47; also *Records of the Courts of Quarter Sessions and Common Pleas of Bucks County, Pennsylvania, 1684-1700* (Meadville, Pa., 1943), 44, 63, 331-333, hereinafter cited as *Bucks Court Records*; Davis, *Bucks County*, 38. For reference to Joseph English, Sr., see Joseph C. Martindale, *History of the Townships of Byberry and Moreland in Philadelphia, Pa.*, (Philadelphia, rev. ed), 229, 270.

[53] This was probably CANAWELL BRITTON who had died intestate by 27 Feb. 1682/3. See *Chester Court Records*, 25, 36, 68, 140.

[54] A survey of 500 acres in Philadelphia Co. for JOHN "SOMMERS" was not returned until 12 7m 1692. *Pennsylvania Archives*, 3rd Series, III, 14, but see Note 60 below.

[55] JOHN DOLE eventually settled in Newton Twp., Gloucester Co., N. J. When he died in 1715, he left a wife Mary and sons John and Joseph Dole. His sister SARAH DOLE, who m. 1st in 1685, Andrew Griscom, and 2nd, John Kaighn, came in indented as a servant. She was the great-grandmother of Betsy Griscom Ross. Apparently another sister m. Jonathan Dickinson who was called "brother-in-law" in John Dole's will, for which see Liber II, 8, abstracted in "Calendar of Wills, 1670-1730, I," *N. J. Archives*, 1st Series, XXIII, 139; *Pennsylvania Archives*, 2nd Series, XIX, 514, 519.

[56] GILES KNIGHT by early historians was said to have come on the *Welcome*. His certificate of removal from Nailsworth Monthly Meeting in Gloucestershire was issued to him 11 2m (April) 1682, less than a month before he loaded goods on the *Society*. Myers, *Quaker Arrivals*, 6. He emigrated with his wife Mary and small son Joseph. Davis, *Bucks County*, 87. Giles and his brother THOMAS KNIGHT were legatees in the will of Thomas Freame who also shipped goods on this vessel. See Note 60 below. ANN KNIGHT, their sister, and the only one who registered her arrival, m. 17 4m 1683, Samuel Dark of Bucks Co., who had arrived in 1680. *PMHB*, IX, 228; Davis, *Bucks County*, 81; Battle, *Bucks County*, 682.

[57] NATHANIEL RICHARDS was possibly the son of Joseph Richards and his wife Jane, mentioned in Note 23 above.

[58] THOMAS BRADFORD by some writers has been placed on the *Bristol Factor* in 1681. A carpenter by trade, he purchased 500 acres in 1685 from William Deverell of Wiltshire, which Robert Summer had died seized of as a First Purchaser. Philadelphia Deed Book C-2-3, 141: 19 3m 1685, William Deverell to Thomas Bradford. The earliest reference to Bradford found is as a witness to the will of John Luffe in 1684, and to Bradford's wife Cicely, in the minutes of the Philadelphia Monthly Meeting, in 1689. *PGSP*, I, 52, and II, 151.

[2 May] JAMES CROFTS: cwt. wrought iron.[59]

[2 May] MATTHEW LAMBERT: 60 lbs. shoes; 6 cwt. nails; 14 lbs. brass manufactured; 2 parcels wares value £2 5s.

[2 May] THOMAS FREAME: 3 cwt. wrought iron; 40 ells English linen; ½ cwt. lead.[60]

[2 May] JAMES FREEMAN: cwt. apothecary wares; 200 English glass bottles.

3 [May] THOMAS PASCHALL: 28 lbs. wrought pewter; 28 lbs. brass manufactured; 2 cwt. wrought iron; 1 firkin butter; 1½ bushels oatmeal; 1 small saddle; 3 parcels wares value £1 1s. 8d.

After this there was a lull, the next ships not arriving until September. The first one, probably a small one called the *Golden Hinde* from London, had arrived by 18 September, when her master signed the protest entered by William Lugger, master of the *Mary*.[61]

The *Golden Hinde* [11]

Edward Reade (Read), master, for Pennsylvania and New Jersey

8 [June] JOHN HIND: for New Jersey, 10 cwt. nails; 20 cwt. iron; 120 lbs. shoes; 4½ cwt. brass; 2½ cwt. cordage; ¼ cwt. haberdashery; 2 horse collars; 1 doz. shod shovels.[62]

9 [June] FRANCIS COLEMAN: for Pennsylvania, 6 doz. felt hats.

[9 June] WILLIAM GIBBS: for New Jersey, 1 pr. millstones at £10.

10 [June] JOHN HIND: for New Jersey, 9 small minikin bayes; 9 doz. men's woolen hose; 20 yds. flannel; 45 goads cottons; 8 lbs. silk; 1 barrel net-lines at £7.

[10 June] THOMAS MATTHEWS: for New Jersey, 19 cwt. wrought iron; cwt. brass; cwt. lead shot; ¼ cwt. gunpowder; 50 lbs. wrought leather; 1 doz. men's worsted hose.[63]

14 [June] EDWARD READ: for New Jersey, 60 lbs. shoes; tin and turnery wares value £12.

15 [June] THOMAS MATTHEWS: for New Jersey, ½ cwt. cordage; 4 horse collars.

16 [June] FRANCIS PLUMSTEAD: for New Jersey: 3½ cwt. wrought iron; 1½ cwt. wrought brass.[64]

59 There was a James "Craft" who apparently came in as a servant to Samuel Dark in 1680. A warrant for surveying land for JAMES CROFTS "& ors." was granted 17 7m 1682, to be laid out in Chester Co. See *PMHB*, IX, 228, and *Pennsylvania Archives*, 3rd Series, III, 115. He was apparently the same man who was indebted to Thomas Freame in the amount of £6, according to the latter's will. See below. James Croft, Sr., was settled in New Jersey by 1691. See *Burlington Court Book*, 130.

60 THOMAS FREAME of "Avon, in the County of Gloster," wrote his will 5 Sept. 1682; it was probated 10 8m 1682, and was the first will entered in Philadelphia records. Witnesses were John Somers, Thomas Maddox, Thomas Williams and William Herrin, the first two of whom proved the will. For possible reference to William "Heron" see *Pennsylvania Archives*, 2nd Series, XIX, 717, and for abstract of Freame's will see *PGSP*, I, 45. Ann Knight, sister of Giles and Thomas Knight, was named executrix and residuary legatee.

61 For the protest, see Stillwell, *Miscellany*, 5, cited in Note 35 above. The loadings for the *Golden Hinde* are from London port book E 190/109/1, PRO.

62 John Hind (Hinde), a London draper and goldsmith, owned shares in the province of West Jersey. John E. Pomfret, "The Proprietors of the Province of West New Jersey, 1674-1702," *PMHB*, LXXV, 142.

63 Thomas Matthews, carpenter from Stoke Newington near London, had also purchased shares in West Jersey. *Ibid.*, 131-132. See his letter to George Fox in *ibid.*, XVII (1893), 195.

64 Francis Plumstead, ironmonger of the Minories, London, and F.P. of 2500 acres, is not known to have ever come to Pennsylvania. His country land was not taken up until after 1700. See *Pennsylvania Archives*, 2nd Series, XIX, 324, 495.

Another ship in the Thames, the *Samuel*, finished putting on goods for Pennsylvania before the *Golden Hinde* began to load. It came in to Falmouth on the southeastern coast of Cornwall, on 10 June 1682, bound for Pennsylvania with 180 passengers, according to the Falmouth correspondent of the *London Gazette*. This would have been a last stop for fresh food and water. Although one passenger reported the *Samuel* came into the Delaware on 22 September 1682, the master, John Adey, signed the protest of William Lugger, and must have dropped anchor by 18 September.[65]

The *Samuel* [12]
John Adey (Adie, Adee), master, for Pennsylvania

12 [April] JOHN SHEENE (Shinn): 18 cwt. wrought iron; 8000 tiles; 1 chaldron grindle stones.[66]

13 [April] JOHN BARNES: 13½ cwt. lead; 14 cwt. wrought iron; 12 cwt. nails; cwt. cordage.[67]

26 [April] JOHN SHEENE: 15¼ cwt. wrought iron; 23 cwt. nails; 50 lbs. shoes; 8½ doz. children's hose; 10 lbs. serges; 16 cwt. lead shot; 12 small minikin bayes.

10 [May] ROBERT YOUNG: 7 doz. woolen hose; 5 cwt. iron; 5 cwt. nails; 4 doz. shod shovels; 2 chests window glass.[68]

---

[65] See the *London Gazette*, Numb. 1733, issue of 29 June 1682, in Henry E. Huntington Library, San Marino, Calif., for the Falmouth item. RICHARD AMOR of Bucklebury, Berkshire, and William Amor were joint F.P. of 250 acres. Richard was reported as having arrived on the *Samuel* 22 7m (Sept.) 1682, but as he died "about the latter end" of 9m (Nov.) 1682, his date of arrival was heresay; the register of arrivals was not begun until 1684. Battle, *Bucks County*, 681; *PMHB*, IX, 233. For abstract of his administration see *PGSP*, I, 213.

EDWARD JEFFERSON, maltster of Ashwell, Herefordshire, and F.P. of 1500 acres, with his wife Mercy, were passengers on the *Samuel*, aboard which Edward died, as per his administration, abstracted in *Pennsylvania Genealogical Magazine* (PGM), XIX, 253. See also Note 86 below. Jefferson's widow subsequently m. Thomas Phillips, for whom see *Pennsylvania Archives*, 2nd Series, XIX, 374, 428, and Note 43 above.

HENRY PAXSON of Bycot house, parish of Slow, Oxfordshire, his wife and children John, Henry and Elizabeth, and his brother Thomas Paxson were also on the *Samuel*. Henry's wife, two sons and brother Thomas died on shipboard, the daughter Elizabeth not long after their arrival. Henry Paxson m. 13 Aug. 1684, Margaret Plumley, said to have been the widow of William Plumley, brother of Charles, for whom see Note 48 above and Davis, *Bucks County*, 162. Henry gave the time of his arrival as the middle of September. See *PMHB*, IX, 227, and Davis, *Bucks County*, 57. For the loadings of the *Samuel* see London port book E 190/109/1, Exports of Woolen Cloth E 190/113/1, PRO.

[66] John Sheene (Shenn, Shinn) had been a resident of Burlington Co. since 1680. See *Burlington Court Book*, 1, cited in Note 18 above.

[67] There were two men named John Barnes, both First Purchasers. One of them, a tailor of West Chiltington, Sussex, was joint F.P. of 1250 acres with John Songhurst. Barnes' step-daughter Sarah Fuller was granted a warrant dated 10 12m (Feb.) 1682/3, for 300 acres to be laid out in Philadelphia Co. *Pennsylvania Archives*, 3rd Series, II, 705. The other John Barnes, merchant of Bristol, had his city lot surveyed at the southwest corner of Second and Chestnut Streets on 28 12m 1682/3; he shipped goods on the *Bristol Merchant* which arrived in Feb. 1682/3. *Ibid.*, III, 390. He would not have sailed from London, but from Bristol; if he had arrived on one of the earlier ships from Bristol he might have ordered goods from London. The shipment of wrought iron, lead and nails seems somewhat unusual for a tailor, whose goods would more likely have been haberdashery wares. JOHN BARNES of Sussex, and his family, however, would have sailed from London.

[68] ROBERT YOUNG started suit against Captain Adey (Adye) 7 Nov. 1682, but withdrew his action. *Burlington Court Book*, 14.

46

12 [May] JOHN MARTYN (Martin): cwt. haberdashery; 6 lbs. wrought silk; 2 doz. children's, 2 doz. men's woolen hose; 1½ cwt. lead shot; 10 cwt. wrought iron; 6 cwt. nails; ¼ cwt. brass; ¼ cwt. gunpowder. From the Wool Book: 1 long cloth.[69]

16 [May] ROBERT CARTER: 18 cwt. cheese; 24 lbs. shoes; 10 cwt. iron; 4 cwt. nails; 15 doz. men's worsted hose; 2 chests window glass; ¼ cwt. gunpowder; cwt. lead shot.[70]

18 [May] JOHN BURGESS: 2¼ cwt. brass; 3 cwt. wrought iron.

19 [May] THOMAS HOTTEN (Hooten, Hooton): 2 small minikin bayes; 4 cwt. cheese; 6 small gross tobacco pipes; 46 lbs. serges; 1 chest window glass; cwt. copper.[71]

20 [May] THOMAS HOOTEN: 1 small minikin baye; 10 goads cottons; 30 lbs. Dornix hangings [silk, wool or linen material from Dornick, Flanders, the French Tournai]. From the Wool Book: 30 lbs. woolen cloth.

A third passenger ship to arrive that month was the *Friend's Adventure* which is said to have dropped anchor 28 September 1682, but must have arrived earlier.[72]   It brought emigrants from Cheshire and Staffordshire.

The *Friend's Adventure* of Liverpool [13]

Thomas Wall, master

31 [May] WILLIAM YARDLEY: 3 bundles, 2 tubbs, 3 chests, 1 pack, 2 boxes qty. 2 cwt. wrought iron; ½ cwt. pewter; 30 lbs. woolen cloth; 100 ells English linen; 40 lbs. new shoes; 2 cwt. nails; ½ chest window glass; ½ cwt. haberdashery wares.[73]

---

69 This was probably JOHN MARTIN, tailor, who m. 17 Dec. 1685, Elizabeth Simms, former servant of William Penn, five months after her certificate of removal had been granted. Myers, *Quaker Arrivals*, 10; *Pennsylvania Archives*, 2nd Series, VIII (1880), v; *ibid.*, XIX, 70, 72, 360, and 3rd Series, I, 44.

70 Possibly the ROBERT CARTER who obtained a warrant for 250 acres which were laid out in Bucks Co. 12 2m 1684. *Ibid.*, III, 61. He was elected a constable of the county in 1685. See *Bucks Court Record*, 34, cited in Note 52 above. In 1686, when Carter's son John set fire to a haystack of Henry Paxson, Carter was fined £5 and cost of suit. *Ibid.*, 70-72.

71 Thomas Hooton of Black Friars, London, was a proprietor of West Jersey, and had arrived on the *Kent* in 1677; his wife and family came at a later date. He had moved to Philadelphia by 1684, and died in 1689, not 1694, as recited in PMHB, LXXV, 129. For abstract of his will see PGSP, I, 75.

72 The original of the Bucks County Register of Arrivals plainly gives the date of arrival of the *Friend's Adventure* as 28 Sept. 1682; see also PMHB, IX, 223, 224, 229. But as Thomas Wall, the presumed master of the ship, signed the Lugger protest of 18 Sept. 1682, the two dates would seem to be irreconcilable. Stillwell, *Miscellany*, II, 5. Since the register was not begun until 1684, perhaps the memories of the registrants were faulty.

Three servants sent over on the *Friend's Adventure* by Randolph Blackshaw who came later this year, were WILLIAM BEASY, RALPH NUTTALL and RALPH COWGILL. Cowgill, presumed son of Ellen Cowgill, probable passenger on the *Lamb* of Liverpool, later m. 1st, Sarah, daughter of Randolph Blackshaw, and 2nd, Sarah Pancoast of Burlington Co. PMHB, XXX (1906), 482. Early in 1695 Blackshaw sold Cowgill 112 acres of land, and then in 1697 made over 200 acres in trust for Cowgill's minor sons Abraham and Nehemiah. *Bucks Court Records*, 292, 311. According to the original Bucks County Register, it is quite clear that a fourth servant was also on the *Friend's Adventure*: WILLIAM SMITH, whom Phinehas Pemberton sent over. Cf. PMHB, IX, 230, which includes a Joseph "Stew"[art] who, however, was on the *Submission*; see Note 126 below. For the loadings of the *Friend's Adventure*, see Liverpool port books E 190/1344/1 and E 190/1345/11, PRO.

73 WILLIAM YARDLEY from Ransclough near Leek, Staffordshire, "late of Congleton Monthly Meeting," and F.P. of 500 acres, his wife Jane and children Enoch, Thomas and William Yardley were on the *Friend's Adventure*. With them came their servant ANDREW HEATH, aged ca. 20 years in 1685, indented

[31 May] JOHN CLOWES (Clows): 2 chests, 3 packs, 1 barrel, 2 bundles, 1 box qty. ½ cwt. haberdashery; 4 pcs. English linen; 112 lbs. woolen cloth; 15 lbs. Norwich stuffs; 2¼ cwt. nails; 2 cwt. iron; 1 chest window glass; 2 cwt. cast lead; ¼ cwt. gunpowder.[74]

1 [June] JOHN BROCK: 5 doz. woolen stockings.[75]

---

for four years, to be "Loose the 29th of the 7th Mo. 1686." He became the third husband of William Venables' widow Elizabeth, for whom see Note 80 below. *PMHB*, IX, 223; *Bucks Court Records*, 32; *Pennsylvania Archives*, 2nd Series, XIX, 261, 291. The Yardley's certificate of removal, for which see photostatic copy of Falls Monthly Meeting Certificates of Removal, 1682-1729, 12, GSP, was dated 2 6m 1682. Those who signed it said the Yardleys' "absence is a great loss to us," plainly indicating the certificate was sent after they had left.

From the same general neighborhood and on the same ship came LUKE BRINDLEY (Brinley, Brinsly), mason of Leek, Staffordshire. His certificate of removal, dated 1 3m 1684, and entered in Falls Monthly Meeting Certificates, 19, said that he "gave us knowledge of his intentions Long before he went." He was sheriff of Bucks County in 1684, and ranger in 1689. *PMHB*, IX, 223; *Bucks Court Records*, 3, 117; *Pennsylvania Archives*, 2nd Series, XIX, 228; Davis, *Bucks County*, 57.

[74] This was JOHN CLOWS, JR., of Gosworth, Cheshire, son of John Clows, a F.P. of 1000 acres, who came in 1683. *PMHB*, IX, 224, 226. Application for certificates of removal for the young man, his brother JOSEPH CLOWS and sister SARAH CLOWS, George Glave, Daniel and Joseph Milnor, Robert Smith and John Brock, was made at Morley Monthly Meeting in Cheshire 2 6m 1682. *PGSP*, III, 231. A joint certificate for the Yardleys, the young Clows, John Brock, George Glave and Daniel Milnor, was signed the same day. Of the Clows it said that all three "had the consent of their parents in their leaving this country and did not depart hence for any debt." John Clows, Jr., died in 1683, and the servant he brought, HENRY LINGART, soon after, according to Davis, *Bucks County*, 57. The sister Sarah Clows m. John Bainbridge 15 6m 1685. *Pennsylvania Archives*, 2nd Series, IX (1880), 221.

George Glave (Gleave) "of Knutsford" and his wife Ann "went clear away out of these parts with ye consent of relatives and friends," according to the above-mentioned joint certificate. A weaver by trade, he had. m. at Thomas Janney's 6 6m 1679, Ann Duncalfe of Hale Bowden Parish, and had one son John, b. 14 9m 1680. See Digested Copy of Registers of Quarterly Meeting of Cheshire and Staffordshire, 1655-1837, GSP. It may have been he who was in Bucks Co. in 1686, where he was fined 10s. for assaulting Edmund Bennett. *Bucks Court Records*, 58. There was also a George Gleave in Chester Co. who m. in 1687 Esther, widow of Joseph Powell, mentioned in Note 30 above, and was dead by 1 1m 1689/90, when Esther Gleave was directed to bring in an inventory of his estate. She m. in 1691, Joseph Ware, according to Smith, *Delaware County*, 465. See also *Chester Court Records*, 60, 101, 197, 218, 245. In 1683 a George Gleave and wife Isabella came in as servants to John Hough and by 1695 were settled in Burlington Co., for whom see *Burlington Court Book*, *passim*. For the arrival of John Hough and this couple, see Battle, *Bucks County*, 674, or *PMHB*, IX, 229, wherein Gleave's name is given as *Glaire*.

[75] JOHN BROCK of Bramhall, according to the certificate mentioned in Note 74 above, was single. "The goods he hath are his own being given him by his parents as his portion," the certificate noted. He contracted with Charles Pickering in Liverpool "in the yeare 1682" for Pickering to "bring [over] a passenger for this province," but was "dispointed of the sd passenger as he was not brought as above." As a result, Brock brought suit in Bucks Co. in 1686 to recover the £5 12s. 6d. he had paid Pickering for the passenger's fare, and which William Yardley and Thomas Phillips, arbitrators, had awarded Brock in 1683, but which Pickering had so far neglected to pay. *Bucks Court Records*, 35, 36. Brock m. Thomas Wynne's step-daughter Elizabeth Rawden in 1684, when he was sheriff of the county. *Ibid.*, 9.

JOB HOULE and ELIZA EATON (Heaton?) came on the *Friend's Adventure* as servants to John Brock. Houle (Howell) appears to have been the son of Thomas Howell (Hould) who settled in Southampton Twp., Bucks Co. See *Pennsylvania Archives*, 2nd Series, XIX, 58, 675; *Bucks Court Records*, 177, 203, 274, 378.

DANIEL and JOSEPH MILNOR, for whom certificates of removal were requested in August, 1682, as recited in Note 74 above, were brothers and joint F.P. of 250 acres. A certificate for Daniel was granted at the same time as for the Yardleys and the others, on which record it was stated he "was born of honest parents and had the consent of his mother and friends" for his removal. This joint certificate was signed, among others, by Joseph Milnor, whose identity has not been determined for this record. Daniel's brother Joseph Milnor, a smith by trade, m. at Middletown Meeting 10 5m 1690, Pleasant Powlin (Pawlin?), having taken up land in Makefield Twp., Bucks Co. He was deceased by 1701 when Pleasant Milnor m. Francis Haige on 8 11m 1700/1701, at Falls Monthly Meeting. *Pennsylvania Archives*, 2nd Series, IX

3 [June] GEORGE POWELL (Pownell): 2 chests, 1 coffer, 3 boxes, 1 bag, 2 bundles qty. 40 lbs. new shoes; 1½ pcs. English linen; 3 doz. woolen stockings for men; 2 cwt. wrought iron; 2 cwt. nails; ½ cwt. cast lead; ¼ cwt. gunpowder; ½ chest window glass; 3½ doz. felts.[76]

[3 June] SHADRACH WALLY (Whaley): 2 bundles qty. 30 ells English linen; 14 lbs. haberdashery; cwt. wrought iron.[77]

20 [June] CHARLES PICKERING: 4 casks, 4 boxes, 2 chests qty. 2 doz. felts, English making; 80 lbs. leather manufactured; 25 lbs. serges; 100 ells English linen; ½ chest window glass; 2 cwt. cast lead; ½ cwt. gunpowder; 2 doz. woolen stockings foreign; 2 cwt. cheese; 3 cwt. wrought iron.[78]

22 [June] SAMUEL BUCKLEY (Bulkly): 1 barrel, 1 roulett [roll], 2 boxes, 3 bundles qty. ¾ cwt. & 14 lbs. haberdashery; ½ cwt. cast lead; ½ cwt. nails; 1½ doz. woolen stockings for men; 4 ordinary saddles; 10 felts English making; 12 lbs. new shoes; 4 bundles, 14 lbs. wrought iron; 1½ pcs. English linen; 14 lbs. woolen cloth; 5 lbs. Norwich stuffs; 1 pott qty. ¼ barrel butter; 1 bundle brown paper; 3½ doz. looking glasses value 35s.[79]

4 [July] CHARLES PICKERING: 1 box qty. 20 felts, English making.

224, 241. See also *ibid.*, XIX, 428, 653-654, for Milnor's heirs, and index of *Bucks Court Records, passim*, for references to Joseph. ROBERT SMITH, the fifth person named in the Morley Meeting minutes, as mentioned in Note 74 above, may have been the man of this name, noted in Smith, *Delaware County*, 503, reputedly from Sawley in Derbyshire. He bought land from John Blunston in 1686. *Chester Court Records*, 84.

76 GEORGE POWELL (Pownall) from Layloch, Cheshire, F.P. of 1000 acres, brought his wife Ellenor and children Reuben, Elizabeth, Sarah, Rachel and Abigail to Pennsylvania on this ship. *PMHB*, IX, 223. According to Davis, *Bucks County*, 58, he was killed by the fall of a tree one month and two days after his arrival; a son George was born twelve days later. See also Battle, *Bucks County*, 681, and *Pennsylvania Archives*, 2nd Series, XIX, 467, 634. With him and his family came three servants, MARTHA WORRALL, ROBERT TAYLOR (?) and JOHN BREARLY, each to serve four years. For notices of Brearly (Brierly, Bryerley), see *Bucks Court Records*, 30, 79-80, and *Burlington Court Book, passim*. Martha Worrall m. 6 12m 1685/6, at Middletown Meeting, Samuel Dark, whose first wife had been Ann Knight, mentioned in Note 56 above. Battle, *Bucks County*, 682.

77 SHADRACH WALLEY, innholder of Bickley in Cheshire and F.P. of 250 acres, had his land laid out in Newtown Twp., Bucks Co. Davis, *Bucks County*, 230. Naomi Walley, said to be his daughter, obtained a certificate of removal from Frandley Monthly Meeting, Cheshire, on 5 6m 1684 "to Carry along with her into Pensilvaniah In America." She m. 9m 1686, at Pennsbury, William Berry of Kent Co., according to Battle, *Bucks County*, 682; Shadrach Walley m. at Middletown Meeting 12 1m 1688/9, Mary Sharpe, at which time Hannah, Damaris and Abraham Walley were among the signers of the certificate, for which see Middletown Monthly Meeting Records, 26, cited in Note 26 above. See also *Pennsylvania Archives*, 2nd Series, XIX, 328-330, 605, and *PGSP* I, 231.

78 CHARLES PICKERING, from Halton, Cheshire, F.P. of 1000 acres, was part owner of the *Friend's Adventure*. The ship's seamen, who were refused their wages until they brought all the goods landed at Upland, up to Philadelphia, petitioned the Provincial Council for redress, but were ordered to comply with their contract. When they had done that, the Council decided they should have six months pay "and 5lb. given them over & above." *Colonial Records*, I, 63-64, 72-73, cited in Note 25 above. When Pickering died in 1694, he left a widow Ann, brother Richard Pickering and sister Mary Lancaster. For abstract of his will, see *PGSP*, II, 16. Did his brother and sister come with him?

79 SAMUEL BUCKLEY (Bulkly, Bulkley) and his brother Thomas were joint F.P. of 500 acres. Thomas released his moiety in the land to his brother in 1684. Samuel m. Ann Jones, daughter of Matthew Jones, at the Center Meeting House in Philadelphia on 12 2m 1693, ten years after he was involved with Charles Pickering in coining "new bits" and fined £10. For the trial, see *Colonial Records*, I, 84-89; for land records, *Pennsylvania Archives*, 2nd Series, XIX, 225, 594. After Samuel's death, his widow m. in 1704, Joseph Growden, whose first wife had died in 1699. See Martindale, 250, cited in Note 52 above.

[4 July] JOHN HYNCK (Heycock, Hiccock): cwt. wrought iron; 6 qtrs. malt; cwt. cheese.[80]

11 [July] SAMUEL BUCKLEY: per post in foreign bulk 6 cwt. untarred cordage; ½ doz. woolen stockings for men; 4 doz. straw hats value 25s.

The end of the month, the *Providence* of Scarborough arrived in the Delaware. Its voyages for 1682 can be traced in different port books. A small ship, less than 50 tons burden, it came from Norway in April with shipbuilding material, went to the small port of Sunderland, then up to Newcastle. There the master put on 62 chaldrons of coal, and with a sealed document known as a cocket, to show he had paid export duty, he sailed down the east coast and up the Thames, arriving in July. After loading there, it called in at Falmouth 8 August, where the correspondent of the *London Gazette* wrote it was bound for Pennsylvania with "several passengers." It arrived in the Delaware 29 September 1682.[81]

The *Providence* of Scarborough [14]

Robert Hooper (Hopper), master

13 [July] PHILIP FORD: 36 cwt. nails; 18 cwt. iron; 400 lbs. cordage.

[19 July] ROBERT HOOPER: 6 cwt. iron; 6 cwt. nails; 1 doz. shod shovels; 80 lbs. shoes; cwt. haberdashery wares; 7 lbs. wrought, 4 lbs. thrown silk; 2 small minikin bayes; ¼ cwt. clockwork; 8 doz. men's woolen hose; cwt. gunpowder; cwt. lead shot.

The last of the September ships to arrive in the Delaware appears under six different names in the London port books, ranging from the *Isabella Ann & Katherine*, to the *Ann*, or the *Elizabeth*. The master's name was always the same, however, and it is obviously the same ship. It arrived 29 September 1682, the same day as the *Providence*. A month

[80] This must have been JOHN HEYCOCK of Slin, Eccleshall Parish, Staffordshire, who brought with him a servant, JAMES MORRIS, indented for four years service. PMHB, IX, 224. With Thomas Barret, Heycock, had bought from Penn in April, 1682, 875 acres, part of which he took up in Falls Twp., Bucks Co. See *Pennsylvania Archives*, 2nd Series, XIX, 261, 523. Thomas Barret was a brother of Elizabeth, wife of WILLIAM VENABLES of Chathill, Eccleshall Parish, Staffordshire, who came with their daughters Joyce and Frances Venables, on the *Friend's Adventure*. PMHB, IX, 224. Upon Venables' death, his widow m. 2nd Lawrence Bannor, and 3rd, Andrew Health, former servant of William Yardley, mentioned in Note 73 above. See *Pennsylvania Archives*, 2nd Series, XIX, 243, 261, 326-327, 523; for Heath's later activities in Hopewell Twp., N. J., see *Bucks Court Records*, 228, 258, 261.

[81] Entries indicating the *Providence's* voyages are found in the port books for Scarborough, E 190/325/10; for Newcastle, E 190/325/1; London Coastal, E 190/109/1, PRO. The Falmouth item is in the *London Gazette*, Numb. 1747, Huntington Library. The date of arrival, as printed in PMHB, VIII, 333, the transcript of the Philadelphia County Register of Arrivals, original of which is in HSP, is given as 29 Sept. 1683, an obvious misprint for 1682. The record says WILLIAM CARTER arrived in the ship with a servant, JOHN LASH. Carter, a turner of Wapping in Middlesex Co., and F.P. of 500 acres, was granted a warrant for his city lot 12 4m (June) 1683, which was surveyed two days later on the west side of Second Street, between Walnut and Chestnut. *Pennsylvania Archives*, 3rd Series, II, 679; ibid., III, 390. ROBERT HOPPER, master "of ye Providence of Scarbrugh," witnessed a money order executed by Griffith Jones 18 Oct. 1682, was defendant in a suit brought by Thomas Hutchinson in August, 1688, and was dead by 4 June 1690, Richard Guy and James Marshall having acted as administrators of his estate. Stillwell, *Miscellany*, II, 5; *Burlington Court Records*, 90, 104.

later it was still at anchor in the Delaware; as soon as William Penn arrived, he sent a horse on it, care of the master, to a friend in Barbados.[82]

The Elizabeth Ann & Catherine of London [15]

Thomas Hudson, master, for Pennsylvania

1 [July] PHILIP ALFORD: 240 lbs. shoes.[83]

4 [July] WILLIAM CLERK (Clark): 1 small minikin baye; 100 goads cottons; 2 doz. felt, 10 castor hats; 70 lbs. shoes; 1 chest window glass; 6 cwt. lead shot; 28 lbs. stuffs; 8 cwt. iron; 4 cwt. nails; 100 pcs. earth[en]ware; 5 doz. candles; 4 doz. shod shovels; 2 doz. men's woolen hose; 25 small gross tobacco pipes. From the Wool Book: 1 kersey; 80 lbs. woolen cloth.[84]

10 [July] ISAAC MARTYN (Martin): 1 small minikin baye; 2 doz. men's woolen hose; 5 doz. candles; 8 cwt. nails; 5 cwt. iron.[85]

17 [July] JOHN DAY: 8 cwt. wrought iron; 8 cwt. nails; 80 lbs. shoes; 4 doz. men's woolen hose; 1 lb. thrown silk; 5 lbs. wrought silk; 4 cwt. lead shot; ½ cwt. gunpowder; 4 chests window glass. [86]

---

82 For date of arrival, see <i>PMHB</i>, VIII, 337, wherein is the registration of Robert Kent who arrived on this vessel as servant to Philip Oxford (Alford). Kent, a "cordwayner" like his master, m. Margaret Thompson, widow, 5 Aug. 1686, with consent of the Philadelphia Meeting. He died early in 1689. <i>Pennsylvania Archives</i>, 2nd Series, VIII, vi, cited in Note 69 above. For abstract see <i>PGSP</i>, I, 73. James Claypoole on 5 6m (Aug.) 1682 wrote that of three ships preparing to leave for Pennsylvania, "ye 3d is Tho. Hutson a great ship gone yesterday with passengers." <i>PMHB</i>, X, 197. For mention of the horse to be shipped on Hudson's vessel, see Penn's letter to William Markham, dated 28 9m 1682, in <i>ibid.</i>, VI (1882), 466. Loadings for the <i>Elizabeth Ann & Catherine</i> are from London port books E 190/109/1 and E 190/112/1, PRO.

83 Philip Alford or Oxford, as his name is variously given, was a F.P. of 125 acres. By a warrant from William Markham dated 7 6m 1682, land was laid out for him 21 6m 1682, on the Neshaminy in Middletown Twp., Bucks Co., a circumstance which seems to indicate he had come over on an earlier ship. At the same time and by a warrant similarly dated, Ralph Ward, another shoemaker, had the same amount of land laid out adjoining Alford's tract; the inference here is that the two men were in partnership. <i>Pennsylvania Archives</i>, 2nd Series, XIX, 309-310. Alford m. 8 Dec. 1686, Sarah Jones, daughter of Henry Jones of Moyamensing. Ibid., VIII, vii; Davis, <i>Bucks County</i>, 163.

84 These goods may have been consigned to, or shipped by William Clark who had been justice of the peace at the Whorekills in 1680, and clerk of the courts there in 1681. However, a William Clarke witnessed the will of GEORGE PALMER, of Nonsuch, Surrey, written 4 Sept. 1682, "on board the Ship called Isabell Anne Katherine, Thomas Hutson being the Master thereof and bound for Pennsylvania." Palmer, a F.P. of 5000 acres, had with him his wife Elizabeth, who later m. Thomas Fitzwater, for whom see Note 111 below, daughter Elizabeth Palmer, and four sons, George, John, Thomas and William, the last two being twins. George Palmer, Sr., apparently died on shipboard before reaching Pennsylvania, but his will was not recorded until many years later. See <i>Roberts-Walton Ancestry</i>, 205-206. The William Clarke who, with Thomas Hudson, the ship's master, and an unidentified person, witnessed George Palmer's will, could have been a seaman.

85 ISAAC MARTIN, London grocer and F.P. of 5000 acres, owned part of a propriety in West Jersey, as did William Clark of the Whorekills. <i>PMHB</i>, LXXV, 133, 135-136. Martin called himself a bolt-maker of Philadelphia in his will date 24 Nov. 1682 and proved 18 5m 1683. For abstract see <i>PGSP</i>, I, 46. He left a widow Katherine who m. John Sibley, and a daughter Elizabeth Martin.

86 There were two men named John Day who settled on opposite sides of the Delaware. John Day of Burlington Co. was a juryman there 8 6m 1683, and had 100 acres in Burlington Co., and was an overseer of the highways in the First Tenth 15 10m 1685. <i>Burlington Court Records</i>, 19, 31, 54. It seems likely that it was he who, with Edward Jefferson, for whom see Note 65 above, obtained a certificate of removal from Ashwell Monthly Meeting, Hertfordshire, 12 3m 1682. Myers, <i>Quaker Arrivals</i>, 6. Jefferson's widow Mercy, and her 2nd husband, Thomas Phillips, conveyed land to John Day in 1685, which he,

18 [July] THOMAS DAY: cwt. haberdashery; 4 chests window glass.

24 [July] JOHN MASON: 2 doz. felt hats; [?] lbs. shoes.[87]

27 [July] THOMAS MERRITT: 6 cwt. nails; 6 cwt. iron; 1½ doz. men's woolen hose; 18 lbs. haberdashery; cwt. shot; ½ cwt. gunpowder; 3 cwt. cheese; 2 bushels meal.

[27 July] JOHN HARWOOD: 18 cwt. nails; 9 cwt. iron; 72 lbs. serges; 3 small mini-kin bayes; 6 doz. men's, 3 doz. children's woolen hose; 6 doz. felts; 150 goads cottons; 200 yds. flannel; ¼ cwt. haberdashery; 2 lbs. wrought silk; 4 cwt. cordage; 4 double bayes.[88]

31 [July] JOHN HARWOOD: 1 single baye; 15 lbs. linsey woolsey. From the Wool Book: 1 Spanish cloth; 6 kersies; 2 penistone friezes.

Another ship, the *Hopewell*, probably a small vessel, in the early part of July was loading in the Thames with some goods intended for Pennsylvania. From mid-July to 29 July, five different merchants put on goods for Maryland, Virginia and Carolina. Precisely when it arrived in the Delaware is not known, but it should have sailed up the river during the first week or so of October, 1682. More is known of the ship's master, Michael Yoakley. He is said to have started life as a shepherd boy, made a fortune as a mariner, and then willed his London house for use as a home for "aged, poor women." Drapers, his farm near Margate in Kent, he also left for use as a charity home. These charitable establishments have grown with the centuries.[89]

The *Hopewell* [16]

Michael Yoakley, master,
for Pennsylvania, Maryland, Virginia and Carolina

10 [July] MICHAEL YOAKLEY: 30 cwt. iron; 1 doz. new wool cards [metal-toothed instruments for combing wool].

"then of the County of Burlington, yeom.," sold in 1691 to Henry Paxson. *Pennsylvania Archives*, 2nd Series, XIX, 374. John Day, London carpenter and F.P. of 1250 acres, with his wife Hannah and two children, John and Hannah, settled in Philadelphia. Digested Copy of the Registers of Marriages of the Quarterly Meeting of London and Middlesex, 1657-1719, and of Births, 1644-1719, GSP. In 1692, when he was about to go on a voyage, he wrote his will, naming his children Hannah, Grace and Sara, the son John apparently having died. He was lost at sea and no certain knowledge of his death had come by 1695. See PGSP, II, 28, for abstract of his will, and *ibid.*, IV, 199. His widow Hannah m. 2nd, James Atkinson, for whom see *Pennsylvania Archives*, 2nd Series, XIX, 205, and Note 118 below. Dr. George E. McCracken, Des Moines, Ia., pointed out the difference between these two Day emigrants.

[87] JOHN MASON from Farington Monthly Meeting, Berkshire, his wife Mary and three sons John, Robert and Richard Mason, came with a certificate of removal from the meeting dated 27 2m 1682. Myers, *Quaker Arrivals*, 6. He died before 2 6m 1683, when administration on his estate was recorded in Philadelphia; it was the first such entered in Philadelphia records. See PGM, XIX, 250, and PGSP, I, 258. He had purchased 1000 acres in England before leaving for Pennsylvania. *Pennsylvania Archives*, 2nd Series, XIX, 205, 762. The surviving son Richard probably settled in Aston Twp. Chester Co. See *Chester Court Records*, 106, 109, 124.

[88] There was a Thomas Harwood who was a "Tydable" at "Marr: Kill"— now Marcus Hook—in 1677. Perhaps the John Harwood, by whom these goods were shipped, was of this family. See Smith, *Delaware County*, 114.

[89] The best account of the Yoakley charities is found in *The Journal of the Friends Historical Society* (London, 1917), XIV, No. 4, 146-156. For loadings on the *Hopewell*, see London port book E 190/109/1, PRO.

12 [July] JOHN RICHARDSON: 3½ cwt. gunpowder.[90]

Probably the next ship to arrive in the Delaware was a relatively small one of 130 tons burden, the *Lamb* of Liverpool. Presumably it had been chartered by a group of Friends who belonged to the Monthly Meeting at Settle in western Yorkshire, which issued one certificate of removal dated 7 4m 1682, for about thirty people, members of seven families. A few others from Lancashire, further west, who shipped goods on the vessel, were probably included among its passengers. It appears to have arrived 22 October 1682.[91]

The *Lamb* of Liverpool [17]

John Tench (French), master, for Pennsylvania

26 [June] CUTHBERT HAYHURST: 2 casks, 1 pack, 1 box, 1 bag qty. 8 cwt. wrought iron; 7 cwt. nails; 35 doz. woolen stockings for men; 5 doz. felts [hats] English making; 35 pots qty. 3½ barrels butter; 462 cheeses qty. 3 tons; 2 cwt. cheese; 40 grindle stones qty. 2 chalders; 5 millstones; 3 doz. sieves value £5.[92]

---

[90] Probably the same man mentioned in Note 25 above, who had shipped goods on the *Amity*.

[91] The Settle certificate, as printed in Isaac Comly, "Sketches of the History of Byberry . . . ," *Memoirs HSP*, II (1827), 182, was for Cuthbert Hayhurst, Thomas Wrightsworth (Wigglesworth), Thomas Walmsley, Thomas Croasdale, Thomas Stackhouse, Nicholas Waln, Ellen Cowgill and their families; only three of them shipped dutiable goods on the *Lamb*. For another version of the certificate, see James Bowden, *History of the Society of Friends in America* (London, 1854), II, 15, also the transcript in Middletown Monthly Meeting Records, 46, cited in Note 26 above. The arrival of the *Lamb* "in 8th Mo." is noted in *PMHB*, IX, 233; Davis, *Bucks County*, 83, gives the date as 22 8m 1682. The *Lamb's* tonnage is given in *Rise of the Port of Liverpool*, 70, cited in Note 36 above. For the loadings of the *Lamb*, see Liverpool port book E 190/1345/11, PRO.

[92] CUTHBERT HAYHURST (Hurst, Hairst), from Easington, Yorkshire and F.P. of 500 acres, by early writers has been considered a passenger on the *Welcome*. See J. Thomas Scharf and Thompson Westcott, *History of Philadelphia, 1609-1884* (Philadelphia, 1884), I, 99, hereinafter cited as Scharf & Westcott. Hayhurst's name headed the Settle certificate, possibly because of his close relationship to the other members of the meeting listed on it. For the relationships, see *PMHB*, XXXI, 440-441. He brought with him his wife Mary Rudd and children William, Margery, John, Cuthbert and Alis; see Middletown Monthly Meeting Records, 123, and *Pennsylvania Archives*, 2nd Series, XIX, 229, 525. He died 5 March 1683, aged 50, according to Davis, *Bucks County*, 66. JOHN COWGILL, his servant who came with him, m. 19 8m 1693, Bridget Croasdale, daughter of Thomas, who presumably was on the same ship. *PMHB*, XXX, 483; *Pennsylvania Archives*, 2nd Series, XIX, 586.

THOMAS CROASDALE of New Hay, Yorkshire, F.P. of 1000 acres, was included in the Settle certificate, as were his wife Agnes and six children, William, John, Elizabeth, Mary, Bridget and Alis, though the children, listed in Middletown Monthly Meeting Records, 123-124, as "born in England," were not named. Croasdale, like Hayhurst, has been considered a passenger on the *Welcome*. He obtained a warrant for the city lot appurtenant to his purchase of country land on 25 11m 1683/4, but died in less than a year, letters of administration being granted to his widow Agnes 10 10m 1684. *Pennsylvania Archives*, 2nd Series, XIX, 255, 260; for the administration see *PGSP*, I, 203.

Part of Croasdale's purchase of land, 250 acres, was "for the account of THOMAS STACKHOUSE," who, with his wife Margery Hayhurst, were included in the Settle certificate. She has been thought to be a sister of Cuthbert, and had only just married Thomas Stackhouse; they had declared their intentions of marriage in April and May, 1682. *Pennsylvania Archives*, 2nd Series, XIX, 429; *PMHB*, XXXI, 440-441. The marriage was of short duration, for she died 5 11m 1682/3, a little more than a year after their arrival. Thomas Stackhouse, Jr., their nephew, who may have been with them, m. 5 5m 1688, Grace Heaton, daughter of Robert. Thomas Stackhouse, Sr., by a warrant from William Markham dated 12 8m (October) 1682—ten days before the *Lamb* is said to have arrived—had his 250 acres laid out on the Neshaminy

[26 June] WILLIAM HALL: 1 box, 1 bundle qty. 5 cwt. wrought iron.[93]

[26 June] JAMES DILWORTH: 2 rashes [container possibly woven of rushes], 1 cask, 1 bundle qty. 150 lbs. woolen cloth; 50 lbs. Norwich stuffs; 1/4 cwt. haberdashery; 200 lbs. new shoes; 8 doz. woolen stockings for men; 6 cwt. cheese.[94]

[26 June] RICHARD COULBOURNE: 1 cask qty. 6 cwt. wrought iron; cwt. nails; 2 cwt. cheese.

[26 June] ROBERT EATON: 1 pack qty. 350 ells English linen.[95]

[26 June] CHARLES LEE: 1 pack qty. 40 yds. English linen; 5 cribbs [osier or wickerwork baskets, or crates] 2 chests window glass.[96]

[26 June] THOMAS WIGELWORTH: 1 cask qty. 2 cwt. gunpowder; 6 pigs qty. 10 cwt. lead; 1 bundle qty. 1/2 cwt. brass manufactured.[97]

---

in Bucks County on 19 8m 1682, the same day Cuthbert Hayhurst had his land surveyed by a warrant similarly dated. See returns of surveys in Warrants and Surveys of the Province of Pennsylvania, 1682-1759, Municipal Archives, Department of Records, City Hall, Philadelphia, III, 150, hereinafter cited as Warrants and Surveys. Did the *Lamb* arrive earlier than 22 October, or did these Yorkshire emigrants delegate friends who had already come over, to take up land for them?

[93] William Hall was possibly the merchant and innholder of Salem, N. J., noted in *Pennsylvania Archives*, 2nd Series, XIX, 487. He m. Elizabeth, daughter of Thomas Pile of Pile Grove, as recited in Salem Deeds, No. 5, 200: 17 Aug. 1692, Thomas Pile to William Hall, abstract in *N. J. Archives*, 1st Series, XXI 598, cited in Note 22 above.

[94] JAMES DILWORTH of Thornbury, Lancashire, arrived with his wife Ann Waln, sister of Nicholas, infant son William and a servant, Stephen Sands, indentured for one year, according to *PMHB*, IX, 233, and Battle, *Bucks County*, 680. Dilworth had purchased 1000 acres in April, 1682, of which 500 were laid out 19 7m 1682, on Neshaminy Creek, by a warrant from Markham dated 10 9m 1682. *Warrants and Surveys*, III, 143; *Pennsylvania Archives*, 2nd Series, XIX, 429. Christopher Sibthorp, who had married the widow of Francis Fincher, after her death in 1699 married James Dilworth's widow Ann.

STEPHEN SANDS, the Dilworth's servant, m. 25 8m 1685, at Nicholas Waln's house, Jane Cowgill. Sands' certificate of removal from Lancaster Monthly Meeting and filed at Middletown Monthly Meeting, was dated 18 4m 1682. It stated he "goes with consent of his mother, sister and relatives," and was signed among others, by Isabella Sands, probably his mother. The original Bucks County Register of Arrivals states he was to be free from his indenture 22 8m 1683.

His wife Jane Cowgill was undoubtedly a daughter of ELLEN COWGILL, probable sister of Thomas Stackhouse, who, with her family, was included in the Settle certificate, though her family was not named. Her children were apparently John Cowgill, servant to Cuthbert Hayhurst; Ralph Cowgill, who came on the *Friend's Adventure*; Edmund Cowgill, who m. 29 3m 1702, at Middletown Meeting, Catherine Blaker; the above-mentioned Jane Cowgill, and Jennet Cowgill, who m. 2 12m 1687/8, at Burlington, Bernard Lane, for whom see *PMHB*, XXX, 482-483, and *ibid.*, XXXI (1907), 441.

[95] This was surely ROBERT HEATON whose separate certificate from Settle, also dated 7 4m 1682, three weeks before his goods were loaded on the *Lamb*, included his wife Alice and children, not named, but who were Grace, who m. 5 5m 1688, at Middletown Meeting, Thomas Stackhouse, Jr., Robert Heaton, Jr., James, Agnes and Ephraim Heaton, as entered in Middletown Monthly Meeting Records, 126. He was not a First Purchaser, but bought Robert Holdgate's original purchase of 250 acres on 19 3m 1686. *Pennsylvania Archives*, 2nd Series, XIX, 308, 429. According to Davis, *Bucks County*, 161, 163, Heaton built the first mill in Middletown Twp., Bucks Co.

[96] CHARLES LEE's certificate of removal from Clitheroe, Lancashire, was dated 30 2m 1682. Myers, *Quaker Arrivals*, 6. He m. Ann Barrett in 1684 with consent of the Philadelphia Meeting, and died about a year later. For declaration of intentions, see *PGSP*, I, 266, 267; for abstract of will, *ibid.*, 54.

[97] THOMAS WIGELWORTH, or Wrightsworth, as his name was given in the Settle certificate, had m. Alice Hayhurst, sister of Cuthbert. She was not named in the certificate. When Thomas wrote his will 13 9m 1682, he was living "upon Neshaminah Creek"; he was dead by 4 12m 1685/6, when his widow proved the will, for abstract of which see *PGSP*, I, 210. See also *PMHB*, XXXI, 440, for the relationship to Cuthbert Hayhurst.

[26 June] NICHOLAS WALNE: 1 cask qty. 7 cwt. wrought iron.[98]

8 [July] JOHN DODSWORTH: 50 lbs. woolen cloth; 3 cwt. cheese.

13 [July] THOMAS CLAYTON & CO: 2 casks. 3 boxes, 3 crates, 3 bales qty. 180 lbs. new shoes; 41 pcs. English linen; 1½ cwt. haberdashery; 4 doz. felts, English making; 1 doz. worsted stockings for men; 1½ cwt. nails; cwt. wrought iron; 160 lbs. woolen cloth; 10½ doz. woolen stockings for men; 15½ doz. ditto for children; 7 rugs for beds; 60 small gross tobacco pipes; 40 yds. flannel; 9 pcs. calico; 100 neck cloths value £6 2s. 6d.[99]

17 [July] THOMAS CLAYTON & CO: per post in foreign bulk, 72 lbs. new shoes.

Meanwhile the *Bristol Factor*, the first Pennsylvania-bound ship, had returned to its home port laden with tobacco from Virginia. Toward the end of July it began taking on goods for another voyage across the Atlantic. Its last load, which was for Virginia, went on 2 September, but there was always some delay before the actual time of sailing, and more days before reaching the open sea. Its precise date of arrival is not known, but one man, Evan Oliver, who shipped goods on this vessel, wrote that his seventh child was born 24 October "within sight of the Capes of Delaware." As it would have taken at least three days, probably more, to come up the Delaware, this family has been said to have come on the same ship as Penn, himself, since the arrival times were nearly coincidental.[100]

The *Bristol Factor* [18]

Roger Drew, master, for Pennsylvania and Virginia

26 [July] TOBIAS LEACH (Leech): 1 old mill for glover (sic) value £3.[101]

---

98 NICHOLAS WALN, said to have been a passenger on the *Welcome*, his wife [Jane] and three children [Jane, Richard and Margaret] were included in the Settle certificate of 7 4m 1682, the bracketed names being supplied from Middletown Monthly Meeting Records, 123. A nephew of Cuthbert Hayhurst's wife Mary Rudd, Waln had purchased from Penn 1000 acres in April, 1682, part of which was laid out at the same time as the Hayhurst and Stackhouse lands. Warrants and Surveys, III, 143: see also *Pennsylvania Archives*, 2nd Series, XIX, 292, 424.

THOMAS WALMSLEY of Waddington Eaves, Yorkshire, his wife Elizabeth Rudd, and their six children were included in the Settle certificate, and also have been said to have been passengers on the *Welcome*. Of the children, Margaret, Mary, Henry, Thomas, Elizabeth and Rosamond, only three survived the trip: Henry, Thomas and Elizabeth. Thomas himself, was bur. "about" 11 10m 1682, said to have been aged 40. See *Roberts-Walton Ancestry*, 282-283, cited in Note 26 above, and PGSP, I, 202, for administration on and inventory of his estate. In 1686, Nicholas Waln conveyed to Ezra Croasdale in trust for Thomas Walmsley's sons Henry and Thomas, 250 acres. *Bucks Court Records*, 73.

99 THOMAS CLAYTON obtained a warrant for 100 acres in Chester County 25 10m 1682. *Pennsylvania Archives*, 3rd Series, III, 114. He was probably the same man who, as a "clark" of Philadelphia Co., died intestate before 4 1m 1699/1700, when letters of administration were granted his brother and next of kin, John Clayton. See abstract in PGM, XIX, 273. He may have belonged to the family of William Clayton of Chester Co., for which see Smith, *Delaware County*, 452, or of James Clayton who came on the *Submission*, q.v.

100 See Scharf & Westcott, I, 99, cited in Note 92 above, for the reference to the birth of Evan Oliver's child. For loadings for the *Bristol Factor*, see Bristol port book E 190/1143/1, PRO.

101 TOBY LEECH, as he was always called, John Ashmead, Everard Boulton (Bolton) and Richard Wall, purchased 1000 acres jointly after they arrived in Pennsylvania, Toby's share being 300 acres. *Pennsylvania Archives*, 2nd Series, XIX, 86, 263, 474. Toby Leech of Cheltenham had m. at Gloucester Meet-

9 [August] WILLIAM BROWN: 4 cwt. nails; 4 cwt. wrought iron; 120 goads cottons; 2 cwt. gunpowder; 1¾ cwt. cheese; 1¼ cwt. cordage; 11 cwt. lead shot; 56 lbs. brass manufactured; 28 lbs. wrought pewter; 170 ells English-made linen; 2 small saddles; 48 lbs. serges; 2 Spanish cloths; 2 doz. & 4 pairs woolen stockings; 1 firkin butter; ⅛ part of a chalder grindle stones; 2 bags, 1 chest wearing apparel; 1 lb. English thrown silk; 28 lbs. haberdashery wares; 9 parcels of several sorts of wares value £14.[102]

11 [August] HUMPHREY ELLIS: 4 felt hats; 8 pairs woolen stockings; 10 yds. English ticking; 19 garments of apparel; ¾ bushel oatmeal; cwt. cheese.[103]

14 [August] TOBIAS LEACH: 5 cwt. nails; 3 cwt. wrought iron; 3 cwt. shot; 50 lbs. leather manufactured; 2 cwt. haberdashery wares; 6 coverlets of wool and hair; 20 made garments; 28 lbs. brass manufactured; 20 bushels malt; 80 lbs. gunpowder; 300 ells English-made linen; ½ chest window glass; 40 lbs. serges; 3 doz. men's woolen stockings; 20 pcs. English fustians; 10 doz. plain sheepskin gloves; ½ cwt. cheese; ¼ chalder grindle stones.

14 [August] EVAN OLIVER: ¾ cwt. wrought iron; 1½ bushels oatmeal; 1 firkin butter; 3 pails; 2 cwt. nails; 14 cwt. cheese; 1¾ cwt. iron; 2 cwt. nails; 10 lbs. brass manufactured; 1 doz. felt hats; ¼ cwt. English soap; 18 lbs. shoes; 15 lbs. pewter; 2 cwt. nails more.[104]

---

ing 26 10m 1679, Esther Ashmead, and with their small son Tobias undoubtedly came over with the others. JOHN ASHMEAD, his presumed father-in-law, was also supposed to have 300 acres, but appears to have gotten only 250 acres. In his will, dated 16 9m 1688, and proved a year later, he mentioned his "now" wife Mary Ashmead, children John, probably born in England, and Mary and Nicholas. Letters of administration, c.t.a., were granted to Toby Leech and "Edward" Bolton; see PGM, XIX, 256, 258.

EVERARD BOULTON, from Ross, Herefordshire, brought a certificate of removal dated 18 5m (Aug.) 1682. Myers, Quaker Arrivals, 5. His wife Elizabeth, and two small children, Everard and Elizabeth, accompanied him. See Roberts-Walton Ancestry, 20-23, cited in Note 26 above, for account of this family. RICHARD WALL of Stoke Orchard, Gloucestershire, had m. 1 8m 1658, Joane Wheel at Gloucester Meeting. His certificate of removal was dated 26 4m 1682; presumably his wife, son RICHARD WALL, JR., and his wife Rachel, and their daughter Sarah emigrated with him. Myers, Quaker Arrivals, 7; Benjamin H. Shoemaker, Genealogy of the Shoemaker Family of Cheltenham, Pennsylvania (Philadelphia, 1893), 9. Richard Wall, Jr., died intestate and letters of administration were granted his father 17 2m 1689. PGM, XIX, 254. The father's will, proved in 1701, devised his estate to his wife Joane and granddaughter Sarah, now wife of George Shoemaker. For abstract of the will see PGSP, III, 249. This Wall family is not to be confused with that of the Richard Wall whose will, proved in early 1695, named his three children Richard, Mary and John Wall, for abstract of which see PGSP, II, 23.

[102] This was possibly the WILLIAM BROWN from Northampton Co., England, who settled in Chichester Twp., Chester Co., and in 1684 m. Ann Mercer of Chester Meeting. See Smith, Delaware County, 450, and Pennsylvania Archives, 2nd Series, XIX, 280, 346, 347.

[103] Humphrey Ellis, son of Thomas Ellis of Wales, acquired land in the Welsh Tract from his father and others. But Thomas Ellis's certificate from Redstone Meeting, Pembrokeshire, for his wife and family was dated 2 7m 1683, and filed at Haverford Meeting. Did Humphrey come over before his parents? A Humphrey Ellis and Gwen Rees were m. 10 12m 1683/4, it being the first entry in Haverford Monthly Meeting records. Browning, 201, 241, 245, 581, cited in Note 36 above; Pennsylvania Archives, 3rd Series, I, 15-17.

[104] Evan Oliver and David James, whose name does not appear on the port books, brought a certificate from Bristol dated 26 6m (Aug.) 1682, obtained at the last moment before the Bristol Factor finished loading goods for Pennsylvania. EVAN OLIVER, who originally came from Glascombe, Wales, and is said to have taken passage on the Welcome, brought his wife Jean (Jane), and probably six children: David, Elizabeth, John, Hannah, Mary and Evan. A seventh child, Seaborn, was born within sight of land, as mentioned in the text. Myers, Quaker Arrivals, 7; Browning, 214, 499; Pennsylvania Archives, 2nd Series, XIX, 371, 426, 456. DAVID JAMES, of Llandegley and Glaseram, Radnorshire, weaver, was included in Oliver's certificate, but his wife Margaret James and daughter Mary had to write back to Wales for theirs.

16 [August] ROBERT LANCASTER: 20 lbs. serges; 1 pc. kersey; 25 lbs. shoes.

[16 August] JOHN BLUNSTON: 20 lbs. serges; 30 lbs. Norwich stuffs; 20 made garments; 14 coverlets of wool and hair; 60 ells English-made linen; 1½ cwt. haberdashery wares; 2 cwt. wrought iron; cwt. shot; ½ chest window glass.[105]

17 [August] JOHN JONES: 24 lbs. serges; 2 pcs. English fustians; 2 parcels of wares value £6.[106]

19 [August] JOHN CHILDE: 20 lbs. shoes; 2 doz. woolen stockings; 60 lbs. serges; cwt. wrought iron; 2 cwt. nails; 3 pcs. English fustians; 40 ells English linen; 6 pcs. kersey; 100 goads cottons.[107]

26 [August] JOHN CHILDE: 2 doz. felt hats; 6 gross tobacco pipes.

Early in July the most famous of the 1682 ships, the 284-ton *Welcome*, was being loaded in the Thames with goods for Pennsylvania. William Penn, its most celebrated passenger, was not listed in the London port book, since he did not bring goods for barter or sale. He boarded the vessel 29 or 30 August when it was in the Downs, off Deal; departure would have been soon after. Among the other passengers were two dozen or more from Sussex who were old friends and neighbors of the Penns. Those who survived the smallpox epidemic which plagued the voyage would settle near Pennsbury in the expectation they would continue to be neighbors of the proprietor. The *Welcome's* first landfall was probably about the same as the *Factor's;* certain it is they dropped anchor

See Browning, 227, and *Pennsylvania Archives*, 2nd Series, XIX, 341; also *PGM*, XIX, 242, for the women's certificate.

John Evans and David Kinsey, both from the parish of Nantmel in Radnorshire, brought certificates from Bristol also dated 26 6m 1682. Myers, *Quaker Arrivals*, 5. For mention of JOHN EVANS of Nantmel, see Browning, 214-216, 225. DAVID KINSEY, carpenter, may have brought his wife Magdalen and two sons John and Edmund with him; he died intestate, letters of administration being granted his widow 30 Nov. 1689. For an account of him, see Clarence V. Roberts, *Early Friends Families of Upper Bucks . . .* , (Philadelphia, 1925), 325, 606-607. All four of these Welshmen, Oliver, James, Evans and Kinsey, bought part of the Richard Davies land in the Welsh Tract before leaving England.

105 John Blunston, F.P. of 1500 acres, was from Little Hallam, Derbyshire; Breach Meeting gave him a certificate of removal dated 13 5m (Aug.) 1682, three days before he loaded goods on the *Bristol Factor*. He brought to Pennsylvania two daughters, Sarah, aged 12, and Katherine, aged 10, and probably his 2nd wife, believed to be Sarah Bickerstaff, whom he had probably just married. Why he shipped goods on the *Factor*, sailing from Bristol over 100 miles away, when the *Lamb* was loading goods in Liverpool, considerably nearer, is not clear. See *Lloyd Manuscripts*, 32-84, for an account of Blunston; also Smith, *Delaware County*, 447, which accounts do not agree in all respects. By a warrant dated 24 6m 1682, to John Blunston "& ors." to lay out sundry tracts, there was surveyed on 10 7m 1682, two separate tracts for Blunston of 350 acres and 150 acres. The same day by similarly dated warrants adjoining tracts were laid out, all in Chester Co., to Samuel Bradshaw and Thomas Worth, both of whom were from Oxton, Nottinghamshire, not far from Little Hallam. Had they acted as agents for Blunston? See Warrants and Surveys, III, 528-530, and Smith, *Delaware County*, 448, 516.

106 These goods were possibly shipped by John Jones, linen draper of Bristol, joint F.P. with Michael Jones, grocer of Bristol, of 1000 acres.

107 These goods may have been shipped for John Child, a juryman at Upland Court 14 March 1681/2, and in subsequent years. See *Chester Court Records*, 10 *et passim;* also *Pennsylvania Archives*, 2nd Series, XIX, 448. He may have been the same man mentioned in Note 7 above, who married Elizabeth Evans, daughter of Nathaniel.

first at New Castle 27 October, and finally at Upland the next day, 28 October 1682.[108]

The *Welcome* [19]

Robert Greenway, master, for Pennsylvania

7 [July] DANIEL WHARLEY: 17 cwt. wrought iron; 1 mill at £53 16s. 9d. [Duty] £3 2s. 4d.[109]

19 [July] DENNIS ROCHFORD: 14 cwt. wrought iron; 1½ cwt. haberdashery; 2 bushels pease; 3 flitches bacon; 1 chest window glass; 6 lbs. shoes; 1 great saddle; cwt. wrought pewter. [Duty] 16s. 1½d. From the Free List: 7 parcels of apparel.[110]

---

[108] The exact tonnage for the *Welcome* is found in C.O. 13/14, 15, PRO. For newspaper notices of the *Welcome's* sailing, see *PMHB*, LXXV, 153, 154. For its arrival at New Castle, see *Records of the Court of New Castle on Delaware* (Meadville, 1935), II (1681-1699), 21. For discussion of the *Welcome* passenger list, see Marion Balderston, "The Real *Welcome* Passengers," *The Huntington Library Quarterly*, XXVI (1962), 31-55, and George E. McCracken, "*Welcome* Notes," *The American Genealogist*, Vol. 38 (1962), Vol. 39 (1963). The loadings for the *Welcome* are from London port book E 190/109/1, and Export of Woolen Cloth E 190/113/1, PRO.

[109] Daniel Wharley, London woolen draper and merchant, was not a passenger on the *Welcome*. He carried on an extensive trade with the West Indies, and had married Mary Penington, half-sister of William Penn's first wife. *PMHB*, XXI (1897), 11n; *Pennsylvania Archives*, 2nd Series, XX, 730. The mill he sent was probably that set up in Chester Co. by Richard Townsend, and which Caleb Pusey operated. See Smith, *Delaware County*, 147. RICHARD TOWNSEND, carpenter of London and F.P. of 250 acres, with his wife Ann and daughter Hannah, were passengers, although they shipped no dutiable goods. He came in as a salaried employee of the Free Society of Traders, and brought with him three indentured servants of his own: WILLIAM SMITH, NATHANIEL HARRISON, and BARTHOLOMEW GREEN, each to serve him seven years. *PMHB*, VIII 339.

BENJAMIN CHAMBERS, turner of Bearsted, Kent Co., and F.P. of 1000 acres, another passenger, brought a certificate of removal from Rochester, dated 18 5m 1682. Myers, *Quaker Arrivals*, 5. He succeeded Dr. Nicholas More as president of the Free Society of Traders. *Pennsylvania Archives*, 2nd Series, XIX, 19. He was an executor of the will of WILLIAM WADE of the parish of Hankton, Sussex, written 20 Sept. 1682, and proved 6 6m 1684. For abstract see *PGSP*, I, 49-50. Witnesses to Wade's will, written on board the *Welcome*, included RICHARD INGELO, GEORGE THOMPSON, a grocer, and WILLIAM LUSHINGTON. Ingelo (Ingels) in 1685 was granted 800 acres to recompense him for his services as secretary of the Provincial Council. See *Colonial Records*, I, 131, 133, 144, 149, 154. For George Thompson, see Note 111 below. ZECHARIAH WHITPAIN, son of Richard Whitpain, citizen and butcher of London who acquired 7000 acres by purchase from various First Purchasers, also witnessed William Wade's will, as evidenced by the original in Office of the Register of Wills, Philadelphia City Hall. See *Pennsylvania Archives*, 2nd Series, XIX, 397-399 for Richard Whitpain's purchases.

[110] The date of DENNIS ROCHFORD's arrival is given as "about" 24 8m 1682; see *PMHB*, VIII, 334. A grocer of Brighthelmston, Sussex, he brought his 2nd wife Marie, daughter of John Heriott, with him, two daughters, Grace and Mary, who died on shipboard of smallpox, and two servants, THOMAS JONES and JEANE MATHEWES. When Rochford died intestate in 1693, he was living in Philadelphia County; see *PGM*, XIX, 263 for abstract of administration. His servant Thomas Jones may have been the man who was constable of Upper Providence Twp., Chester Co., in 1691. See *Chester Court Records*, 233.

THOMAS HERIOTT, Rochford's brother-in-law, of Hurstpierpoint, Sussex and F.P. of 5000 acres, died on the *Welcome*. *PGSP*, I, 46. Witnesses to his will were George Thompson, Dr. Thomas Wynne, David Ogden and Joshua Morris. JOSHUA MORRIS, a "Tynn-plate-worker," died intestate and letters of administration were granted 18 Jan. 1696/7 to Samuel Nicholls, sawyer, on behalf of Morris' brothers, Henry, Richard and John Morris. *PGM*, XIX, 267. DAVID OGDEN, weaver, brought a certificate of removal from London, dated 26 11m 1681/2. Myers, *Quaker Arrivals*, 7. He settled in Providence Twp., and in 1686 m. Martha Houlston, daughter of John, according to Smith, *Delaware County*, 489. See also *Pennsylvania Archives*, 2nd Series, XIX, 245. DR. THOMAS WYNNE, of Caerwys, Flintshire, Wales, with John ap John of Denbighshire, were joint F.P. of 5000 acres. Though a Welsh Tract purchaser, Wynne settled in Lewes, Sussex Co. See Browning, 181-193, and *PGM*, XXII, 222-225, for corrections regarding Wynne's wife Elizabeth, who probably accompanied him.

27 [July] THOMAS FITZWATER: 4 cwt. iron; 4 cwt. nails. [Duty] 3s.[111]

10 [August] ROBERT SMITH: 5½ cwt. gunpowder. [Duty] 11s.

11 [August] JOHN WEST: 22 cwt. red and white lead; tinware value £24 10s.[112]

11 [August] PHILIP FORD: from the Free List, 400 lbs. of apparel; 12 dozen bodices; 20 fustians; 100 oz. [silver] plate. From the Wool Book: 2½ single cloths; 12 kerseys; 3 penistones friezed.

12 [August] PHILIP FORD: 10 cwt. hard soap; 3 chests window glass; 29 cwt. wrought iron; 46 cwt. nails; 2 cwt. wrought pewter; 100 doz. candles; 20 cwt. lead shot; 600 yds. flannel; 2 cwt. cordage; 4 doz. Monmouth caps; 18 small minikin bayes; 300 goads cottons; 60 doz. men's, 30 doz. children's woolen hose; 3 cwt. & 28 lbs. shoes; 60 horse collars; 4 cwt. cordage; 120 lbs. stuffs; 24 lbs. stuffs with silk; 220 lbs. serges;

111 THOMAS FITZWATER of Hanworth, near Hampton Court, Middlesex, lost his wife Mary and children Josiah and Mary on the *Welcome,* presumably from smallpox. Their other two children, Thomas Jr., and George, either did not get it, or survived the epidemic, as did the Fitzwater's servant, JOHN OTTEY, misprinted as "Hey" in *PMHB,* IX, 228. See also *Roberts-Walton Ancestry,* 60-65, for account of the Fitzwaters. Perhaps it was to console Fitzwater in some small measure that he was left £5 by ISAAC INGRAM of Garton, Surrey, who also died on shipboard. Other bequests made by Ingram in his will included £5 to JANE (incorrectly transcribed as "James") BATCHELOR who m. 1 2m 1684, Richard Tucker, with consent of the Philadelphia Meeting; £10 to John Songhurst; and to the children of Ingram's "lately deceased" sister Miriam Short: ADAM, MIRIAM and ANNE SHORT, all his goods on board the ship. *Pennsylvania Archives,* 2nd Series, IX, 203; *PGSP,* I, 48-49. Ingram's niece Miriam Short had m. George Thompson, the grocer, mentioned in Note 109 above, by the following February, 1683, when he and she were hailed into Chester Court for having been married by the Swedish Lutheran minister "Contrary to the Lawes of ye Province." Apparently Thompson died within two years, for in January, 1685, the inhabitants of Concord, Bethel and Chichester in Chester County were instructed by the court to decide on "how to Provide a maintenance for Miriam Thomson and her Child." *Chester Court Records,* 23, 49.

JOHN SONGHURST, carpenter and legatee of Isaac Ingram, from Chiltington, Sussex, and F.P. with John Barnes of Sussex of 1250 acres, came with his daughter Elizabeth, wife of JOHN BARBER of Shipley, Sussex, who died on shipboard. In Barber's will he left to his mother [Mary] a "broad piece of gold," to his brother Edward, and sisters Mary, Sarah and Hannah each "one guney a piece." It was witnessed by Thompson, the grocer, Joseph Woodrooffe and Thomas Gillett. *PGSP,* I, 48. THOMAS GILLETT obtained a warrant for 200 acres in New Castle Co. 5 Feb. 1682/3, for which see *Pennsylvania Archives,* 2nd Series, VII, 193. JOSEPH WOODROOFE (Woodruff) may have gone to Salem, N. J., where this family name was already established. Samuel Smith, *The History of the Colony of Nova Caesaria, or New Jersey* (Trenton, N. J., 1890), 152.

112 John West, tinman of London and F.P. of 1250 acres, also had invested in the Free Society of Traders. For list of subscribers, see *PMHB,* XI (1887), 175-180. His daughter Hannah had married Benjamin East, son of William East, master of the *Hester & Hannah,* mentioned in Note 35 above. See transcript of Registers of London and Middlesex Quarterly Meeting, cited in Note 86 above. While John West may not have been a passenger on the *Welcome,* certainly JOHN ROWLAND of Billinghurst, Sussex, his wife, the former Priscilla Shepherd, and THOMAS ROWLAND, John's brother, were, since they registered their arrival. *PMHB,* IX, 225. Both men were First Purchasers, John of 1250 acres, and Thomas of 2500, while Priscilla had purchased 500 acres in her own name. With them came a servant girl, HANNAH MOGDRIDGE, (Maugridge), indented to serve till May, 1684, who married Thomas Rogers, who came in as a servant to the Free Society of Traders. *Pennsylvania Archives,* 2nd Series, XIX, 671-672. See also *Bucks Court Records,* 94, 99, for the theft of some of Rogers' goods by a run-away slave.

WILLIAM PENN brought his secretary, PHILIP THEODORE LEHNMAN (Thelmain, Lemain), a F.P. of 1000 acres from Bristol. The young man remained in Pennsylvania when Penn returned to England in 1684, and died in December, 1687, possessed of three plantations: Green Spring in Sussex Co., one at Broad Creek in the same county, and one in Kent Co., which he left to Thomas Holme, William Penn and Charles Pickering, respectively. *PGSP,* I, 62-63.

Also passengers on the *Welcome* were WILLIAM BUCKMAN, carpenter of Billingshurst, Sussex, his wife Sarah and daughters Sarah and Mary. It is said William's widowed mother Joan, his brothers Edward and Thomas Buckman, F.P. of 300 acres, and their sister RUTH BUCKMAN accompanied him, but only Ruth survived the trip. She m. 4 3m 1687, Richard Harrison in Nottingham Twp., according to George E. McCracken in *The American Genealogist,* Vol. 38, 154-157, cited in Note 108. His account clarifies the account in Davis, *Bucks County,* 85.

10 bushels oatmeal; 10 cwt. books; 6½ lbs. glue; 4 cwt. brass; 4½ cwt. clockwork; 3 cwt. haberdashery; 5½ cwt. gunpowder; 4 lbs. thrown silk; 6 firkins butter; 3 cwt. cheese; 24 shod shovels; 2 cwt. earth[en]ware. [Duty] £12 12s. 6½d.

15 [August] DENNIS ROCHFORD: 11 cwt. wrought iron; 10 cwt. nails; 6 small, 2 great saddles; cwt. cordage; 20 small gross tobacco pipes; cwt. cheese; 4 firkins butter; 12 cwt. shot; 1½ cwt. pewter; 6 castors, 6 felts [hats]; 1 doz. shod shovels; 2 cwt. shoes; 2 cwt. wrought copper; 2 doz. men's worsted hose; 2 cwt. haberdashery; 1 doz. candles. [Duty] £4 8s. 4d.

[15 August] DANIEL WHARLEY: from the Wool Book, 4 kerseys; 1 short cloth.

16 [August] DANIEL WHARLEY: 275 goads cottons; 1 small minikin baye; 3½ cwt. brass; 14 cwt. nails; 20 cwt. wrought iron; 3 doz. shod shovels; 2 chests window glass; 7 doz. candles; 1½ cwt. gunpowder; 4 cwt. lead shot; 3¼ cwt. pewter; 60 lbs. serges; ½ cwt. haberdashery. [Duty] £2 2s. 9½d. From the Free List: 7 parcels of apparel.

[16 August] PHILIP FORD: 20 lbs. stuffs; 100 lbs. shoes; 56 felts; 4 cwt. iron; 4 cwt. nails; ½ cwt. pewter. [Duty] 13s. 4d.

17 [August] DANIEL WHARLEY: 50 lbs. shoes; ½ cwt. cordage; 2 horse collars. [Duty] 2s. 4d.

21 [August] JOHN WILMER: 410 yds. flannel. [Duty] 1s. 6d.

Probably before the end of October the next ship, the *Jeffrey*, of about 500 tons, arrived in the Delaware. Aboard her were the president of the Free Society of Traders in Pennsylvania, Dr. Nicholas More; John Goodson, "chyrrugeon" to the Society, Ralph Withers, deputy treasurer of the Society; skilled workmen hired by the Society, and probably some settlers. Several London merchants put on goods for Virginia the first week in September, and the last loading was on 12 September of goods intended for that place. Eleven days later it was reported in the Downs "bound for Pennsylvania." After it had actually set sail, it made the voyage in twenty-nine days.[113]

[113] For references to the *Jeffrey's* sailing, see *PMHB*, LXXV, 153, 154, items from the *Epitome of the Weekly News*, Numb. 2, and *Domestick Intelligence*, Numb. 137, both of which papers are in Huntington Library. See also extracts from James Claypoole's letters, *PMHB*, X, 197, 199, 200, 269. He wrote that "above 50 servts" belonging to the Free Society, which chartered the ship, were sailing on it, but no complete record of their names has survived. Aside from Richard Townsend who came on the *Welcome*, and Joshua Tittery who came in 1683, the names of only six known servants have been found. These were ABRAHAM, JANE, THOMAS and JOHN PRATT, who applied for their headland in 1703; SAMUEL MILES who applied for his in 1705, and THOMAS ROGERS of Bensalem, mentioned in Note 112 above. *Pennsylvania Archives*, 2nd Series, XIX, 409, 462, 672. For the charter of the Free Society, see *PMHB*, V (1881), 37, or Hazard, *Register*, I, 394, which last also includes a brief account of an early meeting of the Society's founders.

ISAAC WHEELDON of "Llanroost," Denbighshire, glover, to whom James Claypoole sent his love in a letter dated 21 7m 1682, addressed to John Goodson, when the *Jeffrey* was in the Downs, had purchased a share of the John ap John-Thomas Wynne purchase of 5000 acres. Wheeldon obtained a warrant for 156 acres to be laid out in Chester County 16 3m 1683, having already gotten a warrant for a city lot the month before. In 1695 he assigned his rights in his original purchase to Samuel Lewis of Darby. Browning, 176; *Pennsylvania Archives*, 3rd Series, III, 50, 176, 179. In the same letter Claypoole asked to be remembered to NATHANIEL WATSON, also on board the *Jeffrey*. When Watson died in 1688, he left bequests of £20 "at least," to his kinsman Router of Burlington; to Robert and Ann Eyres £4 "or five if it will be spared"; to Samuel Bulkley £5, and to Hannah Decow £20. For abstract of his will see *PGSP*, I, 68-69, and for mention of the two men, see the original Claypoole Letter-Book, HSP. For loadings of the *Jeffrey*, see London port book E 190/109/1, PRO.

The *Jeffrey* [20]

Thomas Arnold (Arnall), master, for Pennsylvania and Virginia

29 [August] THE SOCIETY OF PENNSYLVANIA: 133 cwt. wrought iron; 12 cwt. nails; 6 cwt. cordage; 6 doz. shod shovels; 3 cwt. wrought brass; 3 fodders [fodder: 19 pigs of 123 lbs. each] lead; 2 cwt. lead shot. [Duty] £7 18s. 2½d.

31 [August] THE OFFICERS AND SOCIETY OF PENNSYLVANIA: 54 horse collars; 2 cwt. cordage; 1½ cwt. lead shot; 3 cwt. haberdashery wares; 9 lbs. thrown, 12 lbs. wrought silk; 4 cwt. wrought iron. [Duty] 11s. 1d.

1 [September] THE SOCIETY OF PENNSYLVANIA: 16 cwt. nails; 5 doz. shod shovels. [Duty] 5s.

8 [September] NICHOLAS MOORE: for Pennsylvania and Virginia, 11 cwt. lead shot; 6 small minikin bayes; 140 yds. flannel; 100 goads cottons; 60 lbs. stuffs; cwt. wrought leather; 2 doz. men's woolen hose; 4 cwt. cheese; 4 firkins butter; 2½ cwt. pewter; 9 cwt. red ochre; ¼ cwt. starch; 7 doz. felt, 5 doz. castor hats; 1 quarter wheat flour; 16 pairs men's worsted, 8 doz. men's woolen hose; 8 doz. plain gloves; ½ cwt. haberdashery wares; 24 doz. candles; 110 lbs. wrought silk; 6½ pcs. English linen; 12 coverlets, wool and hair; cwt. wrought copper; 5 cwt. wrought iron; 3 cwt. books; 3 cwt. apothecary wares; ½ chest window glass. [Duty] £5 17s. 11d.[114]

9 [September] JOHN FORDHAM: 2 doz. castor hats; 2 cwt. wrought iron; cwt. nails; 24 small gross tobacco pipes; ½ chalder grindle stones; 10 small saddles; 1½ doz. bridles; 1 doz. bellows. [Duty] 9s. ½d.

[9 September] ROBERT SMITH: 10½ cwt. gunpowder. [Duty] £1 1s.

[9 September] JAMES CLAYPOOLE: 3 cwt. wrought iron; 4 cwt. nails; 4 shod shovels; 6 lbs. shoes. [Duty] 2s. 2d.[115]

[9 September] THE SOCIETY OF PENNSYLVANIA: 840 yds. flannel; 122 cwt. wrought iron; 10¾ cwt. wrought pewter; 6 cwt. wrought copper; 4 cwt. books; 14,000 bricks; 42 cwt. nails; 42 small saddles; 14 doz. bridles; 48 cwt. cordage; 100 doz. candles; 3 chests window glass; 15 doz. felts [hats]; 56 lbs. hard wax; cwt. alum; 8 cwt. glue; 9 cwt. starch; 5 doz. castor hats; 570 lbs. shoes; 3½ cwt. lead; 32 doz. men's, 10 doz. children's woolen hose; 10 bushels oatmeal; 10 doz. plain Monmouth caps; 31 small minikin bayes; 16 cwt. ochre; 600 goads cottons; 187 lbs. stuffs; 2 pcs. hair cloth; 150 lbs. linsey woolsey; 4 cwt. apothecary wares; 9 cwt. russetting [a brown material]; tin and nursery wares, nets, 2 pair smith's bellows, painter's colours, red lead, value

114 DR. NICHOLAS MORE of London, F.P. of 10,000 acres and president of and substantial investor in the Free Society, probably brought his family with him: his wife Mary Hedge, and children Samuel, Nicholas, Mary, Sarah, and possibly Rebecca. For further notes on Dr. More, see *PGM*, XXI, 96n.

115 James Claypoole, treasurer of the Free Society, sent over RALPH WITHERS of Bishops Canning, Wiltshire, F.P. of 500 acres, as deputy treasurer until Claypoole himself should come over. Withers died soon after his arrival, however, and letters of administration on his estate were granted 12 1m 1683, to John Bezer, one of the Society's commissioners. *PGM*, XIX, 250; *Pennsylvania Archives*, 2nd Series, XIX, 383. Claypoole also sent over EDWARD COLE, a brickmaker by trade, indented to Claypoole for four years, who had instructions to build the Claypooles a house in the town to be laid out in the province. *PMHB*, X, 197-200.

JOHN GOODSON, "chyrrugeon" of Bartholomew Close, London, and F.P. of 500 acres, with his wife Sarah Pococke, and probably their three children: Sarah, Job and Lydia, sailed on the *Jeffrey*. His certificate from Peel Monthly Meeting was dated 30 6m 1682. Myers, *Quaker Arrivals*, 6; *PMHB*, X, 197. In the original letter to Goodson, cited in Note 113 above, Claypoole sent his love "to thy wife and maid Mary," but did not mention the children. Was Mary a servant, a child not listed in the records of the London and Middlesex Quarterly Meeting, or a young friend of the family?

£44 15s. [Duty] £24 9s. 8d. From the Free List: 100 pcs. fustian. From the Wool Book: 6 penistones friezed; 7 kersies; 4½ short cloths.

11 [September] PETER DELINE (Deliens, Deluna?): 4 doz. felt hats; 4 doz. men's woolen, 1 doz. worsted hose; cwt. shot; 6 doz. pairs gloves. [Duty] 5s. 10d.

[11 September] NICHOLAS MOORE: 55 lbs. linsey woolsey; 2 cwt. apothecary wares; 3 cwt. wrought iron; 1½ doz. shod shovels. [Duty] 9s. 5½d.

No known ships with passengers arrived in the Delaware during November, but in December two sailed up river. The first of these was the *Antelope*, bringing Irish passengers. Naturally it does not appear in the English port books, but some of the passengers registered their arrival as being on 9 or 10 December 1682.[116]

The *Antelope* [21]

Edward Cooke, master, from Belfast

ANN MILCOME (Mallcum) of Armagh in Ireland, "with her Children Jane Greaves, Mary Milcome." [117]

---

[116] In February, 1683, James Claypoole wrote that he had heard "there had been 21 sail ships arrived last summer in Delaware," and that Penn "had held a Court in Pensilvania and was gone to hold another in New Castle. . . ." The court or assembly at Upland opened 4 Dec. 1682, and adjourned 7 Dec. 1682 "for 21 days." *Votes*, I, 1, 11. By then, summer was certainly over; with the arrival of the *Antelope*, 21 known ships had come in with passengers, and the variant dates of arrival, as given in *PMHB*, VIII, 329, and *ibid.*, IX, 224, are close enough in time to account for the news Claypoole had heard.

[117] ANN MALLCUM (Milcome, Millcom), of Killmore parish, Ballyhagan Meeting, Ireland, brought a certificate of removal dated 1 1m 1682. Possibly the widow of John Malcom, she and her daughter JANE GREAVES (Greer) of Loughall, because they had "no man in their family, except they might get a servant or servants, and having no want of things necessary for a livelihood," had decided to emigrate as early as 9 4m 1681, the mother being unwilling to part with her daughter who particularly wanted to go. The certificate seems to have included, though not by name, "her other daughter," and "another daughter of hers, and her husband and children," and mentioned that "several neighbors also" intended to "adventure." See Falls Monthly Meeting Certificates of Removal, 15, cited in Note 73 above; also Myers, *Immigration*, 300, cited in Note 6 above. In February, 1684, it was reported to Falls Meeting that Ann "Millcom doth keep disorderly house and Sell Strong Liquors to English and Indians Suffering them to drink till they be drunk. . . . Also about her Daughter Mary's Loose Carriage which is reported she is addicted to." See photostats of Falls Monthly Meeting Minutes, 8, GSP. For the Widow Millcom's further activities, see *Bucks Court Records*, 7, 18, 19. Her daughter Jane Greaves, as Jane *Graves* m. 8 6m 1685, Maurice Leiston (Liston), a mariner of New Castle Co. *Pennsylvania Archives*, 2nd Series, IX, 222; *ibid.*, XIX, 361.

Who the neighbors were who "adventured" with the widow Mallcom remains undetermined. But at least three men from Ireland arrived that year, probably on the *Antelope*. John Low and Joseph Low of Ballyhagan, parish of Kilmore, Armagh, brought a joint certificate dated 31 5m 1682. Myers, *Quaker Arrivals*, 6. John Low, and presumably his wife, were deceased by 2 9m 1685, when the Philadelphia Meeting had a letter from William Berry of Kent Co., mentioned in Note 77 above, "concerning the children of John Lowe, deceased." Arrangements were made for the children to be sent up from the Lower Counties; Archibald Mickel took the boy, Griffith Jones "the middle Girl," and the youngest was "to be disposed of" by the women friends. *PGSP*, I, 290, 295, 297; *Ibid.*, II, 94, 98.

Archibald Michael (Mickle, Mickell, Mitchell), cooper from the Men's Meeting at Richard Boyes' house near Lisburn, Antrim, Ireland, brought a certificate of removal dated 2 6m 1682. Myers, *Quaker Arrivals*, 6. He probably brought his wife Sarah and sister Hannah who m. Abraham Carliel, with him, and on 16 2m 1683, obtained a warrant for a city lot on rent. *Pennsylvania Archives*, 3rd Series, II, 750. He later acquired a lot in Chestnut Street and other property in the city, but when he died in 1706 was of Newton, Gloucester Co., N. J. His will was witnessed by Sarah Low. Liber I, 149, Liber II, 95, abstracts in *N. J. Archives*, 1st Series, XXIII, 317, cited in Note 55 above. It seems possible that the Joseph Low who brought a certificate of clearness from Newton in 1713, with intentions of marrying Elizabeth Taylor, was the son of John Low, noted above. Myers, *Quaker Arrivals*, 55.

FRANCIS SANDERS, servant to Ann Milcome, to serve four years; "loose the 10th of the 10 M^o 1686."

JAMES ATTKINSON, from Clanbrazill, County Armagh, arrived here "1682 9 10 mo." [118]

JOHN ASHBROOKE, servant to James Atkinson, arrived here "1682 9 10 mo."

In all probability the next ship to appear in the Delaware was from Bristol. This was the 300-ton *Unicorn*, bearing goods for both Pennsylvania and Virginia. The first mention of this ship was in the *London Gazette* of 22 June 1682, where, under the Bristol dateline of 17 June it was announced the ship was "now ready to take in Goods and Passengers and to Sail the next month" for "Pensilvania and New-Jersey." Those wishing to take freight or passage were directed to apply to Thomas Goldney or John Dudlestone "in High-street" or to the commander.

Not until the beginning of the last week in August was any cargo loaded for Pennsylvania; Virginia goods went on after that up to 2 September. But the ship did not sail immediately, and on 5 October 1682, the *London Impartial Mercury* noted that in Bristol a ship was "fitting out for Pensylvania on board which 40 Quakers together with their families will imbarq." The paper reported that "'tis said they carry over with them 300 pounds-worth of Half-pence, and Farthings which in that Collony go current for twice their value and 'tis added that some discontented Presbyterians will Likewise accompany them." Twelve days later the same paper reported that a ship from Bristol "full fraught with Quakers bound for Pennsylvania, is ready to sail." There seems little doubt it arrived before the end of December when Penn wrote of the arrival of twenty-three ships. [119]

The *Unicorn* of Bristol [22]

Thomas Cooper, master, for Pennsylvania and Virginia

25 [August] WILLIAM CLOUDE: 4 cwt. wrought iron; 3 pieces qty. 120 yds. English linen; cwt. lead shot; 3 doz. bodices; 150 made garments; 1½ cwt. brass and copper

---

118 JAMES ATKINSON's certificate from Drogheda Meeting was dated 23 8m 1681. He lived for a time with Griffith Jones in Philadelphia where Friends, early in March, 1683, questioned his leaving Clanbrazill "contrary to the Consent of friends," who "signifyed [him] to be very much in Debt, &ca." Apparently matters were cleared up, however, for he declared intentions of marriage with Hannah Newby of New Jersey in 1684, and was given a certificate of clearness to that place. *PGSP*, I, 255-257, 271-272. By 1701 he had married Hannah Day, widow of the carpenter John Day, mentioned in Note 86 above. *Pennsylvania Archives*, 2nd Series, XIX, 205, 458.

One other family might have been on the *Antelope*, that of Valentine Hollingsworth. He was from Ballenisckcrannel, parish of Sego, Armagh, and is said to have brought his wife Ann, daughter Mary and her husband Thomas Conway of Lisburn, Antrim; daughter Catherine, who m. in 1688 George Robinson; probably sons Thomas and Samuel, and an indentured servant, John Musgrave. For an account of this family, see Myers, *Immigration*, 311-313, 318, cited in Note 6 above.

119 For notices of the *Unicorn*, see *PMHB*, LXXV, 152, 154-155. For the loadings, see Bristol port book E 190/1144/1, PRO.

manufactured; ½ cwt. pewter; 3 small saddles; 3 pieces English fustians; 2 cwt. nails; 6 doz. Irish stockings.[120]

[25 August] ANTHONY ELTON: 3 cwt. nails; 15½ cwt. wrought iron; ½ cwt. brass manufactured; ½ cwt. haberdashery wares; cwt. pewter; 60 lbs. serges; 1 short cloth; 2 chests window glass; cwt. steel; ½ cwt. gunpowder; 1½ cwt. lead shot; cwt. wrought iron; 200 lbs. leather manufactured; ½ chalder grindle stones.[121]

[25 August] JAMES HILL: 20 lbs. shoes; 10 pairs wool cards; cwt. iron; 120 suits wearing apparel; 60 lbs. serges; cwt. wrought pewter; ½ cwt. brass manufactured; 3 cwt. shot; ½ cwt. gunpowder; 4 cwt. nuts; cwt. wrought pewter.[122]

26 [August] ANTHONY ELTON: cwt. wrought iron; ½ cwt. cordage.

The last ship to arrive from England before the year was out was the *Submission*. From its log, which survives in part, comes its date of sailing from Liverpool: 6 7m (September) 1682, the passengers having embarked the day before. The voyage was a stormy one, as a result of which in all probability, the vessel came into Chesapeake Bay, rather than into the Delaware. The passengers landed at Choptank, on the Eastern Shore of Maryland on 2 9m (November) 1682, and word of their arrival certainly reached Penn before the end of the year. Most of the passengers had made their way to Appoquiminy Creek, twenty miles south of New Castle, by mid-February 1683.[123]

---

[120] WILLIAM CLOUD (Clowde) from Seene, Wiltshire, F.P. of 500 acres, had his land laid out on the south side of Naaman's Creek in Chester Co. His son Joseph Cloud had come in as a servant to John Bezer who had loaded goods on the *Bristol Factor* in October, 1681, for whom see Note 7 above. In 1691, William Cloud conveyed 200 acres to Joseph and John Cloud; three years later Joseph conveyed his rights to "his Brother John Cloud." Other brothers, who presumably came with the father, were William, Jr., Jeremiah and Robert Cloud. *Chester Court Records*, 255, 326; Smith, *Delaware County*, 453. Jacob Willis was probably on the *Unicorn*, also. He claimed he had come "into the Country at the first Settling of it" as servant to William Cloud. James Widows and Elizabeth Clayton, servants to John Bezer, may have been on the ship. Widows in 1685 took up on rent 2000 acres in New Castle County which he sold to Henry Pierce in 1703. Christian Steward, who came in a servant to Nathaniel Allen, also cited in Note 7 above, may have been on this ship. She later married John Pullen; both she and James Widows sold their headrights to Isaac Taylor. *Pennsylvania Archives*, 2nd Series, XIX, 265, 406, 470.

[121] ANTHONY ELTON, mason of Yatesborough, Wiltshire, and F.P. of 500 acres, was one of the twelve commissioners sent over by the Free Society of Traders to reside in the province. Probably with him were his wife Susanna, daughter Mary who m. 25 10m 1684, Thomas Kendall, sons George, Anthony, Jr., who m. Elizabeth Revell 20 Feb. 1688/9, and Thomas who d. in 1696. Though the father had land laid out in Bucks Co., he settled in Evesham Twp., Burlington Co., where he was deceased by 1686. See Stillwell, *Miscellany*, II, 13, 26, 37, 38, cited in Note 35; *Burlington Court Book*, 182, 187; *Pennsylvania Archives*, 2nd Series, XIX, 319.

[122] JAMES HILL, shoemaker of Beckington, Somersetshire, and F.P. of 500 acres, was certainly related to John Hill, shoemaker of "Bermington," Somersetshire, who was also a F.P. of 500 acres. James obtained an order for survey from the Proprietor dated 13 9m (Nov.) 1682, for part of his 500 acres which was laid out in Falls Twp., Bucks Co. Had the *Unicorn* arrived by that date? He settled in Burlington Co., however, where he was sheriff in 1685 and 1692, and had died by 1698. His only son and heir, Richard Hill, cordwainer of Bristol Twp., Bucks Co., and wife Agnes sold the Bucks Co. land in 1712 to Richard Hill, merchant of Philadelphia. *Burlington Court Book*, xli, 211; *Pennsylvania Archives*, 2nd Series, XIX, 530-531.

[123] For the log of the *Submission*, original of which is in the Society Miscellaneous Collection, HSP, and names of the passengers, see *PGSP*, I, 7-13; for the passengers' arrivals, see Battle, *Bucks County*, 674-675, or the original Bucks County Register in which the date of arrival is clearly 2 9m 1682. In Capt. Settle's defence, it might be noted that he had on board goods to sell, and if he wished to trade them for

The *Submission* [23]

James Settle, master, from Liverpool

16 [August] PHINEAS PEMBERTON: 2 cases, 3 boxes, 1 chest, qty. 3 cwt. wrought iron; 4½ cwt. nails; 80 ells English linen; 25 lbs. Norwich stuffs; 20 lbs. new shoes; ½ cwt. haberdashery; 1 cask qty. 2 barrels oatmeal; ½ cwt. cheese; 1 doz. men's woolen stockings; 2 demi-castors [beaver hats] English making; 1 lb. silk manufactured; 20 lbs. gunpowder.[124]

22 [August] RALPH PEMBERTON: 2 TTs [2 fatts] qty. 100 lbs. woolen cloth; ½ doz. new wool cards.[125]

[22 August] JAMES HARRISON: 1 chest, 1 trunk, 1 cask; 1 pack qty. 100 ells English linen; 3 doz. felts English making; 100 lbs. new shoes; ½ cwt. wrought iron.[126]

26 [August] THOMAS WINN (Wynne): 2 sacks, 3 tubs, 1 pot qty. ¾ cwt. cheese; ½ barrel butter; 1½ bushels oatmeal; 5 yds. frieze; 6 lbs. woolen cloth; 3 coverlets, wool and hair; 1 tub salt; cwt. dressed hemp; 1 pannier qty. 50 glass bottles; 1 twisting mill value £4 10s.[127]

Maryland or Virginia tobacco, he had to sail up the Chesapeake. Pemberton, however, naturally was annoyed at being left on the wrong side of a peninsula in winter, and felt the ship's master had been dishonest. *PMHB*, IX, 229-230. For the *Submission's* loadings, see Liverpool port books E 190/1344/1 and E 190/1345/1, PRO.

[124] PHINEAS PEMBERTON, aged 33, grocer from Bolton in Lancashire, brought his wife Phoebe, daughter of James Harrison, and young children Abigail and Joseph Pemberton. Their certificate from Hartshaw Meeting, filed with Falls Monthly Meeting, was dated 18 5m 1682, a month before Phinehas, as he spelled his name at this time, started loading goods on the *Submission*. He was not an original purchaser, but in right of his wife became heir to James Harrison's land. *Pennsylvania Archives*, 2nd Series, XIX, 525, 540, 556. The Bucks County Register of Arrivals was compiled by him in his capacity as deputy register for Bucks Co. Its transcription in *PMHB*, IX, is unfortunately confusing, and does not correspond in all details to the list of passengers in the log. From the transcript of the latter, in *PGSP*, I, it would appear that he brought over five servants: Joseph Mather, Elizabeth Bradbury, Jane Lyon, Allis Dickinson and Lydia Wharmsby. The transcript in Battle, *Bucks County*, assigns Elizabeth Bradbury to Phinehas' father Ralph, and Allis Dickinson and Jane Lyon to Phinehas' father-in-law, James Harrison. They were all to be free in November, 1686. Of these, JOSEPH MATHER, aged 18, eventually m. the only daughter and heiress of John Russell, in right of whom Mather took up a lot on the south side of Sassafras (Race) Street in Philadelphia. *Pennsylvania Archives*, 2nd Series, XIX, 589, 605; ibid., 3rd Series, III, 399.

[125] RALPH PEMBERTON, aged 72, was Phinehas' father. The ELIZABETH BRADBURY, aged 16, assigned to him in Battle's transcript, was probably a daughter of Roger and Ellenor Bradbury, servants of Randolph Blackshaw, for whom see Note 128 below.

[126] JAMES HARRISON, aged ca. 54, according to the log, was a shoemaker of Bolton, Lancashire and F.P. of 5000 acres. He brought his wife Ann, and aged mother Agnes Harrison, then 80 years old, as well as a number of servants. Of these, ROBERT BOND, son of Thomas of Waddicar Hall, near Garstang, Lancashire, died not long after arrival. JANE LYON, attributed by Battle as one of the Harrison servants, became the 2nd wife of Robert Lundy, for whom see Note 14 above. ALLIS (Alice) DICKINSON, on the log given as a servant to Phinehas Pemberton, m. Edmund McVeagh, who had come in as a servant to Thomas Holme, for whom see Note 20, above. RICHARD RADCLIFFE, aged 21, servant to the Harrisons, was probably the son of James Radcliff who came over with his family in 1685. *Pennsylvania Archives*, 2nd Series, XIX, 525; *PMHB*, XXX, 496-498. JOSEPH STEWARD (Steward), aged ca. 15, and Lydia Wharmsby, aged ca. 42, were also servants. Stewart may have m. in 1694, Alice Wright at Chesterfield Meeting. *PMHB*, IX, 347.

[127] Thomas Wynne's daughter REBECCA WYNNE, aged 20, and stepdaughters, JANE and MARJERY MAUD (Mode), were on the *Submission*, according to the log; no mention is made of Wynne's wife, but "FFARCLIF" HEDGES, "apprentice to Thomas Winn," appears on the original Bucks County Register, and with ELLEN HOLLAND, also a servant, is included in the log. Also on the *Submission* was ELLIS JONES, aged 45, from "Denby, or Flint." With him came his wife

29 [August] JAMES SETTLE: 1 pack, 1 bundle, 1 hhd., 1 barrel qty. 170 ells English linen; 170 lbs. woolen cloth; 12 lbs. new shoes; 3 doz. men's woolen stockings; 14 lbs. haberdashery; cwt. pewter; 60 lbs. Norwich stuffs; 4 barrels strong beer qty. ½ tun exported in English-built shipping; 2 bundles hand sieves qty. 5 doz; 18 milking pales [pails] value £2 10s.

30 [August] RANDLE (Randolph) BLACKSHAW: 4 fardels, 2 bundles, 5 barrels, 2 casks, 2 bags qty. 118 lbs. woolen cloth; 150 ells English linen; 90 lbs. new shoes; 56 lbs. silk manufactured; 6 lbs. thrown silk; ½ cwt. & 10 lbs. haberdashery; 5½ doz. men's woolen stockings; 2 doz. men's worsted stockings; 1 doz. Yorkshire cushions; 2 cwt. nails; 2 cwt. wrought iron; 6 cwt. cast lead.[128]

30 [August] PHINEAS PEMBERTON: per post in foreign bulk 5 ells Hollands [linen from Holland for sheets, handkerchiefs, etc.] value 12s. 6d.

31 [August] RANDLE BLACKSHAW: an old mill stone value 8s.

[31 August] ANTHONY WOOD: 2 pairs cart wheels value £7.

1 [September] JAMES SETTLE: per post in foreign bulk 154 lbs. woolen cloth; ¼ cwt. pewter; 29 lbs. new shoes.

Though the *Submission* did not actually come up the Delaware, its passengers were destined for that river, and did cross the Atlantic before the end of the year, to complete Penn's total of twenty-three ships with passengers, as distinct from trading vessels; these would have been from the West Indies and small coastal vessels. Pennsylvania, with its steadily increasing population, was a good market as well as a religious haven.

It is now appropriate to say something about a wholly imaginary ship which was supposed to have left London in the fall of 1681 and taken thirty weeks to reach the Delaware, having been blown off course to the West Indies. It was said to have arrived finally on 16 April 1682, a date so positive as to give credence to the story.

The tale comes from a well known letter written by John Jones, the son of a young Welsh emigrant named Thomas Sion [John] Evan. According to this letter, Thomas Evan came in a ship called the *William Penn* which sailed from London. He had waited there some weeks for it to sail, having made a previous trip to town to find out about the pro-

---

Jane, aged 40, and children Barbara, 13, Dorothy, 10, Isaac 4 mos., and Mary Jones, 12. They were servants of the Proprietor: Ellis Jones was Penn's miller. Probably for his services he was granted a warrant for a city lot 17 4m 1683, and acquired land in Chester Co. *PMHB*, VIII, 95; *Pennsylvania Archives*, 3rd Series, II, 730; *Chester Court Records*, 238.

128 RANDOLPH BLACKSHAW, aged 60, of Hollinger, Cheshire, his wife Alice, aged 43, and children Phebe, 16, Sarah, 14, Abraham, 10, who died at sea; Jacob, 8, Mary, 6, Nehemiah, 3, and Martha, 1, all were on the *Submission*, according to the log. They brought as servants ROGER BRADBURY and his family, but of these, his wife Ellenor, sons Jacob, Joseph and Roger Bradbury were apparently sold in Maryland for their passage, while only Roger himself, his 14-year old daughter Martha, and 8-year old daughter Sarah, came to Pennsylvania with the Blackshaws. *PMHB*, IX, 229-230. The Blackshaws had sent over other servants on the *Friend's Adventure*, for which see Note 72 above.

The fifth family on the *Submission* was that of JAMES CLAYTON, aged 50, from Cheshire. With him came his wife Jane, aged 48, and their children James, 16, Sarah, 14, John, 11, Mary, 8, and Joseph and Lydia "Cleaton," both aged 5. He obtained a warrant for 250 acres in Chester Co. on 24 6m 1683. *Pennsylvania Archives*, 3rd Series, III, 114.

posed colony. During the tedious thirty-week voyage, Thomas Evan learned to speak English.

The letter was apparently written about 1725, eighteen years after the death of Thomas Evan; his son put down what he remembered of what his father had remembered, thereby causing writers a great deal of work trying to reconcile the various dates mentioned in the letter. The father no doubt left London, as he said, in the fall of 1681, but in one of the many ships sailing to the West Indies, where he would have waited for trans-shipment to Pennsylvania in the spring. Norton Claypoole had done just this a short time before, as no doubt many other adventurous young men did.[129]

All evidence points to the inaccuracy of the account. In the first place, young Evan need not have gone all the way to London from Wales to learn about the new colony; there was plenty of talk and knowledge there among Friends about Pennsylvania, and sales of land to be laid out in the new province had already been made. Second, the port books show no ship named *William Penn*, and no ship of any name leaving London for Pennsylvania in the fall of 1681, except the *John & Sarah,* which did not take thirty weeks. Furthermore, it is most unlikely that William Penn would have permitted a ship to be called after him, as witness his wish to have his colony called simply Sylvania. In addition, owners in those days never used a first and surname when naming their ships. Finally, as a rule colonists took whatever ships were in the colonial trade.

Reference to a second apparently mythical ship appeared in the summer of 1682 in a London newspaper. Datelined Plymouth, 10 July 1682, the London *Domestick Intelligence* carried this notice: "This day a Ship sailed hence for the Island of Pensilvania, on Board which were 28 Quakers bound for that Island, having on Board all their Portable goods, resolving to Plant themselves there, there being as we hear 3000 of the Brethren already inhabitted in those parts." [130]

The Plymouth port books have no entries for Pennsylvania-bound ships at this time, but they do show ships being loaded for the island of Barbados, to which Quakers were still emigrating.[131] Who can blame that distant journalist for dressing up his item? Pennsylvania was news that summer, Barbados an old story. It would not have been the first

---

129 The letter may be found in Thomas Allen Glenn, *Merion in the Welsh Tract* (Norristown, Pa., 1896), 40-44, or in Myers, *Narratives,* 451-459, cited in Note 4 above. For Norton Claypoole, see John Camden Hotten, ed., *The Original Lists of Persons of Quality . . . 1600-1700* (New York, 1931), 357. For brief abstract of the will of Thomas John Evan who died in 1707, see *PMHB,* XV (1891), 198. See also Smith, *Delaware County,* 459, for short notice of Evan.

130 For the newspaper notice, see *PMHB,* LXXV, 152, issue Numb. 119 of the *Domestick Intelligence.*

131 The Plymouth port book E 190/1046/4, PRO, was examined for ship entries relating to Pennsylvania.

time liberties had been taken with the facts. Or the correspondent might have been honestly confused by these strange new names, or had heard a rumour that Quakers were sailing, and assumed it to have been to Pennsylvania.

In recapitulation, then, the following is a list of those ships known to have brought passengers and their goods up the Delaware in that first year of Pennsylvania's founding:

1. The *Bristol Factor*, Roger Drew, master, arrived 15 December, 1681.
2. The *John & Sarah*, Henry Smith, master, from London; arrived by 11 March 1681/2.
3. A ship from New England, name unknown; arrived 19 May 1682.
4. The *Amity*, Richard Dymond, master, from London; arrived 3 August 1682.
5. The *Freeman*, George Southern, master, from Liverpool; arrived 5 or 6 August 1682.
6. The *Hester & Hannah*, William East, master, from London; arrived 8 August 1682.
7. The *Lyon*, John Compton, master, from Liverpool; arrived 13 August 1682.
8. The *Friendship*, Robert Crossman, master, from Liverpool; arrived 14 August 1682.
9. The *Mary*, William Lugger, master, from Fowey; arrived 15 August 1682.
10. The *Society*, Thomas Jordan, master, from Bristol; arrived in August 1682.
11. The *Golden Hinde*, Edward Reade, master, from London; arrived by 18 September 1682.
12. The *Samuel*, John Adey, master, from London; probably arrived by 18 September 1682.
13. The *Friend's Adventure*, Thomas Wall, master, from Liverpool; probably arrived by 18 September 1682.
14. The *Providence*, Robert Hooper, master, from Scarborough; arrived 29 September 1682.
15. The *Elizabeth Ann & Catherine*, Thomas Hudson, master, from London; arrived 29 September 1682.
16. The *Hopewell*, Michael Yoakley, master, from London; probably arrived in October, 1682.
17. The *Lamb*, John Tench, master, from Liverpool; arrived 22 October 1682.
18. The *Bristol Factor*, Roger Drew, master, arrived late in October, 1682.
19. The *Welcome*, Robert Greenway, master, from London; arrived 28 October 1682.
20. The *Jeffrey*, Thomas Arnold, master, from London; probably arrived late in October, 1682.
21. The *Antelope*, Edward Cooke, master, from Belfast; arrived 9 or 10 December 1682.
22. The *Unicorn*, Thomas Cooper, master, from Bristol; arrived in December, 1682.
23. The *Submission*, James Settle, master, from Liverpool; arrived Choptank, Md., 2 November 1682.

NOTES TO WILLIAM PENN'S 23 SHIPS

A ship not included in this article, which loaded for Pennsylvania from London on 16 September 1682, was the <u>Adventure</u>, Moses Locke master. This ship was apparently not registered from London, and appears to have sailed from another east coast port, running up the Thames to take on cargo for James Cox, a London merchant who did not himself come to America. No passengers are known to have come to Pennsylvania on the <u>Adventure</u>, but since all these vessels did carry passengers there seems a good chance that some will some day be identified.

There are several references in contemporary correspondence to a group of 24 Quakers sailing from Plymouth for Pennsylvania during this period. However no vessel is found in the Port Books that seems a likely candidate. There are no Plymouth loadings for Pennsylvania at the proper time, nor yet for other nearby colonies for which these Quakers could have shared the transportation. It is possible that this group coasted to the Downs and transhipped to a vessel there in rendezvous.

W. L. S.

CORRECTIONS AND ADDITIONS

The reader's attention is called to the following errors, both typographical and factual, which appear in Numbers 2 and 3 of this present Volume. The Editor is indebted to Miss Ida C. Townsend, Mr. Walter Lee Sheppard, Jr., Mrs. Mary S. Patterson, Dr. George E. McCracken and Mr. Conrad Wilson for their notices of these errors.

p. 38, Note 30: For Joseph Powel, read *Powell*.

p. 42, Note 48: Charles Plumley, joiner, b. 9 12m 1674; d. 1708, was a son of Charles Plumley, Sr., of Wells Parish, Somersetshire, and his wife *Margery* (not Margaret, as given on p. 45, Note 65, under Henry Paxson) Page, of Butcomb Parish, who were m. 11 12m 1665. Their other children, in addition to the above Charles, were: William Plumley, b. 7 10m 1666; James Plumley, b. 22 6m 1668, who d. young; James Plumley (2nd), b. 3 2m 1669; Joseph Plumley, b. 31 8m 1671, all of whom were born in Wells Parish; John Plumley, b. 8 7m 1677; George Plumley, b. 14 4m 1680, both born in Priddy Parish, Somersetshire. The elder Charles Plumley's death occurred in late 1682 or early 1683 in Pennsylvania; his widow m. 13 6m 1684, Henry Paxson as his 2nd wife. The "brother-in-law" Henry Paxson, mentioned in the will of Charles Plumley, the younger, in 1708, was presumably the son of Plumley's mother's second husband. See Gilbert Cope Collection, Vol. Co 65, 79-109, Collections of the Genealogical Society of Pennsylvania (GSP).

p. 48, Note 76: For Robert Taylor, read *Laylor*.

p. 49, Note 80: For Andrew Health, read *Heath*. Last line: Change Bucks Court Records to read *Burlington Court Book*.

p. 50, Note 86, line 3: Change Burlington Court Records to Burlington Court *Book*.

p. 52, Note 91: The Settle certificate, as recorded in Transcript of Records of Middletown Monthly Meeting, Bucks Co. (Bu 32F), 46, GSP, was for Cuthbert Hayhurst, wife and family; Nicholas Waln, wife and three children; Thomas *Wiglesworth* and wife Alice; Thomas Walmsley, wife Elizabeth and children; Thomas Croasdill, wife Agnes and six children; Thomas Stackhouse and wife; Ellin Cowgill, widow, and children, and William Hayhurst, the latter a brother of Cuthbert Hayhurst and a widower; he died not long after his arrival in Pennsylvania.

p. 53, Note 97: See correction above for Thomas *Wiglesworth*'s name (*not* Wrightsworth).

p. 57, Note 108: The exact tonnage for the *Welcome* is now found in C.O. 13/14/19, and C.O. 33/14/26, Public Record Office, London. These folios, distinguished by the last numbers 19 and 26, were rebound and renumbered in the summer of 1963, too late to insert this present correction.

p. 58, Note 112: Benjamin East, who m. Hannah, daughter of John West, was a *brother* of William East, master of the *Hester & Hannah, not* a son, as stated in this note. Benjamin and William East were sons of William East, Sr.

p. 64, Note 126: For Robert Lundy, read *Richard* Lundy, also referred to on p. 34, Note 14. For Joseph Steward (Steward), read (*Stewart*).

p. 65, Note 128: For James Clayton's son Joseph, read *Joshua* . . . "Cleaton."

THE *LYON* OF LIVERPOOL IN THE CHESTER PORT BOOKS, 1682

By Marion Balderston *

In the often quoted letter to his partner John ap John, written 26 6m (August) 1682, shortly after his arrival in the Delaware, Dr. Edward Jones wrote that "most of the things [he and his fellow passengers had brought with them] will not be sold until you come over because so many things had previously been brought here." [1] When Jones wrote this, at least six ships had arrived at Upland since the first of that August, and no doubt their cargoes, piled up on the river's bank, made an impressive sight.

The ship on which Jones had sailed, the *Lyon*, had been registered in and come from Liverpool. The only goods mentioned in the Liverpool port books for that year of 1682 for that ship were put on board for the master, John Compton. Yet four Welsh families numbering sixteen persons are known to have come on this trip, while the ship transported forty passengers in all, including servants. [2] Who were the other passengers, where were they from, and what were their goods?

* Mrs. Balderston points out that she is *not* a Dame of the British Empire, as incorrectly stated in the asterisked note at the foot of page 27 of this Volume. She was, however, awarded the King's Medal (K.M.), and was made a *Member* of the Order of the British Empire (M.B.E.).

[1] For the letter, see Charles H. Browning, *Welsh Settlement of Pennsylvania* (Philadelphia, 1912), 65-70.

[2] For John Compton's goods stowed on the *Lyon*, see *The Pennsylvania Genealogical Magazine* (PGM), XXIII, 39, and for the four known Welsh families, *ibid.*, Note 39.

72

Fortunately, two books for the small port of Chester exist for 1682. These give the names of five additional shippers, and list enough merchandise to fill that 90-ton vessel. From these books it becomes obvious that John Compton, having loaded his own goods at Liverpool on 22 April 1682, sailed out of the estuary of the Mersey to the Irish Sea, veered west and then south and then eastward and up the Dee to Chester, in all only a few days' sail. He and other Liverpool captains often stopped there at Chester between longer voyages to load coal from the Welsh mines which they then transported to Dublin or Cork.

The following entries from these Chester port records are from the Collector's Book and the Searcher's Book.[3] The Collector totalled the duty to be paid by each shipper, itemizing the dutiable goods, and entering the "value in toto" of the shipment. The Searcher was interested in the number and size of bundles and packages, since he had to stow them in the ship. He therefore entered the goods, item by item, in his records, thereby providing a more complete list of goods belonging to the shipper than the Collector had noted. These two lists are hereinafter combined, the Searcher's list being entered first, then the Collector's, in which the duty and "value in toto" are shown.

The *Lyon* of Liverpool
John Compton, master, for Pennsylvania

2 [May 1682] OWEN FOULKE: 1 bundle qty. [quantity] 60 yds. flannel; 2 sacks qty. 8 Winchester bushels oatmeal. [Duty] 2s. 4½d.[4]

5 [May] JOHN WOOD: 1 cwt. wrought iron; 2 cwt. nails; 6 single bayes [narrow wool cloth]; 1 pail qty. ½ cwt. of butter; 1 barrel qty. 9 measures of oatmeal and groats; 1 hhd. qty. 3 cwt. biscuits; 1 flitch

---

[3] The Chester port books are in the Public Record Office, Chancery Lane, London: the Collector's Book, E 190/1344/13, the Searcher's Book, E 190/1344/6.

[4] OWEN FOULKE, tanner from Bettws-y-Coed, Caernarvonshire, Wales, had purchased on 23 1m (March) 1681/2, for £3 2s. 6d. a two-thirtieth share of the 5000 acres sold to John ap Thomas and Thomas Wynne by William Penn. See Philadelphia Deed Book C-1, 291: 23 1m 1681[/2], John ap Thomas *et al.* to Owen Foulke. On 12 4m 1683, Foulke obtained a warrant for laying out 200 acres of this purchase. The survey was returned into the surveyor general's office five days later on 17 June 1683. (*Pennsylvania Archives*, 3rd Series, III, 125.) On 13 July 1686, Foulke obtained another warrant for 400 acres to be laid out in New Castle Co. (*Ibid.*, 2nd Series, VII, 196.) On 27 4m 1692, as Owen "folke," he sold 150 acres in Darby Twp. (now Delaware Co.) to Samuel Levis. (*Records of the Courts of Chester County, Pennsylvania, 1681-1697* [Philadelphia, 1910], 268.) Listed as a person "not a Friend," Owen "Folk" was buried 5 6m 1695. (W. W. Hinshaw, *Encyclopedia of American Quaker Genealogy* (Ann Arbor, Mich., 1938), II, 444.) In 1719, one Ellenor "Fowke," widow of Duck Creek Hundred, Kent Co., possibly the relict of Owen Foulke, wrote her will. Mentioned therein were her son Henry Fowke, daughter Ann, grandchild Ann, widow of Thomas Gillett; Mary Owens, John, Stephen, Lydia, James and Peter Sanders, John Owens, Ellenor Fowke, Owen, Stephen and Sarah Fowke, Rebecca Banto and Jane Gano, the last of whom was named executrix. See *Calendar of Delaware Wills*, 1682-1800 (Wilmington, 1911), 22.

bacon; 34 yds. English linen. From the Collector's Book: 7 lbs. pewter. [Duty] 11s. 6d. Value in toto, £11 9s. 9d.[5]

[5 May] THOMAS TAYLOR: ¼ cwt. butter; 1 barrel salt; ¼ cwt. gunpowder; 14 lbs. lead shot; ½ cwt. haberdashery; 2 cwt. nails; 2 cwt. wrought iron; 98 yds. flannel; 10 yds. English linen; 1 cwt. & 2 quarters cheese; 8 lbs. Norwich stuffs [wool]; ¼ cwt. lead shot. From the Collector's Book: 2½ barrels, 1 firkin, 1 stound [a woolen vessel], 1 tub, 2 churns, qty. 8 Winchester bushels oatmeal, and other wares. [Duty] 9s. 4d. Value in toto, £9 6s. 2d.[6]

[5 May] EDWARD JONES & CO: For Dublin: 120 yds. flannel; 63 yds. English linen; 1 firkin soap; 40 lbs. leather manufactured [skins already dressed]; 12 lbs. Norwich stuffs; 22 doz. men's woolen hose; 40 yds. flannel; 14 lbs. haberdashery; 1 quarter & 2 lbs. oatmeal; 2 flitches bacon; 6 lbs. shot; 16 lbs. manufactured leather. From the Collector's Book: 20 bundles, 8 cases, 2 trunks, 8 boxes, 2 panniers, 7 tubs, 4 sacks, 1 barrel, qty. 2¾ cwt. wrought iron, and other wares. [Duty] £1 13s. 7d. Value in toto, £33 11s. 11½d.[7]

15 [May] RICHARD CROSBY: 2 chests, 1 box qty. 4 cwt. wrought iron; 3 doz. plain leather gloves; 20 lbs. new shoes; 1 box qty. 16 doz. men's woolen hose; 1 box qty. 1 chest window glass; ¼ cwt. gunpowder; ½ cwt. cast lead; 2 parcels, 1 bundle qty. apparel and bedding; 1 sack

---

[5] John Wood was not a purchaser of land from any of the Welsh companies, and has not been identified. If he was the representative from Bucks County at the Assembly held 12 1m 1682/3, and again on 24 8m 1683, he was almost certainly the John Wood of Sheffield Parish, Yorkshire, who had arrived in 1678 in the *Shield* of Hull with his family. He had taken up 478 acres in what became Falls Twp., in Bucks Co. See "Votes and Proceedings of the House of Representatives of the Province of Pennsylvania," *Pennsylvania Archives*, 8th Series, I, 13, 44; also W. W. H. Davis, *The History of Bucks County.* . . . (Doylestown, Pa., 1876), 36.

[6] This was probably THOMAS TAYLOR of Worthenbury, Flintshire, bapt. 30 March 1628, who married by 1674, Frances, b. 1644, daughter of John Yardle. Taylor purchased 500 acres of John ap John; the warrant of survey for 450 acres was returned into the surveyor general's office 9 Dec. 1682. See Browning, 175, cited in Note 1 above, and *Pennsylvania Archives*, 3rd Series, III, 171. Thomas Taylor must have died shortly thereafter, for on 5 12m (February) 1682/3, Chester Monthly Meeting agreed "yt widdow Taylor have alowed her towards widdow Stedmans dyet ten shillings Starling by ye quarter," and on 11 4m 1683, agreed that she was to be paid 8s. for the "widdow Steedman's quarteridge & 2s. more for Thomas Colborn." See Digest of Minutes of the Business of the Monthly Meeting of Chester, 1681-1720, 274, 276, Collections of the Genealogical Society of Pennsylvania (GSP). On 5 9m 1683 and 10 3m 1683, Widdow Taylor and John Worrall proposed their intentions of marriage, and passed meeting. As Frances Worrall, she died 13 10m 1712, in Middletown Twp., Chester Co., aged "about 68 years." Thomas Taylor and his wife Frances had issue three children: 1. *Thomas*, b. 4 5m 1675, who m. 9 11m 1700, Rachel Minshall; 2. *Phoebe*, b. 3 2m 1677; 3. *Philip*, b. 5 10m 1680, who m. in 1705, Ann, daughter of Thomas and Mary Conway. See Gilbert Cope Collection, Vol. Co79, 63, and George Smith, *History of Delaware County.* . . . (Philadelphia, 1862), 507.

[7] From Edward Jones' letter, quoted in Browning, as cited in Note 1 above, it is known that a quantity of merchandise was brought over by him on the *Lyon*. It is therefore puzzling that his goods entered in the Chester port books were marked for Dublin. However, many Liverpool and Chester ships stopped at Dublin, taking on passengers there—the *Lyon* in 1683 picked up Robert Turner there, for instance. Possibly Jones' goods were sold in Dublin, and a fresh cargo loaded there, of which there is no record.

74

meal; 1 cwt. bread for private use. From the Collector's Book: 144 cheeses qty. 8 cwt., and other wares. [Duty] 14s. 11d. Value in toto, £14 18s. 8d.[8]

22 [May] JAMES TAYLOR: 2 pcs. single bayes; 1½ pcs. calico; 21 lbs. haberdashery; 14 lbs. wrought iron; 1 trunk qty. 1/3 of a short cloth. From the Collector's Book: 1 parcel qty. 40 yds. frieze, and other wares. [Duty] 3s. 6d. Also 1/3 of a short cloth. [Duty] 1s. 1½d. Value in toto, £3 10s.[9]

---

[8] This was RICHARD CROSBY (Crosbie) of Moore in the parish of Runcorn, hundred of Bucklow, in the Northern Division of Cheshire. Not a member of any of the Welsh companies, though a First Purchaser of 1000 acres from William Penn, he had m. 15 3m 1670, Ellinor Done, by whom he had two children: *John*, b. 8 6m 1672, and *Katherine*, b. 19 10m 1675. See Digested Copy of Records of Quarterly Meeting of Cheshire and Staffordshire, GSP. With his wife and two children he settled in Middletown Twp., Chester (now Delaware) Co., having obtained two warrants of survey. The first, dated 10 7m (Sept.) 1682, was granted by William Markham, and the second, dated 13 9m 1683, was from the Proprietor. Pursuant to these warrants 750 acres was laid out in two tracts along Chester Creek. (Warrants and Surveys of the Province of Pennsylvania, 1682-1759, III, 155-156, Municipal Archives, Department of Records, City Hall, Philadelphia.) Richard Crosby's city lots, appurtenant to his purchase of 1000 acres, he sold to Robert Turner, for which see Philadelphia Deed Book E-1-5, 667: 1 12m 1687/8, Richard *Crusby* to Robert Turner. His land transactions, because of the peculiarities of seventeenth century calligraphy, often have been confused with those of Richard Corsley, of Bristol, who was also a First Purchaser of 1000 acres from William Penn. Corsley (sometimes *Croslie*), however, assigned his purchase to Thomas Holme 1 Oct. 1688, and died in Bristol in 1694. See Digested Registers of Quarterly Meeting of Bristol and Somersetshire, GSP, and *Pennsylvania Archives*, 2nd Series, XIX, 155-156, 301. Corsley's widow Sarah m. at Bristol 15 6m 1695, Charles Jones, Jr., father of Mary Jones who became the wife of William Penn, Jr. See Howard M. Jenkins, "The Family of William Penn," *The Pennsylvania Magazine of History and Biography* (PMHB), XXI (1897), 137-140; for further data on Richard Crosby, see Gilbert M. Cope Collection, Vol. Co21, 147-149, GSP.

[9] James Taylor has not been identified. So far as is known, he was not a First Purchaser, but may have been the man of that name who subscribed £50 to the Free Society of Traders, for which see PMHB, XI, 179.

Pennsylvania's 1683 Ships

And Some of Their Passengers

Marion Balderston

THE exact number of ships bearing passengers who settled in Pennsylvania in 1683 remains uncertain. Twenty-one which did arrive have been identified by name. Of these, sixteen are listed in English port books as having loaded goods for resale in the Province, and of these sixteen, the arrival of ten was entered in the registers of arrivals — kept neither very thoroughly nor very long — in Philadelphia and Bucks Counties.[1] The arrival of three additional ships, for which no port records survive, was also entered in the registers. The names of two more vessels are known, one identified in the minutes of the Provincial Council, and one in a letter from William Penn, bringing the total number of ships known to have arrived with passengers in 1683 to twenty-one.

There seems to be evidence, however, of the arrival of perhaps three or four more ships. One is said to have brought eighty passengers. Another is reported to have arrived at Barbados with a cargo from Pennsylvania, but whether it previously had carried passengers from England to the Province before sailing on to Barbados has not been established. A third may have come from Barbados with passengers from that island. And Penn himself, writing at the end of November, mentioned the safe arrival, among others, of a ship from New Castle.[2] No port books for 1683 survive for New Castle, unfortunately, so that this last ship remains unknown.

Six of the identified 1683 ships came from London, six from Bristol, five from Liverpool, two from the small west-country ports of Fowey and Plymouth, one from Southampton, and one from Scarborough on

---

[1] For transcripts of the registers of arrival, the originals of which are in the Historical Society of Pennsylvania (HSP), see "A Partial List of the Families who Arrived at Philadelphia between 1682 and 1687," *The Pennsylvania Magazine of History and Biography* (PMHB), VIII (1884), 328-340, and "A Partial List of the Families who Resided in Bucks County, Pennsylvania, Prior to 1687, with the Date of their Arrival," *ibid.*, IX (1885), 223-233.

[2] For further discussion of these additional ships, see the text *infra*.

the northeast coast of Yorkshire. This compares with the known 1682 arrivals when nine ships sailed from London for Pennsylvania, six from Liverpool, four from Bristol, one each from Ireland, Fowey and Scarborough.[3] It seems clear that the center of migration was moving westward now that the Proprietor had left London.

Both years practically the same number of people shipped goods to Pennsylvania: 139 in 1682, and 138 in 1683, though of the latter several also had shipped goods in 1682. Of the 1682 shippers, 65 appear to have been actual First Purchasers, that is, had bought land in England from Penn before he had sailed, which was to be located and laid out in Pennsylvania, and 90 of the shippers are believed to have emigrated that year with their families and servants, or were already in Pennsylvania or West New Jersey.

Of the 138 shippers in 1683, only 50 were First Purchasers, but nearly 70 of the 138 are known to have come over. Others, of course, also emigrated but did not transport goods for resale, and so their names do not appear in the port books. However, the names of about 150 adults — men, their wives, sisters, brothers or servants — were entered in the partial registers as 1683 arrivals. The names of only 90 had been registered as arriving in 1682.

These emigrants represented only a fraction of those who did settle in the province, for by August 1683, before the arrival of most of the 1683 ships, Penn guessed that in addition to those who had taken up city lots, "about 300 farmers" had already settled near the town; in November he guessed "3000 soules" had arrived, and the following February he said the number of farmers had increased to "500 farmers strong." [4] Obviously many immigrants had neglected to pay the required registration fee, or had died before the registers were started.

Both in 1682 and 1683, as well as in other years, the goods shipped to Pennsylvania for barter or resale represented only a minute fraction of the goods which went through the English customs offices and which

---

3 For the 1682 ships and their passengers, see Marion Balderston, "William Penn's Twenty-three Ships," *Pennsylvania Genealogical Magazine* (PGM), XXIII (1963), 27-67.

4 Penn to Henry Savell, 30 5m 1683, *Pennsylvania Archives* [1st Series (1852)], I, 69; Penn to John Alloway, 29 Nov. 1683, Swarthmore MSS, VI, #68, Friends' House, London; Penn to Marquis of Halifax, 9 12m 1683/4, *Memoirs of HSP*, I (1864), 446. The reader is reminded that until September 1752, England and her colonies followed the Julian Calendar in computing dates. The historical year began then as now on 1 January, but the church, civil and legal year began on 25 March, which Quakers called the first month (1m). A system of double-dating was therefore in use between 1 January and 25 March: 9 11m 1682/3 was 9 January 1683 historically, and 24 1m 1682/3 was 24 March 1683. In this paper dates for this period not so shown are historical dates. The reader is referred to *PGM*, XXIII, 28-31, *loc. cit.*, for a discussion of the customs procedure in English ports, the port books kept by the custom officials, and First Purchaser (F.P.) lists.

were entered in their books. The goods extracted from these books intended for Pennsylvania, and listed hereinafter, were practical items invariably: things needed for building homes, heavy, long-wearing material for clothing, or staple edible supplies not readily procurable in the New World. Whatever luxury goods reached Pennsylvania during the first years came as personal property, and did not appear in the port records.

In the following lists the identified ships have been placed in the order, or approximate order as near as it can be determined, of their arrival in the Delaware River before Philadelphia. The port books do not give the dates of departure, only the various loading dates. Wind and weather controlled the time of departure, and varied each vessel's speed, nor did all ships make Pennsylvania their first port of call.

The first ship from England to bring settlers to Philadelphia in 1683 was of 300 tons burthen. It had arrived in Bristol from Virginia the previous summer of 1682, finished unloading by September, and had begun taking on goods for both Virginia and Pennsylvania by the end of October. About two months after its last loading on 3 December 1682, it arrived in the Delaware shortly before 9 12m (February) 1682/3, the date on which one of its passengers obtained a warrant for 200 acres.[5]

The *Bristol Merchant* [1]
William Smith, master, for Pennsylvania & Virginia

24 [October, 1682] WALTER KING: 200 lbs. shoes; 16 ends fustian; 36 pr. bodices; ½ cwt. haberdashery wares; 5 doz. Irish wool stockings; 40 yds. English ticking; 6 pr. wool cards [for carding wool]; 16 bushels malt; 4 cwt. cheese; 2 pcs. hair cloth; 100 English glass bottles; 200 pcs. English earth wares; 1½ doz. bridles; 1 small saddle; ½ chalder grindstones; cwt. brass manufactured; ¾ cwt. wrought pewter; 8 cwt. wrought iron; 2 doz. felt hats; 50 goads cotton; ½ chest window glass; 50 lbs. serges; 2 cwt. lead shot; 50 lbs. gunpowder; 1 doz. worsted stockings; 1 short cloth; 13 parcels several sorts of wares valued at £19 [duty] 19s.[6]

---

[5] Loadings for the *Bristol Merchant* are from Bristol port books E 190/1143/1, the Customer's Book, and E 190/1144/1, the Controller's Book, Public Record Office (PRO), Chancery Lane, London, England. The vessel's size is given in Colonial Office Records, C.O. 33/14/19, PRO. Her master, William Smith, was probably the man of that name, called "mariner" of Bristol, who was a F.P. of 1000 acres. For the arrival date, see Notes 9 and 10 below.

[6] WALTER KING of "Haveyard," Somerset, F.P. of 1000 acres, was one of the Committee of Twelve sent over by the Free Society of Traders in Pennsylvania. He was one of their representatives, as a member for Philadelphia, at the first Provincial Assembly held at Philadelphia 12 1m 1682/3. In the Bristol port book, no duty was marked for his complete cargo, only the last item. In the books, wrought or manufactured, as applied to metal, was metal worked so as to be easily welded or shaped; as applied to leather, the skins were dressed. Fustian was a coarse woolen cloth. Most woolens were valued by the pound. A piece (pc.) was so many yards of continuously woven fabric; a short cloth, 28 yards or less. Cotton was measured by the goad: 1½ yards. Chaldron or chalder was about 36 bushels, a quarter (qtr.) about 8 bushels. A "chest" of glass was not the container, but a measure: from 200 to 300 feet. A quarter, when with cwt., was 28 pounds.

78

[24 October] JOHN BARNES: 6 cwt. nails; 2 cwt. wrought iron; 2 qtrs. [quarters] malt; 100 lbs. serges; 20 pr. worsted stockings; 14 lbs. haberdashery; 12 pr. woolen stockings; 60 lbs. shoes; 6 small saddles; 3 cwt. cheese; 8 lbs. brass manufactured; 40 lbs. gunpowder.[7]

26 [October] JOHN BARNES: 6 gross tobacco pipes; 1 bbl. beer; 5 cwt. cordage; 4 parcels several sorts of wares, valued at £8 15s. [duty] 14s. 8½d.

[26 October] STEPHEN WATTS: 150 lbs. serges; 12 Dunster kerseys [ribbed cloth from Dunster, Somerset, each kersey about 18 yds. long]; 1 short cloth; 2 penistones [cloth from Penistone, Yorkshire]; 500 goads cottons; 30 doz. men's woolen, 30 doz. children's woolen stockings; 5 doz. men's worsted stockings; 6 cwt. haberdashery; 200 made garments; 10 doz. felt hats; 1 cwt. cordage; 6 small saddles; 200 lbs. leather manufactured; 100 pcs. English fustians; 4 cwt. shot; 40 coverlets, wool & hair; 5 cwt. wrought iron; 20 cwt. nails; 80 gross tobacco pipes; 40 lbs. pewter; 60 lbs. gunpowder; 150 ells English-made linen [English ell: 45 inches]; 6 doz. [lbs.] tallow candles; 1½ qtrs. malt; 3 cwt. cheese; 2 parcels several sorts of wares, valued at £6 15s. [duty] 6s. 9d.

[26 October] RICHARD PHILLIPS: 20 lbs. wrought iron; 2 cwt. nails; 4 lbs. pewter; 2 coverlets, wool & hair; 20 ells Holland duck [Dutch: *doeck*, a heavy linen], value 30s. [duty] 1s. 6d.; 4 lbs. shoes; 9 lbs. haberdashery; 3 pr. wool cards; 7 gross tobacco pipes.[8]

[26 October] JANE COLLET: 2 cwt. wrought iron; 2 cwt. nails; cwt. shot; 20 lbs. gunpowder; 20 lbs. serges; cwt. cheese; 30 lbs. brass manufactured; 20 lbs. shoes; 2 doz. woolen stockings; 40 garments wearing apparel.[9]

27 [October] FRANCIS CHADSEY [Chadds]: ½ chalder grind stones; 2 cwt. biscuit, value £1 [duty] 1s.; 2 cwt. cheese; 3 firkins butter [firkin: ¼ barrel]; 2 cwt. wrought iron; 4 cwt. nails.[10]

[27 October] WILLIAM CLOUDE: 40 lbs. serges; 15 lbs. linsey woolsey [cheap wool and flax mixture]; 18 lbs. woolen stockings; 14 lbs. haberdashery; 68 lbs. shoes & boots;

---

7 JOHN BARNES of Bristol, F.P. of 500 acres, not to be confused with John Barnes from Sussex, a F.P. of 1250 acres with John Songhurst, obtained a warrant for his city lot on 26 12m 1682/3, which was laid out two days later at the southwest corner of Second and Walnut Streets. Warrants and Surveys of the Province of Pennsylvania, 1682-1759, III, 500, Municipal Archives, City Hall, Philadelphia, hereinafter cited as Warrants and Surveys.

8 According to the list of "Old Rights," *Pennsylvania Archives*, 3rd Series, III, 156, one Rutherd (Richard?) Philip's return of a survey of 200 acres in Chester Co. was dated 18 11m 1683[/4?]. He has not been identified further.

9 Joan May of Devizes, Wiltshire, widow, bought from Penn 14 Sept. 1681, 250 acres for £5. On 20 Sept. 1681, she made Jeremiah Collett, of the same place, fishmonger, her son-in-law (stepson?), her attorney irrevocable "for himself in my name but to his own proper use and behoof" to take up the 250 acres "in the same manner as if he had purchased same." Philadelphia Exemplification Book 5, 591, 599, Department of Records, City Hall, Philadelphia. Jeremiah Collet was in Chester Co. by 13 June 1682, when he served on a jury. Both he and his brother WILLIAM COLLETT obtained warrants for land in Chester Co. on 6 12m 1682/3, for which see *Pennsylvania Archives*, 3rd Series, III, 114, 118. See also *Records of the Courts of Chester County, Pennsylvania, 1681-1697* (Philadelphia, 1910), 15, 90, hereinafter cited as *Chester Court Records*, for notices of Jeremiah Collett and for his wife Jane.

10 FRANCIS CHADDS (Chadsey) obtained a warrant for 200 acres to be laid out in Chester Co. on 9 12m 1682/3, evidence that the *Bristol Merchant* had arrived by that date. *Pennsylvania Archives*, 3rd Series, III, 114. According to George Smith, *History of Delaware County . . .* (Philadelphia, 1682), 452, hereinafter cited as Smith, *Delaware County*, he had moved from Chichester, the place of his first settlement, to Birmingham Twp. when he m. in 1695 Grace Stanfield. See also *Chester Court Records*, 329.

2½ cwt. cheese; 3 cwt. wrought iron; ½ cwt. nails; 8 lbs. gunpowder; 28 lbs. shot; ½ cwt. English soap; 2 cwt. bread, value 23s. [duty] 1s. 2d.[11]

[27 October] JOHN HARDRULT (Hardluft?): 50 lbs. leather manufactured; 160 ells English made linen; cwt. haberdashery; 30 lbs. serges; 1 doz. felt hats; cwt. brass manufactured; 5 cwt. wrought iron; 8 cwt. nails; 2 cwt. shot; ½ cwt. gunpowder; 6 small saddles; 5 cwt. cheese; 4 firkins butter; ½ chalder grindstones; 100 pcs. English earthenware; 2 parcles of wares, value 45s. [duty] 2s. 3d.

[27 October] JAMES RANSOM & Co.: 10 cwt. nails; 1¼ cwt. wrought iron; 6 qtrs. malt; 56 lbs. shoes; 1 doz. woolen stockings; 6 pr. worsted stockings; 14 lbs. haberdashery.

[30 October] JOHN JONES: cwt. cheese; 7 lbs. haberdashery; 2 parcels wares, value £2 19s. 2d. [duty] 2s. 11½d.

[27 October] JOHN TROTTER: 36 lbs. shoes.[12]

31 [October] JOHN MOONE: 3 ends English fustians; 30 lbs. serges; 14 lbs. haberdashery; 2 cwt. cheese; 14 bushels malt; 1 firkin beer; 8 gal. aquavita; cwt. wrought iron; 10 bushels French grass seed; 3 parcels of wares, value £5 10s. [duty] 5s. 6d.[13]

[31 October] WILLIAM BEAKES: 3 cwt. wrought iron; 2 cwt. cheese; cwt. brass manufactured; 3 parcels wares, value £4 10s. [duty] 4s. 6d.[14]

8 [November] WILLIAM BEAKES: cwt. cheese; ½ chest window glass; 20 ends English fustian; 50 lbs. serges; 30 lbs. leather manufactured; 20 garments wearing apparel; 6 doz. woolen stockings; 2 cwt. nails; ½ cwt. haberdashery; ½ short cloth; 20 yds.

---

[11] William Cloude, a F.P. of 500 acres, from Seene, Wiltshire, had shipped goods on the *Unicorn* of Bristol in 1682, for which see *PGM*, XXIII, 62, 63. For a brother Robert Cloud, who on 26 9m 1685, was granted a pass to leave the country, see *Chester Court Records*, 63, 70.

[12] Neither James Ransome, a rich Bristol-Virginia merchant, nor John Jones, probably the linendraper and mercer of Bristol and F.P. of 1000 acres with Michael Jones, grocer of Bristol, are known to have come to Pennsylvania. The goods for John Trotter, and for the above John Jones are marked for Virginia in the Controller's Book E 190/1144/1; in the Customer's Book E 190/1143/1, they are marked for Pennsylvania. This is one of the rare occasions when the two port books disagree.

[13] JOHN MOONE, linendraper of Bristol and F.P. of 500 acres, was granted a warrant on 26 12m 1682/3, for his land which was laid out in Bristol Twp., for which see *Pennsylvania Archives*, 3rd Series, III, 311. According to William C. Braithwaite, *The Second Period of Quakerism* (London, 1921), 411, John Moon(e), Sr., a great friend of Penn, had been let out of prison in 1682 on condition that he leave for Pennsylvania at once. He sold 100 acres of the Bristol Twp. land to his son John Moon, Jr., in 1685. Philadelphia Deed Book E-1-5, 93: 5 6m 1685. Unless otherwise cited, all deeds, wills and administrations are Philadelphia Co. records.

[14] WILLIAM BEAKES of the parish of Blackwell, Somersetshire, and F.P. of 1000 acres, came with his youngest son ABRAHAM BEAKES, bringing a certificate of removal from Portishead Monthly Meeting dated 25 6m 1682, for which see William Wade Hinshaw, *Encyclopedia of American Quaker Genealogy* (Ann Arbor, Mich., 1938), II, 978, and registered their arrival as in 12m 1683, for which see *PMHB*, IX, 224. He had m. 12 3m 1661, Mary Wall of Olverstone, by whom he had four sons: William, Stephen, Samuel and Abraham, for whom see Digested Copy of Registers of the Quarterly Meeting of Bristol and Somerset, GSP. The wife and the three oldest sons presumably came later in the year, for whom see Note 139 below. William Beakes, the father, was dead by 19 7m 1687, and letters of administration were granted his widow Mary 7 9m 1687, for which see "Abstracts of Early Bucks County Wills," *Publications of the Genealogical Society of Pennsylvania* (PGSP), I, 215.

HENRY MARGERUM of Cheverell, Wiltshire, and his wife ELIZABETH MARGERUM registered their arrival at the same time as William Beakes. Both men settled in Falls Twp., Bucks Co. W. H. H. Davis, *History of Bucks County, Pennsylvania* (Doylestown, Pa., 1876), 77, 80, hereinafter cited as Davis, *Bucks County*. Margerum appears to have married a second wife by 1696: Jane, late wife of Robert Rigg of Burlington, for which see "Calendar of New Jersey Records, 1664-1705," *New Jersey Archives*, 1st Series, XXI, 472, hereinafter cited as *N. J. Archives*.

English ticking; 20 lbs. pewter; ½ cwt. English soap; 8 felt hats; 2 small saddles; 3 parcels several sorts of wares, value £2 13s. 4d. [duty] 2s. 8d.

[8 November] ROBERT DUNN (Donne): 5 felt hats; ¾ cwt. apothecary wares; 20 pr. worsted stockings; 40 lbs. books; ½ chest window glass; ½ cwt. pewter; cwt. shot; 1½ cwt. wrought iron; cwt. nails; ½ cwt. haberdashery; 2 pcs. kerseys; 40 lbs. shoes; 20 lbs. brass manufactured; 2 parcels wares, value £2 [duty] 2s.[15]

Probably the second ship to arrive in the Delaware from England in 1683 was the *Thomas & Anne* from London. It had begun loading goods for New York in late 1682, and so continued until mid-January 1682/3, with only one consignment entered for Pennsylvania. James Claypoole sent letters by this ship, one dated 9 11m (January), and the other two days later.[16] In the first one he stated that the ship was to sail either the next day — the tenth — or the day after — the eleventh, but its last loading was on 13 January.

Perhaps stopping at New York first, since the bulk of its cargo was destined for that port, it could have reached Philadelphia by 15 April, when one of its probable passengers, Jane Blanchard, obtained a warrant for a city lot.[17]

The *Thomas & Anne* of London [2]

Thomas Singleton, master, for New York and Pennsylvania

8 [January 1682/3] SIMON BOW: for Pennsylvania, 3 doz. hats.[18]

The *John & Elizabeth* from the Isle of Wight, John King, master, appears to have arrived in Philadelphia some time early in May. A relatively small ship of about 70 tons, it is not known if she brought passengers. When she arrived at Barbados from Pennsylvania 15 June

---

[15] Robert Dunn (Donne) settled in Salem Co. on Alloways Creek in West Jersey, buying from Edward Champneys 100 acres on 17 July 1685, and on 29 July 1685, 30 acres from Joseph White. He was deceased by 30 Oct. 1696, when his executor sold the land. *Ibid.*, 577, 601, 616, 617.

[16] For the Claypoole letters see "Extracts from the Letter-Book of James Claypoole," *PMHB*, X (1886), 201-202. In the second letter to his employe Edward Cole, Claypoole said he was sending a servant boy, PHILIP BROOKS, to assist Cole. Indentured to Claypoole for eight years, the boy was probably about 13 years old. Cole was instructed that if he could not use the lad, he was to "let him worke for some other body for wages," for Claypoole "would not have him idle." He had "sent with the boy more things than he needs, but let him wear his old things out first, and upon those days he does not work his new things."

[17] JANE BLANCHARD brought a certificate of removal from the monthly meeting at Ringwood, Hampshire, dated 11 11m 1682/3, for which see Albert Cook Myers, *Quaker Arrivals at Philadelphia 1682-1750* (Baltimore, 1957), 3-4, hereinafter cited as Myers, *Quaker Arrivals*. Less than a year later on 6 10m 1683, she m. David Breintnall, for whom see Hannah Benner Roach, "Philadelphia Business Directory, 1690," *PGM*, XXIII, 115-116. She had been granted on 15 2m 1683, a warrant for a city lot on rent which was laid out a week later on the south side of Chestnut between Third and Fourth Streets from Delaware. Warrants and Surveys, II, 19, cited in Note 7 above.

[18] These hats may have been consigned to James Claypoole who shipped nothing in his own name through the customs, but brought goods which he reshipped to his brother Edward Claypoole in Barbados. See *PMHB*, X, 276, 277, for his reference to beaver hats. The loadings for the *Thomas & Anne* are from London port book E 190/125/1, PRO. Its size of 100 tons is given in Colonial Office Records, C.O. 33/14/21, PRO.

1683, she carried a cargo of 25 hogsheads of tobacco and 3800 pipe staves.[19] Another large ship, the *Grayhound* of London, which had arrived at Barbados from London 3 January 1683, may also have arrived at Philadelphia sometime in May, since she was back in Barbados from Pennsylvania 17 July 1683. While cargo loaded at London on this ship is entered in the London port books, none was for Pennsylvania, and it is not known if she brought any passengers to the Delaware.[20]

About the middle of June a ship reputedly from Plymouth brought 80 passengers to Philadelphia. The only known one of these was Roger Longworth, a well-known "travelling" Friend, who was not a settler. In a letter apparently dated 12 5m (July) 1683, from Longworth to Pieter Hendricks in Europe, Longworth, then in Philadelphia, says he had "departed from Plymouth" with "about 80 passengers who set out for Pensylvania. We were six weeks on the way from Plymouth to the River Delaware," and that the "first place where I trod was the city of Philadelphia. . . ." He continues to tell how he "was at William Penn's for dinner with 6 Indian kings, and after dinner we went to meeting, they along with us. . . ." [21] In so writing he gives some indication as to how long he had been in the city, for on 23 June, a Saturday, six Indians signed or witnessed deeds for land between the Pennypack and Neshaminy Creeks, and on 25 June, a Monday, another deed for land on the west side of the Schuylkill above the first falls.[22] Working back from these dates, the ship must have left Plymouth no later than the first week in May. But the *Endeavour* of London, Francis Richardson, master, on which Longworth is alleged to have come, was loading goods 28 May for East New Jersey, and could hardly have arrived in the Delaware in less than a month's time. Thus, the ship with 80 passengers including Longworth, is still to be identified.[23]

---

[19] Her arrival is entered in Colonial Office Records, C.O. 33/14/19, 27. PRO. Her master, John King, took up a lot on rent in Philadelphia in the spring of 1684, for which see Warrants and Surveys, II, 73-4, and later acquired other land in the city and in the lower counties. Deed Book E-2-5, 51: 10 5m 1688, John King to Richard Hillyard; *Pennsylvania Archives*, 2nd Series, XIX, 154, 177, 179, 251.

[20] While the London port books list Joseph Wasey as master of the *Grayhound*, he did not captain that ship, since he brought over the *America*, arriving in August 1683, for which see the text *infra*. It would appear that he was owner or part owner of the *Grayhound*, since the customs officers often put down the owner instead of the actual captain or master in charge of a particular voyage. For the Larbados entries, see C.O. 33/14/24, 28.

[21] For the letter in translation (from a Dutch copy), see William I. Hull, *William Penn and the Dutch Quaker Migration to Pennsylvania* [Swarthmore College Monographs on Quaker History Number Two] (Philadelphia, 1935), 364-5, hereinafter cited as Hull, *Dutch Quaker Migration*.

[22] *Pennsylvania Archives* [1st Series], I, 62-65.

[23] Albert Cook Myers, in his *William Penn, His Own Account of the Lenni Lenape or Delaware Indians, 1683* (Moylan, Pa., 1937), 88-9, placed Longworth on the *Endeavour*, without substantiating documentation. Plymouth port book E 190/1047/13, PRO, lists an *Endeavour* in Plymouth harbor, but the captain's name was Christopher Newham or Newnham.

There remains the possibility of still a fourth ship which might have brought some passengers to Philadelphia, this time from Barbados, in late June or early July. There is a record that Captain Humphrey Waterman of that place on 2 5m (July) 1683, returned into the surveyor general's office a warrant of survey. But whether Waterman was merely on a trading voyage at this time, or was transporting settlers, remains undetermined.[24]

To return to the twenty-one definitely identified ships which brought settlers to Pennsylvania in 1683, the third to drop anchor before Philadelphia, the *Liver* of Liverpool, of 130 tons burthen, was named for the liver bird from which the port and pool of Liverpool took its name.[25] After its last loading there on 24 April, it sailed for Dublin to pick up additional passengers and cargo before crossing the Atlantic. The voyage was uncomfortable according to the passengers, for the ship seems to have run into the same storms which plagued some of the other vessels crossing the ocean that summer. The water supply ran low, the passengers' beer was pilfered by the crew, and the master was so bad-tempered that the passengers on 7 7m (September) protested to the Provincial Council about the treatment they had received at his hands. The ship had arrived by 17 5m (July), however, the date on which Hugh Marsh, one of the protestants, had obtained a warrant for a city lot.[26]

The *Liver* of Liverpool [3]

James Kilner, master

19 [April] JOSEPH MESSEY (Massey): 2 packs, 1 bundle, qty. 8 pcs. English linen;

---

24 For the notice of the return of "a road" see *Pennsylvania Archives*, 3rd Series, II, 48. Waterman eventually took up land in Philadelphia Co. and was deceased by March 1695, when letters of administration on his estate were granted to Philip Richards, principal creditor, for which see PGM, XIX, 265, recorded in Administration Book A, 207, #38:1695. For survey of his Philadelphia acreage see Warrants and Surveys, III, 545.

25 "Lever" and "Leverpoole" were alternate spellings in the seventeenth century. In *Minutes of the Provincial Council of Pennsylvania . . .* , I (1852), 79-80, hereinafter cited as *Colonial Records*, the ship is incorrectly called the *Levee* of Liverpool. For the vessel's loadings, see Liverpool port book E 190/1345/13; for its tonnage, see C. Northcote Parkinson, *The Rise of the Port of Liverpool* (Liverpool, 1952), 70.

26 For HUGH MARSH's warrant, issued nearly two months before the complaint came before the Council, see *Pennsylvania Archives*, 3rd Series, II, 751. He was a son of ROBERT and SARAH MARSH who probably were with their son on the *Liver*. The elder Marsh also petitioned the Council on 29 8m 1683, though on another matter, and on 1 9m 1683, was granted a warrant for a city lot, for which see *ibid.*, 2nd Series, XIX, 288, *Colonial Records*, I, 89, and Warrants and Surveys, III, 511. The father died in Southampton Twp., Bucks Co. between 25 July 1688 and 17 3m 1689, when his will was proved in Philadelphia, for abstract of which see PGSP, I, 76, recorded in Will Book A, 142, #61:1688. Therein he named his wife Sarah, two sons Hugh and Robert Marsh, and a daughter Alice. Hugh Marsh eventually removed to Duck Creek Hundred, New Castle Co., where he died in 1708. In his will he mentioned a former wife and daughter, his present wife Penelopy, sons John, Joseph and Robert, and his brother Robert, for abstract of which see *Calendar of Delaware Wills, New Castle County, 1682-1800* (Wilmington, Del., 1911), 11, recorded in Miscellaneous Will Book 1, 349.

17 doz. wool stockings for men, 4 doz. for children; ½ cwt. haberdashery; 18 lbs. Norwich stuffs. [Duty] 10s. ½d.[27]

[19 April] PHILIP ENGLAND: 3 cayles [or frayles: a basket], qty. 8 cwt. nails; 3 cwt. wrought iron. [Duty] 3s. 6d.[28]

24 [April] AMOS STRETTALL: 3 packs, 1 bundle qty. 27 pcs. English linen; cwt. haberdashery. [Duty] 13s. 9d.[29]

[24 April] JAMES KILNER: 2 hhds. qty. ½ doz. woolen stockings for men; 286 lbs. new shoes; 20 lbs. wool cloth. [Duty] 12s. 3d.

In the late spring of 1683 of two ships riding at anchor in the Thames, one — the *Vine* — was taking on goods and passengers for New England and Pennsylvania, the other goods for Pennsylvania only. The latter was the *America*, of 200 tons burthen and drawing thirteen feet of water. Leaving Gravesend at the mouth of the Thames on 6 June 1683, with some 80 passengers and a crew of twelve, it arrived at Deal the next day. On 10 June 1683, in company with the *Vine*, the *America* sailed from the Downs through Dover Strait, but in the course of a stormy passage parted company with the other ship and did not sight the New World until 16 August. Two days later the *America* entered the "Bay of Delaware" and arrived before Philadelphia "in the dusk of evening" on 20 6m (August) 1683.[30]

---

[27] On 10 5m 1685, Joseph Massey, then master of the ship *Greyhound* of London (Joseph Wasey's ship noted above?), and owner of one-sixteenth part of said ship, sold for £25 his share in the vessel then "riding at anchor in Delaware River." Deed Book E-1-5, 90: Joseph Massey to William Belcher.

[28] PHILIP ENGLAND brought a certificate of removal from Dublin dated 21 May 1683, indicating the *Liver's* stop at Dublin before crossing the Atlantic. Hinshaw, II, 516. On 16 8m 1683, he obtained a warrant for 12 acres in Philadelphia Co. for keeping "an Ordinarie and ferrie att Skuillkill," by order of the Proprietor. Here he established himself and his family, but when he died in 1708 he was living in New Castle Co. In his will, dated 7 7m 1708 and proved 3 Nov. 1708, his 2nd wife Elizabeth Hatton, whom he had married in 1688 after the death of his 1st wife the year before, was also deceased. Surviving were sons Joseph and James England, a daughter Elizabeth Wells, wife of William Wells, and 20 grandchildren: Joseph England's eight, William Wells seven, his son-in-law Absolom Cuff's three, and Hannah Berwick and her child, probably a great-grandchild. For abstract of his will see *Calendar of Delaware Wills*, 14, cited in Note 27, recorded in New Castle Will Book B, 174. For mention of the decease of his wives, see PGSP, II, 140 and Hinshaw, II, 359.

[29] Amos Strettle in 1703 bought the right to the original purchase or 5000 acres of George Shore of Athlone, Dublin, for whom Philip England had acted as attorney after his arrival at Philadelphia. *Pennsylvania Archives*, 2nd Series, XIX, 521. NICHOLAS NEWLIN, another Irish passenger on the *Liver*, brought a certificate from Mountmellick Meeting, County Tyrone, dated 25 12m 1682/3, which included his sons JOHN and NATHANIEL NEWLIN who were "free for marriage." Albert Cook Myers, *Immigration of the Irish Quakers into Pennsylvania, 1682-1750* (Swarthmore, Pa., 1902), 57, hereinafter cited as Myers, *Irish Immigration*. Newlin brought at least one servant, JOHN FOX, whose petition to Chester Court in 1685 against his former master Nicholas "Newland" regarding bad and cruel usage was rejected by the court for want of proof. *Chester Court Records*, 59, cited in Note 9 above. Newlin died in 1699, his wife Elizabeth in 1717. For abstract of his will, see PGSP, III, 21, recorded in Will Book A, 466, #193:1699. Elizabeth Newlin's will is recorded in Chester Co. Will Book A, 48. Three other passengers on the *Liver*, THOMAS BRINKET, EDWARD JONES and GEORGE GREEN, have not been further identified.

[30] At the beginning of that month, Penn, in writing to the Lords of Trade and Plantations, had noted that "six and twenty sail of people within a year" had arrived. If by this he meant since the beginning of August 1682, when the *Amity* had arrived, he was including the 20 ships which had come between August

According to its well known passenger, Francis Daniel Pastorius, who left a description of the voyage, the passengers aboard — beside Pastorius' own party — included "one D. Mediconae with his wife and eight children, a French captain, a pastry-cook, an apothecary, a glass-blower, mason, smith, cartwright, joiner, cooper, hatter, shoemaker, tailor, gardener, peasants, seamstresses, etc." These included those who had "fallen in with the Romish Church, with the Lutheran, with the Calvinistic, with the Anabaptist and with the English, and only one Quaker." [31]

The *America* of London [4]

Joseph Wasey, master [32]

3 [May] EDWARD WEST: 2 chalders grindlestone [firestones for 2 furnaces] value £26. [Duty] £1 12s. 4d.[33]

7 [May] EDWARD HAISTWELL: 8 cwt. nails; 6 cwt. dim. [*diminus:* not quite] wrought iron; 9¾ cwt. lead shot; 5¾ cwt. gunpowder; 8 lbs. wrought leather; 6 shod shovels. [Duty] £1 8s. 2d.[34]

and November of 1682, the *Bristol Merchant, Thomas & Anne* and the *Liver of Liverpool* of 1683, and probably the *John & Elizabeth, Grayhound* and Longworth's unidentified ship, discussed in the text *supra.* For Penn's letter, dated 6 6m 1683, see *Calendar of State Papers, Colonial Series, America and West Indies, 1681-1685* (London, 1898), 467. A similarly phrased letter, dated 14 6m 1683, also to the Lords of Trade, is in Robert Proud, *The History of Pennsylvania in North America . . .* (Philadelphia, 1797), I, 267. For a tabulated list of the 1682 ships see PGM, XXIII, 67.

31 For Pastorius' complete account of the journey, in translation, see Samuel W. Pennypacker, *The Settlement of Germantown, Pennsylvania . . .* (Philadelphia, 1899), 81-99. Pastorius' group included ISAAC DILBECK, a Dutch weaver and Calvinist, his wife MARIEKE BLOMERSE, and their two sons ABRAHAM and JACOB DILBECK; GEORG (Joris) WERTMÜLLER from Berne; JACOB SCHUMACHER, a tanner from Mainz; THOMAS GASPER; CONRAD BACHER (alias Rutter); and FRANCES SIMPSON, an English maid hired by Pastorius at Deal. Identification of the other passengers is only partial: DR. THOMAS LLOYD, the "D. Mediconae," came with his wife MARY, daughter of Roger Jones, and their children, for whom see Charles P. Keith, *The Provincial Councillors of Pennsylvania . . .* (Philadelphia, 1883), (16-17). The French captain possibly was Gabriel Rappe who was naturalized with seven other Frenchmen 10 7m 1683, for whom see *Colonial Records,* cited in Note 25 above, and *Pennsylvania Archives,* 2nd Series, VII, 193. The pastry cook was CORNELIUS BOM of Haarlem, his wife AGNES, and sons CORNELIUS, ABRAHAM and CHRISTIAN, for whom see Deed Book E-2-5, 172: 16 4m 1691, Anthony Morris to Cornelius Bom *et al.* The glassblower was JOSHUA TITTERY, servant to the Free Society of Traders, from Newcastle-upon-Tyne, Northumberland, for whom see PMHB, VIII, 339, and Note 96 below. The mason was WILLIAM PRESTON from the same place where he had known Tittery; for a time he had worked with him. Preston brought his wife ANN, daughter of Edward and Margaret Taylor, and two children, HENRY and REBECCA, for whom see Charles S. Belsterling, "William Preston of Newcastle-upon-Tyne and Philadelphia," PGSP, XI, 106, 113.

32 Joseph Wasey, master of the *America,* obtained a warrant for a city lot 1 7m 1683, and a second warrant on 12 7m 1683, for 250 acres laid out in Dublin Twp., Phila. Co., 19 1m 1683/4. *Pennsylvania Archives,* 3rd Series, III, 48, 50; *ibid.,* 2nd Series, XIX, 450. Loadings for the *America* are from London port books E 190/115/1, and E 190/125/3, PRO.

33 Edward West, F.P. of 2000 acres in two separate transactions, was a London merchant who had invested £50 in the Free Society of Traders, and was on that company's London committee. PMHB, XI (1887), 186; Samuel Hazard, ed., *The Register of Pennsylvania,* I (1828), 397. No land was laid out for him until 1689. Warrants and Surveys, II, 133.

34 Edward Haistwell was in James Claypoole's employ, acting as his agent in London. These goods probably were intended for Claypoole, who emigrated later that summer. PMHB, X, 278, 281.

11 [May] BENJAMIN WHITEHEAD: 8 cwt. nails; 4 cwt. wrought iron; 6 cwt. lead shot; 40 yds. flannel; ¼ cwt. gunpowder; 20 lbs. serges; 3 Irish rugs; 12 doz. [lbs.] candles; 9 cwt. cheese; ¼ cwt. haberdashery; 4 lbs. wrought silk; 8 castors [hats]; 6 doz. plain gloves; 1 chest window glass. [Duty] £1 2s. 7½d.[35]

12 [May] JOHN HALL: 9 cwt. cheese; ¼ cwt. wrought iron. [Duty] 3s. 1½d.[36]

19 [May] EDWARD WEST: 6 cwt. cheese; 22 cwt. wrought iron; 2 cwt. haberdashery; cwt. lead shot; cwt. gunpowder. [Duty] 18s.

24 [May] RICHARD CARTER: 4 small minikin bayes; 34 small saddles; 2 doz. bridles; doz. castors; ¼ cwt. haberdashery; 1 lb. thrown silk; ¼ cwt. cordage; ½ cwt. lead shot. [Duty] £1 1s. 3½d.

31 [May] RICHARD WHITFIELD: 20 cwt. wrought iron; 14 cwt. nails; 3 cwt. dim. lead shot; cwt. dim. gunpowder; 6 cwt. cheese; cwt. pewter; cwt. wrought brass; 4 small saddles; 2 doz. lbs. candles. [Duty] £1 7s. 11d.[37]

[31 May] DANIEL WHARLEY: 2 doz. shod shovels; 12 lbs. haberdashery; 2 single bayes; 40 lbs. serges; ½ lb. thrown silk; 5 single minikin bayes; 3 cwt. lead; 50 yds. flannel; 4 small saddles; 5½ cwt. wrought iron; ½ cwt. wrought brass; 1 doz. child's, 1 doz. men's worsted hose; 2 Irish rugs; 7 lbs. wrought silk; 350 [pcs.] earthware; 6 lbs. shoes. [Duty] £1 14s. 10½d.[38]

[31 May] DANIEL DUCHAIS: 12 cwt. wrought iron; 2½ cwt. lead shot; 1½ bbls. beef; ¼ cwt. pewter. [Duty] 14s. 3½d.[39]

According to Pastorius, "the ship that started from Deal with ours was fourteen days longer on the way." That vessel surely was the *Vine*, bound for New England and Pennsylvania, and appears to have arrived before Philadelphia 3 September 1683, two weeks after the *America* had dropped anchor. Since most of its goods were intended for New England, it probably had stopped there first. No one on it registered

[35] BENJAMIN WHITEHEAD, probably a passenger on the *America* with his daughters ESTHER and ELIZABETH, obtained a warrant for 250 acres on 27 6m 1683. The land was laid out in Bristol Twp. 3 7m following, and patented 27 4m 1684. Exemplification Book 1, 105. A warrant for his city lot was dated 1 7m 1683, as entered in *Pennsylvania Archives*, 3rd Series, III, 49, but *cf.* the date of survey in *ibid.*, 43. When he died in Feb. 1697/8, he left his estate to his two daughters; of these Elizabeth m. John Bezer, Jr. in 1695. *PGSP*, IV, 186-7. For abstract of Whitehead's will, see *ibid.*, III, 12, recorded in Will Book A, 374, #159:1697/8.

[36] Possibly the John Hall who invested £25 in the Free Society of Traders (*PMHB*, XI, 177), and perhaps the uncle of Jason Withers, heir of Ralph Withers, F.P. of 500 acres, for whom see *Pennsylvania Archives*, 2nd Series, XIX, 383.

[37] RICHARD WHITFIELD on 10 10m 1683, bought 200 acres from Peter Yocum at the mouth of Tacony (Frankford) Creek. *Pennsylvania Archives*, 2nd Series, XIX, 343. Possibly from Hartshaw in Lancashire, he and his wife Mary had the care of the children of Humphrey Hodges, apparently Thomas and Faircliff Hodges, from 1690 to as late as 1693. *PGSP*, IV, 170-1.

[38] Daniel Wharley, woolen draper of London, married Mary Pennington, "ye younger," of the Woodside, Parish of Agmondsham, Buckinhamshire. She was a F.P. of 1250 acres, but neither of them ever came to Pennsylvania, and Wharley bought no land in his own right until 1695 when he purchased 3000 acres from Penn "between Delaware and Susquehanna." *Pennsylvania Archives*, 2nd Series, XIX, 443, 730.

[39] Daniel Duchais possibly was related to Jacques Duché, said to have fled from La Rochelle to London in 1682, with his wife Mary and eight children. *Proceedings of the Huguenot Society of Pennsylvania*, XXVIII (1956), 125.

his arrival; Pastorius wrote that "some of the people died" on the voyage.[40]

The *Vine* of London [5]

William Thomson, master, for Pennsylvania & New England

19 [April] ANTHONY TOMKINS: 44 cwt. wrought iron; 36 cwt. nails; 1½ cwt. cordage; ½ cwt. pewter; 10 small, 1 great saddles; 180 lbs. shoes; 12 bushels pease; 12 doz. & 11 castors, 12 doz. felts [hats]; 6 cwt. cheese; 20 lbs. serge; 40 yds. flannel; 3½ qtrs. wheat meal; 14 horse collars. [Duty] £4 3s. 10½d. From the Wool Book: 200 lbs. wool [duty] 10s. 7d.[41]

21 [April] SAMUEL BAKER: 2 chests window glass; 3 cwt. cheese. [Duty] 2s.[42]

The next ship, also from London, which appears to have arrived with some passengers for Philadelphia seems to have been listed in the port books as the *Elizabeth* or the *Eliza & Mary*, her captain as John Bowen or John Bowman. The goods entered in the port books between 24 April and 2 May were not intended for Pennsylvania, but she seems to have taken on one family at least which was bound for the Delaware River, for the head of this family registered his arrival date as 22 7m (September) 1683. Since he no doubt paid the fee of "no more than Three pence a peece," according to the 163rd law of the province, his information as to the name of the ship and of the captain would seem to be the proper ones.[43]

The *Eliza & Mary* of London [6]

John Bowman, master

JOHN COLLY "late of Sauiour Southwork in old England ffeltmaker." [44]

---

40 For Pastorius' comments on the *Vine*, see Pennypacker, 82, cited in Note 31 above. The ship's loadings are from London port book E 190/115/1, PRO.

41 An ANTHONY TOMPKINS was granted a warrant for a city lot 21 12m 1683/4, which was laid out at the north end of Front Street on Delaware side. At the same time and by the same warrant land was surveyed for him in Bucks Co., but by 1687 he had moved to Kent Co. Warrants and Surveys, II, 124, III, 151; Deed Book E-1-5, 588: 21 4m 1687, Anthony Tompkins to Griffith Jones. For notice of a man of the same name, and probably identical, in an account of a sloop run ashore in West Jersey, see H. Clay Reed and George J. Miller, eds., *The Burlington Court Book* (Washington, D. C., 1944), 40, 86.

42 This Samuel Baker has not been identified. But see *Chester Court Records*, 84, 89, 105, 186, cited in Note 9 above, for references to a man of this name frequently brought into court for unseemly behaviour.

43 For the arrival date see *PMHB*, VIII, 330. Loadings for the *Eliza & Mary*, none of which were for Pennsylvania, are entered in London port book E 190/125/1. For the registration fee, see John Blair Linn, ed., *Charter to William Penn and Laws of the Province of Pennsylvania* (Harrisburg, Pa., 1879), 170.

44 JOHN COLLEY probably brought his wife SUSANNA and daughters ANN and SUSANNA with him. In 1686 he bought 200 acres in Philadelphia Co., and in 1692, a bank lot between High and Chestnut Sts. Deed Book E-1-5, 435: 20 9m 1686, William Powell to John Cole (*sic*) and Susanna his wife and daughter Ann; *Pennsylvania Archives*, 2nd Series, XIX, 325. In 1697, when he was styled a hatter, Colley arranged for a life estate for himself and his wife in the bank lot, with reversions one-half to his daughter Ann Naish, the other one-half to his daughter Susanna. Exemplification Book 7, 52: 29 3m 1697, John Colley *et al.* to James Fox *et al.* Susanna m. Henry Carter 9 5m 1703; he was deceased by 1715, leaving issue. *Pennsylvania Archives*, 2nd Series, XIX, 593; Hinshaw, II, 491.

At the very end of September two ships "arrived in Delaware River." One of these did not come up to Philadelphia until October first. The other, a 100-ton ketch from Liverpool, called the *Endeavour*, bore passengers who registered their arrival a year or more afterwards as 29 7m (September) 1683. But whoever transcribed their information wrote in the registry book in error that the ship's home port was London, instead of Liverpool.[45] English port books show that there was a ship of the same name whose home port was London. But her master, Francis Richardson, was taking on goods and passengers for New York at the same time as the Liverpool ship was loading for Pennsylvania goods being transported for her west-country passengers.

The *Endeavour* of Liverpool [7]

George Thorpe, master [46]

15 [June] FRANCIS ROSSEL (Russel): 21 cwt. iron; 6 grindle stones qtm. [*quantum:* quantity is] ½ chalder; 1 roulette & loose qtm. 6½ cwt. gad steel [roulette: a rolled up container; gad steel: steel cut into small bars or wedges]; 2 mill stones value £2. [Duty] £1 10s. 7½d.[47]

16 [June] WILL PEMBERTON: 4 crates; 1 bundle qtm. 500 pcs. earthware; 2 crates qtm. 20 small gross tobacco pipes. [Duty] 1s. 10d.

[16 June] RICHARD HOUGH: 12 pigs qtm. 20 cwt. lead; 8 grindle stones qtm. ½ chalder; 2 chests qtm. 6 cwt. wrought iron.[48]

---

[45] Loadings for the ketch *Endeavour* of Liverpool are from Liverpool port book E 190/1345/13, PRO. Its arrival is noted in *PMHB*, VIII, 330, and *ibid.*, IX, 226; in both citations it is incorrectly called "of London." The ship was still in the Delaware a week later when James Claypoole arrived in the *Concord.* He shipped hats brought from England, French barley and silver-hafted knives to his brother Edward in Barbados by the *Endeavour*, though he called it the *Comfort*, George Thorp, master, in a letter dated 2 10m 1683. *PMHB*, X, 274-7. The *Endeavour's* arrival at Barbados, however, is reported in C.O. 33/14/32, PRO.

[46] ANNE ROBOTHAM, "serv^t to the m^r of the s^d Ketch," was registered as arriving with the other passengers. *PMHB*, VIII, 331.

[47] FRANCIS and MICHAEL ROSSELL (Russell) both from Macclesfield, Cheshire, registered their arrival on the *Endeavour*. *Ibid.*, 330. Francis, a miller, purchased from Joseph English 3 acres in Bucks Co. by deed 10 9m 1683, and on 25 5m 1684 had acquired an additional 25 acres in Bristol Twp. where he erected a mill. *Pennsylvania Archives*, 2nd Series, XIX, 253, 527. When he died late in 1694, he left additional land, bought from William Penn in England, to the children of John Hough, and land "beyond Wrightstown," bought of Robert Lundy, to his servant William Smith. He left directions that he be buried in Burlington, and devised legacies to the poor of Bucks Co. Will Book A, 288, #116:1694/5, abstract in *PGSP*, II, 20. Nothing is known of Michael Rossell.

Also from Macclesfield came a tanner, JOHN OULDFIELD (Oudfield), who was living in Bucks Co. in 1688. *Records of the Courts of Quarter Sessions and Common Pleas of Bucks County, Pennsylvania, 1684-1700* (Meadville, Pa., 1943), 92, hereinafter cited as *Bucks Court Records.* From the same place came JOHN PRIESTNER, a blacksmith, for whom a warrant for 200 acres in Chester Co. was issued 1 Oct. 1683. *Pennsylvania Archives*, 3rd Series, III, 160; *ibid.*, 2nd Series, XIX, 222, 342, 252; *PMHB*, VIII, 331.

[48] RICHARD HOUGH from Macclesfield, brought a certificate from Congleton Monthly Meeting dated 2 3m 1683. *Hinshaw*, II, 989. With him came as servants FRANCIS HOUGH, possibly a nephew or brother, indentured for two years and for whom see *Bucks Court Records*, 29, 30, 57; THOMAS and MARY WOOD or WOODHOUSE, indentured for four and five years respectively, each to have 50 acres of land; and JAMES SUTTON, indentured for four years, to have £3 15s. per year and 50 acres of land at the end of his servitude. *PMHB*, IX, 226-7. Richard Hough was granted a warrant for a city lot 31 8m 1683, having purchased in England 500 acres on 24 Apr. 1683. *Pennsylvania Archives*, 3rd Series, II, 723; *ibid.*,

18 [June] JOHN CLOWES: 3 bundles, 3 claytes [wattle work containers], 1 box, 1 bag, qtm. 70 lbs. weight woolen cloth; 6 lbs. Norwich stuffs; 100 goads cottons; 75 yds. flannel; 7 coverlets wool & hair; 240 ells English linen; 9 doz. wool stockings & 1 doz. worsted stockings for men; 84 lbs. new shoes; 2 doz. felts English making; 100 lbs. haberdashery; ½ doz. leather cushions; 20 cwt. wrought iron. [Duty] £1 6s. 2d.[49]

19 [June] THOMAS JANNEY: 2 bbls. 13 casks, 1 chest, 1 box, 1 bundle, qtm. 70 lbs. woolen cloth; 31 lbs. Norwich stuffs; 14 lbs. haberdashery; ½ doz. wool stockings for men; 200 ells English linen; 5½ cwt. wrought iron; 20 cwt. cheese; 3 iron pots value 22s. [Duty] 18s. 11½d.[50]

22 [June] HENRY MADDOCK: 1 bbl., 4 casks, 2 bundles, 5 packs, 2 hhds., 1 box, qtm. 9 cwt. wrought iron; 13 cwt. cast lead; 8 cwt. nails; 15 lbs. new shoes; 12 doz. felts, English making; 16 cwt. iron; 175 ells English linen; 20 lbs. woolen cloth; 5 tons cheese; cwt. gad steel. [Duty] £4 2s. 4½d.[51]

2nd Series, XIX, 271. For a biographical sketch of him see *PMHB*, XVIII (1894), 20-34. James Sutton by 1696 had land in Bucks Co. on the road from Newtown to Gilbert Wheeler's ferry. *Bucks Court Records*, 303. JOHN CHARLESWORTH, a tanner from Macclesfield, who came on the *Endeavour*, was granted a warrant for 200 acres 14 7m 1684, laid out in Bucks Co. DANIEL SUTTON, a tailor from the same place and possibly related to the above James Sutton, carried on his trade in Bucks Co. *PMHB*, VIII, 331; *Pennsylvania Archives*, 3rd Series, III, 62; *PGSP*, I, 222.

[49] JOHN CLOWS (Clone), F.P. of 1000 acres, late of Gosworth, Cheshire, with his wife MARJORY, and children MARJORY, REBECCA and WILLIAM CLOWS, were included in the Congleton Monthly Meeting certificate of 2 3m 1683, cited above. John Clows had shipped goods on the *Friend's Adventure* in 1682 in the care of his other children, for which see *PGM*, XXIII, 47. His land was laid out in Makefield Twp., Bucks Co., on the Delaware where he died 4 7m 1687, and his wife 2 2m 1698. For abstract of his will, see *PGSP*, I, 219, recorded in Bucks Co. Will Book A-1, 44. See also sketch of Richard Hough, who married Marjory Clows, *PMHB*, XVIII, 32, cited above. SAMUEL HOUGH, one of Clowes' servants, who was aged about 20 in 1685, in 1698 and 1699 was constable for Newtown and Wrightstown. *Bucks Court Records*, 33, 357, 396. JOSEPH CHORLEY, another servant, by 1689 was constable for the district "below the falls to the governors," and in 1697 was granted a license to keep an ordinary at his ferry house. *Ibid.*, 101, 147, 321, 326. JOHN RICHARDSON, the third Clows servant, by 1699 had married Joyce Venables, thereby becoming the stepson (son-in-law) of Andrew Heath who had married the widow of William Venables. *Ibid.*, 394; *PGM*, XXIII, 46, 49.

[50] THOMAS JANNEY (Janeway), late of Pownall Fee and of Styall, Cheshire, his wife MARJORY (Margaret) HEATH, sister of James Harrison's wife Ann and William Yardley's wife Jane, came with their children JACOB, THOMAS, ABEL and JOSEPH JANNEY on the *Endeavour*, registering their arrival. *PMHB*, IX, 226 and *ibid.*, VIII, 330. The well-known Quaker preacher, he had purchased 250 acres on 12 6m 1682, by right of which he obtained a warrant for 300 acres which was laid out in Makefield Twp., Bucks Co. 24 8m 1683. *Pennsylvania Archives*, 3rd Series, III, 78. For a biographical sketch, see *PMHB*, XXVII (1905), 212-237. Janney brought over two servants, JOHN NEILD, indentured for five years and to have 50 acres at the expiration of his time, and HANNAH FALKNER, to serve four years and also have 50 acres. Her right to this land was taken up by James Sutton, who had come with Richard Hough. John Neild bought 236 acres from Samuel Beakes in 1696, married, and when he died in 1747, left to his wife Judith £7 yearly, to his son John 150 acres, to his son James 86 acres, and to his daughters Martha and Jane each £10. See *ibid.*, 216; for his will see Bucks Co. Will Book 2, 186. He presumably is not the F.P. of 250 acres.

[51] Henry Maddock of Loom Hall, Cheshire, F.P. jointly of 1500 acres with his brother-in-law, James Kennerly who had come in the *Friendship* in 1682, for which see *PGM*, XXIII, 40, probably did not come at this time, but did send over two servants, GEORGE PHILLIPS, a tailor, who in 1689 sued James Stanfield for money owing on account of clothes he had made for Stanfield, and RALPH DUCKARD. See *Chester Court Records*, 104-5; see also Note 123 below. JOHN MADDOCK, a joiner, on the same ship, was from Nantwich, Cheshire, as were RICHARD CLOWS (Clone), another joiner, JOHN CLOUS, a shoemaker, and CHARLES KILBECK. John Maddock married with consent granted by the Philadelphia Meeting 28 1m 1690, Margaret Kent. *PGSP*, II, 161, 162. The following year he bought 50 acres in Nether Providence Twp., Chester Co., from Francis Balding, which he sold 10 11m 1692. Possibly he moved away as he had been fined several times for uttering "Scandelous and Dishonourable words" against the Proprietor. *Chester Court Records*, 161, 234, 264, 277.

[22 June] THOMAS JANNEY: ¼ cwt. pewter. [Duty] 1s. 3d.[52]

28 [June] HENRY THORPE: 13 pigs [pig: up to 300 lbs.] qtm. 21¼ & 20 lbs. lead; 3 bbls. qtm. 3 cwt. gunpowder; 3 bundles qtm. 3 doz. wool stockings for men. [Duty] £1 8s. 3d.

2 [July] JAMES FLETCHER: 1 pack, 1 cask, 2 bbls. qtm. 140 lbs. wool cloth; cwt. wrought iron; 130 lbs. new shoes; 90 ells English linen; cwt. hard soap, English making. [Duty] 14s. 10d.

5 [July] FRANCIS STANFORD (Stanfield): 1 crate qtm. 1 chest window glass. [Duty] 6d.[53]

---

[52] JOHN NIXON (Nickson) from "Powell" (Pownall), a F.P. of 500 acres, his wife MARGERY, and children JOHN, THOMAS, JAMES, NEHEMIAH, JOSEPH, FREDERICK, MARY, JANE, MARGERY and ELIZABETH NIXON, all came on the *Endeavour*, bringing with them a servant JAMES WHITAKER. By a warrant dated 6 8m 1683, 300 acres were laid out for Nixon, probably in Providence Twp., Chester Co., of which he was a constable in 1686. Whitaker was on the grand jury in Chester Co. in 1690, but did not take up his headland until 1709. *Chester Court Records*, 86, 216; *Pennsylvania Archives*, 3rd Series, III, 150, 177. See also Note 89 below.

From the same general vicinity of Pownall came JOSEPH MILNER, a blacksmith, his mother ANN MILNER, and her children, SARAH and RALPH MILNER. The mother appears to have been the widow of Robert Milner of Styall in Pownall Fee who died 30 9m 1673, for whom see Digested Copy of the Registers of the Quarterly Meeting of Cheshire and Staffordshire, Marriages, Births, Burials, GSP. Joseph Milner, who with Daniel, his brother, had first come over in 1682 on the *Friend's Adventure*, for whom see PGM, XXIII, 47, had apparently returned to bring over his mother and sisters. The mother died 29 10m 1688, the sister Sarah, 17 10m 1689, and Daniel Milner 3 8m 1685, according to Middletown Monthly Meeting Records, Births and Deaths, Bu2F, 396, GSP. See also *Pennsylvania Archives*, 3rd Series, III, 83, for warrant for Joseph Milner dated 26 Oct. 1683, for 300 acres in Bucks Co.

At the same time came RALPH MILNER, carpenter and wheelwright from Pownall, with his wife RACHEL and son ROBERT. For litigation in which both were involved in 1686, see *Bucks Court Records*, 53, 55-8, 59, 70. From Budworth, southwest of Styall in Cheshire, came JOHN HOWELL, his wife MARY, and daughter HANNAH HOWELL, all of whom registered their arrival on the *Endeavour*. PMHB, VIII, 330. On 27 3m 1680, at Frandley, when he was of Norcott in Over Whitley, Cheshire, he had married Mary Williamson of Stretton, Cheshire, for which see Digested Registers of Cheshire and Staffordshire, cited above. He took up 350 acres in Marple Twp., Chester Co. by warrant dated 20 Oct. 1683. *Pennsylvania Archives*, 3rd Series, III, 136. He died between February and June 1703; for his will see Will Book B, 307, #115:1703. With them came Mary's brother DANIEL WILLIAMSON as servant to Robert Taylor, F.P. of 1000 acres from Little Leigh, Cheshire, who apparently had come in one of the 1682 Liverpool ships, since he returned a warrant of survey for 400 acres into the surveyor general's office 11 Nov. 1682, for which see *Pennsylvania Archives*, 3rd Series, III, 173. His servant and brother-in-law Williamson now brought over Taylor's wife MARY TAYLOR, and children ISAAC, THOMAS, JONATHAN, PHEBE, MARY and MARTHA TAYLOR, the arrival of all of whom was registered. PMHB, VIII, 331. For abstract of Taylor's will, see PGSP, II, 24, recorded in Will Book A, 311, #124:1695. See also Smith, *Delaware County*, 507, and *Pennsylvania Archives*, 2nd Series, XIX, 450.

[53] FRANCIS STANFIELD (Stanford) of Garton, Cheshire, his wife GRACE, and children JAMES, MARY, SARAH, ELIZABETH, GRACE and HANNAH all registered their arrival in the *Endeavour*. PMHB, VIII, 331. On 5 8m 1683, he obtained a warrant for 600 acres which was laid out in Marple Twp., Chester Co., where he was constable in 1684. *Pennsylvania Archives*, 3rd Series, III, 167; *Chester Court Records*, 86. His wife died in 1691, and he in 1692. Smith, *Delaware County*, 504. With them came servants DANIEL BROOM (Browne), constable of Marple in 1695; THOMAS MASSEY (Marsey), who in 1692 married Phebe Taylor, daughter of Robert, noted above, and was supervisor of highways in Marple in 1693 and constable in 1695. The next year he bought 300 acres in Marple from Jonathan Hayes. *Chester Court Records*, 283, 311, 339, 359, 401. Massey died in 1708 in his 45th year, leaving children Esther, Mordecai, James, Hannah, Thomas, Phebe and Mary Massey. Smith, *Delaware County*, 483. Other servants of Stanfield who came on the *Endeavour* were ISAAC BROOKESBY (Brickshaw, Brackshaw, Brookshaw), hailed into court for defaming John Simcock in 1689; ROBERT and THOMAS SIDBOTHAM, the latter called into court in 1696 on suspicion of a felony committed against the sheriff and fined 5s., JOHN SMITH, ROBERT BRYAN and WILLIAM RUDWAY. *Chester Court Records*, 66, 192, 402, 405.

Also on the *Endeavour* were THOMAS PIERSON (Pearson, Person), a mason from Pownall, with his wife

11 [July] HENRY THORPE: ¾ cwt. & 8 lbs. lead. [Duty] 10*d*.

The second ship to enter Delaware Bay the end of September was the *Bristol Comfort*, a Dutch-built but English-owned vessel of 200 tons. The previous April she had arrived at Bristol in old England from Virginia laden with tobacco from that place. On 25 July, a month after the last goods for Pennsylvania had been loaded, she set sail again from the "Kingroad" — the King's Roadstead — at Bristol, arriving in the Delaware on 28 7m (September) 1683, and at Upland 1 8m (October) following. She was the first of five ships said to have arrived that month.[54]

The *Bristol Comfort* [8]

John Read (Reed), master, for Pennsylvania & Virginia

23 [May] GEORGE MORRIS (Maris): 10 doz. dressed calf skins; 1 qtr. malt; 3½ qtrs. wheat; 3 bushels oatmeal; 90 lbs. shoes; ½ cwt. pewter; cwt. brass manufactured; 2 flitches bacon; 20 cwt. wrought iron; 6 doz. woolen stockings; 10 cwt. cheese; 1 bbl. beer; 3 doz. plain sheepskin gloves; 1½ firkins butter; 33 yds. flannel; 11 pcs. English earthware; 1/15 hhd. aquavita; 2¼ cwt. lead shot; ¼ cwt. gunpowder; 20 ells English linen; 10 parcels several wares value £18 10s.[55]

[23 May] ALEXANDER BEARDSLEY: 17 yds. flannel; 4 lbs. worsted stuff; cwt. wrought iron; 34 lbs. brass manufactured; 4 lbs. shoes; 1¼ cwt. cheese; ½ cwt. wrought pewter; 1 firkin butter; 1 castor hat; 20 ells English linen; 3 bushels malt; 7 parcels wares value £4 3s.[56]

MARGARET, incorrectly assigned to the *Welcome* in Smith, *Delaware County*, 491. However, their arrival was registered as being on the *Endeavour*. *PMHB*, VIII, 330. He was constable and supervisor for Marple in 1684. *Chester Court Records*, 38. JOHN PIERSON, his brother, also a passenger, was granted a warrant for himself "& Co." on 6 8m 1683, but he settled in Newtown. *Pennsylvania Archives*, 3rd Series, III, 157; Smith, *Delaware County*, 491. Their sister MARY SMITH came at the same time with them; she was also from Pownall, and may have made her home with one of her brothers.

54 In a letter from Penn, written 10 Nov. 1683, n.s., to an unknown correspondent in England, he is reported by Benjamin Furley to have stated that within the month [*i.e.*, October], "there arrived five vessels, among others one [the *Concord*] which brought many people from Crevelt and neighboring places. . . ." See "Reciieil de Diverses Pieces, Concernant la Pensylvanie [Collection of Various Pieces Concerning Pennsylvania. . . .]," *PMHB*, VI (1882), 323. The arrival of the first of these five ships, the *Bristol Comfort*, is given in the registration of CHRISTIANUS LEWIS, schoolmaster, late of Dudley in Worcestershire. *Ibid.*, VIII, 333. The ship's loadings are from Bristol port book E 190/1146/1, PRO.

55 GEORGE MARIS (Morris) and ALICE his wife of Hadswell, parish of Inkborough, Worcestershire, brought a certificate of removal dated 6 3m 1683, which he presented to Darby Monthly Meeting. He is reported to have bought land from Robert Toomer, a F.P. of 1000 acres, by deed dated 14 May 1683, at which time Maris was of Grafton Flyford. A shoemaker by trade, on 6 8m 1683, he was granted a warrant for 400 acres which were laid out in Chester Co. His wife Alice d. 11 1m 1699, and he d. 15 11m 1705, aged *ca.* 73. The children who came with them were ALICE, GEORGE, ELIZABETH, ANNA, JOHN, and probably RICHARD. For an account of this family see J. Smith Futhey and Gilbert Cope, *History of Chester County, Philadelphia* . . . (Philadelphia, 1881), 649, hereinafter cited as Futhey and Cope.

56 ALEXANDER BEARDSLEY, F.P. of 500 acres, a glover of the city of Worcester, with his wife MARGARET and daughter MARY, brought a certificate dated 14 3m 1683, to the Philadelphia Meeting. On 12 8m 1683, he was granted a warrant for his city lot which was surveyed 19 8m following, between Schuylkill Second and Third Streets south of Walnut. Warrants and Surveys, III, 261; Myers, *Quaker Arrivals*, 5, cited in Note 17 above; Hinshaw, II, 461. On 27 8m 1683, Beardsley assigned his rights in his 500-acre purchase to

24 [May] ROBERT BURROWS: cwt. wrought iron; ¾ cwt. cheese; 34 lbs. wrought pewter; 20 lbs. brass manufactured. [Duty] 2s. 6d.[57]

25 [May] ELIZABETH SMITH: 4 bushels malt; 30 lbs. pewter; 30 lbs. wrought iron; ½ cwt. brass manufactured; 28 lbs. cheese; 2 parcels wares value 30s. [Duty] 3s. 6½d.[58]

26 [May] FRANCIS YARNALL: 1¼ cwt. shot; 3 doz. wool stockings; 40 ells English linen; ¼ cwt. gunpowder. [Duty] 3s.[59]

2 [June] JOHN WAYTE (Waite): 1 chest window glass; 12 doz. wool stockings; 2 doz. children's wool stockings; 5 cwt. lead shot; 56 lbs. gunpowder; 3 cwt. English soap; 14 lbs. starch; 84 lbs. hops; 2 hhds. aquavita; 7 parcels wares value £20 15s.[60]

[2 June] JOHN GRANT: 20 lbs. shoes; 2 doz. wool stockings; cwt. wrought iron; 30 goads cottons; 10 lbs. serges; 6 lbs. Norwich stuffs; ½ cwt. haberdashery; 6 ends fustians.

[2 June] MILLISENT HOPKINS (Hodgkins): 1 qtr. malt; ½ cwt. pewter; 1½ cwt.

FRANCIS FINCHER, also a glover from Worcester, who had shipped goods the previous year on the *Society* of Bristol. *PGM*, XXIII, 42. Fincher brought a certificate, bearing the same date as Beardsley's, for himself and presumably his wife MARY who, after Fincher's death, m. Christopher Sibthorp. *Pennsylvania Archives*, 2nd Series, XIX, 351; Deed Book E-2-5, 271: 18 9m 1693, Christopher Sibthorp to Jonathan Ducket; Hinshaw, II, 523. THOMAS BOWETER, indentured to Fincher for three years, accompanied his master. He took up his headland in Edgmont Twp., Chester Co., and in 1686 m. Sarah Edge who died in 1692. On 2 March 1695/6, he bought from John Fox, former servant to Nicholas Newlin, 100 acres in Edgmont which he had previously sold in 1693 to Charles Thomas. He m. 2nd in 1701, the widow Frances Barnet, and in 1720 removed to New Garden. *Chester Court Records*, 233, 303, 375; Smith, *Delaware County*, 448.

Other certificates issued 14 3m 1683, from Worcester, included one for SEMERCIE ADAMS, another glover from Worcester. He m. with consent of the Philadelphia Meeting granted 28 8m 1687, the widow Mary Britt, and died intestate by 21 Oct. 1699, when his brother Joseph Adams renounced his right to administer on the estate. *PGSP*, II, 122, 125; *PGM*, XIX, 271, Administration Book A, 290. A certificate of the same date was given JOHN PRICE, a probable passenger on the *Comfort*, but he has not been identified further. Myers, *Quaker Arrivals*, 5; Hinshaw, II, 450, 627.

[57] ROBERT BURROWS, and perhaps his wife Dorothy, settled first in Chester Co. where he was on the grand jury 7m 1686. *Chester Court Records*, 75, 117, 243. He removed to Philadelphia after 1691, and in 1701 bought a lot in Chestnut St. between Fourth and Fifth. *Pennsylvania Archives*, 2nd Series, XIX, 488. He was a witness to or legatee of numerous Philadelphia wills. *PGSP*, III, 34-5, 149; *PGM*, XIX, 263. Letters of administration on his own estate were granted 1 Dec. 1714, to his widow Deborah. *PGM*, XX, 52, recorded in Administration Book B, 110, #17:1714.

[58] ELIZABETH SMITH, widow, was granted a warrant 12 8m 1683, for a lot which was laid out on the west side of Schuylkill Fourth south of Mulberry (Arch) Street. Warrants and Surveys, III, 228. She m. Edward Luff, a cordwainer from Market Levington, Wiltshire, with consent of the Philadelphia Meeting granted 5 6m 1684. *PGSP*, I, 268, 270. He died in 1688, and on her death in 1694, Robert Burrows and his wife Deborah became residuary legatees. *Ibid.*, 68; *PGM*, XIX, 263, recorded in Administration Book A, 181, #16:1693. See also Note 68 below.

[59] FRANCIS YARNALL was granted a warrant for 100 acres 6 8m 1683, which had been laid out in "Springtown" (Springfield Twp.), Chester Co., by the following 17 Oct. 1683. *Pennsylvania Archives*, 3rd Series, III, 180. Fifty acres of this he sold to George Maris, Jr. on 1 1m 1685/5, and that year m. Hannah Baker, daughter of Joseph Baker. *Chester Court Records*, 64, 182. For data on their children, see Futhey and Cope, 778-9, cited in Note 55 above. Philip Yarnall, brother of Francis, may also have been on the *Comfort*. For references to his activities, see Futhey & Cope, *loc. cit.*, and *Chester Court Records, passim.*

[60] JOHN WAITE of Worcester on 5 3m 1683, acquired from William Pardoe, also of Worcester and F.P. of 1250 acres, Pardoe's rights to the land. *Pennsylvania Archives*, 2nd Series, XIX, 474. From Samuel Richardson, Waite acquired a 17-foot lot at the northeast corner of Second and High Sts., where he was living at the time of his death. Recited in Deed Book E-2-5, 252: 3 10m 1692, William Harwood to William Kelly. For abstract of Waite's will, recorded in Administration Book A, 220, #88:1689, see *PGSP*, III, 166. He had m. Magadalen Morris with consent of the Philadelphia Meeting granted 28 7m 1688. *Ibid.*, II, 142.

brass manufactured; 2 cwt. wrought iron; 28 lbs. cordage; cwt. cheese; 8 bushels wheat meal at 2s.; 2 cwt. nails.[61]

[2 June] THOMAS PEERSON (Peirson, Pierson): 5 doz. wool stockings; 6 cwt. wrought iron; 28 lbs. brass manufactured; 14 lbs. wrought pewter; 40 yds. frieze; 12 lbs. serges; 50 lbs. shoes; ½ chest window glass; cwt. cheese; 5 pcs. English fustian; 3 parcels wares value £3 1s. 5d.[62]

[2 June] ENOCH FLOWER: 4 cwt. wrought iron; ½ cwt. wrought pewter; cwt. brass manufactured; 72 lbs. shoes; ½ cwt. gunpowder; 1½ cwt. shot; 10 bushels malt; 1 Spanish cloth; 2 flitches bacon; 2 cwt. cheese; 3 parcels wares value £5 15s. [Duty] £1 7½d.[63]

4 [June] WALTER STEPHENS: 440 ells English linen; 40 yds. flannel; 5 pcs. English fustian; 40 lbs. serges; 12 gross tobacco pipes; 30 lbs. wrought iron; 60 ells coarse linen value 35s. [Duty] 11s. 3½d.

[4 June] RALPH SMITH & WILLIAM BROWNE: 4 lbs. haberdashery; 1 pc. kersey; 1 penistone [frieze]; 4 cwt. nails; 20 lbs. shoes; 3½ cwt. cheese; 1 doz. felt hats; 12 yds. flannel; 1 Spanish cloth; 2 parcels wares value £9 3s. 4d.; 150 goads cottons; 5 cwt.

---

61 MILLICENT HODGKINS (Hopkins) is also said to have come from Worcester, presumably with her daughter BRIDGET HODGKINS who m. 26 9m 1686, William Fisher, for an account of whom see J. Bennett Hill and Margaret Howe Hill, "William Fisher, Early Philadelphia Quaker . . . ," PGM, XXI, 253. On 12 8m 1683, Millicent Hodgkins was granted a warrant for a city lot laid out 28 12m 1683/4, at the southwest corner of Schuylkill Fourth and Mulberry, adjoining the lot laid out to Elizabeth Smith, noted above.

62 The 1683 voyage of the Bristol Comfort is noted in "Queries," PMHB, XXI (1897), 506, in the account of THOMAS PEIRSON, one of the passengers. He says he had finished his apprenticeship in 1675, journeyed from Bristol to London early in 1675/6, and in 7m (Sept.) of that year, sailed for Maryland on the Joseph & Benjamin, Mathew Pain, commander, in company with one William Dixson, for notice of whom see Myers, Irish Immigration, 319, cited in Note 29 above. On 14 12m 1681/2, Peirson left Maryland in the Comfort, then commanded by Thomas Whitop, and arrived back at Bristol 20 March 1681/2, a date confirmed by the Bristol port books. "On or about" 25 July 1683, he embarked once more in the Comfort, and arrived, he says, at Upland (probably in error for New Castle) 28 Sept. 1683. He appears to have m. Rachel Sharply by authority of Newark Monthly Meeting at New Castle granted in 8m 1686. She d. 2 7m 1687, and was bur. at Newark burying place in Brandywine Hundred, New Castle Co. He m. 2nd, Rose Dixson in 1690, according to Newark Monthly Meeting records. He appears to have been the deputy surveyor for New Castle Co. appointed 10 7m 1684. Colonial Records, I, 120.

63 ENOCH FLOWER, a schoolmaster of 20 years' standing, and F.P. of 500 acres for himself and 1500 acres for six others, brought a certificate dated 21 3m 1683, from Brinkworth Monthly Meeting, Wiltshire. Myers, Quaker Arrivals, 5; Warrants and Surveys, I, 375. By a warrant dated 5 8m 1683, a lot on Delaware Front St. was surveyed for him on 12 8m 1683, between Walnut St. and the Dock. Ibid., III, 508. On 25 8m 1683, he was among those impanelled on the grand jury which found a true bill against Charles Pickering for coining "New Bitts." On 26 10m 1683, he was engaged as schoolmaster in Philadelphia. The terms agreed upon were: "to Learne to read English 4s. by the Quarter, to Learne to read and write 6s. by ye Quarter, to learne to read, Write and Cast accot 8s. by ye Quarter, for Boarding a Scholler, that is to say, dyet, Washing, Lodging & Scooling, Tenn pounds for one whole year." Colonial Records, I, 87, 91. The school was of short duration, for he died the following year. For abstract of his will, dated 21 6m 1684 and proved 25 7m 1684, see PGSP, I, 51, recorded in Philadelphia Will Book A, 17, #13:1684. With Enoch Flower came his nephew HENRY FLOWER, a barber by trade, and son of Seth Flower of Middlesex, also a barber. Henry apparently had two wives, Elizabeth, and Ann who survived him. Hinshaw, II, 443. For his will see Philadelphia Will Book E, 366, #439:1736. See also Pennsylvania Archives, 2nd Series, XIX, 287-8; Deed Book E-1-5, 194: 2 12m 1685/6, Henry Flower to James Pellar.

JOSEPH BUSHEL, who had purchased 250 of the 1500 acres for which Enoch Flower was acting as agent, came at the same time as Enoch and Henry Flower, with certificate from Brinkworth Meeting of same date. His 2nd wife Sarah Webb, and children Jane, who m. Walter Martin and Abigail who m. Nicholas Pyle, may have accompanied him. On 5 8m 1683, Bushell was granted a warrant for 250 acres to be laid out in Chester Co. Pennsylvania Archives, 3rd Series, III, 108. A barber by trade, originally from Culherne Parish, Wiltshire, he died in Concord Twp. in 1708. For his will see Philadelphia Will Book C, 101, #81:1708. For an account of his family, see Alfred R. Justice Collection, Ju4, 79, GSP, and Smith, Delaware County, 451.

cheese; 2 firkins butter; 2 bushels wheat; 5 cwt. wrought iron; cwt. steel; 8 chalders grind stones; 6 bushels hay seed & dust. [Duty] £1 5s.[64]

[4 June] JOHN GIBBONS: 60 lbs. shoes; 8 doz. wool stockings; 120 lbs. serges; 2½ cwt. cordage; 6 bushels malt; 56 lbs. wrought pewter; 4 bushels pease; cwt. brass manufactured; 3 doz. plain sheepskin gloves; cwt. wrought iron; 3 cwt. cheese; 1 firkin butter; 3 parcels wares value £8. [Duty] £1 11s. 10½d.[65]

5 [June] EDWARD BEAZER: cwt. shot; ¾ cwt. wrought pewter; cwt. brass manufactured; cwt. nails; 28 lbs. gunpowder; 4½ cwt. wrought iron; 34 lbs. shoes; 1¾ cwt. cheese; 1 bbl. pork; ⅛ chalder grindlestones; 2 pcs. kerseys; ½ short cloth; 24 lbs. serges; 4 parcels wares value £9 10s.[66]

6 [June] ANNE SMITH: 1½ cwt. cheese. [Duty] 6d.[67]

[6 June] JOHN LUFFE: 6 cwt. wrought iron; 4 doz. felts; 40 lbs. wrought pewter; cwt. brass manufactured; 72 lbs. shoes; 1 pc. kersey; 20 lbs. gunpowder; 2 cwt. lead shot; 36 lbs. serges; 2 parcels wares value £4 10s. [Duty] £1 1s. 3½d.[68]

---

[64] William Brown of Bristol, merchant and F.P. of 1000 acres, was probably he who had shipped goods on the *Bristol Factor* in 1682, for which see *PGM*, XXIII, 55; whether he is identical with the William Brown cited therein who settled in Chester Co. is still uncertain. City lots had been laid out for the merchant Brown 9 5m 1683. Warrants and Surveys, II, 18. Ralph Smith, who had a share in the 1683 goods, had obtained warrants, dated 12 4m 1683, for 300 acres each to be laid out in Bucks Co. *Pennsylvania Archives*, 3rd Series, III, 93. He was the "gouernors gardiner" and was bur. "att the burying place in the point" 5 3m 1685. For abstract of his will, see *PGSP*, I, 209-210.

[65] This was the JOHN GIBBON, shoemaker of Warminster, Wiltshire and F.P. of 500 acres, who had shipped goods on the *Amity* in 1682, for which see *PGM*, XXIII, 35. Since he did not obtain a warrant for his land, laid out in Bethel Twp., until 12 3m 1683, it now seems likely he was a passenger on the *Bristol Comfort*, the 1682 goods probably having been sent over in the care of his servant, Reuben Ford, for whom see *Pennsylvania Archives*, 2nd Series, XIX, 409, and Futhey and Cope, 564, cited in Note 55 above, reciting a letter of William Coole of Devizes to his sister Sarah, widow of William Bezer, dated 24 12m 1683[/4]. In this letter it is implied that Gibbon, Robert Pyle and Edward Beazer all came to Pennsylvania together. Gibbon brought his wife MARGERY, and sons JOHN and JAMES GIBBON. Smith, *Delaware County*, 464. ROBERT PYLE (Pile), malster of Horton, Bishops Canning, Wiltshire, his wife ANN, and infant daughter SARAH PYLE, b. 27 11m 1682/3, settled in Bethel Twp., Chester Co. where by 1685 he was a justice of the county court. He had been granted a warrant for "part of 250 acres" 12 8m 1683, and was on a jury in Chester County with Edward Beazer 14 10m 1683. *Chester Court Records*, 34, 55 *et passim*. He sold to his brother Nicholas Pyle 100 acres in Concord Twp. 27 9m 1686, but whether the brother came with him or not has not been determined. *Ibid.*, 83. See also Smith, Delaware County, 495.

[66] EDWARD BEAZER, mason and carpenter from Rowde, Wiltshire, F.P. of 500 acres and brother of John Beazer who had come on the *Bristol Factor* in 1681, for whom see *PGM*, XXIII, 32, was granted a warrant for his 500 acres 12 8m 1683, which was laid out in Bethel Twp. *Pennsylvania Archives*, 3rd Series, III, 103; Smith, *Delaware County*, 446. Dying in 1688, Edward Beazer left a widow Ann and orphan children, either seven or eight in number, the eldest of which was Edward, Jr. *Chester Court Records*, 169, 196, 223, 229. A servant, JAMES HAYWARD, probably had emigrated with the family in 1683. *Pennsylvania Archives*, 2nd Series, XIX, 610.

[67] Ann Smith has not been positively identified. She may have been the wife of Francis Smith whose daughter Ann was the wife of Robert Eyre. See *ibid.*, 229; *Chester Court Records*, 73, 104.

[68] JOHN LUFF, with his brother Edward, were shoemakers and sons of Edward Luff of Market Levington, Wiltshire, a F.P. of 500 acres. By a warrant dated 6 8m 1683, a lot was surveyed for John Luff at the southeast corner of Third and Chestnut, in right of a half part of the 500 acres of his father. Warrants and Surveys, II, 77; Deed Book C-1, 13, 14: 14, 15 Sept. 1681, Edward Luff to John Luff. John Luff probably brought his wife JANE with him, and probably his father EDWARD LUFF who m. Elizabeth Smith in 1684, for whom see Note 58 above. Both men were on the Pickering jury 26 8m 1683. *Colonial Records*, I, 87. John Luff died between 27 7m 1684 and 17 12m 1685/6, when his will was proved, leaving a widow Jane and a minor son John, and naming his father Edward Luff and William Clayton overseers. For abstract of the will see *PGSP*, I, 52, recorded in Will Book A, 20, #15:1686. The widow Jane m. Philip Howell, for whom see Note 110 below, with consent of the Philadelphia Meeting granted 3 3m 1686. *PGSP*, I, 297; *ibid.*, II, 94.

21 [June] JOHN WAYTE: cwt. English glue. [Duty] 10*d.*

25 [June] JOHN WAYTE: cwt. nails; 150 lbs. worsted stuffs; 28 lbs. haberdashery. [Duty] 12s. 9d.

26 [June] EDWARD HACKETT: 1¼ cwt. clover seed. [Duty] 2s.

The second ship to arrive in October was probably the *Bristol Factor.* Its exact arrival date is uncertain since no passenger registered his arrival on it. However, although it was only about 100 tons burthen, in 1682 its voyage from Bristol to Pennsylvania had been made in less than two months, evidence it was a fast sailer. This year its last loading, which was for Virginia, went on 7 August 1683, so that its arrival at Philadelphia by 4 October 1683, the date one passenger obtained a warrant for survey, would not be improbable.[69]

The *Bristol Factor* [9]

Roger Drew, master, for Pennsylvania & Virginia

6 [July] JOHN BEVAN: 3 doz. woolen stockings; 1½ doz. child's woolen stockings; 50 yds. flannel; 2/3 of a short cloth; 40 lbs. haberdashery; 20 suits wearing apparel; 5 cwt. wrought iron; 7 firkins butter; 1 barrel beef; 30 yds. flannel; ½ cwt. English soap; 2 parcels wares value £4 15s. [Duty] 14s. 3d.[70]

16 [July] SAM PACKER for CHARLES JONES: 4 cwt. wrought iron. [Duty] 2s.[71]

24 [July] STEPHEN WATTS: 30 coverlets, wool & hair; 6 Dunster kerseys [from Dunster, Somerset], [duty] 5s. 6d.; ½ a short cloth; 100 goads cottons; 150 made garments; 30 pcs. English fustians; 2 cwt. haberdashery; 100 lbs. serges; 8 small saddles; 14 doz. men's woolen stockings; 100 lbs. shoes & leather manufactured; 2 cwt. shot; 3 cwt. wrought iron; 6 cwt. nails; 6 doz. felt hats; 30 gross tobacco pipes; 1½ cwt. brass manufactured; ½ cwt. pewter; 6 cwt. wrought iron; 3 parcels wares value £10 5s.

---

69 For the *Factor's* 1682 loadings and passengers, see *PGM*, XXIII, 54-56. The 1683 loadings are from Bristol port book E 190/1146/1, PRO. Its arrival by 4 8m 1683, is suggested by the warrant granted John Holland who loaded goods on the ship 31 July, for whom see Note 77 below.

70 It has been claimed that JOHN BEVAN, F.P. of 2000 acres as agent for a group of Glamorganshire, Wales, purchasers, arrived in November 1683, in the *Morning Star* from Liverpool. It hardly seems logical for him to have transported his goods, family and servants from the south of Wales to the extreme north part, over 100 miles away, when a ship was loading at Bristol, within a few miles of his home at Cardiff. However, his certificate of removal from Treverig, Glamorgan, dated 10 7m (Sept.) 1683, issued by the mens' meeting both at Cardiff and Treverig and filed at Radnor Monthly Meeting, speaks of the "loss we and others have sustained in the removal of our deare friends to wit John ap Bevan and Barbara,: with their tender family into Penn Silvani *about ye 4th day of this Instant* . . . their small weakly family along with them." In like manner a certificate bearing same date was issued for RALPH LEWIS of Eglwysilan, Glamorgan, and his family "passing ye same time with our friend John ap Bevan for Pennsylvania," and one for JOHN RICHARD "of small abilitie," for WILLIAM SHARPUS who was "looked on" as "a harmless man, low in the outward," and for JOHN LLOYD "yt goeth as a servant to John ap Bevan." Transcript of Records of Radnor Monthly Meeting, 1680-1733, Del5F, 23-25, GSP. For accounts of these families, see Thomas Allen Glenn, *Merion in the Welsh Tract* (Norristown, Pa., 1896), *passim*, and Charles H. Browning, *Welsh Settlement of Pensylvania* (Philadelphia, 1912), *passim*.

71 Charles Jones, soap boiler of Bristol, and Charles Jones, Jr., merchant of Bristol, father and son, were joint F.P. of 2000 acres. Ann, daughter of the younger Charles, m. William Penn, Jr. in 1698/9. *PMHB*, XXI (1897), 137. Sam Packer, who was acting as agent for Jones, in 1691 was involved with other Bristol merchants in accusations of customs frauds. See *Merchants and Merchandise in Seventeenth-Century Bristol*, [Bristol Record Society's Publications, XIX (1955)], 222.

[24 July] ROGER DREW: 50 lbs. shoes; 2 pcs. kersey; 2 doz. wool stockings; 10 goads cottons; 4 small saddles; cwt. nails; 10 gross tobacco pipes; 10 lbs. serges; 6 pcs. English fustian; ½ cwt. wrought iron; 4 shod shovels; 3 parcels wares value £3 13s. 4d. [Duty for Watts and Drew] £2 19s. 1½d.[72]

26 [July] PHILIP JAMES: 2 cwt. cheese; ½ cwt. wrought iron; 2 chalders grindstones; 200 pcs. English earthware; ½ cwt. nails. [Duty] 2s. 8½d.[73]

[26 July] EDWARD HARFORD: ½ cwt. haberdashery; 175 lbs. shoes; 4 coverlets, wool & hair; 2 doz. felt hats; cwt. English soap; 1 chest window glass; 11 doz. wool stockings; 30 lbs. serges; 36 suits wearing apparel; 150 made garments; cwt. wrought iron; 2 cwt. nails; cwt. cheese. [Duty] 16s. 1d.[74]

[26 July] JOSEPH BAUGH: 20 ells English made linen; 1 pc. English fustian; 8 lbs. shoes; 5 lbs. haberdashery; 2 parcels wares value 30s. [Duty] 2s. 2d.

[26 July] ANTHONY STURGIS: cwt. lead weights; cwt. cheese; 1 firkin butter; 18 lbs. shoes; 1 doz. felt hats; 3 cwt. biscuit value £1 13s. 4d. [Duty] 6s. 6d.[75]

[26 July] WILLIAM SMITH: 10 cwt. cheese; 30 suits wearing apparel; 1 doz. woolen stockings; 30 coverlets wool & hair; 40 lbs. shoes; 30 small saddles; 2 cwt. wrought iron; 16 cwt. nails; 200 goads cottons; 2 flock beds value £2. [Duty] £2 3s.[76]

28 [July] NICHOLAS DOWNING: cwt. nails; 14 lbs. shoes; 12 lbs. serges. [Duty] 1s. 7d.

31 [July] CHARLES JONES: 1½ cwt. wrought iron; ½ cwt. steel. [Duty] 1s. 3d.

[31 July] JOHN HOLLAND: 2 pcs. English fustians; 12 lbs. serges; 2 parcels wares value £4 6s. 8d. [Duty] 5s. 1d.[77]

1 [August] WALTER STEPHENS: 30 lbs. serges; 3 pcs. calicoes value 30s. 1 doz. wool stockings; 20 lbs. shoes; 5 lbs. haberdashery; 1 pair worsted stockings. [Duty] 4s. 6½d.

---

[72] Roger Drew, master of the *Factor*, was a F.P. of 500 acres. Thomas Jacques on 22 9m 1683, obtained a warrant in Drew's right, for Drew's city lot which was surveyed the next day at the northeast corner of Schuylkill Front and Race Streets. Warrants and Surveys, II, 34, III, 224. Drew also acted as factor for Stephen Watts, a very rich exporter.

[73] PHILIP JAMES, a cooper by trade, was granted a warrant for a city lot on rent 6 8m 1683. Warrants and Surveys, III, 241. His 1st wife Sarah d. in 1698, and he m. 2nd, Esther (Willcox) Freeland, dau. of Barnabas Willcox and widow of William Freeland who had d. in March 1697/8. For abstract of Freeland's will see PGSP, III, 13, recorded in Will Book A, 376, #160:1697/8. After James' death in 1702, his 2nd wife m. 3rd, the first Edward Shippen. For James' will see Will Book B, 200, #74:1702.

[74] Edward Harford, probably a son of Charles Harford of Bristol who was a F.P. of 1000 acres, m. Elizabeth Jones, daughter of Charles Jones, Sr., cited in Note 71 above. See PMHB, XVII (1893), 75.

[75] ANTHONY STURGIS, feltmaker, took up a lot on rent by warrant dated 2 9m 1683. Warrants and Surveys, II, 116. He died in 1702 leaving a wife Dorothy, son Cornelius, daughters Sarah, wife of Mathew Holgate, Esther Huntsman, and son-in-law Peter Long, for whom see Note 88 below. Will Book B, 221, #83:1702.

[76] This entry included a note by the customs official: "cheese being at 3s. 4d., saddles 4s. 6d., etc." This William Smith was probably identical with the master of the *Bristol Merchant*, a F.P. of 1000 acres, for whom see Note 5 above, who by 1703 was called a merchant. *Pennsylvania Archives*, 2nd Series, XIX, 440. A city lot was laid out for him on Schuylkill side adjoining the city lot of the Harfords (Warrants and Surveys, II, 115), and he would appear to have been one of the merchants later involved with Samuel Packer and the Harfords in the customs scandal, noted above.

[77] JOHN HOLLAND, shipwright, was the son of Joshua Holland, mariner, of Chatham, Kent, who had purchased 5000 acres from Penn 15 Aug. 1682. The following May the father had given his son 1000 acres of the purchase, in right of which John Holland was granted a warrant of survey for a city lot 4 8m 1683. Warrants and Surveys, I, 468; *Pennsylvania Archives*, 2nd Series, XIX, 545. John Holland returned to England where he died subsequent to 29 5m 1695, the date of his will, for account of which see *ibid.*, 3rd Series, I, 97.

The third ship to arrive in the Delaware in October, the *Concord*, is reported by its best known passenger, James Claypoole, to have carried a crew of forty, mounted twenty-six guns, was 132 feet long and 32 feet broad. Claypoole also said it was "about 500 tunns" burthen and could transport 140 passengers in comfort. When ready to sail from Gravesend it had been victualled for 120 passengers, a number of whom — "the friends from Crevilt" — had been late in arriving at London. When they did finally come on board, they found "many convenient Cabins made and private rooms for familys and 14 Excellent Oxen killed and 30 Tunn beer & abundance of bread and water already stowed away." [78]

Claypoole and his family went on board at Gravesend 24 5m (July) 1683, but the last sight of England was not until about three weeks later. After a "verry comfortable passage" of 49 days, land was once more sighted, and on 1 8m (October), some of the passengers, including Claypoole, went ashore for the first time, possibly at Lewes. Philadelphia, however, was not reached until a week later. Some of the German passengers gave their date of arrival as 6 October, Claypoole his arrival as "8th or 10th" October.[79]

The *Concord* of London [10]

William Jeffries, master, for Pennsylvania & Virginia

26 [June] JOHN GARDNER: 4 doz. castor, 5 doz. felt [hats]; 2 pcs. English linen; 2 cwt. haberdashery; 24 lbs. wrought & 6 lbs. thrown silk [1 lb. silk: 24 ounces]; 1 doz. men's worsted hose; 1 doz. plain gloves; 7 chests window glass; 14 cwt. lead & shot; 4 cwt. cordage; 86 lbs. shoes & wrought leather; 20 cwt. wrought iron; 40 horse collars; 10 cwt. nails; 6 small & 3 great saddles; 1½ cwt. pewter; 400 pcs. glass & earthenware;

---

78 Of the 13 heads of families from Crefeld who came on the *Concord*, bringing 33 persons in their group, only three registered their arrival. These were LENART ARENTS (Aratts), a weaver, his wife, AGNISTAN (Agnes), and LEONARD TEISON (Tyson), said to have been the "brother" of Lenart Arents. *PMHB*, VIII, 331. The heads of the other Crefeld families were JOHANNES BLIJKERS (Bleickers), ABRAHAM OP DEN GRAEFF, a weaver, his brothers DERICK and HERMAN OP DEN GRAEFF, both weavers, PIETER KEURLIS, an innkeeper, THONES KUNDERS, JAN LENSEN, another weaver, JAN LUYKENS (Lückens), JAN SIEMES, REYNIER TEISSEN, ABRAHAM TUNES, and WILLEM STREYPERS (Strepers). See Hull, *Dutch Quaker Migration*, 403-406, *et passim*, cited in Note 21 above, for discussion of these emigrants.

79 JAMES CLAYPOOLE registered his arrival, that of his wife HELENA, and 7 children, though these not by name. He brought 5 servants, but only listed four: HUGH MASLAND and wife, indentured for 4 years, but who was granted a warrant for 200 acres in New Castle Co. 31 8m 1684, for which see *Pennsylvania Archives*, 2nd Series, VII, 193; CICELY WOOLEY, indentured for 4 years, m. Joshua Tittery, passenger on the *America*, cited in Note 31 above; EDWARD COLE, JR., indentured for 7 years, son of the man Claypoole had sent over in 1682 to build the Claypooles' house; he apparently also went to New Castle Co. where he eventually m. Martha, the daughter of Ambrose Baker, for abstract of whose will see *Calendar of Delaware Wills*, 11, cited in Note 26 above, and recorded in New Castle Co. Will Book B, 57. See also *Pennsylvania Archives*, 2nd Series, XIX, 467; *PMHB*, VIII, 331. The fifth Claypoole servant was ELIZABETH BENNETT, daughter of William Bennett who arrived in the *Jeffrey* the next month. For a notice of her see *PGM*, XXIII, 34; for her arrival on the *Concord*, *PMHB*, IX, 232. For data on the *Concord* and the voyage, see *ibid.*, X, 270, 273-5, 403, 406. The loadings are from the London port book E 190/125/3, PRO.

3 cwt. wrought brass & copper; 40 yds. flannel; 3 doz. thread hose; 1 fishing net, value £7 10s. [Duty] £3 14s. ½d.[80]

30 [June] JOHN VINER (Vines?): 10 bbls. strong beer. [Duty] 1s. 8d.[81]

2 [July] WILLIAM HARD: cwt. wrought iron; 1½ cwt. wrought brass; cwt. & 3 qtrs. pewter; tinware value £5 2s. 4d. [Duty] 13s. 1½d.[82]

3 [July] PHILIP CROOK: 8 cwt. lead; 3 chests window glass; 1½ cwt. wrought iron. [Duty] 9s. 9d.

[3 July] DANIEL STYLES: 10 chaldrons sea coal, London measure; 1 chaldron grindle-stones [chaldron: usually 36 bushels; London bushel: 80 gals. water; Winchester bushel: 77 gals.]. [Duty] 10s. 8d.

[3 July] JOHN ALLEN: ½ cwt. wrought copper; 4 cwt. wrought iron; 2 horse collars; 10 lbs. wrought leather; ¼ cwt. cordage; ¼ cwt. haberdashery; parcel hatmakers tools value £2. [Duty] 5s. 3d.[83]

6 [July] JOHN GARDNER: 18 doz. child's, 15 doz. men's wool & 10 doz. men's worsted hose; 40 yds. flannel; 1 single baye; 25 goads plains [plain backs: coarse wool woven in imitation of cotton]; 30 cwt. cheese; 10 doz. [lbs.] candles; 30 lbs. wrought silk; 4 small saddles; 2 cwt. lead; cwt. pewter. [Duty] £1 16s. 5½d.

11 [July] EDWARD BLAKE: 4 cwt. wrought iron. [Duty] 2s.[84]

14 [July] JOHN GARDNER: 6 bbls. beer; 2 cwt. wrought brass & copper; 20 lbs. wrought silk. [Duty] 4s. 4d.

17 [July] JOHN GARDNER: 4 chests glass & turney wares value £16 5s.; cwt. nails; 10 lbs. wrought silk; cwt. hard soap; cwt. cheese; 20 lbs. shoes; 2 cwt. wrought iron. [Duty] £1.

21 [July] HUGH LAMB: 8 cwt. apothecary wares; 8 cwt. books; 11 cwt. wrought iron; 120 lbs. stuffs; 1 small minikin baye; 18 doz. men's woolen, 7 doz. men's worsted hose; 1½ tun strong beer; 24 lbs. serges; 4 cwt. haberdashery; 3 cwt. wrought brass;

---

[80] John Gardner (Gardiner) was no doubt the merchant and exporter who acted as agent or attorney for James Claypoole's business. He lived two doors away from Claypoole at the corner of Bush Lane and Scots Yard. *PMHB*, X, 268. He should not be confused with the John Gardner who came with William Harmer in 1682 bringing a certificate from Purton Monthly Meeting, Wiltshire, dated 5 4m 1682. Myers, *Quaker Arrivals*, 5.

[81] A John Vines was sheriff of Sussex Co. early in 1683, and a member of the Provincial Assembly in 1686. *Colonial Records*, I, 57; *Pennsylvania Archives*, 8th Series, I, 71.

[82] WILLIAM HARD, a cordwainer, was granted a warrant 2 9m 1683, for a city lot on rent, which was laid out 24 10m following on the east side of Third St. between High and Arch. Warrants and Surveys, III, 228. He may have brought a servant, JOHN JONES, with him; Jones' right to 50 acres of headland was taken up by Philip Howell in 1702. *Ibid.*, I, 475, #1153. Hard died intestate in 1697; for administration on his estate see *PGM*, XIX, 267, recorded in Administration Book A, 239, #171:1697. See also *PGM*, XXIII, 113, for his wife Elizabeth, sister of Alce Guest.

[83] Possibly the John Allen who on 23 9m 1686, was granted a warrant for 400 acres in Bucks Co. and was deceased by 1697 when his widow was the wife of Ralph Boome. *Pennsylvania Archives*, 3rd Series, III, 54; *Bucks Court Records*, 214, 215, 217, 332.

[84] EDWARD BLAKE of London, turner, a F.P. of 250 acres, appears to have settled in New Castle Co. where he had a plantation and a lot in the town. *Pennsylvania Archives*, 2nd Series, XIX, 40, 48, 376; *ibid.*, VII, 196. As agent for himself and Henry Sleighton, another F.P. of 250 acres, also a turner of London, Blake had land laid out in Middletown Twp., Chester Co., by warrant granted 17 11m 1683/4, and returned into the surveyor general's office the following April. *Ibid.*, 3rd Series, III, 105, 168. Blake's wife Hannah died in 1699 (Hinshaw, II, 338), and by 1701 he had m. 2nd, one Sarah, called sister-in-law by Abraham Decow, for abstract of whose will see *PGSP*, III, 151, recorded in Philadelphia Will Book B, 124, #49:1701.

98

cwt. pewter; 10 lbs. stuffs with silk; cwt. lead; 1 chest window glass; 3 qtrs. wheat meal; 10 doz. [lbs.] candles; 4 small saddles; 9 bushels oat meal. [Duty] £3 6s. 9½d.[85]

16 [August] JOHN HARWOOD: 6 bushels oatmeal; 2 small saddles; 2 cwt. nails; tinware, value £5. [Duty] 6s. 9½d.[86]

Within the next week, a 90-ton ship from Liverpool dropped anchor in the Delaware, the fourth of the ships to arrive that month. With the same master it had brought the first contingent of Welsh settlers to Pennsylvania in August of the previous year. Its late arrival this year was partially due to its scheduled stop at Dublin, where most of its passengers embarked. Its arrival date was between 8 8m (October) 1683 and 14 8m 1683.[87]

The Lyon of Liverpool [11]

John Crumpton (Compton), master, for Pennsylvania

22 [June] HENRY LUCAS: 1 chest qty. 28 ells [English linen]; 14 lbs. pewter; ½ cwt. nails; 7 lbs. new shoes; 1 box qty. ½ chest window glass. [Duty] 1s. 8d.

[22 June] JOHN CRUMPTON: 2 pails, 3 fatts, 2 hhds., 2 bbls. qty. 9 old saddles; 2 doz. bridles; 42 lbs. leather manufactured & new shoes; 1 doz. old wool cards; 2½ cwt. nails; ¾ cwt. wrought iron; 420 lbs. woolen cloth; 340 ells English linen; 114 lbs. pewter; ¼ cwt. haberdashery; 250 goads cottons; 1 doz. stocks [cravats?] value 7s. [Duty] £2 1s. 10d.[88]

---

85 Hugh Lamb, hosier of St. Martin's-in-the-Field Parish, London, was a F.P. of 2500 acres who lived about where Trafalgar Square now is. In addition to his initial purchase, he bought 2000 acres more in 1682, and 2500 acres in 1685 from other original purchasers, or their heirs. By his will, dated 20 8m 1686, all the land descended to his brother Daniel who died intestate. Another brother, Joseph Lamb, heir of Daniel, in 1711 sold the entire 7000 acres to James Logan. *Pennsylvania Archives,* 2nd Series, XIX, 518-19.

86 This is a curious item, and may have been dated in error, since Claypoole said the *Concord* had left Gravesend 25 July, and the passengers had lost sight of England in about three weeks time, or approximately 13 August. John Harwood had sent goods over in 1682, for which see *PGM,* XXIII, 51.

87 For the 1682 loadings of the *Lyon* and notices of some of its passengers, see *ibid.,* 39-40, 251-254. The 1683 loadings are from Liverpool port book E 190/1345/13, PRO. The inclusive dates of arrival derive from an entry in the minutes of the Board of Property (entered in 1701), giving what was probably the date the ship entered the Delaware Capes, and the registration date given by some of the chief passengers. *Pennsylvania Archives,* 2nd Series, XIX, 200; *PMHB,* VIII, 334-5. The names of 37 passengers are known, of which all but 9 were servants indentured for periods ranging from 2 to 13 years. ROBERT TURNER, of Dublin, F.P. of 5000 acres, accompanied by his daughter MARTHA, brought 17 of these servants: ROBERT THREWECKS and his probable son, ROBERT, aged about 8; HENRY FURNACE (Furniss) and his family consisting of JOHN, JOSEPH, KATHERINE, and DANIEL (Samuel?); ROBERT SALFORD, a brickmaker who died in 1688 only a year after he was free, and for whose administration see *PGM,* XIX, 253, recorded in Administration Book A, 45, #102:1688; BENJAMIN ACTON, a weaver who by 1686 was buying land in Salem, West Jersey, and was settled there by 1688, for which see *N. J. Archives,* XXI, 581, 589, 594, 610, *et seq.*; JOHN REEVES who took up a lot on rent early in 1685 "on the Governor's Land" on the north side of Vine St. (Warrants and Surveys, III, 250); HENRY HOLLINGSWORTH, indentured for 2 years, son of Valentine who had come over in 1682; RICHARD CURLIS, ROWLAND HAMBRIDGE, LEMUEL BRADSHAW, ROBERT LLOYD, WILLIAM LONG, and ALICE CALES.

88 While John Crumpton's name was generally spelled Compton in the 1682 port books, in 1683 it more often appeared as Crompton or Crumpton. The second cabin passenger he brought was JOSEPH FISHER, F.P. of 5000 acres, from Stillorgin near Dublin, "born in Elton in Cheshire," as he registered his

23 [June] HENRY LUCAS: 14 lbs. Norwich stuffs. [Duty] 2d.

[23 June] JOHN NIXON: 1 chest, 1 bundle, 2 packs, 2 casks, qty. 4 cwt. wrought iron; 4 cwt. nails; 3 cwt. iron; 3 cwt. cast lead; 2 cwt. & ½ gunpowder. [Duty] 15s. 11d.[89]

25 [June] FRANCIS TUCKER: 2 horses. [Duty] 10s.

Just before the end of October, a small ship, less than 50 tons burthen, came from Scarborough on the east coast of Yorkshire. It had crossed the ocean the year before, having first stopped at London to pick up a passenger or two and some cargo for Pennsylvania. This time it skipped London — no mention of goods loaded on it consigned to Pennsylvania is to be found in the London port books — and apparently headed directly for the Delaware.[90]

Aboard were at least two families, both of which registered their arrival, giving the date as 10 9m (November) 1683. But warrants of survey had been granted to the two families ten days before on 31 8m 1683, for land which was surveyed in Bucks County 7 9m 1683. These must have been obtained when the ship first dropped anchor, and the arrival date they gave was when they were actually on their own land in Falls Township.[91]

---

arrival. With him came his wife ELIZABETH, and children MOSES, JOSEPH, MARY and MARTHA FISHER. Of the 11 servants Fisher brought, one, ROBERT KILCARTH, was aged about 13, while PETER LONG, who was a carpenter, had only 2 years to serve. He had removed to West New Jersey by 1688 when he bought 100 acres in the "Second Tenth" from Anna Salter, and was of Burlington the next year when he bought from Robert Turner another 100 acres. N. J. Archives, XXI, 425, 439 et seq. See also Note 75 above for reference to Long. Another servant, BENJAMIN CLIFT, whose probable sister Isabel had come in as a servant in 1682, and apparently m. Christopher Lobb, a woolcomber, may be identical with the Benjamin Cliffe who settled in Darby Twp. and died in 1750, leaving most of his estate to Benjamin Lobb, "my sister's son." Pennsylvania Archives, 2nd Series, XIX, 450; Chester Co. Will Book C, 198; Smith, Delaware County, 453. EDWARD DOYLE, another Fisher servant, in 1699 was deputy sheriff in Bucks Co., for whom see Bucks Court Records, 391, et passim. PHILIP PACKER (Parker), also a servant, m. 10 Nov. 1685, less than 2 months after he was free, Hannah Sessions, and administered the estate of her mother Ann in 1689. Pennsylvania Archives, 2nd Series, VIII, v; PGM, XIX, 255. THOMAS TERWOOD (Tearwood) acquired 200 acres in Dublin Twp. where the Fishers settled, and left it to Joseph Fisher's son Joseph, Jr., and daughters Mary and Martha. For abstract of his will, see PGSP, II, 30, recorded in Will Book A, 349, #146:1696/7. Other servants were EDWARD LANCASTER, WILLIAM ROBERTSON, WILLIAM CONDUIT, MARY TOOLE and ELEAZAR JOHNSON. One free person who registered her arrival was MARGARET COLVERT (Calvert), presumed daughter of Thomas Calvert of Chester Co. whose nuncupative will was recorded in Philadelphia Will Book A, 30, #23:1685, for an abstract of which see PGSP, I, 55. See also Myers, Irish Immigration, 316, cited in Note 21 above.

[89] This John Nixon is presumed to be the same person as he who registered his arrival on the Endeavour of Liverpool, for whom see Note 52 above. Why he sailed on one ship, but sent his goods on another remains unexplained. With the possible exception of John Bevan, this is the only known instance of a person travelling separate from his goods.

[90] For the 1682 passengers and their goods, see PGM, XXIII, 49; for the date as it was registered of the Providence's arrival in 1683, PMHB, IX, 227-8. The ship's arrival, without date, is also entered in ibid., VIII, 322.

[91] For the warrants, see Warrants and Surveys, III, 593. Each was for 250 acres.

The *Providence* of Scarborough [12]

Robert Hopper (Hooper), master [92]

JOHN PALMER of "Cheadland [Cleveland] in Yorkshire, husbandman, and CHRISTIANA his wife.[93]

JOSHUA HOOPES "of Skelton in Clunland" [Cleveland], Yorkshire, husbandman and ISABELL his wife. Children: DANIEL, MARY and CHRISTIAN HOOPES.[94]

Although Penn in November wrote that five ships had arrived within a month, a sixth ship had arrived at the very end of October. It was a large 300-ton vessel from Bristol which in 1682 had brought over forty Quaker families and other emigrants, a few of whom had loaded goods for resale in Pennsylvania. This year none of its Pennsylvania-bound passengers did so, and there was only one consignment of goods to the province, all others being for Virginia. However, one family, the Painters from Haverford West in Pembrokeshire, southwest Wales, registered their arrival, giving the date as 31 8m (October) 1683.[95] Since ships from Bristol sailed past Milford Haven, the port for Pembrokeshire, other families from the area known to have come this year may well have embarked there also.

---

92 As in the case of John Crumpton (Compton), Hopper's name was spelled in various ways in the port books. During Hopper's stay in the Delaware in 1682, he had bought a house and lot in Burlington. The following spring, back in England, he bought one-sixth of a share in West Jersey. Now, back in the Delaware, on 8 and 9 November 1683, Hopper bought additional land, part of a one-twelfth share. The following 21 Jan. 1683/4, again back in England, he sold one-quarter of his three-one hundreths of a share in the Yorkshire Tenth, or "Scarborough" property previously purchased. See *N. J. Archives*, XXI, 398, 402, 404, 410. He was deceased by 1690, when his administrators asked to be discharged from their trust. *Burlington Court Book*, 104, cited in Note 41 above.

39 JOHN PALMER and his wife CHRISTIANA brought a certificate dated 4 May 1683, from "Gilburgh, Rowsby" — Guisborough, Roxby, in the North Riding of Yorkshire, which was entered in the records of Falls Monthly Meeting. Hinshaw, II, 1018, 966. He died on 11 6m 1726, and his widow 28 7m 1740; they are said to have had 14 children, all born after their emigration, for whom see Miers and Henry Busch, Records of Families of Palmer, Cutler, Hayhurst, Cornish, Fort, Jeffries . . . (1910), GSP.

94 JOSHUA HOOPES brought a certificate, also dated 4 May 1683, from "Gainsborough, Rowsby" which was recorded at Falls Monthly Meeting. Hinshaw, II, 1002. His wife d. 15 April 1684, according Davis, *Bucks County*, 87, cited in Note 14 above. On 8 10m 1696, Joshua made over to his son Daniel 125 acres in Bucks Co. (*Bucks Court Records*, 309), and two days later Daniel m. Jane Worrilow, dau. of Thomas and Jane Worrilow of Edgmont Twp. Chester Co. They subsequently settled in Westtown Twp., Chester Co. and had 17 children, for whom see Futhey and Cope, 605-6, cited in Note 55 above. A JOHN ROBINSON, not otherwise identified, brought a certificate from the Monthly Meeting in "Gainsborough" to Falls Meeting, and must have come on the *Providence*. Hinshaw, II, 1023.

95 GEORGE PAINTER from Haverford West, Pembroke, registered the arrival of his family in the *Unicorn*; with him were his wife ELLINOR, and children SUSAN and GEORGE PAINTER, JR. *PMHB*, VIII, 334. According to Smith, *Delaware County*, 490, these children did not survive their father who was bur. (at Haverford) 27 5m 1687, leaving a widow Eleanor who was also bur. at Haverford 23 11m 1689, and two children, Daniel and Deborah Painter. See Radnor Transcripts, De15F, 466, 488, cited in Note 70 above, but *cf.* Browning, *Welsh Settlement*, 103, cited in same note, wherein it is stated that Edward Roberts, son of Hugh Roberts, m. as his 1st wife Susanna Painter, dau. of George, and that she d. 3 10m 1707. The Painters brought three servants with them, two men named MATHEW and LEWIS, and JANET HUMPHRIES. The loading for the *Unicorn* is from Bristol port book E 190/1146/1, PRO.

The *Unicorn* of Bristol [13]

Thomas Cooper, master, for Pennsylvania & Virginia

6 [July] SAM PACKER for WILLIAM PENN: 18 hhds. of earth for making glass, value £2 12s. 8d. [Duty] 2s. 7½d.[96]

By 7 November 1683, a week after the arrival of the *Unicorn*, a ship bearing the name *Mary of Southampton* appears to have arrived in the Delaware from that port on the south coast of England with some passengers.[97] After it had been bruited about town that her papers seemed not to be in order, on 21 November Penn and his Council, acting as an informal court of admiralty, with John Test as "Prosecutor," heard the complaints. After "a full hearing . . . and by the Ingenious acknowledgement of the Master and some of ye Owners" — apparently among the passengers — "and Especially by the Goulden Breif that was produced by one of them," the ship was found "to be the *Alexander* of Inverness, of ye Kingdom of Scotland." She was therefore "a Scottish Bottom and noe ways made ffree to trade to any of his Majesty's Plantations in America."[98] As prescribed by the navigation laws she was thereupon condemned and sold. John Swift, one of the passengers, who had loaded goods on her both for himself and other Southampton merchants, was among those who bought her in for a sum variously reported at £161 10s., or at £300, and she was finally allowed to sail.[99]

---

[96] These hogsheads of earth for making glass were no doubt intended for the use of Joshua Tittery, broad-glass-maker, who had come over on the *America* as servant to the Free Society of Traders, for whom see Note 31 above. The consignment, put on board the first day the ship began loading, was the only one for Pennsylvania, though other goods continued to be loaded until 15 August. It therefore seems probable that HANNAH HARDIMAN was another passenger. She brought a certificate dated 2 6m 1683, from Haverford West, and certainly could have reached Milford Haven in time to board the ship. Myers, *Quaker Arrivals*, 9. When she and Samuel Carpenter declared their intentions of marriage 4 9m and 2 10m 1684, at the Philadelphia Meeting, Ellinor Painter was one of her sponsors. PGSP, I, 274-5.

[97] The arrival time of the *Mary of Southampton* is derived from the date of the warrant granted John Swift for a city lot. Warrants and Surveys, III, 245.

[98] See *Colonial Records*, I, 90-91. English navigation laws decreed that only English ships, owned and largely manned by Englishmen, were free to trade with English colonies. Foreign ships had to stop first at an English port, have their cargo examined, pay duty on it, and "strangers' duty" as a ship of alien registry. A "cocket" or certificate was then granted showing the ship was "free." Scotland, before the Act of Union of 1707, was a foreign country, hence the ship was not free. In Scotch law, a "breif" was a writ. In December 1682, as the *Alexander* of Inverness, William Geddes, master, she had arrived at Southampton from Portugal "in distress and necessity" and was allowed a brief stay without paying dues. Southampton port book E 190/832/9, PRO. She managed to load a quantity of salt, took on 2000 cheeses for one John Ware, and in January 1683, left for Rochelle. She returned as the *Mary of Southampton* in June, Anthony Pryor, master. In addition to the goods loaded for John Swift & Co. for Pennsylvania, she may also have taken on merchandise for one Robert Leigh, but its destination is not clear in the port books. *Ibid.*, 190/832/13, PRO.

[99] For Penn's report to the Lords of the Treasury of the sale and its amount, one-third of which in all such cases went to the King, subsequent correspondence giving the different sums, and the ship's later history, see Calendar of Treasury Books, VII, 1681-1685, Part 2, 1455; VIII, 1685-1689, Part 1, 106, 212-13; Part 2, 1009; C.O. 33/14/34; Southampton port book E 190/833/2, PRO. For the vessel's earlier history as the *Recovery*, see Calendar of Treasury Books, VI, 1679-1680, 197, PRO; J. C. Hotten, *Original Lists of Persons . . . to the American Plantations* (New York, 1931), 405, 410.

The *Mary of Southampton* [14]

otherwise called

The *Alexander* of Inverness

Anthony Pryor, master

18 [July] JOHN SWIFT & Co.: 3 hundred wtt. [weight] wrought iron; 56 pounds boots & shoes; 10 dozen stockings for men; 1 pc. ½ cloth rashes [smooth fabric of wool or silk] & 4 lb. overwtt; one pc. kersey; 3 casks cont. 3 qtrs. malt; 2 barrels cont. 3 cwt. wtt. honey val. £3; one pc. English linen; ¼ cwt. soap; 4 pcls. [or 400 pieces] earthenware; 10 chests window glass; one basket cont. 4 dozen hour glasses; ½ cwt. old iron casements; 3 cwt. cheese; ½ a ton lead; 9 cwt. nails; 15 cwt. biscuit in 6 hhds. val. £10; ½ a hhd. cont. four bushels white salt, val. £6; ¼ cwt. worsted, val. £3; one rundlet [a cask] cont. 4 gals. oatmeal; one basket cont. 2 dozen [lbs.] candles; one barrel cont. one hundredweight gunpowder; six grindlestones qty. [amounting to] ¼ chaldron; 4 loads household goods, val. £8; several pcls. wearing apparel; 3 rundlets cont. 23 gallons brandy; 1 rundlet cont. 8 gallons linseed oil; 6 iron pots.[100]

That same week another ship must have dropped anchor in the Delaware. In 1682 it had been loaded with goods in London for the Free Society of Traders in Pennsylvania, and had brought over the society's president, Nicholas More.[101] This year the goods consigned to Pennsylvania were all put on by well-known London exporters. While the ship probably carried a good number of passengers as well — it was about 500 tons burthen — only one registered the date of his arrival. This was William Bennet who gave the date simply as in the ninth month (November). A warrant in Bennet's name, dated 8 9m 1683, indicates the ship probably had arrived during the previous week.[102]

The *Jeffrey* of London [15]

Thomas Arnold, master, for Pennsylvania, New Jersey & Virginia

28 [July] WILLIAM WOODBY (Woodley?): 20 cwt. wrought iron; 40 cwt. nails;

100 JOHN SWIFT's partners appear to have been Edward Pritchard, F.P. of 2500 acres, a glover in 1682 of Almely, Pembroke, but in 1686 of the parish of Almele, Hereford; George Jackman, grocer of Alsford, Kent, and F.P. of 500 acres; and Joseph Jones, blacksmith of Southampton, F.P. of 500 acres. See *Pennsylvania Archives*, 2nd Series, XIX, 313, 321, 455, 459; Deed Book E-1-5, 592; 24 4m 1686, Edward Pritchard to John Eckley. A glazier by trade and F.P. of 500 acres, John Swift is reported to have m. 11 12m 1673/4, FRANCIS GRANT, who d. in Jan. 1716/17. Swift m. 2nd, Elizabeth, widow of Patrick Robinson and Griffith Jones, and d. in 1733. Two children JOHN and MARY SWIFT, came with their parents. See Lewis D. Cook Collection, I, GSP.

101 For the *Jeffrey's* 1682 loadings and passengers, see PGM, XXIII, 59. The 1683 loadings are from London port book E 190/125/3, PRO.

102 WILLIAM BENNETT, from Hammondsworth, Middlesex, registered his arrival with his wife REBECCA. PMHB, IX, 228. He obtained a warrant for 400 acres to be laid out in Bucks Co. on 8 9m 1683. *Pennsylvania Archives*, 3rd Series, III, 104. His daughter Elizabeth Bennett had left earlier on the *Concord*, indentured as a servant to James Claypoole, for whom see Note 79 above. William Bennett died 19 1m 1684/5, leaving his widow Rebecca, a son William, daughter Mary, wife of Thomas Chandler, the abovesaid Elizabeth, now wife of Richard Lundy, Rebecca, Anne and Sarah. Possibly the last three daughters came with him. For abstract of his will see PGSP, I, 204, recorded in Bucks Co. Will Book A-1, 9.

3 doz. felt hats; 60 cwt. cheese; 3¼ cwt. pewter; 2¼ cwt. wrought brass; 2 chests window glass; 5 pcs. hair cloth; 18 pcs. sacking; cwt. russeting [brown color cloth]; ¼ cwt. alum; 2 cwt. cordage; 3 fodders [about 19½ cwt.] lead; cwt. books; 12 horse collars; 2 chalders grindlestones; ¾ cwt. flax; cwt. haberdashery; 100 glasses; 2 cwt. wrought leather; 2 pcs. ticking; 40 yds. dimity; 60 bushels oatmeal; 9 bushels flour; 3 small minikin bayes; 232 lbs. serges; 8 lbs. Norwich stuffs; 12 coverlets wool & hair. [Duty] £9 4s. 4½d.

30 [July] WILLIAM WOODBY: 20 pcs. English linen. [Duty] 2s.

31 [July] JAMES CAREY: 12 cwt. & ¼ nails; 11 cwt. wrought iron; 1 doz. plain Monmouth caps; 223 lbs. shoes & wrought leather; ½ cwt. cordage; 1 cwt. & ¼ & 14 lbs. pewter [154 lbs.]; 8 doz. children's, 23 doz. men's woolen, 4 doz. men's worsted [stockings]; 6 doz. Irish hose; 6 small minikin bayes; 310 goads cotton; 1 pc. hair cloth; 10 doz. felt, 1 doz. castor hats; 23 lbs. wrought silk; 14 doz. plain gloves; 160 lbs. serges; 30 lbs. stuffs; 2 cwt. haberdashery; 50 glasses; 3 horse collars; 1 Irish rug; 2 cwt. lead shot; 1 lb. thrown silk; 4 bundles turnery wares [wooden ware]; 90 lbs. lace; 2 doz. milk pans; 1 pr. blankets; upholstery ware value £14 5s. [Duty] £5 3s.

3 [August] WILLIAM SHARDLOW: 10 chaldrons sea coal, London measure. [Duty] 10s.[103]

6 [August] JOHN FIRTH: 4 tons strong beer. [Duty] 4s.

7 [August] JOHN HARWOOD: 3 cwt. cheese; 2 cwt. wrought iron; 18 castors; 300 pcs. earthenware; ½ cwt. wrought brass; 1½ qtrs. wheat meal; 25 doz. [lbs.] candles; 1½ cwt. gunpowder; 3 cwt. lead; cwt. nails; ½ cwt. pewter; 4 firkins butter. [Duty] £1 8s. 5d.

9 [August] WILLIAM WOODBEE [sic]: 22 cwt. wrought iron; 10 horse collars; ¾ cwt. cordage; 280 lbs. wrought leather; 7½ doz. felts; 15 doz. men's woolen hose; 12 small saddles; 160 lbs. stuffs; 1½ bbls. soap; 10 doz. [lbs.] candles; ½ cwt. starch; ½ cwt. alum; ½ cwt. books; 60 yds. flannel; 21½ pcs. English linen; 3 pcs. English ticking; ¾ cwt. pewter; ¾ cwt. wrought brass; 2½ cwt. lead; 3 doz. shod shovels; 1½ cwt. haberdashery; tin and turnery wares value £6 17s. [Duty] £3 14s. 9d.

10 [August] WILLIAM WOODBEE: 12 horse collars; 19 small saddles; 3 doz. & 11 felts; 102 lbs. wrought leather; ¾ cwt. cordage; 14 cwt. wrought iron; 1½ pcs. English linen; cwt. pewter; 35 lbs. haberdashery; 1 firkin soap; 15 shod shovels; 14 lbs. books; 70 lbs. wrought copper; 1 doz. plain Monmouth caps; 2 cwt. lead; 1 doz. bridles; 1 chest window glass; 100 glasses; 4 doz. men's woolen hose; 5 doz. [lbs.] candles; cwt. wrought brass. [Duty] £1 9s. 11d.

[10 August] THOMAS CRANDALL: 6 small minikin bayes; 5½ doz. castors; 5 cwt. white & cwt. red lead; ½ cwt. blacking; ¾ cwt. blueing value £6 17s. [Duty] £1 15s. 10d.

[10 August] PHILIP FORD: 3 small minikin bayes; 30 lbs. wrought silk. [Duty] 11s. 6d.

---

[103] William Shardlow, joint F.P. with WILLIAM WOOD of 5000 acres and a subscriber for £100 in the stock of the Free Society of Traders, never came to Philadelphia, although his partner Wood did, bringing a certificate from Nottingham dated 5 6m 1683. He may have been on this ship. Wood was granted a warrant for himself and Shardlow for 100 acres of land in Philadelphia County on the west side of the Schuylkill 27 10m 1683. Logan Papers, XVI, 14, 15, HSP. William Wood was deceased by 6 1m 1687, and his widow Susanna by 4 9m 1689, when letters of administration were granted to the eldest son Joseph, leaving issue Joseph, John, Jonathan and Susanna. *Chester Court Records*, 122, 230. See also Smith, *Delaware County*, 515. For the administration on estate of William and Susanna Wood, see *PGM*, XIX, 256, recorded in Administration Book A, 93, #99:1689.

13 [August] HUGH LAMB: 1600 pcs. glass & earthenware; 5 cwt. nails; 6 cwt. wrought iron; cwt. cordage; cwt. lead; ¼ cwt. haberdashery. [Duty] 8s. 8d.

17 [August] CLEMENT PLUMSTED: 4 cwt. cheese; 3 cwt. nails; 4 cwt. wrought iron; 6 lbs. serges. [Duty] 4s. 5½d.[104]

During the last half of July and up to the last week in August, a good-sized ship was being loaded with goods for a group of Quakers from the northern part of Wales. Most of them had purchased land from the John ap Thomas and Edward Jones company, and intended to join their friends who had emigrated on the *Lyon* of Liverpool in 1682.

Called the *Morning Star* of Liverpool by those passengers who registered their arrival, the ship was loaded with goods which had passed through the customs at Chester, rather than at Liverpool, while some of the passengers apparently boarded the vessel at Mostyn (Mosson), in the estuary of the Dee, just before the voyage began.[105] Conflicting statements have been made as to who of the Welsh Quakers, besides those who shipped goods on it, were passengers on this ship. These consigners in themselves represented better than seventy individuals; it is possible others came on it who brought no dutiable goods. Still others could have sailed on some of the other Liverpool ships. Of the more than seventy known passengers, only five registered their arrival, four of them giving it as 20 9m (November) 1683.[106]

---

104 This Clement Plumstead was possibly the draper and merchant of London who was an original Proprietor of East Jersey. *N. J. Archives*, XXI, 55, 122, 305. Whether he is identical with the Clement Plumstead, ironmonger of the Minories, London, the birth of whose children, Robert, Frances, Mathew and Mary, born between 1663 and 1670, are entered in the records of the London and Middlesex Quarterly Meeting, has not been established. Certainly neither are to be confused with the Clement Plumstead (1681-1745), whose father William was one of William Penn's jury in 1670 (not 1668 as given in *Pennsylvania Archives*, 2nd Series, XIX, 576). See *PMHB*, XIV (1880), 376, and Catherine Owens Peare, *William Penn: A Biography* (Philadelphia, 1957), 112.

105 Though called "of Liverpool," no ladings in 1683 are entered in the Liverpool port books for the *Morning Star*. For the Chester ladings, see Chester Searcher's Book E 190/1345/1, and Customer's Book E 190/1345/16, PRO. These books were carelessly kept, the Customer's Book often including items not listed in the Searcher's Book, and are difficult to decipher. The embarkation of some of the passengers at Mostyn is cited in Browning, *Welsh Settlement*, 95, without documentation, and of others at Chester in *ibid.*, 117. The Mostyn embarkation, however, appears to be corroborated in the letter from Penn, dated 29 Nov. 1683, cited in Note 4 above, in which he speaks of "one shipp from Moston [*sic*] in Wales. . . ."

106 Relatively few warrants of survey granted these Welsh Friends survive to pinpoint the time of their arrival, and not all of them filed certificates of removal. In the Penn letter, cited above, he says that the ship from Mostyn was the only one which had "lost with the bloody flux 22 of 100 w[ch] was caught by taking on a p[sn] sick of it at Dublin." It is known that some of Hugh Roberts' party — the children of John ap Thomas — died on the voyage (Browning, 118, *loc. cit.*), but who the Dublin passengers were remains unknown. Perhaps they all died on the voyage. HENRY ATHERLY, shoemaker, was one of the five passengers who registered their arrival "from Leverpoole." *PMHB*, VIII, 329. Atherly "came first" to the house in Philadelphia of Ralph Ward, another shoemaker, "and there departed this life . . ." in 10m 1686, as per letters of administration granted 20 10m 1683 to Ward, his principal creditor, for which see *PGM*, XIX, 252, entered in Administration Book A, 26, #79:1686. JOHN LOFTUS also registered his arrival "from Leverpoole." When he executed his will 31 6m 1695, he described himself as being "late of Chester County, now of Phil[a] planter," and appears to have been unmarried. The will was proved by his executors, Thomas Powell of Chester and James Jacobs, for abstract of which see *PGSP*, II, 26, recorded in Will Book A, 324, #135:1695.

The *Morning Star* of Liverpool [16]

Thomas Hayes, master, for Pennsylvania

19 [July] HUGH ROBERTS: 2 bags, 2 bundles, 2 firkins, 4 rundles [round containers], qty. 4 cwt. 2 qtrs. [or 56 lbs.] & 14 lbs. wrought iron. Other wares value £35 9s. 2d. [Duty] paid. From the Customer's Book: Value in toto, £15 8s. 7d. [Duty] 15s. 5d.[107]

[19 July] JOHN ROBERTS: 1 trunk, 3 boxes, 1 chest, 2 bundles, 1 basket, qty. 3 cwt. 1 qtr. & 14 lbs. wrought iron; 3 lbs. brass manufactured, & other wares value £3 8s. 4d. [Duty] paid.[108]

[19 July] WILLIAM JONES: 1 cask, 1 trunk, 1 bundle, 3 rundles, 1 churn, 2 bbls. qty. 2 qtrs. & 21 lbs. wrought iron, and other wares value £9 14s. 2d. [Duty] paid.[109]

[19 July] DAVID DAVIES: 10 casks, 2 bundles, 1 case, 1 churn, 4 tubs, 1 rundle, qty. 2 cwt. 3 qtrs. & 9 lbs. wrought iron & other wares value £25 11s. 8d. [Duty] paid.[110]

[19 July] ROBERT DAVIES (David): 1 cask, 1 trunk, 1 bundle, 4 rundles, 2½ firkins, 3 bbls., 1 churn, qty. 2 qtrs. & 14 lbs. wrought iron & other wares value £8 15s. [Duty] paid.[110a]

[19 July] JOHN ROBERTS: 4 bags, 1 trunk, 1 box, 2 firkins, qty. 2 cwt. wrought iron & other wares value £19 19s. 2d. [Duty] paid.[111]

[107] HUGH ROBERTS of Ciltagarth, parish of Llanvawr, Merionethshire, near Bala, brought a certificate dated 2 5m 1683, for his wife JANE, and children ROBERT, ELLIN, OWEN, EDWARD and WILLIAM, though the wife and children were not named therein. Radnor Transcripts, De15F, 8, cited in Note 70 above; see Browning, *Welsh Settlement*, 96, for account of his family. He had purchased 625 acres of the Thomas-Jones lands.

[108] This JOHN ROBERTS was probably from Llun, Caernarvonshire, a maltster by trade, who brought a certificate, dated 18 5m 1683, from Penllyn Meeting which described him as "free of marriage." Radnor Transcripts, De15F, 10. He had purchased 150 acres from Richard Davies, F.P. of 5000 acres, which he took up in Merion and called "Pwencoid." He brought one servant with him, name unknown, and m. at Merion Meeting 20 1m 1683/4, Gainor Roberts, a fellow passenger, for whom see below and Browning, *Welsh Settlement*, 125.

[109] WILLIAM JONES (William ap John) of Bettws, Merionethshire, had bought 156¼ acres of the Thomas-Jones lands. No certificate of removal has been found, but he came with his wife ANN REYNOLD (Renault), and children JOHN, ALICE, KATHERINE and GWEN. He was bur. at Merion, having d. 20 9m 1683, apparently on shipboard; his wife Ann was bur. 5 8m 1685, also at Merion, and his will was proved 1 1m 1685/6, for abstract of which see PGSP, I, 55, recorded in Will Book A, 37, #24:1685/6. See also Radnor Transcripts, De15F, 491, and Browning, *Welsh Settlement*, 104, which states he was a widower when he came over.

[110] DAVID DAVIES (Davis), "son of Richard Davis of Welchpoole, in the County of Montgomery, Chirurgeon," registered his arrival "in this river" as 14 9m 1683, which was probably when the ship entered Delaware Bay. PMHB, IX, 233. He is said to have m. Margaret Evans 8 March 1686, d. 23 March 1683, and was bur. "at Nicholas Walne's burying place." Davis, *Bucks County*, 83, cited in Note 14 above. See also *Bucks Court Records*, 14-15, 42-3, 62-3. When he emigrated he brought a servant PHILIP HOWELL, tailor, who "served about a Year, [then] bought off the remainder of his time." *Pennsylvania Archives*, 2nd Series, XIX, 316. He m. in 1686, Jane Luff, widow of John Luff who had come on the *Bristol Comfort*, for whom see Note 68 above; also PGSP, I, 297, and II, 94.

[110a] ROBERT DAVIES (Davis, David) of Tuyn y Nant, Merionethsire, filed at Radnor a certificate from the Penllyn Meeting dated 18 5m 1683, for himself, his wife and children, not named. Radnor Transcripts, De15F, 11. He may have been the innholder "at the Queen's Head," in Philadelphia, for which see PGM, XXII, 264, 268, and *Pennsylvania Gazette*, 21 Sept. 1733; but cf. Browning, *Welsh Settlement*, 84.

[111] This JOHN ROBERTS may have been the miller of Pen y Clwyd, Denbighshire, who bought from John ap John and Thomas Wynne 500 acres in July 1682. He is reported to have come over as a single man, and not married until he was 60 years old. See Browning, *Welsh Settlement*, 178-9, and PMHB, LXI (1937), 455-457, an account written by his descendant Jonathan Roberts.

26 [July] DAVID DAVIES: 2 fatts qty. 2 cwt. & 13 lbs. nails & other wares value £3 14s. 7d. [Duty] paid. From the Customer's Book: 1 chalder grindstones.

27 [July] GEORGE EDGE: 1 bbl. qty. 4 measures oatmeal. [Duty] paid.[112]

30 [July] EDWARD JONES: 2 casks, 2 packs, 3 bundles, 2 rundles, 2 bbls. qty. 3 flitches bacon & other wares value £14 15s. 1d. [Duty] paid. From the Customer's Book: 3 cwt. cheese, etc.[113]

1 [August] RICHARD THOMAS: 1 chaldron, 1 hhd., 2 rundles qty. cwt. 3 qtrs. wrought iron & other wares value £11 7s. 6d. [Duty] paid.[114]

3 [August] JOHN EDWARDS: 4 hhds., 3 straw baskets, 2 small casks, 1 chest, 7 bundles, qty. 5 cwt. cheese & other wares value £15 13s. From the Customer's Book: value £13 19s.[115]

---

[112] George Edge and his wife Joan of "Barrow," had a son John, b. 20 10m 1648, and a son Joseph, b. 9 10m 1654, according to the Digested Registers of Cheshire and Staffordshire, cited in Note 52 above. A George Edge of Barrow who d. 22 3m 1676, may have been another child or the father of these two children. John Edge, F.P. of 125 acres, listed in Pennsylvania Archives [1st Series] I, 44, may have been the son of George of Barrow; he hardly seems to have been the John Edge of St. Andrews, Holborn, Middlesex, who was deceased by 1707, leaving a widow Frances, as per Digested Copy of Registers of the Quarterly Meeting of London and Middlesex, GSP. The F.P. is probably identical with the John Edge and wife Jane of Little Mollington, Cheshire, whose daughter Martha was bur. in 1681, as per Digested Registers of Cheshire and Staffordshire, and with the emigrant to Chester Co. whose 1711 will names his wife Jane, and brother Joseph. The latter served his time with Thomas Mincher, as per Chester Court Records, 89, 261, 338-9, 351. John Edge's will is recorded in Will Book C, 247, for an abstract of which see Chester County Collections, No. 9 (Jan. 1938), 343. For accounts of John Edge, see Smith, Delaware County, 458, and Futhey and Cope, 527-8, in which he is confused with the John Edge of Middlesex.

[113] If these goods were not consigned to Edward Jones, the immigrant of 1681, it is possible they were for the EDWARD JONES of St. Harmon, Radnorshire, who bought 250 acres of the Richard Davies land. A lot at the northwest corner of Fifth and Chestnut Sts. was surveyed 30 9m 1683, for one of these two men. Pennsylvania Archives, 3rd Series, III, 395; Browning, Welsh Settlement, 214, 221. Letters of administration were granted 10 Nov. 1699, to Jeremiah Collett, principal creditor, on the estate of an Edward Jones, for which see PGM, XIX, 272, entered in Administration Book A, 302, #128:1699.

[114] RICHARD THOMAS (Richard ap Thomas), F.P. of 5000 acres, late of "Whitford Geordon," Flintshire, Wales, on 18 9m 1683, being then sick and weak of body and "now arrived in Penna," devised his wearing apparel to Thomas ap Richard, for whom see below, and to Edward Jones, one of the men noticed last above. For abstract of Thomas's will see PGSP, III, 165, and PGM, XIX, 265, entered in Administration Book A, 217-219. With him came his son RICHARD THOMAS, JR., and it is said servants, not named. For an account of this family see Futhey and Cope, 740-741. THOMAS OLDMAN, carpenter, who in 1693 testified for Richard Thomas, Jr., apparently was also a passenger on the Morning Star, and probably one of the Thomas servants. He first settled at Lewes, Sussex Co., where he m. 20 1m 1687/8, Elizabeth Sykes, daughter of James Sykes. Oldman d. in Philadelphia early in 1715; for his will see Will Book D, 29, #35:1714/15, and for that of his wife Elizabeth, Will Book D, 400, #319:1724.

[115] JOHN EDWARDS (John ap Edward) of Nant Lleidiog, Merionethshire, bought 312½ acres of the Thomas-Jones lands. His will, obviously written on shipboard and dated 16 8m 1683, was not proved until 8 2m 1686, by his brother William Edwards of Merion. Named in it as executors were Hugh Roberts, David Davis, John Robert, and Hugh John Thomas, all of whom except the latter, shipped goods on the Morning Star. It was witnessed by GABRIEL JONES, and William Morgan, for whom see below. The inventory of his estate was dated 3 1m 1683/4, indicating his death shortly after his arrival. Will Book A, 37, #27a, and Will Book B, 270, #101. With him came his minor children ELIZABETH, SARAH, EDWARD and EVAN who assumed the surname Jones. Of the four servants he brought, in addition probably to Gabriel Jones, two were HUMPHREY EDWARDS and MARY HUGHES, for whom see Pennsylvania Archives, 2nd Series, XIX, 315-16, 332. Cf. Browning, Welsh Settlement, 47-8, 55, 87-92. HUGH JOHN THOMAS, also of Nant Lleidiog, one of John ap Edwards' executors, brought a certificate dated 18 5m 1683, from Penllyn Meeting for himself and his wife, described therein as "a friendly woman." Radnor Transcripts, De15F, 10. He had purchased 156¼ acres of the Thomas-Jones lands which were laid out in Merion; these he sold early in 1708 and removed to Plymouth Twp. were he d. as Hugh John or Jones in 1727, according to Browning, Welsh Settlement, 108. For his will, see Will Book E, 74, #77:1727.

[3 August] KATHERINE ROBERTS: 5 hhds., 4 crates, 10 small vessels, 1 box, 7 chests, 1 desk (chest?), qty. 4 cwt. cheese & other wares value £22 15s. [Duty] paid.[116]

[3 August] CADWALLADER MORGAN: 3 hhds., 2 straw flasketts [long narrow basket, from the Welsh *fflasged*], 5 casks, 5 bundles, qty. 2 cwt. cheese & other wares value £9 6s. 2d. [Duty] Paid. From the Customer's Book: value £7 2s. 5d.[117]

[3 August] ROBERT DAVIES: 4 hhds., 2 bbls., 7 casks, 1 chest, 3 bags, 1 sack, qty. 2 cwt. cheese & other wares value £14 10d. From the Customer's Book: value £11 15s. 10d.

[3 August] JOHN ROBERTS: 1 hhd., 4 small casks, 1 chest, 2 bundles, qty. cwt. cheese & other wares value £1, 10s. 10d. [Duty] paid. From the Customer's Book: 5 bushels oatmeal, 20 yds. flannel, kerseys.

[3 August] THOMAS LLOYD: 2 hhds., 2 casks, 1 bundle, qty. cwt. cheese & other wares value £1 10s. 10d. [Duty] paid.[118]

[3 August] GAYNOR ROBERTS: 1 hhd., 2 cases, 2 chests, 1 bundle, qty. 2 qtrs. cheese & other wares value £1 10s. 10d. [Duty] paid.[119]

[3 August] HUGH ROBERTS: 2 hhds., 2 chests, 6 casks, 3 bundles, qty. 1 qtr. wrought iron & other wares value £16. [Duty] paid. From the Customer's Book: value £6 14s. 5d. 1 kersey, 4 millstones value £7.

7 [August] WILLIAM MORGAN: 6 cases, 2 firkins, 1 rundle, 3 boxes, 1 trunk, 1 churn, 2 tubs, 2 bundles, 1 sack, 1 chest, qty. 14 lbs. haberdashery & other wares value £6 7s. 6d. [Duty] paid.[120]

11 [August] DAVID DAVIES: 1 anvil, 1 cask, 1 box, qty. 2 cwt. wrought iron & other wares value £7 4d. [Duty] paid.

20 [August] WILLIAM JONES: 1 chest, 1 cask, qty. 30 bushels oatmeal & other

---

[116] KATHERINE ROBERTS (Katherine Thomas), widow of Llaithgwm, Merionethshire, "a plaene woman," brought a certificate for herself and children dated 18 5m 1683. Radnor Transcripts, De15F, 11. Widow of Edward Jones' partner, John ap Thomas, who had died the previous May, she brought with her 7 children, two of whom, SYDNEY and MARY, died at sea. *Ibid.,* 491. The other children were EVAN, CATHERINE, THOMAS, ROBERT and CADWALLADER, for an account of whom see Browning, *Welsh Settlement,* 120-123. Her party is said to have numbered twenty, twelve of whom were servants.

[117] CADWALADER MORGAN of Gwernfel, Merionethshire, brought a certificate dated 8 5m 1683, from Penllyn Meeting, for himself, his wife JANE and at least two children, MORGAN and EDWARD MORGAN. For an account of this family, see *ibid.,* 105-107.

[118] THOMAS LLOYD, yeoman of Llangower, Merionethshire, mentioned in minutes of the Welsh purchasers as "not the Presid'" to distinguish him from the man who came on the *America,* had purchased 156¼ acres of the Thomas-Jones lands. See Browning, *Welsh Settlement,* 47, 48, 134, 137, 246-7, for conflicting statements about this man.

[119] GAYNOR ROBERTS of Ciltagarth, sister of Hugh, and purchaser of 156¼ acres of the Thomas-Jones lands in her own right, brought a certificate dated 18 5m 1683, declaring her free of marriage. Radnor Transcripts, De15F, 12. She m. her fellow passenger John Roberts (of Pencoid) at Merion Meeting, for whom see Note 108 above. She d. 20 12m 1722, aged 69. Browning, *Welsh Settlements,* 125. With her came her mother, KATHERINE ROBERTS, not to be confused with Katherine, the widow of John ap Thomas; she is said to have d. in 1699, and was bur. at Merion. *Ibid.,* 96.

[120] WILLIAM MORGAN and his wife ELIZABETH, "both free," registered their arrival "from Leverpoole" as being in 9m 1683. PMHB, VIII, 329. He is perhaps the man who, on 30 1m 1688, obtained permission from the Philadelphia Meeting to keep his school in the meeting house (*PGSP,* II, 133), but died in less than a year, leaving a child and his widow to whom letters of administration on his estate were granted 4 11m 1688, for which see PGM, XIX, 254, entered in Administration Book A, 50, #70:1688. She m. 2nd William Walker *ca.* 1689 (*PGSP,* II, 156-7); he was deceased by 24 May 1697, when his will was proved, for abstract of which see *ibid.,* 31, recorded in Will Book A, 356, #150:1697. His wife Elizabeth Walker and a daughter Elizabeth survived him, but whether the girl was his, or William Morgan's, has not been determined.

wares. [Duty] paid. From the Customer's Book: 4 cwt. cheese, 60 yds. flannel, ½ of a Norwich kersey, value £8 10d.

[20 August] THOMAS PRITCHARD: 1 sack, 1 cask, qty. 6 Winchester bushels oatmeal, 3 flitches bacon. [Duty] paid.[121]

[20 August] RICHARD THOMAS: 4 bags, 3 sacks, qty. 18 Winchester bushels oatmeal & other wares value £4 15s. [Duty] paid.

23 [August] JAMES PRESCOTT: 8 chests, 2 bbls., 1 hhd., 2 boxes, qty. 160 lbs. serges & other wares value £156 3s. 3d. [Duty] paid. From the Customer's Book: value £89 10s. 2d. 48 narrow kerseys, 16 short cloths, 4 broad cloths. [Duty] £3 6s. 8d.

The fifth and last ship known to have come from Liverpool in 1683, the *Friendship*, had arrived in the Delaware by 21 9m (November) 1683, when several of its passengers obtained warrants for land to be laid out in the province. A small ship of 60 tons burthen, with a crew of six, its passage this year was a quick one of less than two months — the last goods went on 13 September — making better time, apparently, than it had the year before.[122]

The *Friendship* of Liverpool [17]

Robert Crossman, master, for Pennsylvania & Virginia

3 [August] HENRY MADDOCK: 9 casks, qty. 2½ qtrs. malt; 2 chests, qty. 4½ qtrs. wheat; 3 pots & 1 tub, qty. ½ bbl. butter; 2 hhds. salt value 20s. [Duty] 6s. 9d.[123]

[3 August] JOHN HODKINSON (Hodskins): 3 cayles, qty. 3 cwt. cheese; 3 pots, qty. ½ bbl. butter. [Duty] 1s. 6d.[124]

6 [August] THOMAS PEMBERTON: 1 cask, qty. 48 lbs. pewter. [Duty] 2s. 2¼d.[125]

---

121 THOMAS PRITCHARD of Nant Lleidiog, yeoman, a purchaser of 156¼ acres of the Thomas-Jones lands, is said in Browning, *Welsh Settlement*, 136, not to have emigrated. But a warrant was issued for a city lot for a Thomas Pritchard (Prichard) on 23 9m 1683, and another 2 10m 1684, for which see *Pennsylvania Archives*, 3rd Series, II, 757, 759. By virtue of the last warrant, a lot was laid out at the northeast corner of Broad and Chestnut Sts., for which see Warrants and Surveys, III, 252. For an account of this man, a cordwainer by trade, see *PGM*, XXIII, 113-14; also *N. J. Archives*, XXI, 649, 665, 674.

122 For the 1682 passengers and goods on the *Friendship*, see *PGM*, XXIII, 40. The 1683 loadings are from Liverpool port book E 190/1345/13, PRO.

123 HENRY MADDOCK had also shipped goods on the *Endeavour*, for which see Note 51 above. These on the *Friendship* may have been brought to the customs too late to go on the earlier ship, or perhaps Henry himself had not been able to leave so early. It seems likely he came on the *Friendship*, for he was returned an assemblyman from Chester Co. 10 3m 1684, and a warrant for 300 additional acres in Chester Co. was issued in his name 20 10m 1683. *Pennsylvania Archives*, 3rd Series, I, 47; *ibid.*, 3rd Series, III, 149.

124 John Hodkinson was granted a warrant for 240 acres in Chester Co. 21 9m 1683, but as it appears he also had been granted a warrant 9 2m 1683, for a city lot, the exact time of his arrival remains uncertain. *Pennsylvania Archives*, 3rd Series, 130; Warrants and Surveys, III, 238.

125 Thomas Pemberton had been granted a warrant 29 March 1682, for 1000 acres in Kent Co. by the court at St. Jones (later Kent Co.). *Pennsylvania Archives*, 2nd Series, VII, 199. He was returned a member of the Provincial Assembly from Kent Co. in 1687, and was deputy surveyor for the county. *Ibid.*, 8th Series, I, 78, and 2nd Series, XIX, 193, 197, 384. Possibly he was related to the nonconformist apothecary of Liverpool, John Pemberton, for whom see William Irvine, ed., *Liverpool in King Charles the Second's Time* (Liverpool, 1899), 119.

7 [August] JOHN PENNINGTON: 5 tubs, qty. ½ qtr. wheat; ½ bbl. butter; ½ qtr. barley meal; ½ cwt. wrought iron; 13 cwt. cheese; 1 bbl. fat. [Duty] 5s. 11½d.[126]

[7 August] JONATHON SCAFE (Scaife): 1 pack, 3 casks, 3 pots, qty. 250 ells English linen; 152 lbs. woolen cloth; cwt. nails; cwt. cast lead; 40 lbs. pewter; 1½ cwt. wrought iron; ½ cwt. brass manufactured; ½ bbl. butter; 3 grindlestones qty. ½ chalder; [1] iron pot; 1 tub salt value 2s. 8d. [Duty] 16s. 6d.[127]

[7 August] JOSEPH DRAKE: 2 pots, qty. ¼ bbl. butter. [Duty] 3d.

[7 August] JOHN HOUGH: cwt. & 50 lbs. woolen cloth; 140 ells English linen; 1 doz. felts, English making; 1½ doz. woolen stockings for men, 1 doz. ditto for children; 4 coverlets, wool & hair; 4 casks, 1 bundle, 1 bbl. qty. ¼ cwt. brass manufactured; 28 lbs. new shoes; ½ cwt. gunpowder; ¼ cwt. haberdashery; 1 chest window glass; 5 cwt. cheese; ¾ bbl. butter; ½ qtr. wheat; 4 cwt. wrought iron; cwt. flour; 2 old saddles; 2 iron pots; 2 bbls. salt value 10s. [Duty] 16s. 3¼d.[128]

13 [August] HENRY MADDOCK: 1 bundle, 5 hhds., 1 chest, 1 box, 11 casks, qty. 2¼ cwt. goads Taunton & Norwich cottons; 400 ells English linen; 60 lbs. serges; 70 lbs. woolen cloth; 15 cwt. cheese; 40 lbs. new shoes; cwt. hard soap, English making; 10 lbs. leather manufactured; 4 neck collars; 2 packetts; 1 cart saddle [put over a horse's back to support the shafts of a cart] value 15s. 14 lbs. printed books; 14 lbs. haberdashery; ¼ cwt. wrought iron; 1 tub, qty. ¼ bbl. butter; ¼ cwt. brass manufactured; 16 lbs. Norwich stuffs; 30 felts, English making; 6 doz. woolen stockings for men, 4 doz. ditto for children. [Duty] £1 10s. 1¾d.

[13 August] JONATHON HEYES (Hayes): 2 bbls., 3 tubs, 11 casks, 1 box, 2 bundles, qty. ½ qtr. malt; cwt. nails; 19 cwt. cheese; 3 flitches bacon; ½ chest window glass; ½ qtr. wheat; ½ qtr. oatmeal; ½ cwt. pewter; ½ bbl. salt value 20d. [Duty] 13s. 10d.[129]

---

126 Warrants for survey were issued for John Pennington & Co. 8 and 13 7m 1683. John Pennington (1655-1710), eldest son of Isaac and Mary Pennington, and step-brother of Penn's first wife Gulielma Maria Springett, was a F.P. of 1250 acres, but did not emigrate. Since he was of Buckinghamshire, the John Pennington who shipped goods on the *Friendship*, may have been another of the same name. *Pennsylvania Archives*, 3rd Series, II, 767; *PMHB*, LXX (1946), 358.

127 JONATHAN SCAIFE of Idle in the parish of Kalverly, Yorkshire, brought a certificate of removal dated 28 4m 1683, from Askwith, Yorkshire, which was filed at Middletown Meeting. His wife ANN and children MARY, JEREMIAH and WILLIAM, b. 30 5m 1683; d. 12 12m 1683[/4], came with him. Transcripts of Records of Middletown Bucks County Monthly Meeting: Marriages 1684-1780; Removal Certificates 1682-1715; Condemnations: 1686-1721; Births 1664-1806; Deaths 1687-1807, Bu32F, 56, 126, GSP. He was one of the peacemakers in Bucks Co. in 1685, and coroner between 1697 and 1699. He was bur. 1 5m 1709; his wife Ann 8 8m 1723. Middletown Births and Deaths, Bu2F, 404, cited in Note 52 above; *Bucks Court Records*, 25, 285, 269, 316, 358, 391.

128 JOHN HOUGH of Hough, Cheshire, his wife HANNAH and son JOHN, came on the *Friendship*, registering their arrival as in 9m 1683. *PMHB*, IX, 229. He was granted a warrant 21 9m 1683, for 125 acres to be laid out in Chester Co., but he settled in Middletown Twp., Bucks Co. *Pennsylvania Archives*, 3rd Series, III, 130; *Bucks Court Records*, 269, 375. He is not to be confused with the John Hough, brother of Richard, who came on the *Endeavour*. See *PMHB*, XVIII, 20n. Servants who came with the Houghs were GEORGE and ISABELLA GLEAVE (Glaire), both indentured for 4 years, and their son GEORGE, until he was 21. They eventually settled in Burlington Co. where Gleave was a wheelwright by trade. For notices of them, see *N. J. Archives*, XXI, 514; *Burlington Court Book*, 185, 176, 267, 269, 304. See also *PGM*, XXIII, 47n. THOMAS HOUGH, another servant of John Hough, indentured for 4 years, was settled "above the Falls of Delaware" in Burlington Co. by 1699, for which see *N. J. Archives*, XXI, 518. The other Hough servant, NATHANIEL WATMOUGH (Wattmore), may have removed to Chester Co. after his indentures had expired; for possible reference to him see *Chester Court Records*, 298.

129 JONATHAN HAYES of Edington, and ANN WILLIAMSON of Crewood Hall were m. 14 11m 1675, according to Digested Registers of Cheshire and Staffordshire, GSP, cited in Note 52 above. She no doubt

[13 August] GILBERT WOOLAMS (Woolman): 8 casks, qty. 4 cwt. cheese; ¾ cwt. brass manufactured; cwt. wrought iron; ½ qtr. oatmeal; ½ qtr. wheat meal; 21 lbs. pewter; ¼ bbl. butter; 14 lbs. gunpowder; 1 bbl. salt value 2s. 6d. [Duty] 5s. 2¼d.[130]

[13 August] SAMUEL BORGES (Burges): 2 hhds., 1 chest, qty. 1 qtr. wheat; ½ cwt. lead; 10 lbs. new shoes; 1 doz. bridles; cwt. cheese; ½ cwt. wrought iron; 2 lbs. Norwich stuffs; ¼ cwt. haberdashery; ½ chest window glass; 14 lbs. gunpowder; ½ doz. woolen stockings for men, 2 doz. ditto for children; 6 felts, English making. [Duty] 4s. 10½d.[131]

[13 August] JOSEPH CLAYTON: 2 bundles, qty. ½ cwt. wrought iron; ¼ cwt. gunpowder. [Duty] 9d.[132]

17 [August] SIMON ELLIS: 1 fatt, 1 box, qty. 160 lbs. woolen cloth; 30 lbs. serges; 40 ells English linen; 14 lbs. haberdashery; ¼ cwt. wrought iron; 2 coverlets, wool & hair. [Duty] 11s. 1½d.[133]

23 [August] JOHN SHARPLES: 5 casks, 1 chest, qty. 10 cwt. cheese; 2 narrow Yorkshire kerseys; 6 lbs. serges; 40 ells English linen; 14 lbs. haberdashery; 2 yds. Holland [fine linen] value 25s. [Duty] 7s. 10d.[134]

[23 August] ROBERT CROSSMAN: 3 chests, 1 hhd., 1 bbl., 1 bale, qty. 10 narrow Yorkshire kerseys; 2 short cloths; 3 Penistones [wool from Penistone in the West Riding of Yorkshire]; 20 yds. frieze; 4 pcs. Manchester double bayes; 2 pcs. Manchester single bayes; 20 lbs. silk manufactured; 90 lbs. Norwich stuffs; 300 lbs. serges; cwt. haberdashery; 24 lbs. new shoes; 9 coverlets, wool & hair; 2 doz. old wool cards; 5 cwt. wrought iron; 2 doz. bridles; 20 lbs. leather manufactured; 6 under saddles; 3 cwt. nails; 1 doz. plain sheep leather gloves; 880 ells English linen; 76 ells Holland; ½ doz. whips; 3 pcs. calico value £6 10s. [Duty] £4 3s. 5d.

---

came with him, as well as their children JONATHAN, MARY and ELIZABETH. They settled in Marple Twp. Chester Co., on 600 acres for which a warrant had been granted Hayes 21 9m 1683. *Pennsylvania Archives*, 3rd Series, III, 131. The daughter Mary m. Evan Lewis, Elizabeth m. Richard Maris, son of George Maris of the *Bristol Comfort*, and the son Jonathan Hayes m. Jane Rees. He was murdered, allegedly by Hugh Pugh; for administration on Jonathan's estate see *PGM*, XX, 53, entered in Administration Book B, 112, #19½:1714. For mention of the other children see *Pennsylvania Archives*, 2nd Series, XIX, 670, 701-2; Smith, *Delaware County*, 467.

130 A warrant of survey for Gilbert Woolamin (sic) had been granted 1 7m 1683, by virtue of which 250 acres were laid out 15 2m 1684, in Chester Co. by Darby Creek, in right of Thomas Briggs, of Hedelston, parish of Acton, Cheshire, a F.P. of 500 acres. Warrants & Surveys, III, 605. Other warrants were issued Woolman, but no evidence has been found he emigrated. See *Pennsylvania Archives*, 3rd Series, II, 52, and III, 176.

131 SAMUEL BURGES was undoubtedly of the family of Pownall Fee in Cheshire, where Alice Burgis m. Randle Blackshaw of the 1682 *Submission* at John Worthington's 9 8m 1661, for whom see *PGM*, XXIII, 65; where Sarah Burgis m. Edward Pierson at Thomas Potts' house 6 1m 1671, presumed to be the settler in Falls Twp., for whom see *Bucks Court Records*, 269; where Hugh Burgess and Martha Janney were m. at Thomas Janney's house 12 12m 1672, for all of whom see Digested Registers of Cheshire and Staffordshire, GSP, cited in Note 52 above. Samuel Burges bought 200 acres in 1685 "between Randulph Blackshaw and the great timber Swamp" in Bucks Co., and in 1697 was constable of Falls Twp. A brother Isaac Burges was of Salem Co., West Jersey in 1694. *Bucks Court Records*, 33, 301, 327; *N. J. Archives*, XXI, 606.

132 JOSEPH CLAYTON, for whom a warrant was issued 20 [*blank*] 1683, for 100 acres in Chester Co., was of New Castle Co. by 1689. See *Pennsylvania Archives*, 3rd Series, III, 117; *Chester Court Records*, 60, 156, 161.

133 This Simon Ellis appears to be identical with the Simeon Ellis of Gloucester Co., N. J., clothier, who bought 200 acres southwest of the north branch of Cooper's Creek in 1691. See *N. J. Archives*, XXI, 659, 666-7.

134 John Sharples from Hadderton, Cheshire, had emigrated in 1682 on this same ship, for whom see *PGM*, XXIII, 40.

3 [September] JOHN HOUGH: 20 lbs. pewter; 3 cwt. wrought iron. [Duty] 2s. 5¼d.

[3 September] SIMON ELLIS: 14 lbs. serges. [Duty] 10½d.

4 [September] JONATHON SCAFE: 1 cask, qty. 5 cwt. cheese. [Duty] 1s. 8d.

During the first half of September, two ships at Bristol were loading goods intended for both Pennsylvania and Virginia. One may have sailed a few days earlier than the other — most of its goods were intended for Virginia — but both ships appear to have arrived in the Delaware at almost the same time. The one which probably sailed first, the *Society* of Bristol, had made the trip to the Delaware the year before with the same master during the summer months. This year, loading between 1 and 17 September, it had only one consignment of goods for Pennsylvania.[135]

The *Society* of Bristol [18]

Thomas Jordan, master, for Virginia

13 [September] WILLIAM ALLOWAY & WILLIAM SALLOWAY, for Pennsylvania: 2 cwt. wrought iron; cwt. gunpowder; ½ doz. bellows; 190 lbs. serges; 5 lbs. brass manufactured; 20 lbs. lead. [Duty] 15s. 7d.[136]

The other Bristol ship, the *Samuel & Mary*, which was loading goods in September did not finish loading until 19 September, two days after the last goods had been stowed on the *Society*. A fairly large ship of 250 tons burthen, she was the last Bristol vessel to arrive in the Delaware in 1683. Though her departure date probably was a little later than the *Society*'s, she seems to have made a good crossing, for a warrant for a city lot was granted 26 9m (November) 1683 for one of her passengers.[137]

The *Samuel & Mary* of Bristol [19]

Thomas Skeves, master, for Pennsylvania & Virginia

3 [September] WILLIAM SALLOWAY & WILLIAM ALLOWAY: 1¾ cwt. brass manu-

---

135 For the *Society*'s 1682 passengers and goods, see *PGM*, XXIII, 41-44. The 1683 consignment is from Bristol Port Book E 190/1146/1, PRO.

136 WILLIAM ALLOWAY, the first of these two shippers, was a tallow chandler by trade, and possibly the son of John Alloway of Taunton and Ilchester, to whom Penn wrote at the end of November reporting on the arrival of ships from England, for which see Note 4 above. Both William and John Alloway on 27 and 28 June 1683, had witnessed the two sales to Matthew Perrin by William Salloway and Francis Herford, each of whom was a F.P. of 250 acres, of their original purchases from Penn, for which see Deed Book C-1, 276, 281. For a notice of William Alloway, see *PGM*, XXIII, 119; for his death between 30 Aug. and 11 7m (Sept.) 1699, of yellow fever, see *Correspondence Between William Penn and James Logan* (Philadelphia, 1870), I, lviii.

137 The tonnage of the *Samuel & Mary* is given in Acts of the Privy Council (Colonial), 1680-1720, 119, PRO. Therein the master's name is variously given as Thomas Skeves or John Skuse. The ship's loadings are from Bristol port book E 190/1146/1, PRO. In Penn's letter of 29 Nov. 1683 to John Alloway, he reported that the *Samuel & Mary*, as well as the *Factor* and *Unicorn*, and ships from London, "Leverpoole," New Castle and Southampton had all come "well with Theire passengers." For the *Samuel & Mary*'s arrival some days earlier, see Note 148 below.

factured; 2½ cwt. wrought pewter; 2 cwt. alum; cwt. lead weights; 28 lbs. haberdashery; 1 lb. silk manufactured; ½ cwt. books; 2 parcels wares value £1 16s. 8d. [Duty] 18s. 4½d.[138]

8 [September] SAMUEL BEAKES: cwt. shot; 3 cwt. cheese; 5 bushels malt; 5 cwt. wrought iron; 60 lbs. shoes; cwt. biscuit value 13s. 4d. [Duty] 8s.[139]

[8 September] JOSEPH KIRLE: 1½ cwt. cheese; ⅙ hhd. aquavita; ¼ cwt. wrought iron; 28 lbs. shoes; 1 bushel pease; 1 firkin butter; 200 bbls. hoops; 2 parcels wares value £2 1s. 8d. [Duty] 4s. 9d.[140]

[8 September] JOHN PERET (Perrot, Parrot?): 1 doz. woolen Irish stockings; 1 lb. brass manufactured; 5 yds. bengal [silk]; 2 lbs. haberdashery. [Duty] 7½d.[141]

11 [September] JOHN HUGHS: 8 cwt. cheese; ½ cwt. shot; 4 bushels malt; 3 firkins butter; ½ chest window glass; 84 lbs. English soap; 56 lbs. pewter; 56 lbs. shoes; 12 lbs. gunpowder; 8 cwt. wrought iron; 4 parcels several sorts of wares value £6 15s. [Duty] £1 8d.[142]

12 [September] THOMAS SKEVES: 30 goads cottons; 2 remnants kersey, qty. 1¼ pieces; 18 lbs. serges; ½ cwt. haberdashery; 10 ends English fustians & 1 doz. bodices; 3 parcels wares value £3 3s. 4d. [Duty] 6s. 9½d.

[12 September] JOHN BATCHELOR: 40 ends English fustians; 100 ells English ticking; 40 lbs. serges; 150 lbs. linsey woolsey; ½ cwt. haberdashery; cwt. brass & copper manufactured; cwt. wrought pewter; 2 qtrs. malt; 1 hhd. aquavita; 6 doz. [lbs.] tallow

---

138 WILLIAM SALLOWAY (Salway), brought a certificate of removal from Taunton Monthly Meeting, Somerset, dated 13 6m 1683. Myers, Quaker Arrivals, 4. A sergemaker by trade, and F.P. of 250 acres which he had sold to Matthew Perrin, he nevertheless was granted a warrant for a city lot on Schuylkill side 28 9m 1683, which was laid out at the southwest corner of Schuylkill Second and Walnut Sts. Warrants and Surveys, III, 224. In 1684 he bought 115 acres in Tacony at the mouth of Frankford Creek where he set up a fulling mill. Exemplification Book 1, 131: 22 3m 1685, Patent to William Salway. In 1688 he m. Sarah Pennock, dau. of Christopher Pennock, and d. between 12 Nov. 1694 and 1 Feb. 1694/5, as per his will recorded in Will Book A, 302, #121:1694/5, abstracted in PGSP, II, 23. He left a son Samuel and two daughters, Mary who m. Isaac Warner, and Hannah who m. Thomas Skelton. Deed Book F-3, 64: 6 Jan. 1719, Isaac Warner et al. to Jonathan Dickinson. William Salway had a brother Thomas, a weaver of Salem Co., N. J., who was deceased by 1694, for whom see N. J. Archives, XXI, 597, 606.

139 SAMUEL BEAKES was the third son of William Beakes, for whom see Note 14 above. Presumably with him were his mother MARY, and older brothers WILLIAM and STEPHEN BEAKES who registered the family's cattle mark in 1684. Davis, Bucks County, 77. For notices of Samuel as sheriff of Bucks Co., see Bucks Court Records, passim. He m. Joanna Biles in 1695. Hinshaw, II, 978.

140 JOSEPH KIRLE, cooper of Bristol, on 29 Aug. 1683, bought for £6 5s. from William Lovell of Bristol, mariner, 625 acres, half of the original purchase of Richard Collins and Richard Wood. Of this Kirle sold 300 acres to William Salway for £17 early in 1686, as endorsed in Deed Book E-1-5, 209: 29 Aug. 1683, William Lovell to Joseph Kirle. He may be identical with the Joseph Kirle, mariner, who appears in Colonial Office records at Barbados in ships of 25 to 45 tons, as per C.O. 33/13/21, 24, and C.O. 33/14/45, PRO, and who sailed the 25-ton Joseph to Barbados from Philadelphia in 1689 to marry Mary Brett, dau. of John and Mary Brett of Michael's Parish at Bridgetown Meeting. Hinshaw, II, 574. He d. 24 7m 1704, and his widow two months later on 28 9m 1704. Ibid., 386.

141 One John Perrot signed a certificate of removal, filed at Haverford Monthly Meeting about 1684/5, for Allice Lewis, dau. of James Lewis of Llardevy, Pembroke, according to Browning, Welsh Settlement, 197. No evidence has been found that he emigrated.

142 These goods may have been consigned to the John Hewes (Hughes) of the parish of St. Clemens in the suburbs of the city of Oxford, collarmaker and F.P. of 500 acres, whose country land had been laid out in Oxford Twp. by a warrant dated 17 6m 1682. A warrant for a city lot, dated 30 9m 1683, was issued either for this man or another of the same name. Exemplification Book 5, 473; Pennsylvania Archives, 2nd Series, XIX, 302; ibid., 3rd Series, II, 723.

candles; 2 bbls. beer; ½ chest window glass; 50 yds. frieze; 6 doz. woolen stockings; 14 parcels several sorts of wares value £139 10s. [Duty] £8 6s. 5d.[143]

[12 September] JAMES WEST: 20 yds. blue linen value 10s. 2 cwt. wrought iron. [Duty] 2s. cwt. cheese; ½ firkin butter; cwt. biscuit value 13s. 4d. [Duty] 8d. 50 pcs. English earthenware; ¼ chaldron grindstones. [Duty] 2d. ½ bushel oatmeal. [Duty] 1s. 11½d.[144]

[12 September] WILLIAM ALLWAY & WILLIAM SALLWAY [sic]: 19 cwt. wrought iron; 3 cwt. shot; 16 gross tobacco pipes; 7 firkins butter; ½ doz. bellows; 11 felt hats; 12 lbs. shoes; 1½ chests window glass; 2 bbls. beef [Duty] 6s. 180 lbs. serges; 2 ends English fustians; ¼ cwt. wrought iron; 3 parcels wares value £1 8s. 4d. [Duty] £1 15s. 11½d.

[12 September] JOHN ARMSTRONG: 10 lbs. wrought iron; 25 goads cottons; 1 doz. woolen stockings; 3 lbs. shoes; 2 pcs. English fustians; 4 suits wearing apparel; 2 felt hats; 2 parcels wares value £1 8s. 4d. [Duty] 2s. 10½d.

14 [September] JOHN PARROTT [sic]: ¼ cwt. & 14 lbs. wrought pewter; ¾ cwt. brass manufactured; ½ cwt. wrought iron; 2 flitches bacon; 2 bushels malt; 2 firkins butter; ½ cwt. cheese; 1 bushel pease; 2 parcels several sorts of wares value £1 15s. [Duty] 6s. 5½d.

[14 September] HENRY DAVIS: 7 suits wearing apparel; 50 pcs. earthenware. [Duty] 1d.[145]

[14 September] JOHN MOONE: 20 doz. whisks value £1. 3 cwt. English made soap; 30 lbs. shoes; 14 lbs. gunpowder; ¾ cwt. lead shot; ¾ cwt. cheese; 10 gross tobacco pipes. [Duty] 5s. 6d.[146]

15 [September] THOMAS MASTERS: 3 cwt. cheese. [Duty] 1s.[147]

[15 September] EDWARD COMLY: 10 lbs. serges; ½ pc. kersey; 100 lbs. linsey woolsey; 4 cwt. cheese; 2 cwt. wrought iron; ¼ hhd. aquavita; ½ cwt. brass manufactured; 2 parcels wares value £2 3s. 4d. [Duty] 13s. 4d.[148]

---

[143] For references to merchants in Bristol named Batchelor, and to a John Batchelor who became prominent in the 1690s, see *Records Relating to the Society of Merchant Venturers of the City of Bristol in the Seventeenth Century* [Bristol Record Society's Publications, XVII], *passim*.

[144] For notice of JAMES WEST, shipwright, see *PGM*, XXIII, 122-3. He was first granted a warrant for a city lot on rent 29 10m 1683, which was laid out on the north side of Mulberry (Arch) between Schuylkill Fourth and Fifth Sts. Warrants and Surveys, III, 259. He was deceased by 1 Oct. 1701, when letters of administration on his estate were granted his widow PRUDENCE, who probably came with him; see *PGM*, XIX, 275, entered in Administration Book A, 343. With West and his wife when they emigrated was at least one child, their son JAMES, JR., b. in Bristol 12 5m 1681, for whom see Starr and Cooper Notes, Mary R. Scattergood Collection, HSP.

[145] This small duty was paid on the earthenware only; wearing apparel and fustian were duty-free.

[146] This shipper probably was identical with the Bristol linendraper who had shipped goods on the *Bristol Merchant* earlier in the year, for whom see Note 13 above. In this case, whisks were women's neckerchiefs, though they were also utensils for beating eggs.

[147] For notice of THOMAS MASTERS, carpenter, see *PGM*, XXIII, 106. He was granted a warrant 25 2m 1684, for a lot laid out the next day on the west side of Schuylkill Third between Vine and Sassafras (Race) Sts. Warrants and Surveys, II, 82.

[148] HENRY COMLY of Bedminster, near Bristol, weaver and F.P. of 500 acres, his wife JOAN, and son HENRY, JR., are said erroneously to have come with Penn in 1682 on the *Welcome* by Joseph Martindale in his *History of the Townships of Byberry and Moreland . . .* (Philadelphia, rev. ed.), 270. But he was granted a warrant for 200 acres 26 9m 1683, and the next day another warrant for a city lot which was laid out 29 9m 1683, on the east side of Schuylkill Second between Walnut and Chestnut Sts. *Pennsylvania Archives*, 3rd Series, II, 679; Warrants and Surveys, III, 503. An indentured servant, GEORGE SHEAVE,

[15 September] JOHN BRISTOW: ½ cwt. iron; ½ cwt. brass manufactured; $\frac{1}{12}$ hhd. aquavita. [Duty] 10*d*.[149]

[15 September] JOSEPH BLEASE (Bliss?): 1½ cwt. wrought iron. [Duty] 8*d*.

[15 September] JOSEPH BROWNE: 20 lbs. wrought pewter; 60 lbs. serges; ½ cwt. brass manufactured; cwt. shot; cwt. wrought iron; 2 cwt. cheese; 14 lbs. soap; 1 doz. [lbs.] tallow candles; ¼ chalder grindstones; 2 parcels wares value 11*s*. 8*d*. [Duty] 8*s*. 6*d*.[150]

17 [September] CHRISTOPHER MATHEWS: 12 gross tobacco pipes; 1 pair linsey woolsey curtains & valences; 6 pair woolen stockings. [Duty] 1*s*. 8½*d*.

19 [September] JOHN WYSE: 80 goads cottons. [Duty] 1*s*. 8*d*.

There is no direct evidence that the next ship actually came up the Delaware to Philadelphia. She arrived in Maryland from Plymouth in November 1683, bearing at least two passengers who were "from thence transported to this river" (the Delaware) by some means. The situation of these two men who "arrived here in 10ᵗʰ Mᵒ 1683," is reminiscent of the *Submission* passengers of the year before. They had been landed at Choptank on the Eastern Shore of Maryland early in November, and did not reach Philadelphia until considerably later.[151]

The port books show no goods were transported in the 1683 vessel which were intended for Pennsylvania, but since she had passengers bound for the province, she may have dropped them off on her way back to England.

The *Daniel & Elizabeth* of Plymouth [20]

William Ginney, master

GEORGE STONE of Frogmore, in the parish of Charlton in the County of Devon, "serge wavor" [weaver].[152]

---

may have come with the family, for whom see *Colonial Records*, I, 92. Henry Comly d. in Bucks Co. 13 3m 1684, leaving his widow Joan, son Henry and daughter Mary, not mentioned by Martindale. For abstract of his will see PGSP, I, 203, recorded in Bucks Co. Will Book A-1, 8. His widow Joan m. 26 2m 1685, Joseph English, for notice of whom see PGM, XXIII, 43; she was bur. 20 10m 1689, as per Martindale, 271. See also *Bucks Court Records*, 42-3, 287; *Pennsylvania Archives*, 2nd Series, XIX, 311. The Edward Comly who took these goods through the customs presumably was a relative.

149 The arrival of John Bristow of Bristol, on this ship is uncertain. A F.P. of 500 acres, his first warrant of record was dated 31 8m 1684. For an account of him in Chester Co., see Smith, *Delaware County*, 449-50, wherein he is called an edge-tool maker.

150 JOSEPH BROWNE, brickmaker, was granted a warrant for a city lot 28 9m 1683, which was not laid out until 1686. Warrants and Surveys, II, 17. By that time he had been in partnership with George Guest, and had taken out letters of administration on Guest's estate 6 11m 1685/6, for which see PGM, XIX, 250, entered in Administration Book A, 7, #60:1685. For notice of Browne, see PGM, XXIII, 111-12.

151 The arrival date of the two passengers is given in PMHB, IX, 226. For the *Submission* passengers and goods, see PGM, XXIII, 64-5, 274.

152 GEORGE STONE brought a certificate dated 24 6m 1683, from Kingsbridge Monthly Meeting in Devonshire to Falls Monthly Meeting in Bucks Co. Hinshaw, II, 1030. On 19 8m 1699, he acknowledged himself indebted to his former servant Thomas "Dure" in the sum of £13 18s. and promised payment of same. See *Bucks Court Records*, 399.

THOMAS DYER, [his] servant, to serve 4 years; loose the 9th M°. To have 50 acres of land.[153]

One more vessel bringing a few passengers should have arrived in 1683, but did not come up the Delaware until nearly the end of January 1683/4. This was the *Mary* of Fowey which had transported goods in the summer of 1682 for the Growdens of Cornwall. The Fowey port books for 1683 show the vessel arrived back in England with a cargo of tobacco from Maryland. Then in September it had begun taking on goods for the Growdens under a new master, Joshua Dalton, but the details of that merchandise have been lost.

A letter from Penn, dated 24 11m (January) 1683/4, reports the arrival of the vessel, and its chief passenger Joseph Growden, at New Castle. Penn found "him weary wth nineteen weeks' passage & ye care of an intire ship & Cargo of his own. . . ."[154]

The *Mary* of Fowey [21]

Joshua Dalton, master

JOSEPH GROWDEN of St. Austell in ye County of Cornwall, Gent.[155]

While a few others, still unidentified, also came up the Delaware in 1683, the arrival of the *Mary* of Fowey brings the total of identified ships known to have brought settlers to Pennsylvania since December 1681, to forty-four. Not all their passengers are known, and records are lacking which place others, known to have arrived, on identified ships. By the end of November, 1683, Penn had claimed that 3000 "soules" had arrived, a figure which probably included those who had come prior to the arrival of the 1682 fleet. It remains, nevertheless, a truly remarkable figure in view of the perils of seventeenth century transportation.

To recapitulate, the following is a list of those identified ships which brought passengers and goods up the Delaware in 1683:

---

[153] THOMAS DYER (Dure) sold 50 acres — probably his headland, 1 10m 1696, to William Darby. *Ibid.*, 305. He had m. Elhenah or Ellen Baines (Beanes) at Middletown Meeting 26 7m 1694, for which see *Pennsylvania Archives*, 2nd Series, IX, 222. The births of 8 children are entered in Falls Meeting records: Mary, Deborah, John, Thomas, Hannah who d. in infancy, Joseph, Ellen and Eliza. Hinshaw, II, 958, 977, 994.

[154] For the letter, see *Pennsylvania Archives*, 2nd Series, VII, 4. The 1683 port book for Fowey, E 190/1047/2, consists of three folios only; details of merchandise shipped have been lost.

[155] JOSEPH GROWDEN, F.P. of 5000 acres, is called of St. Austell in Keith, *Provincial Councillors*, 222, cited in Note 31 above, but he was of Trevose in 1681 when he and his father each purchased land from Penn, for which see *Pennsylvania Archives*, 2nd Series, XIX, 403. His 1st wife ELIZABETH probably came with him; she d. 4 9m 1699, and he m. 2nd Ann, widow of Samuel Bulkley, 10 11m 1704/5. Keith, *Provincial Councillors*, 222; Hinshaw, II, 537. Probably his two oldest children, JOSEPH and GRACE, also came with their father. Joseph Growden, Sr., d. 10 9m 1730, and his wife Ann was deceased by 28 Aug. 1736 when letters of administration on her estate were granted Joseph Growden, Jr., for which see *PGM*, XXII, 271, entered in Administration Book C, 330, #25:1736. In 1713 Joseph Growden said he had brought over about 45 servants, but no record of these has been found. *Pennsylvania Archives*, 2nd Series, XIX, 550.

1. The *Bristol Merchant*, William Smith, master; arrived by 9 February 1682/3.
2. The *Thomas & Anne* from London, Thomas Singleton, master; probably arrived by 15 April 1683.
3. The *Liver* of Liverpool, James Kilner, master; arrived by 17 July 1683.
4. The *America* of London, Joseph Wasey, master; arrived 20 August 1683.
5. The *Vine* of London, William Thomson, master; arrived 3 September 1683.
6. The *Eliza & Mary* of London, John Bowman, master; arrived 22 September 1683.
7. The *Endeavour* of Liverpool, George Thorpe, master; arrived 27 September 1683.
8. The *Bristol Comfort*, John Read, master; arrived 1 October 1683.
9. The *Bristol Factor*, Roger Drew, master; arrived by 4 October 1683.
10. The *Concord* of London, William Jeffries, master; arrived by 6 October 1683.
11. The *Lyon* of Liverpool, John Crumpton, master; arrived by 14 October 1683.
12. The *Providence* of Scarborough, Robert Hopper, master; arrived by 31 October 1683.
13. The *Unicorn* of Bristol, Thomas Cooper, master; arrived 31 October 1683.
14. The *Mary of Southampton*, Anthony Pryor, master; arrived by 7 November 1683.
15. The *Jeffrey* of London, Thomas Arnold, master; arrived by 8 November 1683.
16. The *Morning Star* of Liverpool, Thomas Hayes, master; arrived 20 November 1683.
17. The *Friendship* of Liverpool, Robert Crossman, master; arrived by 21 November 1683.
18. The *Society* of Bristol, Thomas Jordan, master; probably arrived the end of November 1683.
19. The *Samuel & Mary* of Bristol, Thomas Skeves, master; arrived by 26 November 1683.
20. The *Daniel & Elizabeth* of Plymouth, William Ginney, master; arrived in Maryland in November 1683.
21. The *Mary* of Fowey, Joshua Dalton, master; arrived by 24 January 1683/4.

Appendix*

Among the settlers who must have been passengers in 1683 on the above ships, some thirty are known to have brought certificates of removal which were entered in the records of various monthly meetings in Pennsylvania. In the following list of these emigrants, their names have been grouped chronologically together under the dates on which the certificates were granted, since such certificates were usually given just before the individual sailed. As the voyage across the Atlantic averaged between eight and ten weeks, an approximate date of arrival can be established from the dates of the certificates.

8 12m (February) 1682[/3], entered in Darby Monthly Meeting records:
EDMUND CARTLIDGE and wife [Mary], from Riddings, Derbyshire, "Breath House" Monthly Meeting. A F.P. of 250 acres, he was granted a warrant for a city lot 2 5m (July) 1683.[1]
THOMAS HOOD from "Breson" (Breaston), Derbyshire. A survey in his name for

---

* By the Editor.
1 Digest of a List of the Births, Marriages, Removals and Burials Recorded in the Books of the Darby Monthly Meeting of Friends, 1682-1891, De13F, 223, GSP, hereinafter cited as Digest of Darby Records. Warrants and Surveys, II, 29. For the origins of 1683 settlers in Darby Twp., see "The Names of the Early Settlers of Darby Township, Chester County, Pennsylvania," PMHB, XXIV (1900), 182-3. This is, to some extent, the Darby Twp. counterpart of the partial registers of arrivals for Philadelphia and Bucks Cos., but includes arrivals up through 1760.

150 acres in Chester County was returned into the surveyor general's office 12 July 1683.[2]

THOMAS HOLLAND and wife [Mary] from "Breath House." They are probably identical with the Thomas and Mary Holland of Milnhay, Derbyshire, whose daughter Mary had married ca. 1675, John Hallowell, as his second wife.[3]

19 12m 1682[/3], entered in Darby Monthly Meeting Records:
JOHN HALLOWELL [of Hucknall, Nottinghamshire], Mansfield Monthly Meeting. His wife Mary and children, Sarah, Thomas and Mary came with him. Both he and Thomas Hood may have been sent over by Joseph Potter, F.P. of 250 acres, to take up Potter's land, for which a warrant was granted 3 5m 1683.[4]

22 12m 1682[/3], entered in Darby Monthly Meeting records:
RICHARD BONSALL and family, from [Mouldridge, Derbyshire] Ashford Monthly Meeting. The family included his wife Mary, said to have been a daughter of George Wood, a F.P. of 1000 acres, and several children, probably Elizabeth, Rachel, Ann, Abigail and Obadiah.[5]

16 2m (April) 1683, entered in Philadelphia Monthly Meeting records:
DANIEL MEDLICOTT from [Ratlinghope, Salop] Salop Monthly Meeting. He was granted a warrant for 100 acres in Chester County 27 6m (August) 1683, and was buried at Radnor 1 9m 1693.[6]

13 3m (May) 1683, entered in Philadelphia Monthly Meeting records:
MARTHA SANKEY from Salop Monthly Meeting. She married with permission of the Philadelphia Meeting, granted 2 10m 1684, the abovenamed Daniel Medlicott. After his death she married secondly, 13 March 1698, James Keite (Kite), who died 6 September 1713, and thirdly, Jonathan Cogshall in 1715.[7]

6 2m (April) 1683, entered in Falls Monthly Meeting records:
THOMAS WOLF (Woolfe) from Kingsworth Monthly Meeting, "Hartford County." A F.P. of 250 acres, he was granted a warrant for the survey of his land in Bucks County 18 7m (September) 1683. He died in 1688, leaving his property to his sister Sarah and her husband Abraham Cocks (Cox).[8]

4 3m (May) 1683, entered in Falls Monthly Meeting Records:
SARAH WOLF from Kingsworth Monthly Meeting, "Hartford County." Sister of the abovenamed Thomas Wolf, she married at Middletown Meeting Abraham Cox on 26 9m 1686.[9]

---

[2] Digest of Darby Records, De13F, 240; *Pennsylvania Archives*, 3rd Series, 131. *Cf.* Smith, *Delaware County*, 469.

[3] Digest of Darby Records, De13F, 240; Smith, *Delaware County*, 469; Clarence V. Roberts, *Ancestry of Clarence V. Roberts & Frances A. (Walton) Roberts* (Philadelphia, 1940), 109.

[4] *Ibid.*, 109-11; Digest of Darby Records, De13F, 240. Both Hood and Hallowell bought part of the Potter land, for which see *Chester Court Records*, 152, 319. See also *Pennsylvania Archives*, 3rd Series, III, 156.

[5] Digest of Darby Records, De13F, 214; William B. Evans, "Early Settlers of Darby: The Original Bonsall," (newspaper clipping), Chester County Historical Society, West Chester, Pa. Smith, *Delaware County*, 447.

[6] Myers, *Quaker Arrivals*, 9. Exemplification Book 5, 518: 23, 24 March 1681/2, William Penn to Daniel Meddlecott. *Pennsylvania Archives*, 3rd Series, III, 149; Radnor Transcripts, De15F, 485, cited in Note 70 above.

[7] Myers, *Quaker Arrivals*, 9, 63-4; PGSP, I, 275. Browning, *Welsh Settlement*, 595; Glenn, *Merion*, 84, both cited in Note 70 above; *Pennsylvania Archives*, 2nd Series, XIX, 379.

[8] Hinshaw, II, 1040; *Pennsylvania Archives*, 3rd Series, III, 100; *ibid.*, 2nd Series, XIX, 453.

[9] Hinshaw, II, 1040; *Pennsylvania Archives*, 2nd Series (1880), IX, 229.

2 5m (July) 1683, entered in Falls Monthly Meeting records:

ABRAHAM COCKS (Cox) from "Hangar Hill" Monthly Meeting, Buckinghamshire. Six months before his marriage to the abovenamed Sarah Wolf, he leased on 8 3m 1686, from Joseph English, Jr., the ferry house "over against" Burlington, and 32 acres adjacent.[10]

6 5m 1683, entered in Darby Monthly Meeting records:

THOMAS BRADSHAW from "Exton" (Oxton), Nottinghamshire. He is presumed to be the brother of Samuel Bradshaw of the same place, F.P. of 500 acres, who had emigrated in 1682.[11]

"Last day of 3m 1683," entered in Falls Monthly Meeting records:

JOHN BAINBRIDGE of Lindley in Obley Parish, Yorkshire, the younger, from Askwith Monthly Meeting. A carpenter by trade, he obtained a warrant for 300 acres in Bucks County 21 9m (November) 1683, and in April 1684, one for 200 acres in West Jersey.[12]

26 5m 1683, entered in Middletown Monthly Meeting records:

JOHN TOWN of Hartwith, Yorkshire, linen weaver, from Askwith Monthly Meeting. He obtained a warrant for 200 acres in Bucks County 21 12m (February) 1683[/4].[13]

20 5m 1683, entered in Radnor Monthly Meeting records:

STEPHEN EVAN of parish of Llanbister, Radnorshire, Wales, for self, wife Elizabeth and children John and Phoebe. They may have come in as servants of one of the large Welsh purchasers, since they acquired no land until 1691.[14]

DAVID MEREDITH, weaver, of parish of Llanbister, Radnorshire, Wales, his wife Katherine and children Richard [Moore], John [Moore], Mary [Moore], Meredith and Sarah [Meredith]. A warrant for a city lot was granted him 22 9m 1683.[15]

JOHN JARMAN (German) from Llangerig, Montgomeryshire, his wife Margaret and daughters Elizabeth and Sarah. A warrant in his name for a city lot was granted him 22 9m 1683.[16]

27 5m 1683, entered in Philadelphia Monthly Meeting records:

SAMUEL MILES from the monthly meeting in the parish of Llanfihangel Helygen,

---

[10] Hinshaw, II, 987; *Bucks Court Records*, 43-45, cited in Note 44 above.

[11] Digest of Darby Records, De13F, 214; Smith, *Delaware County*, 448; Futhey and Cope, 774. Samuel Bradshaw's certificate from "Exton," entered in Digest of Darby Records, *loc. cit.*, was dated 20 1m 1682. See also *PGM*, XXIII, 56n.

[12] Certificates of Removal, Falls Monthly Meeting, Bucks County, Bu29F (photostats of originals), GSP. *Pennsylvania Archives*, 3rd Series, III, 105; *N. J. Archives*, XXI, 359, cited in Note 14 above. He m. Sarah Clows, daughter of John, at Middletown Meeting 15 6m 1685 (*Pennsylvania Archives*, 2nd Series, IX, 219), and on 20 Jan. 1685/6, as John Bainbridge, the younger, carpenter, of near Chesterfield, West Jersey, acquired from George Hutcheson 250 acres in the First Tenth. *N. J. Archives*, XXI, 419. When he d. in Maidenhead Twp., Hunterdon Co. (formerly Burlington Co.) in Feb. 1732, he had been aged 74 the previous 2 Nov. 1731. His wife, who d. 25 March 1731, had been in her 67th year. "Calendar of Wills, Vol. II, 1730-1750," *N. J. Archives*, 1st Series, XXX, 30.

[13] Middletown Transcripts, Bu32F, 58, cited in Note 127 above. *Pennsylvania Archives*, 3rd Series, III, 97. He m. Deborah Booth at Middletown Meeting 28 9m 1691. *Ibid.*, 2nd Series, IX, 228.

[14] Radnor Transcripts, De15F, 14, cited in Note 70 above. For his purchase of land see *Pennsylvania Archives*, 3rd Series, I, 14; Browning, *Welsh Settlement*, 227-8.

[15] Radnor Transcripts, De15F, 14; Warrants and Surveys, II, 81. For an account of David Meredith and his step-children, surnamed Moore, see *PGM*, XIX, 217-242, and corrections in *ibid.*, XX, 61.

[16] Radnor Transcripts, De15F, 13; Warrants and Surveys, II, 53. In 1688 he bought 100 acres from John Evans. *Pennsylvania Archives*, 3rd Series, I, 13.

Radnorshire, Wales. He had married there on 24 4m 1682, Margaret James, spinster, a purchaser of 200 acres from Richard Davies.[17]

JAMES MILES from the monthly meeting in the parish of Llanfihangel Helygen, Radnorshire, Wales. He is believed to have been the father of the abovesaid Samuel Miles, and of Richard and Griffith Miles.[18]

> 27 5m 1683, entered in Radnor Monthly Meeting records:

ELIZABETH HUMPHREY, widow, of Llanegrin in Merionethshire, with her children Benjamin, Lidia, Anne, Humphrey and Gobeitha. Widow of Samuel Humphrey, her eldest son Daniel had emigrated the year before.[19]

JOHN HUMPHREY of "Llwundu" in Merionethshire, and Joan his wife, members of the meeting for twenty-three years. Brother-in-law of Elizabeth Humphrey abovesaid, he had purchased 312½ acres from Charles Lloyd and Margaret Davies, joint F.P. of 5000 acres.[20]

RICHARD HUMPHREY, bachelor, of "Llangyuin, Merioneth." He had purchased 156¼ acres from Richard Davies which he devised to his brother-in-law John Humphrey, husband of his sister Joan abovesaid.[21]

JOSHUA OWEN, bachelor, of "Llwyndu," parish of "Llangylyuin," Merionethsire, who was emigrating with his "relations' consent." His sister Elizabeth Owen was she who married John Roberts "of the Mill."[22]

REES PETTER (Peters) of Machanlleth, Montgomeryshire. A cordwainer by trade, he was granted a warrant for a city lot on Schuylkill side 29 1m (March) 1684, which was laid out between Vine and Sassafras (Race) Streets on the west side of Schuylkill Third.[23]

> 31 5m 1683, entered in Radnor Monthly Meeting Records:

JOHN RHYDDERCH of Hirnant, Montgomeryshire, "clear of marriage." He had purchased 156¼ acres from Charles Lloyd and Margaret Davies, but did not live long to enjoy it. He was buried at "Skoolkill burying place" 27 9m 1685.[24]

THOMAS JONES from "Llanworthin," Montgomeryshire, "clear in life, credit, marriage and engagements." He also had bought 156¼ acres from Charles Lloyd and Margaret Davies, and by letter of attorney 14 August 1683, had been made agent for Mar-

---

[17] Myers, Quaker Arrivals, 4. This appears to have been his second trip, for a city lot had been surveyed for him 31 1m 1683, apparently in right of his wife's purchase, on the north side of Walnut St. between Fifth and Sixth. Warrants and Surveys, II, 83; Pennsylvania Archives, 3rd Series, I, 14. Miles' first purchase in his own right was paid for 29 5m 1684, for which see ibid., 2nd Series, XIX, 450. No evidence has been found that he was identical with the Samuel Miles who came in 1682 as a servant to the Free Society of Traders, for which see ibid., 462, and Deed Book E-3-6, 90: 25 7m 1705, Samuel Miles, cooper of Philadelphia, to Benjamin Chambers; courtesy of Miss Mildred Goshow.

[18] Myers, Quaker Arrivals, 4. According to the researches of Miss Goshow on the Miles family, James Miles went to the Pennypack region, and became a Baptist.

[19] Radnor Transcripts, Del5F, 19; Smith, Delaware County, 471.

[20] Radnor Transcripts, Del5F, 17; Glenn, Merion, 247; Smith, Delaware County, 471; Pennsylvania Archives, 3rd Series, I, 23.

[21] Radnor Transcripts, Del5F, 18; Glenn, Merion, 247. For abstract of his will see ibid., and PGSP, I, 10.

[22] Radnor Transcripts, Del5F, 18. Reported to be a nephew of John Humphrey and his sister-in-law Elizabeth Humphrey, mentioned above, he is said to have m. Martha Shinn and removed to Burlington where he was living in 1739. Glenn, Merion, 249. For his sister Elizabeth Owen, who m. John Roberts "of the Mill," see Note 112 above; Browning, Welsh Settlement, 179.

[23] Radnor Transcripts, Del5F, 16. Warrants and Surveys, II, 92. On 27 6m 1708, a certificate to Dublin Meeting was granted him and his wife by the Philadelphia Meeting, for which see PGSP, IV, 296.

[24] Radnor Transcripts, Del5F, 21, 487; Pennsylvania Archives, 3rd Series, I, 23.

garet Thomas and Thomas Morris to take up their land bought from the same original purchasers.[25]

15 5m 1683, *entered in Philadelphia Monthly Meeting records:*

JOHN JONES, from Plantation Meeting, Island of Barbadoes. A carpenter by trade, he had purchased jointly with John Jennings of Barbadoes, apothecary, land in Pennsylvania, in right of which a warrant for a city lot was granted Jones 13 7m (September) 1683, laid out at the southwest corner of Second and Mulberry (Arch).[26]

23 6m (August) 1683, *entered in Philadelphia Monthly Meeting records:*

SAMUEL CARPENTER from Monthly Meeting at Bridge Town, Island of Barbadoes. A F.P. of 5000 acres, his Front Street lot had been laid out at the end of the previous December, 1682. His liberty land was warranted 2 9m 1683.[27]

2 7m (September) 1683, *entered in Radnor Monthly Meeting records:*

THOMAS ELLIS from the monthly meeting at Redstone in Pembroke, South Wales. With him came his wife Ellen (?), and at least some of their children, probably Ellis, Humphrey and Ellenor. He was a F.P. of 1000 acres, by virtue of which a warrant was granted him 24 1m 1683[/4?] for laying out his land.[28]

2 7m 1683, *entered in Philadelphia Monthly Meeting records:*

JOHN BANT and NICHOLAS PRIME, certificate signed by "Will: Bant & Tho: Bant ffather of ye said John, Thomas Lower, Tho: Salthouse, ffrancis ffox, with several others." John Bant called himself a chirurgeon; he was granted a warrant for a city lot 24 7m 1684, which was surveyed the same month on the north side of "market alley" at the Center.[29]

2 7m 1683, *entered in Middletown Monthly Meeting records:*

THOMAS CONSTABLE of the parish of Diskeard in Cornwall, and sister BLANCHE and JOHN PENQUITE his servant. Thomas Constable was granted a warrant for 500 acres on 2 11m 1683[/4], which were laid out in Bucks County.[30]

WALTER BRIDGEMAN of the parish of Keyne in Cornwall. He married on 2 6m 1686, Blanche Constable, abovenamed, at Middletown Meeting. By a warrant dated 2 11m 1683[/4], 200 acres were laid out for him adjoining the land laid out for Thomas Constable.[31]

13 7m 1683, *entered in Philadelphia Monthly Meeting records:*

ELIZABETH WALTER, her certificate signed by Peter Walter, Peter Walter, Jr., Christopher Holder, Jr., Richard Hill and several others. She married in 4m (June) 1684, with consent of the Philadelphia Meeting, John Gardner of Philadelphia.[32]

---

25 Radnor Transcripts, De15F, 21; *Pennsylvania Archives*, 3rd Series, I, 23. This Thomas Jones, as Thomas John Thomas, is said to have died testate in 1723, as per Glenn, *Merion*, 34n.

26 Myers, *Quaker Arrivals*, 3; Deed Book E-1-5, 222: 4 3m 1686, John Jones to John Jennings.

27 Myers, *Quaker Arrivals*, 9; Warrants and Surveys, II, 25, III, 194.

28 Radnor Transcripts, De15F, 22; *Pennsylvania Archives*, 3rd Series, II, 689. Browning, *Welsh Settlement*, 244-5, but *cf.* Smith, *Delaware County*, 458.

29 Myers, *Quaker Arrivals*, 8-9; the certificate gives no place of origin. Warrants and Surveys, III, 247; *Pennsylvania Archives*, 3rd Series, II, 672.

30 Middletown Transcripts, Bu32F, 61, cited in Note 127 above. *Pennsylvania Archives*, 2nd Series, XIX, 492.

31 Middletown Transcripts, Bu32F, 63; *Pennsylvania Archives*, 2nd Series, IX, 220; *ibid.*, 3rd Series, III, 59; *ibid.*, 2nd Series, XIX, 314.

32 Myers, *Quaker Arrivals*, 4. No place of origin is given on the certificates; she may have come from Maryland. For her marriage to John Gardner, emigrant of 1682, for mention of whom see Note 80 above, see *PGSP*, I, 266-8.

DIGEST OF

SHIP

AND PASSENGER ARRIVALS

IN THE DELAWARE

By
Walter Lee Sheppard, Jr.

1682	Name	Size	Master	Port of Registry
1.	Bristol Factor	100 T	Roger Drew	Bristol
2.	John & Sarah	100 T	Henry Smith	London
3.	unknown	unk.	unknown	home port unknown; last from New England
4.	Amity	200 T	Richard Dymond	London
5.	Freeman	?	George Southern	Liverpool
6.	Hester & Hannah	?	William East	London
7.	Lyon	90 T	John Compton	Liverpool
8.	Friendship	60 T	Robert Crossman	Liverpool
9.	Mary (very small)	46 T	William Lugger	Fowey
10.	Society	100 T	Thomas Jordan	Bristol
11.	Golden Hinde	?	Edward Read	London
12.	Samuel	70 T	John Adey	London
13.	Friends Adventure	?	Thomas Wall	Liverpool
14.	Providence	50 T	Robert Hooper	Scarborough
15.	Elizabeth, Ann & Catharine	?	Thomas Hudson	London
			(Sometimes called Isabella, Ann & Catherine,	
16.	Hopewell	?	Michael Yoakley	London
17.	Lamb	130 T	John Tench (French)	Liverpool
18.	Bristol Factor	100 T	Roger Drew (trip 2)	Bristol
19.	Welcome	284 T	Robert Greenway	London
20.	Jeffrey	500 T	Thomas Arnold	London
21.	Antelope	?	Edward Cooke	Liverpool
22.	Unicorn	300 T	Thomas Cooper	Bristol
23.	Submission	?	James Settle	Liverpool

1683				
1.	Bristol Merchant	300 T	William Smith	Bristol
2.	Thomas & Anne	?	William Singleton	London
(	John & Elizabeth	70 T	John King	Isle of Wight
(	Grayhound	?	?	
(	unknown	?	Capt. Humphrey Waterman	
(	unknown	?	?	Plymouth
3.	Liver	130 T	James Kilner	Liverpool
4.	America	200 T	Joseph Wasey	London
5.	Vine	?	William Thompson	London
6.	Eliza & Mary	?	John Bowman	London
			(also called Elizabeth)	
7.	Endeavor	100 T	George Thorpe	Liverpool
8.	Bristol Comfort	200 T	John Read	Bristol
9.	Bristol Factor	100 T	Roger Drew (trip 3)	Bristol
10.	Concord	500 T	William Jeffries	London
11.	Lyon (trip 2)	90 T	John Compton	Liverpool

Loading Dates	Arrival in Delaware	No. Pass.
28 Sept.- 6 Oct. 1681	15 Dec. 1681	16+
26 Sept.- 24 Oct. 1681	winter 1681/2	?
	19 May 1682	1 known
21 Feb. 1681/2-15 Apr. 1682	3 Aug. 1682	20+
24 May- 7 June 1682	5-6 Aug. 1682	?
1 Feb.- 7 Mar. 1681/2	8 Aug. 1682	?
22 Apr. Liverpool; 2-		
22 May Chester	13 Aug. 1682	?
22-30 May 1682	14 Aug. 1682	?
19 May 1682	15 Aug. 1682	?
12 Apr.- 3 May 1682	-- Aug. 1682	?
8-16 June 1682	by 18 Sept. 1682	?
12 Apr.- 20 May 1682	by 18 Sept. 1682	?
31 May- 11 July 1682	by 28 Sept. 1682	?
13-19 July 1682	29 Sept. 1682	?
1 July- 31 July 1682	29 Sept. 1682	?
sometimes by any of the three names)		
11-12 July 1682	early Oct. 1682	?
26 June- 17 July 1682	22 Oct. 1682	?
26 July- 26 Aug. 1682	last week Oct. 1682	?
7 July- 21 Aug. 1682	28 Oct. 1682	?
29 Aug.- 11 Sept. 1682	end Oct. 1682	?
Loaded at Belfast	9-10 Dec. 1682	?
25-26 Aug., sailed after 17 Oct.	before last Dec. 1682	40+
16 Aug.- 1 Sept., sailed	Choptank, Md., Nov.; pass.	
6 Sept. 1682	overland to Del. arr.	
	Dec. 1682.	?
24 Oct.- 3 Dec. 1682	by 9 Feb. 1682/3	?
Dec.-Jan. 1682/3, sailed		
after 13 Jan.	prob. by 15 Apr. 1683	?
	early May 1683	?
Barbados 3 Jan. 1682/3	perh. to Phila. May 1683	?
from Barbados	prob. late June, early July	?
	mid-June 1683	?
19-24 Apr. 1683; last fr. Dublin	by 17 July 1683	?
3-31 May, sailed 6 June	20 Aug. 1683	80+
19-21 Apr. 1683	3 Sept. 1683	brought Pastorius
	27 Sept. 1683	?
15 June- 11 July 1683	29 Sept. 1683	?
23 May- 26 June 1683	1 Oct. 1683	?
last loaded 7 Aug.	4 Oct. 1683	?
26 June- 16 Aug. 1683	6-10 Oct. 1683	?
22-25 June; last fr. Dublin	8-14 Oct. 1683	?

	Name	Size	Master	Port of Registry
12.	Providence (trip 2)	50 T	Robert Hooper	Scarborough
13.	Unicorn (trip 2)	300 T	Thomas Cooper	Bristol
14.	Mary of South-ampton	?	Anthony Pryor	Southampton
	(otherwise Alexander of Inverness; also Recovery)			
15.	Jeffrey (trip 2)	500 T	Thomas Arnold	London
16.	Morning Star	?	Thomas Hayes	Liverpool
17.	Friendship (trip 2)	60 T	Robert Crossman	Liverpool
18.	Society (trip 2)	100 T	Thomas Jordan	Bristol
19.	Samuel & Mary	250 T	Thomas Skeves	Bristol
20.	Daniel & Elizabeth	?	William Ginney	Plymouth
21.	Mary (trip 2)	46 T	Joshua Dalton (new master)	Fowey

Loading Dates	Arrival in Delaware	No. Pass.
----	last Oct. 1683	?
6 July 1683	31 Oct. 1683	?
	7 Nov. 1683	?
28 July – 17 Aug. 1683	by 8 Nov. 1683	?
19 July – 23 Aug. 1683; also loaded Chester	20 Nov. 1683	70+
3 Aug. – 4 Sept. 1683	21 Nov. 1683	?
1–17 Sept. 1683	ca. 25 Nov. 1683	?
3–19 Sept. 1683	ca. 25 Nov. 1683	?
	arr. Md. Nov.; pass. over-land to Del., arr. Dec. 1683	?
	by 24 Jan. 1683/4	?

GOODS TO START A COLONY

by

Marion R. Balderston

In 1682 some hundreds of families and single persons, totaling more than 1800 people, were forced to face the problem of what to pack to take with them for life in the unknown wilderness of Pennsylvania. They were to sail on any one of the twenty three ships due to leave England that year,[1] to go directly to William Penn's new colony, stopping there first to discharge passengers, before continuing to Virginia or Barbados.

The number — 1800 — is Penn's, and need not be taken too literally. He was notoriously vague when it came to figures. He wrote that "23 ships with passengers" had come that year — this included the Bristol Factor which arrived December 15, 1681 — and he said they averaged 80 people each.[2]

They were not large ships. The Unicorn was 300 tons; the Welcome, 284; the largest, the new fast Jeffrey, was about 500. But the Providence of Scarborough was a coastal ship of 50 tons, and the Mary of Fowey was even smaller than that. They took a surprising amount of goods, and crowded into themselves an incredible number of passengers. It was a luxury to sleep in a gunport, sharing this with only one other person.[3]

The housewives' problem was the easier one. They took the family beds and bedding, for the ships provided nothing in this line. They took quite a lot of food, and small luxuries like butter and sugar to add to the ship's fare, which was usually pretty grim. They took cooking pots, and knives and spoons — many families did their own cooking on the way across. They probably took extra shoes for the growing children, and they added pounds of wool, goads of cotton, ells of linen, to replace worn clothing. The chests they packed their goods in would serve later as tables and chairs. The housewife also packed cheese and oatmeal, which would stay fresh for a long time, soap in buckets, and candles to keep out the dark.

The men's task was more difficult; they had the problem of house-building. Penn had written fairly explicit directions about how to do this. But they needed axes to cut down the trees, iron and pewter and window glass. There are romantic stories that the colonists filled their windows with oiled paper, but they are not true. Seventy-five "chests" of window glass came over that summer, besides what was in the emigrants' personal luggage. A chest contained anywhere from 200 to 300 running feet of glass. There is no way of knowing the width, which in any case probably varied, but it was ample for the three hundred farms and eighty town houses Penn spoke of in letters written that December and the following July.

They needed shovels and spades to break up the earth, in order to plant a garden; a gun, and powder and shot to hunt game. Many took along extra stocks of articles that might be useful; these were for barter and trade with other colonists, for the things they had forgotten. Penn had advised this, and James Claypoole, writing to a friend he was taking over, asked him to bring along whatever he might judge to be "vendible".

These extra articles are the ones we know about, for these had to pass through the customs, the exporter paying a small fee. His personal goods went free, and were often considerable. But he paid the ship's master for these, according to weight. One Bucks County family embarked with 2000 pounds of personal and household goods. Merchants of course paid customs on every item. Or were supposed to! Many preferred paying the clerks to taking their merchandise through customs. James Claypoole was a passed master at this game.

It is interesting to see what articles the colonists thought would be most useful in this new life. Wrought iron — that is, malleable iron — was first choice, and 855-3/4 cwt. went over that first year. The English hundredweight was 112 pounds. Nails were next, 572-1/2 cwt. of them. Then bricks, thousands of them, 48,500.

This is a misunderstood item, for people have written that the bricks came as ballast. But those ships were laden to capacity; they needed no ballast. The bricks were for floors; the housewife wanted a floor she could scrub, and she was used to a brick floor in her kitchen, as English country housewives are today. So the John & Sarah took 10,000 bricks, the Amity 15,000 bricks and tiles from one merchant, 1,000 bricks and 500 tiles from two others; the Samuel took 8,000 tiles; and the Jeffrey 14,000 bricks. The tiles were thick enough for floors. Very soon, suitable clay was discovered around Callowhill Street, and Pennsylvania began to make its own bricks. Philadelphia became, and remained, a city of pleasant red brick houses.

That first summer the colonists took over, for sale, 57 cwt. of gun-powder and 146-1/4 cwt. of shot. Besides, they took lead in bars from which shot could be made. They remembered other essentials, such as 4072 pounds of shoes, which must have amounted to quite a number of pairs, and, very surprisingly, 526-1/2 dozen pairs of men's woolen and worsted hose — did they think the women would have no time to knit? — and 134 dozen pairs of children's stocksings. Most of these, however, were really for women; they called them children's because the duty was lower.

Only 22-1/4 cwt. of soap went that summer, but 165 cwt. of that most valuable food, cheese; this sent mostly from the West Country, around Wales and Bristol. Every farm has to have at least one grindstone, and some of these went, 15-3/8 calders of them. A calder is a large container which, if filled with wheat, would hold eighty bushels. Four or more large grindstones could be packed in each. 5

The colonists looked forward to establishing convenient mills. So the Freeman took two pairs of millstones, the Lamb took five. Richard Townsend brought a complete knocked-down mill on the Welcome, and the customs book for the Submission shows "one old millstone, value 8 shillings."

One thought occurred to many emigrants — the Indians smoked pipes, and the gift of a pipe might make a friend. That summer 239 gross of tobacco pipes were loaded onto the ships, obviously as presents to the Indians. Nearly 35,000 pipes! 6

Actually, the first settlers of Pennsylvania had an easy time, as compared to other colonists, and especially to New England. The Indians here belonged to weak tribes, and on the whole were glad to have the pro-tection of the newcomers. This takes away no credit from Penn, who made friendly gestures to them, both before and after he arrived, on the principle of the Golden Rule, treating them as he would have them treat him. No one in Penn's colony at that time grabbed land; they bargained and paid for it.

New Jersey, across the Delaware, was already being settled and Burlington was a market town. The first arrivals had written long letters home, some of which survive today, and all of which were copied and read in every Meeting in England, where there were people who planned to emigrate. There were many Swedes and a few English already in Pennsylvania, and English over the border in Maryland.

Penn sent out a pamphlet, which he wrote or caused to be written, with directions so explicit it made settling in a wilderness seem easy. Eight trees would be enough to build a "clabbord" house, for instance, to be divided in half for the main room, the other half to be two small bedrooms. A carpenter and two helpers could build this in a few weeks. If lined, the space between was filled with sod and the house was warm. The cost of house and labor would be ₤7, and the nails would be ₤3.10.0, and a shelter for livestock could be built then or later. The house should last ten years without repairs. 7 He urged newcomers to take goods for barter or sale, and to bring as much money as they could. Both increased in value in the colony. (The twelve penny shilling was worth fifteen in Pennsylvania, and James Claypoole expected to double the price of what he exported.)

It was not too bad a life. Penn settled his farmers in groups of ten, the nuclei of villages, which they named after the homes they left — Cheltenham, Abington, Bryn Mawr, etc. The housewife had her snug home, with its clean, scrubable brick floor, friendly neighbors, and new people arriving with every ship. Best of all, freedom to worship, without being thrown into jail, without having your livestock or household goods taken away, often by the local minister.

There were shortages, and one was soap. Any country housewife can make soap of sorts, but more was needed. When the merchant Claypoole arrived in Philadelphia he wrote back to England, telling his agent there not to send shoes, stockings, gloves, glass, wine, hats or lead. He wanted more butter, cheese, the sweet German beer called mum, iron, and nails of the six, eight, and tenpenny sizes. He also wanted more soap.

Pennsylvania became self-supporting in a remarkably short time, but for some years she continued to import the practical items named above, as well as woolen cloth — the Germans in Germantown were growing flax and weaving linen. In those first years only one luxury item appeared in the port books — a dulcimer was taken over in 1684 by a Mistress Hathway. 8

These are the port book figures. But many merchants bribed the underpaid customs' men and put on more than the books show. James Claypoole was a master at this. The men in the "outports" — Chester, Bristol, Liverpool — were careless bookkeepers, and would not have lasted half a day in London. How many small items went into a hundredweight of haberdashery? What does the phrase "and other wares" conceal? The Chester collector used this, first choosing an item the searcher had not put down. Bristol added "------- parcels of wares."

What each ship carried is shown in tabular form. To sum up in more easily remembered round figures, that summer of 1682 the ships carried 850 cwt. of wrought iron, 570 cwt. of nails, 48,500 bricks and tiles, 75 "chests" of glass, more than 4,000 pounds of shoes, more than 530 dozen pairs of men's hose and 135 dozen pairs for women and children, 34,500 tobacco pipes for the Indians, 22 cwt. of soap, 165 cwt. of cheese, 140 cwt. of shot, and

130

57 cwt. of powder, 15 calders (or at least 60) large size grindstones, be-
sides 7 pairs of millstones and a complete knocked-down mill which Daniel
Wharley put on the Welcome for Richard Townsend.
All this in addition to their personal non-dutiable possessions.

NOTES

[1] The first ship, the Bristol Factor, left in the autumn and reached the Delaware mid-December, 1681; the John & Sarah, leaving in October, arrived early in the winter of 1682. Penn wrote the Earl of Sunderland, "We have had with passengers 23 ships," and the same to other friends. Memoirs of the Historical Society of Pennsylvania, vol. 2, p. 245. Hereafter Memoirs.

[2] Richard Townsend wrote that nearly 3000 people came that first year. Samuel Janney, Life of William Penn (Philadelphia, 1852), p. 236.

[3] Ship tonnage from the Colonial Office Records, Barbados, Public Record Office, London; also James Claypoole's Letter book, edit. Marion Balderston, Huntington Library Publications, San Marino, California, p. 150.

[4] To Lord North, 24th, 5th mo. 1683, "about eighty houses are built (in the town), and I suppose above three hundred farms settled as contiguous as may be." Memoirs, supra, vol. 1 (1826), p. 448. He wrote the same to the Earl of Sunderland.

[5] Details of what came in the ships; — from the London port books: E190/99/1 (1681) and E190/109/1 (1682); Bristol, E190/1143/1, E190/1144/1, E190/1144/2; Liverpool, E190/1344/1, E190/1345/11; for the Lyon, E190/1344/4, E190/1344/13; for the Mary, E190/1046/10.

[6] Details of individual emigrants' and merchants' loadings are in the Pennsylvania Genealogical Magazine, vol. XXIII, No. 2 (1963), and XXIII, No. 4 (1964).

[7] Penn wrote, or had someone write for him, that it needed eight trees for a house 30 x 16, divided across for a main room and one half divided again for two small bedrooms. The boards were split and "feather-edged", the house was lined and the space between was filled, probably with sod. Such a house would last ten years without repairs. Labor for a carpenter and three helpers, Ł7, for the barn, Ł5, nails for both, Ł3.10.0. Livestock, Ł24.10.0. Information and Direction to Such Persons as are Inclined to America, Pennsylvania Magazine of History and Biography, IV (1880), pp. 331-342.

[8] The dulcimer, ancestor of the piano, was placed on a table and its wires were struck with leather padded hammers. Mary Hathway took it on the Friendship from Liverpool. Port book E190/1346/9.

GOODS CARRIED

	cwt. iron	cwt. nails	bricks	chests glass	lbs. shoes
Bristol Factor	11	5			40
John & Sarah	40. 75	26	10,000		132
Amity	56	69	16,500	36. 5	192
Freeman	8. 25	3		1	20
Hester & Hannah	18. 50	62			150
Lyon	9. 75	8		1	20
Friendship	11. 75	14			140
Mary					112
Society	78. 75	54		5. 5	500
Golden Hinde					
Samuel	75. 25	50	8,000	5	74
Elizabeth Ann & Catherine	36	44		9	390
Hopewell	30				
Lamb	36	9. 5		2	497
Bristol Factor	10. 75	15		1	62
Welcome	99	78		6	744
Jeffrey	272	75	14,000	3. 5	576
Unicorne	21. 75	5		2	20
Submission	5. 50	6. 5			251
Friends Adventure	11	6. 5		2. 5	92
Providence	24	42			80

BY PENN'S SHIPS

doz. men's hose	doz. child. hose	gross pipes	cwt. soap	cwt. shot	cwt. gun-powder	cwt. cheese	calder grind-stones
6			.50	2	3	1	
41	24			20.75	.50	3	2.50
35	29			6	8	6	7.25
2					5.50	2	
10	8	26			4		
38			.50	.25	.50	1.50	
22			2			12	
			3	9			
111	4	72	5	12.75	.25	12	1.25
24	10.50	6		17.50	.50	22	1
15.50	3	25		11	1.50	3	
					3.50		
54.50	15.50	60			2	73	2
15		6	.25	15		17.25	3/8
62	30	20	10	32	2.75	4	
63	10	24		14.50	11.50	4	.50
6				5.50	10.50		.50
11.50					1	1.25	
12					1	3	
8			1		1		

EARLY SHIPPING
TO THE JERSEY SHORE OF THE DELAWARE

by

Walter Lee Sheppard, Jr. & Marion R. Balderston

As students of history know, the earliest settlements along the
Delaware were those of the Swedes, with the Dutch following closely behind.
There were scattered British trading posts, and probably a few British
trappers lived in the area; there had also been an abortive attempt by the
New Haven Colony to establish a branch on the eastern bank of the Delaware
in 1643/4, close to the present location of the city of Salem. [1] Though it is
possible that some of the early British settlers left descendants in the Delaware Valley, most of them were driven off by the Swedes and Dutch, and few
pre-Penn English settlers or traders have ever been identified on the west
bank, with the exception of a few soldiers who came with Sir Robert Carr in
his campaign against the Dutch in 1665, and who remained behind afterwards
as colonists. A list of the residents on the west bank may be found in the
Upland Court Records by those interested. [2] A list of those on the east bank
who were there in 1675 before the landing of Fenwick's settlers will be found
in Cushing and Sheppard [3], pages 317-8.

Before the arrival of Penn's colonists in 1682, the great bulk of
the Delaware traffic was to New Jersey and the east bank, but for some reason no one has apparently ever seen fit to assemble a record of this shipping.
Of the early works only Samuel Smith's History of New Jersey [4] (Burlington,
1765) gives any information and unfortunately he does not cite his sources.
The quality of his work is good, and it seems probable that when he wrote it
he had access to manuscript material now lost. Some ships and passengers
are also identified in Cushing and Sheppard, cited above, and in Woodward
and Hegeman [5]. The ships on which some colonists arrived are identified
in the Bucks County Book of Arrivals (included in this volume) [6], and in
Hinshaw [7], and in the New Jersey Archives [8]. Mrs. Balderston has gone to
the Port Books for data to supplement or correct the data in these works.
She has covered London, Bristol, and Liverpool, the only three ports for
which these books are available in the period under discussion. The following shipping material is assembled from these sources and many others as
indicated. The content and use of the material in the Port Books has been
discussed elsewhere in this volume and will not be repeated here. The
source of each name is indicated by a superior letter, and the key to these
will be found with the references at the end of this chapter. Superior
numbers are used for reference citations in the text.

It has been stated in many if not most histories that the first ship
to arrive in the Delaware transporting English colonists to New Jersey was
the Griffin, see below, which carried John Fenwick, the Proprietor of the

Salem Tenth and his settlers. However, Mrs. Balderston has noted in
Thomas Shourd's History and Genealogy of Fenwick's Colony [9] a mention of
an earlier one, the Joseph and Benjamin, Matthew Paine master, which he
says anchored at Ft. Elsborg, at the mouth of the Salem River, on 13 Mar.
1675. He lists the following as passengers on this vessel:

> Hippolite Lefever (or Lefevre).
> John Pledger and wife Elizabeth, son Joseph aged 3.
> > (Perhaps he came on the Joseph and Benjamin and his
> > wife and son followed on Griffin.)
> John Butcher.
> Richard Johnson.

As will be seen when we study the Griffin, the first two appear on most lists
for that ship, and the second two appear on none of them. Where Shourds
got this information is now uncertain. He was a farmer and antiquarian,
with a prodigious memory, quite elderly when he published the book, and he
made few if any notes. The book was written almost entirely from memory,
dates and all, and he corrected his proof in the same way, without even
referring to the original manuscript. The book is an astonishing mixture of
error and fact, and contains many things that only Shourd knew, taken from
sources now lost. Those that use this book, do so with caution. On the face
of it then, the Joseph and Benjamin, not seen elsewhere, might not have
existed, but there is a strange confirmation at least of the arrival of Lefevre
and Pledger before the Griffin in two different sources. First, Albert Cook
Myers cites [10] an Indian deed, dated 27 March 1675 referring to land in
Salem, N.J., belonging to Hippolite Lefever and John Pledger (just two weeks
after their alleged arrival on the Joseph and Benjamin). Second, the New
Jersey Calendar of Deeds [11] quoting the first book of Salem Deeds, where
are recorded, the first purchases of Salem lands from John Fenwick, page
561, shows under date of 25 May 1675 "John Pledger, late of Portsmouth,
co. of Southampton, shipcarpenter and Elizabeth his wife", 3,000 acres; and
on the same date "Hipolit Lefever late of St. Martins in the fields, co.
Middlesex, "gentleman and wife Mary," 3,000 acres. Of all the purchases
here recorded, only these two are shown as late of the place of their former
abode, indicating that at the time of recording these purchases they were
no longer living at the English addresses. The Griffin had not at this time
sailed, and all the other persons stated to have been aboard her who are
recorded as purchasing are here listed with their English addresses.
Shourd's statement then may indeed be correct. He seems only to have
missed Lefever's wife Mary, who was certainly with him in Salem.

The next arrival was the Griffin, Robert Griffin of Newcastle,
master, which had been chartered by Fenwick for the voyage. It loaded at
London from 16 June to 20 July, and arrived at Ft. Elsborg on 5 October,
then sailed about 3 miles up stream and landed the settlers on the south
side of the river at the present site of the city of Salem. (Loadings in Port
Book E 190/62/1.) The following passengers are named as having travelled
aboard her. A total of 200 passengers are said to have sailed. [m] In this and
all following lists the passengers have been alphabetized, with servant's
names appearing in brackets [ ] in alphabetical order, and again with the
families with which they travelled. Persons in parentheses ( ) are doubtful,
and may be listed later with another ship.

> John Adams [abhkm] of Redding, Berks, weaver, with wife Eliza-
> beth (Fenwick); children: Elizabeth aged 11, Fenwick aged 9,

Mary aged 4. Sometimes shown as a servant of Fenwick.

[(Jane Allen)] [b]

William Braithwaite [e] loaded goods 16 June.

[(Thomas Brinton)] [b]

[John Burton] [gm]

[Gervase Bywater] [bkm]

John Cann [m]

[Nathaniel Chambless [abgm] (or Champness or Champneys) and son Nathaniel, Jr. [abgm]]

Edward Champneys [hkm] of Thornbury, Gloucs., joyner, wife Priscilla (Fenwick) and children: John and Mary; servants: Mark Reeve, Edward Webb, Elizabeth Waites.

(Edward Cholmoley, prob. a mistake for Champneys, loaded 2 July) [e]

Thomas Duke, loaded 8 July and 20 July. [e]

[Michael Eaton] [km]

John Fenwick [abghkm] with three daughters: [Elizabeth, see under Adams], Ann who later married Samuel Hedge, and [Priscilla, see under Champneys]; ten servants: Gervase Bywater, Michael Eaton, Robert Turner, William Wilkinson, Joseph North, Elinor Geere, Sarah Hutchins, Ruth Geere, Zacharia Geere, and Ann Parsons. There were no loadings recorded for Fenwick. As leader of the expedition, and Proprietor, he must have brought much dutiable baggage. It seems probable therefore that he "bought out" of the customs so that his loadings did not get recorded.

[Elinor Geere] [km]

[Ruth Geere] [km]

[Zacharia Geere] [km]

Francis Gibbon, loaded 25 June [e].

Joanne Grigson [m]

Richard Guy and wife Bridget [abm]

Richard Hancock [abm]

William Hancock [bm] with wife Isabella; sons John and William

John Harding [m]

Richard Hartshorne [a]

Samuel Hayles, loaded 14 July. [e] (Could this be an error for Samuel Hedges?)

Samuel Hedge [am] or Hedges, later married Ann Fenwick, sometimes shown as "servant" of John Fenwick.

Peter Huff [m]

Roger Hutchins [bm] wife Esther [m] (who wrote a letter after arrival saying there were "near 200 passengers") and Esther's mother, not named. [m]

[Sarah Hutchins or Hutchings] [km]

(Hippolite Lefevre, shown above to have arrived before the Griffin) [ab]

Edward Lemon or Loman. His loading on 13 July marked for Virginia. [e]

John Lynd [bm]

Samuel Lynde [bm]

William Malster or Malstiff [bm]

John Matlock or Mallock [ab]

Job Nettleship [m]

Vicessimus Nettleship [m]

(James Nevill [b], but see the Willing Mind.)

John Nichols or Nicholson [m]

Samuel Nicholson, or Nichols [abgm], wife Ann; children: Rachel, Elizabeth, Samuel, Joseph, and Able.

Richard Noble [abhm]

[Joseph North] [km]

William Parker, loaded 21 July. [e]

Roger Pedrick [m], wrote home to wife Rebecca 14 June 1676.

(John Pledger [ab], wife Elizabeth [abm], son Joseph [abm], but see above. It is however possible that his wife did come on the Griffin, while he came on the Joseph and Benjamin.)

[Ann Parsons] [km]

[Mark Reeve] [bhm]

Isaac Smart, a crewman of the Griffin who stayed with the colony. [bgm]

John Smith [abm], wife Martha (Craft); children: Daniel, Samuel, David and Sarah.

[Francis Smithey] [gm]

John Spooner and wife [m]

John Test [m]

[Robert Turner] [km]

Edward Wade [abghm], wife Prudence; servants: Joseph Ware, Nathaniel Chambless, Senr. and Nathaniel Chambless, Jr. Also indentured servants: John Burton, Francis Smithey.

Robert Wade [bm]. He loaded on Kent, which see. Perhaps he returned to England and came again, or perhaps the Kent loading was by an agent, for him in Salem. He wrote a letter from New Jersey in June 1676, N.J. Archives, Ser.I, Vol.I, p.227.

Samuel Wade [abghm]

[Joseph Ware] [bgm]

[Elizabeth Waites] [hm]

[Edward Webb] [hm]

Richard Whitacre of Whitacar [bfm]

[William Wilkinson] [km]

(Christopher White [b]; servants Jane Allen and Thomas Brinton, but see under Kent.)

Mary White [m]

Robert Windham, wife and daughter [b]

John Wood, loaded 28 June. [e]

Edward Wood, loaded 28 June. [e]

Robert Zane [m]

(Mr. Stewart adds "one old woman and one young woman" [unnamed], and "two brothers who died on the voyage". [m]

The next known ship to carry colonists to West New Jersey was the Kent. Gregory Marlow, master, which loaded in London for New Jersey 19 March to 31 March 1677. There followed loadings for other ports, but she sailed before May. (See Port Books: Searcher E 190/66/5, and Surveyor E 190/67/4). The Kent sailed first to New York, arriving 16 August, 12 or 4 August, then after a short stay, sailed across the bay to Perth Amboy, after which she headed south to the Delaware, landing first at the mouth of Raccoon Creek where she is said to have disembarked some 230 passengers of a total of 270. She then moved on to Chygoes Island, now Burlington. Other histories state that she landed at Raccoon Creek after an early June halt at New Castle, then to Burlington on 23 June. However, the arrival time in New York is known from the minutes of the New York government, with which the Commissioners (aboard the Kent) met during their stay there. The Yorkshire purchasors settled the 1st tenth, from Assinpink to Rancocas. The London purchasors settled the 2nd tenth, from Rancocas to Timber Creek. Those known to have been aboard or thought to have been aboard the Kent were:

(Benjamin Acton) [b] *

[John Allin] [b]   ([Jane Allin]) [ab]

(Edward Bradway, wife Mary, children: William, Mary, Susannah; servants: John Allin, Thomas Buckel, William Groom. However see Grayhound, in which he loaded goods after Kent had departed.)

---

* Benjamin Acton actually was a passenger on the Lyon of Liverpool, arrived Philadelphia, October 1683.

([Thomas Brinton]) [ab]   ([Thomas Buckel]) [b]

William Clayton [a]

John Cripps [a]

Richard Davis or Davies [e], loaded 22 March.

Morgan Drewett [ae], loaded 24 March.

William Emley [ad] or Emlen.

Thomas Eves [a]

Thomas Foulke [bd]

Thomas Farnsworth [a]

([William Groom]) [b]

Jonathan Habbuck [e], loaded 31 March.

Thomas Harding [a]

Joseph Helmsley [abd]

(William Hibbs or Hebes) [a]

Henry Jennings [abf]

(John Kinsey [b], actually came on the Greyhound, loading after
   Kent left.)

Samuel Lovett [a]

— Marshall, a carpenter [a]

Thomas Nosster [a]

Thomas Olive [abe], loaded 22 March.

William Peachey [a]

John Penton or Penford [abd]

William Perkins [a] died aboard, and family.

Robert Powell [a]

Christopher Saunders [a]

Benjamin Scott [a]

Robert Stacey [abd]

Robert Wade [e], loaded 19 March. Perhaps he had first come on
   the Griffin and returned as agent for the Colony.

(Christopher White [ab], servants: Jane Allin and Thomas Brinton.
   Perhaps he was on the Griffin instead, which see, however, in a
   separate reference he is stated to have landed in 1677.)

Daniel Wills [a]

John Wilkinson [a], died aboard.

Jonathan Woodhouse [a], loaded 22 March.

William Woodmanson or Woodmancy [a] and family.

John Woolston [a]

It should be noted that many passengers alleged to have been a-board were from Yorkshire, Northamptonshire, and other northern counties. They probably loaded at a northern port, perhaps Hull or Liverpool, before the Kent arrived at London, which is why they do not appear in the London loadings.

Another ship which loaded just after Kent in London was the Greyhound, Joseph Wasey, master. The records show that an unidentified ship g. h. arrived at Wickaco in the Delaware near Old Swedes Church, present Philadelphia, in October, 1677, and this can only be the Greyhound. She loaded from 11 April until 31 May for New Jersey (Port Books E 190/66/5 and E 190/67/4), and added later loadings for Virginia. The following passengers can be identified.

Daniel Allen, loaded 26 May [e].

[John Allen] [g]

Thomas Batting, loaded 19 May [e].

Edward Bradwell [eg] or Bradway, loaded 14 May, brought wife Mary; children: William, Mary, Susannah; servants: John Allin, Thomas Buckel, William Groome.

[Thomas Buckel] [g]

(William Clayton) [d]

David Conyard, loaded 11 April [e].

(John Cripps) [d]

(Morgan Drewett [d], but he loaded on the Kent).

(Thomas Eves) [d]

(Thomas Farnsworth or Fairnsworth) [d]

Edward Griffith, loaded 16 May [e].

[William Groome] [g]

(Thomas Harding) [d]

Jonathan Harwood, loaded 11 May [e].

William Hebes or Hibbs [d]

Benjamin Hewling, loaded 16 May [e].

Zapheniah Hilton, loaded 3 May [e].

(Henry Jennings) [d]

(William Jones, loaded 31 May [e], merchant; may not have come.)

John Kinsey, Sr., loaded 19 May [e].

(Samuel Lovett) [d]

(Edward Mann [e], merchant, loaded goods but almost certainly did not sail.)

(Thomas Nossiter) [d]

(William Peachey) [d]

(Thomas Olive, but see under Kent) [d]

William Pennton [d]

Thomas Pooting, loaded 11 May [e].

(Robert Powell) [d]

(Christopher Saunders) [d]

Jonathan Stone, loaded 9 May [e].

Joseph Taylor, loaded 26 May [e].

(Daniel Wills, but see under Kent) [d]

(John Woolston) [d]

(John Woodmancy) [d]

Christopher White and his servants Jane Allin and Thomas Brinton may have been aboard the Greyhound rather than either Kent or Griffin.

The Willing Mind, John Newcomb, master, loaded in London [ac] though none of its loadings have been identified as for New Jersey. However, she arrived in the Delaware in November of 1677 [a] or January (1678) [g] or 28 Sept. 1677 [c] with 60 or more passengers, of which the following have been identified.

Daniel Brinson of Membary psh., Devon [c].

George Deacon [a]

James Nevill [a]

Henry Salter [a]

The Phoenix or Phenix [c], Matthew Sheare, master, for which we have neither home port nor loading data, apparently sailed from a northern port across the Irish Sea where it loaded, probably at Dublin. It arrived in the Delaware "6 month 1677" (August). The only identified passenger was:

John Purslowe, of Dublin, Ire. [c]

The fly boat Martha from Hull, Thomas Wildbuys or Wildcup, master, cannot be found in the Port Books either. According to Smith she arrived "at the end of summer" 1677, or from the Bucks Arrivals, in 7 month (Sept.) 1677, bringing "114 passengers" [a] for the Yorkshire Tenth, at Burlington. The following are those stated to have been aboard.

John Batts [ad], servant of George Hutchinson.

William Black [adn]

Joshua Boare [e] of Drainfield, Derbyshire. (His wife followed on the Elizabeth and Sarah.)

Richard Dingworth [ad] or Dungworth

Thomas Ellis [ad], servant of George Hutchinson.

William Goforth [ad]

Richard Harrison [ad]

Thomas Hooten [ad], wrote home shortly after arrival. Staying with Thomas Olive.

Marmaduke Horsman [ad]

William Ley [ad]

Nathaniel Luke [ad]

John Lyman [ad]

George Miles [ad]

The family of Samuel Odas [d] (Otis)

William Oxley [ad]

Thomas Schooley [ad]

Edward Season [ad]

The family of Robert Stacy [ad]

Samuel Taylor [ad], and sister Alice, later married William Black [n]

William Wood [ad]

Thomas Wright [ad]. He wrote home to his wife 28 Oct. 1677, having just arrived.

The Mary of Dublin, master's name stated by Shourd [f] to be John Hall, sailed 16 of 9 month (Nov.) 1677, arrived 22 of 12 month (Feb.) 1677/8. The following passengers being identified:

Robert Fairbanks and wife, and daughter Elizabeth [g].

[William Hall, servant to the Thompsons] [f]

Henry Stubbings, son-in-law of Robert Fairbanks. [g]

Andrew Thompson [f] and family from Dublin, with servant William Hall.

John Thompson [f] and family from Dublin.

The Shield of Stockton, (probably sailed from Hull), Daniel Towers (or Towle or Towes), master, no loadings noted, arrived at Burlington in Dec. 1677 with the following passengers identified.

— Barnes [ad], a merchant from Hull.

Francis Barwick [ad]

[Peter Berry or Bury] [k]

John Drewsbury [ad] or Dewsbury

Gawen Drummond [k] and servant, Peter Berry or Bury.

William Emley or Emlen [ad], 2nd trip, with wife and two children, one born at sea; and 4 servants, two men and two women.

Susannah Fairnsworth [ad], children and 2 servants (See Thomas Farnsworth, on the Kent.)

John Fretwell [ad]

Peter Fretwell [ad]

Richard Green [ad]

Godfrey Hancock [ad], wife and children and servants.

John Heyres [ad]

George Hill [ad]

John Lambert and servant [ad]

Thomas Lambert [ad], wife, children, and servants.

Robert Murfin [ad], wife, 2 children

Godfrey Newbold [ad]

John Newbold [ad]

George Parks [ad]

James Pharo [ad], wife and children

Thomas Potts [ad], wife, children

Thomas Revel [ad], wife, children, servants

Robert Schooley [ad], wife, children

Mahlon Stacy [ad], wife, children, servants

Richard Tattersall [ad], wife, children

John Wood [adc] of Attercliffe psh., Sheffield, Yorks., wife, children:
John, Joseph, Ester, Mary, Sarah

Thomas Wood [ad], wife, children

The Success (miscalled Surrey in many records, as Shourd, and in Cushing and Sheppard; and as Surckress in Hinshaw), Stephen Nichols, master (Controller's Book E 190/74/1), loaded for New Jersey at London from 19 Aug. to 7 Sept. 1678; arrived April 1679. [g] probably having first stopped at Bermuda or in the Carribean. It brought:

William Biddulph [e], loaded 27 August.

William Crouch [e], loaded 19 August.

John Dent [e], loaded 4 September.

James Dunson [e], or Dennison, loaded 7 September.

Hugh Hartshorne [e], loaded 21 August.

[Allise Harvey] [g]

John Hawes [e], loaded 30 August.

Joseph Jackson [e], loaded 7 September.

Samuel Jackson [e], loaded 26 August.

Marmaduke Randall [e], loaded 31 August.

Thomas Woodruff or Woodrofe [g] of Gloucs., wife Edith; children: Thomas, Edith, John, Isaac, and Mary born at sea; and servant

Allise Harvey.

John Richardson [e] loaded gunpowder on 28 August, but is known to have come over later. Perhaps he came on this trip and returned. Edward Mann [e], a London merchant also loaded goods but is known to have remained in London. This is probably the "London ship" mentioned in Woodward and Hageman (page 10) and elsewhere, on which came:

Jonathan Eldridge [d]

Abraham Hewlings [d]

William Hewlings [d]

Thomas Kirby [d]

John Petty [d]

From arrival dates and master's name, as stated above, we also identify it as the Surrey on which Cushing and Sheppard (page 321) and Shourd (pages 143, 374) state that the following came.

Richard Durham [bf]

[Thomas Hoaten] [bf]

John Maddox [bf], wife Elizabeth, [daughter Elizabeth and her husband Richard Durham]; and servants: Thomas Oder, Thomas Hoaten, and Mary Stafford.

[Thomas Oder] [bf]

[Mary Stafford] [bf]

The same references state that Thomas Woodruff and his family came on the Surrey.

The Elizabeth and Sarah, Richard Friend, master (also identified as the Elizabeth and Mary) of Wemouth, Dorset, arrived probably 4th of 4th month (June) 1679, though the date of 29th of 3 month (May) appears in the Boare notation. Perhaps this was the date that she paused at New Castle. No loadings are seen for this ship.

William Biles [c] of Dorchester, co. Dorset, wife Johannah; children: William, George, John, Elizabeth, and Johannah; servants: Edward Hancock and Elizabeth Petty.

Charles Biles [c] of Dorchester.

Margaret Boare [c] "now of Norton Bavant, Wilts," wife of Joshua who came on Martha.

[Edward Hancock] [c]

Robert Lucas [c] of Deveral Longbridge, Wilts.

[Elizabeth Petty] [c]

The Jacob and Mary, Richard Moore, master, home port not seen, no loadings shown, arrived 12th of 7th month (Sept.) 1679. Two known families.

[Robert Benson] [c]

[Katharine Knight] [c]

Richard Ridgeway [c] of Welford, Berks, taylor, wife Elizabeth,
    son Thomas (perh. also earlier son Richard who died young.)

[Charles Thompson] [c]

Gilbert Wheeler [c] of London, wife Martha; Children: William,
    Briant, and Martha; servants: Charles Thompson, Robert Ben-
    son, Katharine Knight.

The Content of London, William Johnson, master (Port Book E
190/88/8, wool and leather) loaded 23 June 1680 for William Dpister or
Dempster, a London merchant who remained in England. The two known
passengers may have been loaded in Bristol or some other southern or
western port. She probably made stops at southern ports before she arrived
8th month (October) (though in one record in an obvious error, arrival is
indicated as 4th month (June), probably meaning that they boarded on that
date. Known passengers:

[James Craft] [c]

[Mary Craft] [c]

Samuel Dark [c] of London, calenderer, servants: James Craft, Mary
    Craft.

William Dark [c] of Chipping Camden, Gloucs., glover, (perhaps
    boarded 4th month). His wife Allis and son John came in the
    Charles in 1684.

Elizabeth Lucas [c], wife of Robert who came on the Elizabeth and
    Sarah. (Their children: John, Gile, Edward, Robert, Elizabeth,
    Rebecca, Mary, and Sarah, or just the older ones, may have
    come with their father. If not they came with Elizabeth.)

The Owners Advice of Bermuda, George Bond, master, arrived in
4th month (June) 1680. We do not know from which English port she loaded,
nor when. One passenger is reported.

Lionel Brittain [c] of Alney (Olney), Bucks., blacksmith, with wife
    Elizabeth, daughter Elizabeth who died as the ship came up
    Delaware Bay, buried at Burlington.

The Thomas and Anne, Thomas Singleton, master, loaded (Port
Book E 190/99/1) in London for New York, 3 May 1681 for Edward Mann,
merchant, and on 14 July for Elias Farr [j] already known to be in New Jersey.
There was also a loading on 3 May for Benjamin Hewlings who had gone on
the Greyhound. She sailed in mid-August, the last loading having been made
2 August. Known passengers:

William Biddle, [e] loaded 2 August.

Francis Collins, [e] loaded 26 July.

Thomas Crundall or Crandall [e], loaded 26 May.

Edward Ellis [e], loaded 26 May.

John Essington [e], loaded 3 May.

The date of her arrival is unknown, though probably in October. She then continued to Virginia.

The Owner's Adventure of London, Thomas Lurting, master [j], was chartered by Irish Friends and sailed to Dublin to load. There the master fell ill, and the mate John Dagger brought her to America.* She arrived in West New Jersey 9 month (November) 1681, but whether she unloaded at Perth Amboy and her passengers took the "King's Road" thence to Burlington, or whether she came up the Delaware is unknown. Only one family has been identified as aboard her.

Christopher Carary of Dublin, wife Elizabeth, daughter Rachel.

There undoubtedly were many other vessels that entered the Delaware during these years, and we may subsequently identify more of them. Smith's History (page 150) mentions one ship "of 550 tons" that ran aground in the Delaware in 1682, presumably on its way to Burlington, that the vessel was stranded for eight days, and that it brought 360 passengers. We can probably identify this ship as the Grayhound, Samuel Groome Jr. [j] master, which had come to New Jersey in 1682, stopping at New York and at Perth Amboy, at which latter point Groome landed and eventually built a house. The ship may then have gone on to Virginia, stopping en route in the Delaware. No passengers to the Delaware have been identified for her, but there are no loadings for Burlington in this year, and the Grayhound fits the description.

FINAL NOTE

Since the text above was prepared, the writer has noted in the April 1969 issue of The New Jersey Genesis, vol. 16, page 701, an inquiry numbered 1901 in which the "Quaker John Beals" is stated to have come to America on the Griffin in 1675. Correspondence with the author of the query led me to the source of this statement, which appears to be "Bales Families of East Tennessee" by Clarence A. Bales of Chicago, Ill. and Jefferson City, Tenn. However the author cites no evidence for this statement, and none has been seen by this author. It must therefore be concluded that John Beals above was not aboard this vessel.

---

* This is the same vessel as Ye Owners Choice. See "A Final Note on The Delaware Shipping", page 209.

148

REFERENCES

1. C. A. Weslager, The English on the Delaware, 1610-1682 (Rutgers University Press, 1967. Page 105 lists seven families of English planters in the Salem area "under Swedish jurisdiction", quoting Johnson's Swedish Settlements, 2:709.

2. Records of the Court of Upland 1676-1681, edited by Edward Armstrong, Memoirs of the Historical Society of Pennsylvania VII (1860).

3. History of Gloucester, Salem and Cumberland Counties, N. J., Thomas Cushing and Charles E. Sheppard (1883).

4. Samuel H. Smith, History of the Colony of Novo-Caesaria or New Jersey (Burlington, 1765, reprinted 1890).

5. History of Burlington and Mercer Counties, E. M. Woodward and J. F. Hageman (1883).

6. See pages   to   of this volume.

7. William Wade Hinshaw, Encyclopedia of American Quaker Genealogy (Ann Arbor, Mich. 1938) Vol. II.

8. New Jersey Archives, Series I, vol. I.

9. Thomas Shourd, History and Genealogy of Fenwick's Colony, (Bridgeton, N. J. 1876).

10. William Penn, His Own Account of the Lenni Lenape or Delaware Indians, Albert Cook Myers (Moylan, 1937) pages 60-61.

11. New Jersey Archives, Series 1, vol. XXI, Calendar of New Jersey Deeds, 1664-1703.

12. Woodward and Hageman, cit. page 9.

13. New Jersey Archives Series 1, vol. I p. 239.

Key to Citations on the Names of Immigrants.

a. Samuel Smith's History, cit. pp. 79, 99, 102, 108. Also Thomas Gordon's History of New Jersey (1834) (which quotes Smith) pp. 35, 38, 39.

b. Cushing and Sheppard, cit. pp. 16, 17, 316, 317.

c. Bucks County Arrivals, cit. (See this volume, pp.

d. Woodward and Hageman, cit. pp. 7-10.

e. Port Books, volumes as cited in each section.

f. Thomas Shourd's Fenwick's Colony, cit. pp. 85, 93, 103, 283, 350.

g. Hinshaw, cit. pp. 17, 24, 48.

h. New Jersey Archives, cit. see footnote 8.

j. Claypoole Letter Book, Marion Balderston (Huntington Library, 1967).

k. New Jersey Calendar of Deeds, cit. (footnote 11) pp. 172, 590-1.

m. Maj. John Fenwick, Frank H. Stewart (Woodbury, 1939), pp. 7, 8.

JOHN WEST AND THE *WELCOME*

By WALTER LEE SHEPPARD, JR., F.A.S.G.

Mrs. John Balderston, in abstracting the record books of the Port of London for the dutiable goods carried by the *Welcome*[1] which brought William Penn to the Delaware in October 1682, has noted that one John West shipped (loaded August 11th) red and white lead, and tinware, to the value of £24.10s. This was too small a shipment for a merchant but rather it suggests a stock brought for barter by a colonist.

John West has been identified as one of the First Purchasers of land in the new Colony of Pennsylvania, having bought 1250 acres from Penn. His name appears in group no. 35 in Penn's List,[2] and he also held an investment in the "Free Society."[3] The first warrant under his entitlement was for 500 acres in Oxford Township, and was issued 12th of the 8th month, 1682.[4]

The Friends' records, London Quarterly Meeting,[5] yield the following data:

Rebecca, b. 5 mo. 10d. 1663 parish of St. Sepulchre, London, to John and Mary West of the Peel St. John Street Meeting.
Benjamin, b. 8 mo.19d.1664 [*ibid.*].
Benjamin East of Brooks Wharf, London, sugar baker [elsewhere called "sugar boiler"] son of William East late of Tower St., London, mar. Hannah West, spinster, dau. John West, at the *Bull and Mouth*, 1 mo. 25d.1680.
Mary West, dau. John, citizen & freeman of London, mar. Simon Harris of London, upholsterer, 5mo.17d.1671.
Mary West d. of the plague 6mo.17d.1665, bur. at Bunhillfields.
James West d. 6mo.22d.1675, at St. Sepulchre parish, aged 19, son of John, "of a fever"; "of Westminster Meeting," bur. in Chequer Alley.
Mary, wife of John West, d. 10mo.8d.1680, aged 54 at Snow Hill, London, "of consumption," bur. in Chequer Alley.
Rebecca, dau. of John West, d. 7mo.25d.1682, aged about 19, at Snow Hill, of "a stoppage of the stomache."
John East, son of Benjamin and Hannah East, of [St.] Mary Somerset, London, b. 8mo.21d.1682 at Brooks Wharf.
John West, of London, citizen and girdler, married at Somerset House 22 of 7th mo. 1685, Mary Marsh, widow of Ralph Marsh, citizen & pewterer of London, of Devnshire House Meeting.
Mary, wife of John West of St. Sepulchre's parish, d. "of colleck" 11mo.30d.1698/99 aged 58.
John West, "tinman" d. at Wansworth, Surrey, of an "appoplexy or convulsions," 4mo.18d.1699 aged 76, of Snow Hill. Bur. in Chequer Alley.

John West of the parish of St. Sepulchre, London, citizen and girdler (i.e. member of the Girdlers, one of the ancient city companies of wealthy men of good character), left a will dated 20 May 1698, with a codicil dated 1 Nov. 1698, proven 1 July [1699?] at the Prerogative Court of Canterbury, from which a copy was supplied, 25 Jan. 1745, to the Court of Philadelphia, to be recorded and settle a title dispute over land in Oxford Township. This copy is in file 167 for the year 1747, and recorded in will book H, p. 317. Philadelphia Registry of Wills. This is a long will, of which the following is an abstract:

He directs that he be buried in or near "Bonehill Fields" [Bunhill Fields], co. Middlesex, in the burial place of the Quakers. To his son Benjamin he bequeaths only £5, since he has received his portion to the value of £500. To Sarah wife of son Benjamin £5. To grandson John West, one of the sons of Benjamin and Sarah, when 21, £50. Grandson Thomas Harris, son of Simon and Mary his wife "my daughter," both dead, when 21, £100. Grandson John Harris, one of the other sons of Simon and Mary, when 21 "fourscore" (i.e. £80) To granddaughter Mary West, one of the daughters of Richard and his wife Ann, when 21, £40. Grandson Richard West, son of Richard, when 21, £40. Granddaughter Ann West, one of the daughters of Richard and Ann, when 21, £40. Grandson John East, son of son-in-law Benjamin East deceased and Hannah his wife "my daughter" now residing in Pennsylvania, at 21, £50. Granddaughter Mary East, daughter of said John [obvious error for Benjamin] and Hannah his wife "my daughter" in Pennsylvania, when 21, £50. Grandson Benjamin Street, son of Daniel Street and Hannah his wife "my said daughter," at 21, £50. Said Daniel Street, my son-in-law, £5. If any of said grandchildren John East, Mary East, or Benjamin Street die under 21, their share to the survivors, equally, at 21. If all die under age, their shares to any other surviving children of daughter Hannah at 21. If all her children die under 21, then all their legacies equally divided between children of Benjamin and Richard and daughter Mary, in England, at 21. If all children of Benjamin, Richard and Mary die under age, their shares equally to Hannah's children. If all grandchildren die under 21, their shares to son Richard, heirs and assigns. Loving wife Mary £5. Ann Marsh, her daughter by her former husband, 50s. Mary Sellwood, her other daughter by her former husband, 50s. "My maidservant," 50s. Wife all messuages, lands and tennaments. All real estate whatsoever in America to grandchildren John East, Mary East, and Benjamin Street and heirs equally as tennants in common. Son Richard copyhold, messuage etc. with barn etc., in Wandsworth, co. Surrey, held of lord of said manor, and also freehold messuage in Banbury, co. Oxford, now in the hands of Salathiel Gardner, which testator recommends be sold to pay debts etc. Two leases from the Worshipful Company of Sadlers, for two messuages on Snow Hill parish of St. Sepulchre without Newgate, London, at 40s. rent per annum, one known by the sign of the *Crown*, "now in my tenure," the other by the sign of the *Bull* now in the tenure of Rowland Steward, rents to provide for daughter in law Sarah, wife of Bemjamin and her children. Hannah Street now in Pennsylvania a rentcharge or annuity of £10 out of rent for the *Bull* from Rowland Steward for the term of the lease [not stated] and £7 per annum to Benjamin out of the *Bull*. These two messuages also subject to annuities to son Richard. Bequests to friends John Edge of Hatton Garden, Peter Briggins of Bartholomew Close; £4 to the poor of "Peel Street Meeting" and £16 for putting out four apprentices from poor but honest of Meeting. £4 to the vicar of St. Sepulchre for putting out one poor but honest apprentice. Remits all debts of his brother Thomas West, and nephew Tom Axton, late of Princes Risborn [Risborough] co. Bucks. Debts to be paid by son Richard out of the Wandesborough inheritance. "Son John West stands bound to me by bond," dated 18 May 1675 for £600. [The description of this bond is confusing.] Bond is for property in Croudon in Bucks. John the son was in default of £325. If estate fell short of legal payments, John was to pay £100 of that in default, and was released from the balance of the bond, and of another bond for £50 to "my wife Mary." The codicil indicates a change in the status of this Croudon property which at date of codicil was under bond to Richard for £400, dated 7 Oct. 1698, and this property was now to go equally to son Benjamin and grandson Thomas Harris. [There appears no indication of what happened to the son John. Perhaps he was dead without issue or a wife.]

Benjamin East, John West's son-in-law, was also a First Purchaser of 1250 acres from William Penn.[6] His first survey was made 30th of 6th month [i.e. August] 1682, being 585 acres "up Tacony Creek" in Oxford Township,[7] Philadelphia County. With his wife Hannah, Benjamin East of Philadelphia "mart" [merchant?] sold two lots of land: the first 28th of 1st month (March) 1685, 200 acres in Oxford Township for £20 to Thomas Graves, adjoining William East, part of a grant from William Penn 13 Oct. 1681 [date of his purchase from Penn]. He gave power of attorney, 18 July 1685, to William O'Rion of Philadelphia, blacksmith, to deliver the property to Thomas Graves;[8] the second, 16 Nov. 1685, for £5, two lots in the city of Philadelphia totalling 25 acres, to Barnabas Wilcox, obtained by warrant from William Penn 16 of 5 month 1684. The following day he gave power of attorney to Robert Longshore to make delivery of the property.[9]

On 16 Aug. 1683, Benjamin East "of Brooks Wharf, London, sugar baker," made an agreement with John West of Exeter and Richard West of London, fishmonger, to protect the dowery of his wife Hannah East "in natural love and affection" in case she should outlive him. He mentions 700 acres and messuage in Pennsylvania, part of his 1250 acres allotment as the dower. This was "sealed in the presence of Charles Marshall, John West, and George Shyets," though the place where it was signed is not shown. It was recorded in Philadelphia 3rd day 4th month 1701.[10]

The only Philadelphia deed specifically indexed under the name of John West is one in Book E-7, vol. 9, p. 292, drawn in 1689. This deals with the sale of some land of Richard Whitpain of London to pay his creditors, one of whom was John West.

John West was in Philadelphia when a house lot survey was made to him[11] on the Schuylkill side of Philadelphia between Second and Front and between Mulberry and High Streets, and adjoining a lot surveyed the same day to Benjamin East, who was also present. The two men had a second set of lots, also adjoining each other. Note that the date of the above quoted dower agreement was soon thereafter, and made in England, when Benjamin was called "of London." But he was back in Pennsylvania when additional surveys were made to him in 1684,[12] and he was "of Philadelphia" when he conveyed in 1685. His death must have occurred shortly thereafter since Hannah East married, 16 Jan. 1686/7, at her own house, Daniel Street.[13] Henry A. Street and Mary A. Street in *The Street Genealogy* (1895), state that Daniel was born in 1658 and died Thursday, 20 July 1738, aged 80. Hannah's children by Benjamin East are listed as: John East, born in 1682, and Mary East, born 23 Aug. 1685. The Street children are given as Benjamin, born 26 Feb. 1688, and James, born 26 Aug. 1692; married Mary Griffith, this line continued. The dates are stated to be from a family Bible printed in 1696. Hannah (West) (East) Street is stated to have died in August 1706, "aged 71," which appears most unlikely, as she would have married for the first time at 45, had her first child at 47, and been born when her father was 12. Why John West did not know about and include this youngest grandchild in his will is a puzzle. However, it seems clear that James *was* Hannah's youngest child, since he inherited some of his father's property.

The West lands were apparently subject of litigation nearly a century later, since the Edward Cary Gardner manuscript collection in the Historical Society of Pennsylvania includes notes of a title search made in this period, and some notes of John West's will, adding that of the three named grandchildren, John East died without issue; Mary married Joseph Cook and had four children (though it names only three, to wit: Benjamin, John and Rebecca Miller).[14] Benjamin Street sold 100 acres to Jno. Clayton, and 210 acres in Montgomery County to Thomas, David and John Edwards.

A much fuller history of the interlocking East and West properties is contained in the records of the "Norris of Fairhill Manuscripts" in the same collection. The bulk of the material is found in the volume on Philadelphia County, p. 112 to 121, though they are mentioned on page 36 of the Chester and Montgomery County volume. Besides several of the original warrants and surveys, there are the following two lists of properties for each man.

For John West, "purchaser of 1250 acres:"

Warrant for a front lot   15   4m   1683   surveyed 20th same month.
Warrant for 25 acres of Liberty Land   14   4m   1683   no survey.
Warrant for High Sreet lot   14   4m   1683   surveyed 21st same month.
Warrant for 500 acres   12   8m   1682   [survey date not given].
Warrant for 500 acres   30   7m   1684   [survey date not given].
Warrant for 200 acres   [no date given]   [survey date not given].

Lands laid out for Benjamin East "purchaser of 1250 acres:"

30th of ye 6th mo 1682 five hundred eighty five acres up Tacony Creek by warrent from Thos. Holmes, same month and year, pursuant to order of Governor and Council.
Surveyed 2d of 11mo 1685   640 acres on Neshaminy Creek, Bucks, by warrant from the Governor dated 26 4m 1684.
A warrant dated 19 Dec. 1684 for 200 acres in Newcasle Co. [Delaware, part of Penn's patent] no return of survey found.[15]
Warrant for Liberty Land dated 16   5m   1684. No return.
His lots were laid out on Schuylkill side, one on Front St., the other on High St., 14   4m   1683.[16]

In addition to the properties shown above in the rights of John West and Benjamin East, the Norris papers contain the original of another warrant, dated 5 8ber 1701, from William Penn to Daniel Street, granting him 500 acres in right of John West, purchaser of 1250 acres, "who in his last will and testament devised same to his grandchildren, the children of Hannah his daughter, present wife of Daniel Street. . . . These caused to be surveyed to the said Daniel Street. To Edward Pennington, surveyor."

The Norris papers supply further data (to 1750) on the West grandchildren and their heirs as follows [condensed and abstracted]:

John West's daughter Hannah married Benjamin East and had children: John East who died s. p. at sea, aged about 20 years [actually he was 25]; "Cordwainer," died intestate 1707, unmarried; and Mary East who married Joseph Cook and had three children to wit: John, Mary [later corrected to Rebecca], and Hannah. Benjamin East died and his wife Hannah married secondly, Daniel Street, and had two sons: Benjamin Street, "the father of the present Benjamin Street," and James Street, who had several children. [Due to the wording of the will, James and his descendants did not inherit, and their descendants are not followed]. The share of John East descended to his sister Mary as heir at law [since he died over age, not 20 as the notes indicate]. Both Mary Cook and her husband Joseph died intestate. Their son John Cook died leaving issue, a son John and a daughter Mary "who lives at James Morgan's in Frankford," who had a right to 1/2 of 2/3.[17] "Rebecca, wife of William Miller has right to 1/4 of 2/3. Hannah, wife of Isaiah Atkins has right to same." Benjamin Street [son of Daniel and Hannah] the other devisee died intestate leaving issue a son Benjamin Street, "his only child, who now has a right to 1/3" the lands in Pennsylvania.

At the end of these records are powers of attorney signed by the heirs named, most of them originals, specifically those of Henry Atkins, merchant of Boston,[18] dated 4 Oct. 1745; Isaiah Atkins and wife

Hannah, daughter of Joseph Cook dec'd and Mary, etc., also to Griffiths, dated 7 April 1749 from Barnstable, Mass., signed by both and witnessed by Rebecca Miller; from Henry Atkins, Jr., of Boston, dated 21 April 1750; Benjamin Street of Boston, mariner, 12 May 1746; and Rebecca Miller of Philadelphia, wife of William Miller of Kent County, Del., dated 11 Oct. 1748. Isaac Griffiths of Philadelphia was attorney for all of them. Also included are some of the original deeds of sale, including that of Benjamin East.

Mrs. Balderston has most kindly supplied some interesting information about William East, Benjamin's brother, whose property adjoined that of Benjamin. He was master of the *Hester and Hannah*, which was loading in March, and arrived in the Delaware 8 Aug. 1682. He also was a Quaker and had taken up, by an agent, a city lot for himself, 17 April of the same year. After the arrival of his ship he remained several months in Pennsylvania; subsequently Penn made him the master of his personal ship the *Gulielma* which was named after Penn's wife.[19]

It is clear that Benjamin East was in Pennsylvania by August 1682 to take out his first warrant, the 29th, and to order his first survey on the day following. It is equally clear that his wife was still in England, where she bore his first child at the same time the *Welcome* was sailing up the Delaware. Since the *Hester and Hannah* had arrived just three weeks earlier than his warrant and survey, it seems more than probable that Benjamin sailed to Pennsylvania in his brother's ship. He would then have taken out the first warrant for his father-in-law, John West, at the same time that he took out his own, and probably took out the second for him as well. Presumably he would have turned these over to West upon his arrival, and West himself would have ordered his first survey on 25 Nov. 1682. At all events we know he was in Philadelphia in the following spring when he took out the warrants for his city lots.

John West shipped trading goods on the *Welcome*. The average colonist can not have been too happy about sending goods to America without a responsible person accompanying them. It is certain that he arrived before late spring, and most probable that he was in Pennsylvania by late November. Though there are a number of ships that he might have come on, the *Welcome* would appear the most probable.

REFERENCES

1. "The Real *Welcome* Passengers" by Marian Balderston, The *Huntington Library Quarterly*, November 1962, vol. 26, p.31-56. See especially "The Case for John West," p. 55-6.

2. *Pennsylvania Archives*, 3rd Ser., vol. 3, p. 343; 1st Ser., vol. 1, p. 39 *et seq.*; Samuel Hazard's *Annals of Philadelphia*, p. 637-642.

3. *Pennsylvania Magazine of History and Biography*, vol. 11, p. 179.

4. The "Norris of Fairhill manuscripts" (quoted p. 277) give a tabulation of his warrants but do not include this one. The first warrant there listed is dated 12th the 8th month, 1682, and this was probably taken from the Proprietor's records at Harrisburg though this date may be an error. However, this earlier one is disclosed in the bodies of two survey records, made against it, as follows: "Warrants and Surveys, Province of Pennsylvania, 1682-1759," in the Philadelphia Municipal Archives, vol. 3, p. 590, records under date of 5th of 5th month 1684, the return of a survey of 200 acres in Oxford Township, made 29th of 9th month

1683, to John West "by virtue of a warrant dated 29th day 6th month 1682 to John West." This is the same date as that of the first warrant taken out by Benjamin East (John West's son-in-law, see p. 278), and recorded immediately below this return is that of Benjamin East for 585 acres in the same township, bounded by John West, Henry Waddy, and vacant land, his survey being made on the 30th of the 6th month 1682, against East's warrant of the preceding day. In West's survey, his bounds are shown as Benjamin East, Nehemiah Mitchell, and vacant land. Since East's survey was made first, even though the warrants were issued the same day, it seems likely that these bounds were entered by the surveyor when he made his return, some time later.

John West's earliest survey also appears in these books (not noted in the Norris papers), recorded (*not* a return) in his survey books by Thomas Holme, Surveyor General ("Warrents and Surveys," vol. 6 p. 122), "by virtue of a warrant dated 29th of 6 month 1682 (directed to me)" and shows that he surveyed for West, against this warant on 25th of 9th month 1682, 200 acres in Oxford Township.

5. Taken from the tabulated copies of the London and Middlesex Quarterly Meeting, made by Gilbert Cope, in the files of the Historical Society of Pennsylvania. These transcripts have been abbreviated and given more uniform spelling for the purposes of this article. For instance, the monthly meeting to which the Wests belonged was Peel St. John Street Meeting, often called simply Peel, or Peel Street, sometimes Pell. The parish in which they lived, St. Sepulchre, is written in a variety of ways, including "Pulcher's."

6. Hazard, *op. cit.* p. 637-642; *Pennsylvania Archives*, 1st Ser., vol. 1, p. 39 *et seq.*; 3rd Ser., vol. 3, p. 331, 366.

7. *Ibid*, 3rd Ser., vol. 2, p. 585, 699.

8. Philadelphia Deeds, book E-1, vol. 5, p. 108, 111.

9. *Ibid*, E-1, vol. 5, p. 458, 460.

10. *Ibid*, C-2, p. 159.

11. *Pennsylvania Archives*, 3rd Ser., vol. 1, p. 50, 51; vol. 2, p. 699. Warrant for city lot 14th 4 mo. 1683, and a second the day following. Survey: 20th 4 month [June] 1683. "Warrants and Surveys," *op. cit.*, vol. 3, p. 234, 235; vol. 2, p. 130. Benjamin East's city lots were surveyed the same day and adjoined Wests. Prior to Penn's arrival his deputy, Markham, handled all these warrants and surveys. Rarely did Markham's record indicate whether the documents were issued to the owner or to his agent. However, when Penn arrived and took over, these records became much more complete. Penn was always careful to indicate whether a document was issued to an agent or the actual owner. For this reason, since no agent is shown, we can be certain that John West was present when the warrant was issued for his lots, though he need not necessarily have been present when the actual survey was made. In the case of the first Oxford Township survey, it would appear most likely that he had been given the warrant by East, who had picked it up as his agent, and West had then delivered it to Thomas Holmes to be surveyed.

12. *Pennsylvania Archives*, 3rd Ser., vol. 2, p. 696. He took out a warrant for 640 acres, 26th 4 month 1684, and one for another city lot, 16th 5 month 1684.

13. *Ibid*, 2nd Ser., vol. 8, p. 7.

14. See Lewis D. Cook, "Isaiah Atkins of Truro, Mass., and Hannah Cook of Philadelphia," *The American Genealogist* vol. 20, p. 193-199.

15. See also *Pennsylvania Archives*, 2nd Ser., vol. 7, p. 194.

16. He held an additional warrant, dated 16 5mo 1684, for city lots (*Pennsylvania Archives*, 3rd Ser., vol. 2, p. 696), the same date as above Liberty Land warrant, but apparently Norris did not find this one.

17. This corrects Mr. Cook's article cited above, which states (p. 195) under John Cook "apparently also died intestate and without issue."

18. Isaiah and Hannah (Cook) Atkins had, with others, a son Henry Atkins, b. 4 May 1743 (*The American Genealogist*, vol. 2, p. 198, *op. cit.*).

19. *Pennsylvania Archives*, 2nd Ser., vol. 19, p. 533: Under date of "20th 8ber 1712" "John Test" [*sic*] sold, 23 Apr. 1683, to "William West, master of he Govern ship Gulielma, whose Relict Esther and Sole [surviving] Daughter and heiress Elizabeth, with their present Husbands, Richard Cary, Ciizen and Merchant Taylor of London who married [the] widow and Thomas Jackson of Dartford, coun. Kent, Carpenter, Conveyed the Same by Deeds . . . dat. the 19th and 20th of 7ber, 1711, to James Logan." See also *ibid.*, p. 38; and 3rd Ser., vol. 2, p. 697, for other references to William West.

MRS. THOMAS WYNNE OF PHILADELPHIA AND HER FAMILY:

Corrections to the Pedigrees of Wynne and Maude

By Francis James Dallett, f.g.s.p.

Dr. Thomas Wynne, the Welsh physician who accompanied William Penn to Philadelphia on the ship *Welcome* in 1682 and founded an historic Philadelphia family, has heretofore been credited with three wives: first, Martha Buttall of Wrexham, Denbighshire, Wales, the mother of his children; secondly, a widow Rawden (Rowden); and thirdly, the widow Elizabeth Maud (correctly, *Maude*), whom he married 20 5m 1676, not in Wales but in England, at Rainhill, Lancashire, under the care of the Monthly Meeting of Friends of Hardshaw East in that county, and who followed him to Pennsylvania.[1]

The first marriage is correct. The relationship of Mrs. Wynne as the daughter of Randle Buttall of Wrexham, is established by her father's will.[2]

The name of the so-called "second" Mrs. Wynne has been inferred from the known fact that Thomas Wynne had a stepdaughter, Elizabeth Rowden (Rawden) who was granted liberty by the Philadelphia Monthly

---

[1] The Quaker certificate of marriage from the Lancashire Friends records is printed in Thomas Allen Glenn, *Merion in the Welsh Tract. . . .* (Norristown, 1896), 264. Thomas Wynne, chirurgeon, the groom, was then a resident of Caerwys, Flintshire, Wales. His bride Elizabeth Maud [*sic*] was of Rainhill, Lancashire, seven miles east of Liverpool. There are no ship lists, in the modern sense, for early English arrivals in Pennsylvania, such as are extant for German immigrants. Pursuant to a law passed at New Castle in 1684, however, directing inhabitants then in the Province, and those who should arrive thereafter, to register themselves, an attempt was made to list these first arrivals. For two such extant lists, made between 1682 and 1687, see *The Pennsylvania Magazine of History and Biography*, VIII (1884), 328-340, and *ibid.*, IX (1885), 223-233, hereinafter cited as *PMHB*. For a compiled list from miscellaneous sources of the *Welcome's* passengers, see J. Thomas Scharf and Thompson Westcott, *History of Philadelphia, 1609-1884* (Philadelphia, 1884), I, 99-100. Thomas Wynne's name is included in this list, but not his wife's. For further information on the *Welcome's* passenger list, see George E. McCracken, "Welcome Notes," *The American Genealogist*, Vol. 38 (July, 1962), 152. The log of the ship *Submission*, which sailed at the same time as the *Welcome*, includes a list of passengers "near as cold be well taken;" on this appear the names of Wynne's daughter Rebecca, then aged 20, and step-daughters Marjory Mede, aged 11, and Jane Mede, aged 15, the surname properly being Maude. The inference follows that Wynne's wife came on a later ship, as yet unidentified. See *Publications of the Genealogical Society of Pennsylvania*, I, 9-10, hereinafter cited as *PGSP*.

[2] For abstract of the will of Randle Buttall, see *PMHB*, XL (1916), 239-240. Thomas and Martha (Buttall) Wynne had five daughters and one son, all presumably born in Wales: 1. Mary Wynne, b. *ca.* 1659, who m. *ca.* 1677 in Wales, Dr. Edward Jones of Merion; 2. Rebecca Wynne, b. *ca.* 1662, who m. 1st in Talbot Co., Md., 3m 1685, Solomon Thomas, and 2nd, 23 7m 1692, John Dickinson; 3. Sydney Wynne, who m. in Anne Arundel Co., Md., 20 10m 1690, William Chew; 4. Hannah Wynne, who m. 25 8m 1695, Daniel Humphreys; 5. Tabitha Wynne; 6. Jonathan Wynne, who m. *ca.* 1694, Sarah, surname not proven.

Meeting of Friends on 5 6m 1684, to marry John Brock of Falls Monthly Meeting.[3]

The alleged "third" Mrs. Wynne has been the subject of printed study since at least 1896, not because of her husband Thomas Wynne, but because her former husband, Joshua Maude (1627-1672) of the Cliffs,[4] Wakefield, Yorkshire, was the grandfather of Joshua Fisher (1707-1783), the colonial Philadelphia shipowner.[5] His many descendants have long been aware of their armigerous ancestor Joshua Maude. The interest of the antiquarian-minded Fishers in their family origins has resulted in a series of genealogical studies which, insofar as the earlier generations are concerned, unfortunately contain many misstatements of fact.

It may now be stated in print that each genealogy which has dealt

[3] William Wade Hinshaw, *Encyclopedia of American Quaker Genealogy* (Ann Arbor, Mich., 1938), II, 641, 1024. Thomas Wynne is described, in the old manner, as "father in law" of Elizabeth Rowden, in the intentions of marriage declared before the Philadelphia Monthly Meeting 1 5m 1684, at which time Wynne "together with his wife," was about to depart for England. Minutes of the Philadelphia Monthly Meeting, I, 18-19, quoted in full on pages 14-15 of Alfred R. Justice's "Maude of West Riddlesden, Yorkshire," Alfred R. Justice Collection, Vol. 16, 5, in Collections of the Genealogical Society of Pennsylvania, hereinafter cited as Justice, GSP. Elizabeth Rowden presumably had just arrived in Pennsylvania when she witnessed the will of Richard ap Thomas "late of Whitford garden in flintshire" on 18 9m 1683. *PGSP*, III, 165. The *Morning Star* of Liverpool, on which Thomas, and no doubt Elizabeth Rowden, had sailed, had arrived about 14 9m 1683. *PMHB*, IV (1880), 319; *ibid.*, IX (1885), 233. Charles H. Browning, *Welsh Settlement of Pennsylvania* (Philadelphia, 1912), 209, gives the date of arrival as 16 Nov. 1683.

[4] Son of John and Sarah Maude of Alverthorpe Hall, near Wakefield, Yorkshire, Joshua Maude was bapt. at Wakefield 21 Apr. 1627; in 1663 he was Churchwarden of Wakefield. See Joseph Foster, *Pedigrees of the County Families of Yorkshire* (London, 1874), I, under pedigree of "Maude of Alverthorpe." Letters of administration were granted on his estate 22 Apr. 1672 to his widow Elizabeth. See page 10 of Justice, GSP, Vol. 16, 5, *loc. cit.*, wherein is cited, with misspelling, the Probate Register of Pontefract with Halifax, 1672, folio 78. *Cf.* Anna Wharton Smith, *Genealogy of the Fisher Family, 1682-1896* (Philadelphia, 1896), 14, wherein it is stated Joshua Maude, whose name is incorrectly given as Maud throughout, died in 1675. This work, and the earlier *Recollections of Joshua Francis Fisher: Written in 1864* (not published until 1929 when it was edited by Sophia Cadwalader) both state Joshua Maude inherited the parental home of his father, The Cliffs, whereas the parental home, Alverthorpe Hall, was inherited by Joshua's elder brother Daniel Maude.

[5] Joshua Fisher, son of Margery Maude, daughter of Joshua, and Thomas Fisher, was successively hatter, surveyor and importer; he established in Philadelphia a leading line of trans-Atlantic shipping packets shortly after the middle of the eighteenth century. On land bequeathed to him by his father at Cool Spring, Sussex County, Del., he built a small half-timbered house, nogged with brick and weatherboarded, which is now being restored by Fisher descendants. Harold Donaldson Eberlein has claimed that the house, standing in 1736 when Joshua Fisher sold it, was probably built by Joshua's father, Thomas Fisher. It was, however, the son's project. In the will of the father, written in 1713 just before his death, Thomas Fisher left 500 unimproved acres of the Cold (Cool) Spring land to his son Joshua, and expressed the hope that "when my children comes to age that they shall be admitted to seats on some part of their respective Land. . . ." Smith, *op. cit.*, 18, 19. Thomas Fisher himself lived at Fisher's Island, in Broadkill Marsh, formerly the property of his wife Margery Maude's stepfather, Thomas Wynne. It is interesting to note that Joshua Fisher, the hatter-merchant, was second cousin to the Reverend Sir William Lowther, M.A., 1st Baronet (1707-1788) of Little Preston, Yorkshire, prebendary of York and rector of Swillington, whose son was created first Earl of Lonsdale. The baronet's grandfather, Daniel Maude who inherited Alverthorpe Hall, and Joshua Fisher's grandfather, Joshua Maude, were brothers. See Foster, *op. cit.*

with the marriage of Mrs. Maude and Dr. Wynne has been in error, and that the compounded errors may be wiped out by the simple citation of one printed record which has been available for more than half a century.

"Paver's Marriage Licenses, Volume II" in the *Yorkshire Archeological Society Record Series*, Volume XLIII (1909), page 110, publishes an abstract of the license issued in the year 1667 to "Joshua Maude, gentleman. 38, Wakefield," and "Elizabeth Rawden, widow, 34, Drax." [6] From this it is evident that when the Widow Maude married Dr. Wynne in 1676, she herself had been married not once before, but twice; her first husband had been a Mr. Rawden [7] and her second Joshua Maude. Thus she, not the other vague and actually non-existent second wife of Dr. Wynne, was the mother of Elizabeth (Rowden, Rawden) Brock. Thomas Wynne's supposed third wife was in fact identical with his second wife, but he was *her* third husband.

Equally confused have been the supposed origins of Elizabeth Rawden Maude Wynne herself. It has been claimed that she was born Elizabeth Parr, "a daughter of the Rev. Thomas Parr, who married a sister of John Bradshaw, President of Parliament at the trial and condemnation of King Charles," and that the Reverend Thomas Parr, "chaplain to John Bradshaw, was a Puritan clergyman, and was of the family of Catherine Parr." [8] Unfortunately these fascinating relationships are false, and even

---

[6] When Joshua Maude married Elizabeth Rawden he himself was a widower, with four children, all baptized at Wakefield between 1659 and 1664: Penelope, Joshua, Jr., Sarah and Joyce Maude. Foster, *op. cit.* After his marriage to Elizabeth Rawden, he and she evidently were both soon converted to Quakerism, for their children, Jane Maude, b. *ca.* 1667, and Margery Maude, b. *ca.* 1671, were not baptized in the Established Church. *Jane Maude* m. 1st at Lewes, Del., 15 7m 1687, Isaac Bowde who was deceased by 6 7m 1692, when letters were granted to his widow Jane *Scott.* She m. 3rd, apparently, one Lucas, probably a widower with small children, for her 4th husband, Cornelius Wiltbanck in Feb. 1705 was ordered by Sussex County Court to provide for them, Wiltbanck then being married to Jane (Maude) Bowde Scott Lucas. See PGSP, XII, 195n, and *ibid.*, XVIII, 27. She d. without issue after 21 Jan. 1717/18 and before 1720 when Wiltbanck m. his 2nd wife, the widow Hannah (Kollock) White. *Margery Maude* m. 1st at Lewes, Del., in 1692, Thomas Fisher, who d. between 17 Nov. 1713, when he wrote his will, and 8 2m 1717, when his widow Margery was wife of one *Green. Pennsylvania Archives*, 2nd Series, XIX, 678; Smith, *op. cit.*, 14, 199. Nothing is known of the daughters of Joshua Maude by his first wife, but their brother Joshua, Jr., bapt. at Wakefield 26 Nov. 1662, who inherited The Cliffs (claimed in Smith, 14, to be issue of his father's second marriage, but was in fact of the first marriage) is said to have married Elizabeth, daughter of John Nott of Sheldesley Beauchamp. See page 13 of Justice, GSP, Vol. 16, 5, *loc. cit.*, wherein the reference given is *Familiae Minorum Gentium*, 620. The statement made by Mr. Justice, that they had a daughter Sarah Maude who married a James Miers, is open to question, inasmuch as Margery (Maude) Fisher's son, Joshua Fisher (1707-1783), married Sarah Rowland (1716-1772), of Sussex County, Del., whose mother was Sarah Miers, daughter of John Miers of the same place. The coincidence of these names calls for further investigation.

[7] Rawden was a well known Yorkshire name, but the identity of Elizabeth's first husband is unknown. He may have been the John Rawden of Wistow, whose estate was probated 12 July 1667, the year of Elizabeth's marriage to Joshua Maude. "Index of the Wills and Administrations entered in the Registers of the Archbishops at York, being Consistory Wills, &c.," *Yorkshire Archaeological Society Record Series*, XCIII (1936), 60, citing Register Vol. 33, folio 89. More probably, her first husband, Mr. Rawden, was of Drax, her residence at the time of her remarriage.

[8] Smith, *op. cit.*, 14n.

the identity of the individuals mentioned is much garbled.

There was no traceable clergyman in England in the seventeenth century named Thomas Parr.[9] John Bradshaw's chaplain was *John* Parr who, inasmuch as he was approximately the same age as Mrs. Rawden Maude, could not have been her father.[10] Another writer has stated that Mrs. Maude was "a person possessing considerable property and belonging to an influential family of Flintshire."[11] It is unlikely that Mrs. Maude ever set foot in Wales or had any interest in it until her third marriage to a Welshman.

Alfred R. Justice, one of Philadelphia's leading genealogists a generation ago, states unequivocally in a genealogical study, apparently never heretofore noticed in print, that Elizabeth Rawden Maude Wynne was born Elizabeth Chorley, one of ten children of John Chorley, armiger, of Rainhill, Lancashire, by his wife Elizabeth, daughter of Hugh Ley of Liverpool.[12] Mr. Justice extensively developed the Chorley pedigree. In view of the fact that Elizabeth's marriage to Thomas Wynne took place at John Chorley's house, and that John Chorley, Alexander Chorley and Faith Chorley were witnesses (Justice's theory would make the men her brothers), this statement is quite possibly correct.

It should be noted, however, that Drax, Elizabeth's home as Mrs. Rawden, and Wakefield, her home as Mrs. Maude, were both in Yorkshire, many miles northeast of Rainhill in Lancashire. While it would have been logical for a widow with two families of minor children to return to her parental home, there is as yet no proof that Rainhill, where she married Thomas Wynne in 1676, was such. A closer examination of Yorkshire and Lancashire probate records and other source material would likely solve the question.

---

[9] Prior to the middle of the seventeenth century, when non-conformist clergy began to gain pulpits without Anglican ordination, all English clergy were educated at Oxford or Cambridge. A check of Foster's *Alumni Oxonienses* and of Venn's *Alumni Cantabrigienses*, will always establish a cleric's existence. No clergyman named Thomas Parr is found in either work.

[10] *Dictionary of National Biography* (New York, 1895), XLIII, 354-355. The Regicide's chaplain was of the Parr family of Prescot Par, Lancashire, the parish in which Rainhill is located, and Elizabeth Rawden Maude Wynne's residence in 1676. Possibly her American descendants may have had a tradition of some remote Parr relationship, or the "Par" in the parish name may have been twisted into a family name for her.

[11] T. B. Deem, *The Wynnes, a Genealogical Summary of the Ancestry of the Welsh Wynnes, Who Emigrated to Pennsylvania with William Penn* (Indianapolis, Ind., 1907), 204. This work, the basic Wynne genealogy, should be used with extreme caution; it is full of errors.

[12] See page 8 of "Chorley of Chorley, Lancashire," Justice, GSP, Vol. 5, 75, in which she is #43 of that record.

THE PHILADELPHIA AND BUCKS COUNTY
REGISTERS OF ARRIVALS

Compared, Corrected and Re-transcribed by
Hannah Benner Roach

In 1881, a transcript of the original register of arrivals in the 1680's at Philadelphia (deposited in the Historical Society of Pennsylvania) first appeared in print in The History of Chester County by J. Smith Futhey and Gilbert Cope. It was followed in 1884, in Volume VIII of The Pennsylvania Magazine of History and Biography, by a second transcript of the same register.

In 1885, a transcript of the Bucks County register of arrivals appeared in Volume IX of the latter publication, taken, it was said, from "a certified copy of the original in possession of the Historical Society." Then in 1887, J. H. Battle published in his History of Bucks County, a transcript of the Bucks register which was taken, he stated, from the original in the "Register's Office" in the court house at Doylestown. Except for the form in which he printed it, however, it followed exactly the earlier transcript which had appeared in 1885 in The Pennsylvania Magazine.

None of these transcripts was an exact verbatim et literatum copy of the original records. Of them all, the copy of the Philadelphia record in The History of Chester County was the most accurate so far as the interpretation of proper names is concerned. Whoever transcribed the Philadelphia record for The Pennsylvania Magazine was not sufficiently familiar with the idiosyncracies of seventeenth-century calligraphy, so that a number of names were misinterpreted. With the permission of the Historical Society of Pennsylvania, the following new transcript corrects those errors in spelling.

According to the researches of Dr. George E. McCracken, the Bucks County register exists in two contemporary copies, one in the Historical Society of Pennsylvania, and one in the Bucks County Historical Society at Doylestown. Both are in the handwriting of Phinehas Pemberton and both are largely, though not entirely, identical in text.

The copy now in the Historical Society of Pennsylvania presumably Pemberton sent to the Register General's Office in Philadelphia. The other copy Pemberton retained in his own possession as Register for Bucks County. Upon his death in 1701, the record was not delivered to his successor, but was retained by the family. In 1843, it was held by James Pemberton Park, Esq., who kindly consented to return it to the Bucks County Courts. At that time two careful copies of this original Pemberton record were made — one for Mr. Park and one for Charles Roberts, Esq., who appears to have located the original. In 1938, one of these 1843 copies was bequeathed to the Bucks County Historical Society, where it now reposes, by Miss Elizabeth Ely of Lambertville, Pa. An account of its provenance is appended to it. The original Pemberton record, now carefully laminated,

is also in the custody of the Bucks County Historical Society. According to
Dr. McCracken, it was that version, and not the record sent to Philadelphia
and now in the Historical Society of Pennsylvania, which was followed when
the text was printed in 1885 in Volume IX of The Pennsylvania Magazine.

Since the Bucks register in Philadelphia includes names which do not
appear in the record retained by Pemberton, it has therefore been deemed
advisable to publish it. The original manuscript is arranged in three columns headed "Free Passengers", "Children", and "Servants", with the time
of servitude and wages of the latter indicated. These have been rearranged
so as to run together with appropriate words inserted in brackets where the
meaning otherwise would not be clear. The spelling and capitalization of
the original have been maintained as closely as possible, but superscript
letters and numbers have been lowered. Where necessary, data no longer
entirely legible in the original, but included in the 1885 transcript, are also
placed in brackets. Minor punctuation has been inserted to clarify the
transposition from the original columnar listing.

A PORTION OF

REGISTRY OF ARRIVALS AT PHILAD[A]

1682 - 1686

1682 9 10mo The Antelope of Bellfast arrived here from Ireland.
James Attkinson arrived here and Jno. Ashbrooke his Servant per 5 yr.

The Morning Starr Thomas Hayes master Arrived from Leverpoole in England about the 20th 9 mo 168[3].
Henry Atherly Shoomaker a freeman.
John Loftus Husbandman a ffreeman from Leverpoole.
Wm Morgan & Elizabeth his Wife both free arrived at Philadelphila in the same Ship from Leverpoole in ye 9th Month 1683.

The Jeffries Thomas Arnold m[ast]er from London Arrived 20 1 mo 168[6].
Johannes Cassel a German his Children Arnold, Peter, Elizabeth, Mary, Sarah.
Sarah Shoemaker of the Palatinate Widdow, Georg 23 years old, Abraham 19, Barbary 20, Isaack 17, Susanna 13, Elizabeth 11, Benjamine 10, all her Children.
Joseph Ransted Gardner from London.

28th 11th m 1687 The Margaret from London arrived here from London John Bowman Comander.
Pasco Belitho Servant to John Tizack bound at London for fower years next ensueing his arrival in this province, & Registered in the new office in London erected by Letters Patent for that purpose.

John Colly late of Saviour Southwork in old England ffeltmaker came in the Eliz: & Mary John Bowman M[ast]er arrived here ye 22 7 mo 1683.

In the Endeaver of London a Ketch Geo: Thorp M[ast]er:
Fran: Rosell late of Maxfield in Cheshire in old England Milliner came in the Endeaver of London Geo: Thorp M[ast]er arrived here the 29 7 mo 1683.
Michael Rosell late of the same place Husbandman came in the said vessell.
Tho: Janeway & Margaret his wife late of Poonall in Cheshire Husband-man came in ditto shipp. [Children] Jacob, Thomas, Abell, Joseph Janeway. [Servants] John Neild, Hannah ffalkner.
Jos: Milner & Ann his Mother late of Poonnell blacksmith in ditto. [Children] Sarah, Ralph Milner.
Ralph Milner & Rachell his wife late of Ditto Carpenter came in ditto vessell. [Child] Robt Milner.
Tho: Pierson & Margt his wife late of ditto Mason came in ditto shipp.
John his Brother & Mary Smith his sister all of the same place came

in ditto vessell.

John Nickson & Margery his wife late of Powell in Cheshire husbandman came in ditto vessel. [Children] John, Tho:, James, Nehemiah, Joseph, Shedrick, Mary, Jane, margery, Eliz: Nickson. [Servant] James Witaker.

John Clous & Margery his wife late of Gosworth in Cheshire husbandman came in ditto ship. [Children] Wm., Margery, Rebeckah Clous. [Servants] Jos: Charley, John Richardson, Sam: Hough.

Richard Hough late of Maxfield in Cheshire husbandman Ditto ship. [Servants] ffran Hough, Jam: Sutton, Tho: Woodhouse, Mary Woodhouse.

Fran: Stanfield & Grace his wife late of Garton in Cheshire Hushandman in ditto shipp. [Children] Jam:, Mary, Sarah, Eliz:, Gras, Hannah Stanfield. [Servants] Dan: Browne, Tho: Marsey; Isa: Brookesby, Rob. sidBotham, John Smith, Robt. Bryan, Wm. Rudway, Tho: Sidbotham.

John Maddock Joyner. Richard Clous Joyner. John Clous Shoemaker. Char: Kilbeck Glouver all of Nantwitch in Cheshire came in ditto shipp.

Servants to Henry Madock: Geo: Philipps, Ralph Duckard.

Daniell Sutton Taylor. John Presoner blacksmith both of Maxfield in Cheshire came in ditto shipp & Jo: Charlesworth Taner of the same place.

John Oudfield Taylor of the same place in ditto ship.

John Howell & Mary his Wife late of Budworth in Cheshire Husbandman came in ditto vessell. Hannah his daughter.

Mary Taylor late of Clatterwitch in Cheshire came in ditto shipp. [Children] Isaack, Tho:, Jona:, Pheb, Mary, Martha Taylor.

Anne Robothan servt to the M[ast]er of the sd Ketch.

in Capt Jefferies Shipp:

Leonard & Lionell Aratts & Agnistan his wife late of Crevelt near Rotterdam in Holland came in the [blank] of Lond. Wm. Jeffries Comder arrived here the 6 of 8 mo 1683. Leonard Teison his Brother a freeman.

James Claypoole Merchant & Helena his Wife with 7 Chilldren and 5 Servants viz: Hugh Masland and his Wife to serve 4 year, Siscilla Wooley 4 year, and Edward Cole Juner to serve 7 year.

The Providence of Scarbrough Robt Hopper M[ast]er.

Joshua Hoopes & Isabell his wife late of Cleveland in Yorkshire Husbandman came in ditto ship. [Children] Dan:, Marg:, Christian Hoopes.

John Palmer & Christian his wife late of Ditto place came in ditto ship.

William Preeson M[ast]er of the Viñe of Liverpoole Arived the 17th day of the 7 mo 1684 At Philadelphia ffrom dolyserne nere dolgules in Merioneth shire.

Robt. Owen & Jeane his wife and Lewes their Sone, one Servt Boy Named Edward Edwards for 8: yeares & 4 Servt. Maids named Lowry Edwards for 4 yrs, Margaret Edwards for 4 yrs, Ann Owen for 12 yrs And Hannah Watts for 3 yrs.

From Denby shire

David Davis & Katherine his sister & Mary Tidey her daughter and one servt man named Charles Hues for 3 yrs.

From Maukinleth in Montgomery shire

Hugh Harris & Daniell Harris.

John Richards & Susan his wife & their daughters Hannah & Bridget and one Servant named Susan Griffeth for 8 yeares.

Margaret the wife of Alexander Edwards & her daughters Margaret & Martha and 2 Sones Alexander & Tho:
From Radnor shire
Rees Prees & his wife Ann & their daughters Mary, Sarah and Phebe & two Sones Rich & John.
Jane Evans Widdow & her 4 daughters Sarah, Mary, Alice and Eliza: & one Sone named Joseph.
From Merionith Shire
Res Jones & his wife Hannah & their Sones Rich. & Evan and one Daughter named Lowry.
From Carmarthen shire
Ane Jones & her daughter Ane Jones.
From shropshire
Richard Turner & Margaret his wife & Rebecca their Daughter.
ffrom Prescoe in Lancashire
Griffith Owen & his wife Sarah & their sone Robt. & 2 daughters Sarah & Elinor & 7 Servants named Tho: Armes, John Ball 4 years, Robert Lort for 8 yers, Alexander Edwards, Jeane, Bridget & Eliz: Watts 3 yers
From Walton in Lancashire
Henry Baker & Margaret his wife & their Daughters Rachell, Rebecca, Phebey & Hester and Nathan & Samuel their Sones; Mary Becket & 10 Servts. named John Siddell for 4 yers, Hen: Siddell 4 yrs, James Yates 5 yrs, Jon. Hurst 4 yrs, Tho: ffisher 4 yrs, John Stedman 4 yeres, Tho Candy for Joseph fferror 4 yrs, Deborah Booth 4 yers, Joshua Lort 4 yers.
From Lancashire
Wm. Hatton & Eliza his wife, Rebecca, Martha & Elinor Hall; their servants Tho Harrison for 2 yeares, John Cowp for 4 yeares, Lawrance Parker for 5 yeares, Katherine Owen for 4 yeares, Mary Hall for 8 yers, Eliz: Stedman, Sarah & Judith Buller her Daughters, Jon Stedman her sone, Rebecca Barrow.

The ship Providence from Old England Capt. Robert Hopper Comander Arived here in Delaware River the 29th of the 7th Month 1682.
William Carter. John Lash.

The ship Called the Bristoll Comfort from Old England John Read Master arived here in Delaware River the 28th of the 7th Month & in the same came 1683:
Alexander Beardsly & Margaret his wife & his Daughter Mary the said Alexander is a Glover and he came from Worcester.
Tho: Boweter out of wostershire a servant to ffrancis ffincher out of woster City Glover for 3: yeares they Came in the ship aforesaid.
Richard Hillyard and Mary his Wife and Rich and Philip his sons and John Witt his Servant.
Christianus Lewis late of Dudley in Worstershire in old England Schoolemaster came in the Comfort of Bristow, Capt. Reed arrived here the 1 8 mo 1683.

Geo. Painter & Ellinor his wife late Haverford west in Pembrookeshire in South wales Husbandman came in ye Unicorne of Bristow Tho: Cooper M[ast]er arrived here ye 31 8 mo 1683. [Children] Susan, Geo: Painter. [Servants] Lewis 4 yrs [payment in money] £2, 50 [acres of land; time of freedom] 31 8 mo 1687. Mathes 2 years & wages ye last 2 yeares. Jannet Umphries 4 yrs [payrment in money] ₤2 5s. for ye 2 last yeares [time of freedom] 31 8 mo 1687.

Dennis Rochford son of William Rochford, who was Born in Enisscorfey in the County of waxford in Ireland aboute the yeare 47: And through the goodness and Mercy of the Lord was Convinced of gods blessed truth. Aboute the yeare 62: Went into England & Landed in Whitehaven in Cumberland the 30th of the 3d Month 1675. Dwelt in Brighthelmston in Sussex 3 yeares & kept a grocers shop, And came into this Province of Pennsilvania with Mary his wife Daughter of John Heriott of the Parish of Hostperpoynt in Sussex in old England she was Born on the 14th of the 3d Month 52) in the ship Called the Welcom Robert Greenaway Comander with two servants Tho: Jones & Jeane Mathewes, the said Dennis two Daughters Grace & Mary Rochford dyed upon the Seas in the said ship, Grace being above 3 years old & Mary being 6 Months old the said Dennis Rochford Landed wth his family in Pennsilvania about the 24th day of the 8th Month 1682. Mary Rochford the second Daughter of Dennis & Mary Rochford was born in the Province of Pennsilvania at Egely poynt in the County of Philadelphia the 22th of the 8th Mo 1683 between 10: & 11th at night she being their second Daughter of that name.

Robert Turner late of Dublin in Ireland Mercht. came in ye Lion of Leverpoole John Crumpton M[ast]er arrived here the 14 8 mo 1683. [Child] Marther Turner. [Servants] Robt. Threwecks [to serve] 4 yrs [have] ₤8 [and] 50 acres. Henry furnace [to serve] 4 yrs [have] ₤3 [and] 50 acres. Robt. Selford [to serve] 4 yrs [have] ₤6 10s. [and] 50 acres. Ben: Acton [to serve] 4 yrs [have] ₤3 [and] 50 acres. John Reeves [to serve] 4 yrs [have] ₤6 10s. [and] 50 acres. Row: Hambidge [to serve] 4 yrs [have] 50 acres. Richard Curtis [to serve] 4 yrs [have] ₤3 [and] 50 acres. John Furnace [to serve] 4 yrs [have] ₤3 [and] 50 acres. [All these above named to be free] 14 8 mo 1687. Dan: Furnace [to serve] 9 yrs [have] 50 acres [free] 14 8 mo 1692. Robt. Threwecks [to serve] 13 yrs [have] 50 acres [free] 14 8 mo 1695. Lemuel Bradshaw [to serve] 4 yrs [have] ₤2 10s. [and] 50 acres. Robt. Lloyd [to serve] 4 yrs [have] ₤4 [and] 50 acres. Wm. Long [to serve] 4 yrs [have] ₤3 [and] 50 acres. [The last three abovenamed to be free] 14 8 mo 1687. Hen: Hollingsworth [to serve] 2 yrs [have] 50 acres [free] 14 8 mo 1685. Aiolce Cales [to serve] 4 yrs [have] ₤3 [and] 50 acres [free] 14 8 mo 1687. Kath: Furnace [to serve] 6 yrs [have] 50 acres [free] 14 8 mo 1689. Jos: Furnace [to serve] 4 yrs [have] ₤3 [and] 50 acres [free] 14 8 mo 1687.

Joseph Fisher & Elizabeth Fisher his wife late of Stillorgin near Dublin in Ireland Yeoman borne in in Elton in Chesshire in old England came in ditto ship. [Children] Moses, Joseph, Mary, Marth Fisher. [Servants] Edward Lancaster [to serve] 4 yrs [have] ₤4 10s. [and] 50 acres. Wm. Robertson [to serve] 4 yrs [have] 50 acres. Ed. Doyle [to serve] 4 yrs [have] 50 acres. Ben: Clift [to serve] 4 yrs [have] 50 acres. Tho: Tearewood [to serve] 4 yrs [have] 50 acres. [All these abovenamed to be free] 14 8 mo 1687. Robt Kilcarth [to serve] 8 yrs [have] 50 acres [free] 14 8 mo 1691. Peter Long [to serve] 2 yrs [have] ₤6 [and] 50 acres [free] 14 8 mo 1685. Phill: Packer [to serve] 4 yrs [have] 50 acres. Wm. Conduit [to serve] 4 yrs [have] ₤3 [and] 50 acres. Mary Toole [to serve] 4 yrs [have] ₤3 [and] 50 acres. Eliz: Johnson [to serve] 4 yrs [have] 50 acres. [The last four abovenamed free] 14 8 mo 1687.

Margt Colvert late of Dublin came in ditto Ship.

The Rebeca of Liverpoole James Skinner Commander Arived at philadelphia the 31th of the 8th Month 1685. The passangers names are as followeth & is

John Cutler, Edmond Cutler, Issabell Cutler, Elizabeth Cutler, Thomas Cutler, William Cutler. They came from Bulland in Yorkeshire, freemen. Richard Mather, Cornelious Netherwood, James Myrriall, William Wardle, James Molenex, Eliz: Wingreene, Servants to the said John Cutler.

Thomas Bates: a freeman.

James Ratclife, Mary Ratclife, Richard Ratclife, Edward Ratclife, Rebecca Ratcliffe, Rachell Ratcliffe, free persons: From Mousebury in Lancashire. James Heyworth, Robert Hewet, James Rothwell, Servants to the said Ratclife.

Richard Curetone & Margaret his wife, William Cureton his sone & Jane Cureton his Daughter, free persons. James Holgate & Ann Dugdale, servants to the said Cureton.

Matthew Holdgate & Mary his Daughter, free persons.

John Lathum, Ann Lathum his wife, John Jennings his wifes son, John Lathum his sone, Aron Lathum his sone, Moses Lathum his sone & Ann Lathum his Daughter, free persons.

James Scoles, John Scoles, Hester Rothwell, Free persons.

The Bristoll Merchant John Stephens Comander Arived here the 10th of the 9th Month 1685. The passengers names are as followeth vizt.

Jasper Farmer Senior his Family: Mary Farmer widdow, Edward Farmer, Edward Batsford, Sarah Farmer, John Farmer, Robert Farmer, Katherine Farmer, Charles Farmer.

Jasper Farmer Juniors family: Thomas ffarmer, Katherine ffarmer widdow, Elizabeth ffarmer, Katherine ffarmer Junior.

Their servants are as followeth vzt. Joane Daly, Philip Mayow and Hellen his wife, John Mayow, John Whitloe, Nicholas Whitloe, Thomas Young & his wife, William Winter, George ffisher, Arthur Smith, Thomas Alferry, Henry Wells, Robert Wilkison, Elizabeth Mayow, Martha Mayow, Sarah Binke, Shele Orevan, Andrew Walbridge, all from Ireland.

Thomas Webb and Danniell Webb his son. Thomas Webbs Servants are as followeth: John Beltshire, John Robinson, Richard fford, James Banbury, Thomas Case, Henry fford, John ffox, Derby Haley, Joseph Case, Thomas Burke, John Garrell, John Mehone, David Quinn, Mary Widdam, Prudence Stuart, Katherine Robinson, Richard Muske.

Nicholas Scull, free. his servants are as followeth: Samuell Hall, Cornelious Davye, George Gooding, Miles Morin, Daniell Morin, John Ward, Mary Cantwell.

Tho: Carters family: Thomas Carter Senior, Frances his wife, Thomas his Sonn, Henry his Sonn, John his sonn, Ann his Daughter.

Jonathan Thatcher.

Arrived here the 29th of the 7th month 1682 the Ship called the Elizabeth, Anne & Catherine from old England Thomas Hudson Commander.

Robert Kent servt to Phillip Orford.

Arrived here the 6th of the 6th month 1685 the ship Charles from London

Edmond Pane Commander.
John Marlton servt. to Robert Kent.

The ffrancis and Dorothy ffrom London, Richard Bridgeman Commander
Arived at Philadelphia the 12th of the 8th Month 1685. The Passengers
names are as ffolloweth:
Isaac sheepheard and Gertrude his wife and Margaret his Daughter.
John Peter Umstat and Barbara his wife, John his sonn, Margaret and
Eave his Daughters.
Garret Hendrix and Mary his wife and Sarah his Daughter. Henry Fry
his servant.
Peter Shoomaker and Peter his Sonn, Mary his Daughter & Sarah his
Cosen. Frances and Gertrude his Daughters.
Henry Pookeholes and Mary his wife.
Aron Wonderley.
John Saxby and Eliz: his wife & John and Thomas his sons and Elizabeth,
Lucy, and Ester his Daughters.

The Unicorne from Bristoll Arived here the 16th of the 10th Month 1685,
Thomas Cooper Commander. The Passengers Names are as followeth:
Daniel fflower. Mary Bradwell, Mary Bradwell Juner, Sarah Bradwell.
Thomas Mixon, Tho: Mixon Juner. Philip Doling. Mary Townsend. Hannah
Smith. Tho: Martin, Margery Martin, Mary Martin, Sarah Martin, Hannah
Martin, Rachell Martin. Tho: Hopes, John Hopes. Moses Mendinhall. God-
den Walter. Joshua Chart, Jane, Sam:, Jane Juner Chart. John Roberts,
Joseph Morgan, Benjam: Morgan. Tho: Tutlin [?] Anne Morgan. Faith Wot-
ten. Eliz. Philpot. Henry Laking, Sarah Laking, Susanna Laking, Moses
Laking. John Ironmonger.

The ship the Desire ffrom Plymouth in old England Arived here the 23th of
June 1686. James Cock Comander.
ffrancis Rawle sener, ffrancis Rawle Juner. his servants are: Thomas
Janveiries als January, ffrancis Jervice, John Marshall, Samuell Rennell,
Isaac Garnier, Elizabeth Saries.
Richard Grove. his Servants are: David Savanplane, David Bonifoye.
Nicholas Pearce. his servants are: Richard weymouth, John ffox.
James ffox & Elizabeth his wife. George & James his Sonns, Elizabeth
& Sarah his Daughters. his Servants are: Richard ffox, stephen Nowell,
Christopher Lobb, Richard Davis, Nathaniell Christopher, Abraham Rowe,
Mary Lucas, Sarah Jefferies.
John Shellson & Naomie his wife. his servants are: John Hart, John
Cocker, Justinian ffox, Mary welsh.
James shaddock & Joane his wife. his servts are: Jacob Coffin, Eliz:
Giles.
John Holme his servts are: William Hayes 5: yeares, Richard Besti-
traser 9: yeares, George Gwinop: 5: yeares from the arivall of the Desire
afresd.

The America Joseph Wasey m[ast]er from London Arrived 20 6 mo 1683.
Jacob Shoemaker borne in ye Palatinate in Germany Servant to Danll.
Pastorius & Compa[ny].

Joshua Tittery servant to ye society broad Glass maker from New Castle upon Tine to serve four yeare at £88 per ann.

The Wellcome Rob Greenway master from London arrived at Upland about the end of ye 8th Month 1682.

Richard Townsend Carpenter servant to ye society for 5 years to have £50 per ann. salary. Anne Townsend his Wife & Hannah their Daughter. Wm. Smith, Natha: Harrison, Barthol: Green his Servants each for 7 year.

The ship Delaware From Bristoll in Old England John Moore Comander Arived here the 11th of the 5th Month 1686.

Thomas Greene Husbandman & Margaret his wife, Thomas and John Greene his sons. Mary Guest his servant for 7: yeares to come from the third day of May 1686.

Richard Moore Brick maker & Mary his wife & Mary his Daughter & John Moore his sone. Sarah Searle his servant for 4: yeares to come from the 3d of May 1686.

Henry Guest Sawyer & Mary his wife & Henry his sone.

The Amity Richard Dymond master from London arrived in Pensylvania the 15th 5 Month 1686.

David Lloyd borne in the year 1656 in ye Parish of Manavan in ye County of MountGomery in North Wales. Sarah Lloyd his Wife borne in ye year 166[?] at Cirensister in Glocester Shire in England.

Christofer Sibthorp and Barbara his Wife of London Brasier. Tho: Peppitt & Barbara Peppitt the Children of Christopher Sibthorps Wife Barbary and Wm. Pike their Servant bound in London for 7 year and had about 4 year to serve when they arrived here wch was in Ship above written ye 23 3 mo 1685.

The Registers office of all persons
Resideing or Inhabiting within the
County of Bucks as well ffreemen as
servants and the time of the said
servants freedome and wages

ffrom old England – William yardley and Jane his Wife Came from Ransclough neare Leeke in the County of Staford – yeoman in the Ship the friends adventure The master Thomas Wall arrived in Delaware River the 28th day of the 7th month 1682 – with their Children Enoch, Thomas, William yardley. Andrew Heath Servant to sd wm yardley to Serve 4 yeares & to have meate drink & apparrel & passage & land accustomed. Loose the 29th day of the 7th month 1686.

george pownal and Ellenor his wife of Lostock in the County of Chester yeoman Came in the afforesd Ship Calld the friends adventure of Liver poole & arrived at the aforementioned day in this River Delaware – with their Children Ruben, Ellizabeth, Sarah, Rachel, Abigall pownal And theire servants John Brearele, Thomas Leister & martha Worrall. To Serve foure yeares a peice, wages passage dyet & apparrel dureing the Said terme & Land accustomed – free from theire Servitude the 29 day of the 7th mo 1686.

Luke Brindley Came from Leek in the County of Staford in [the aforesaid Ship.]

John Clows Son of John Clows of goses worth in the County of Chester as allso Joseph Clows & Sarah Clows – the son & daughter of the sd John Clows Senior Came in the aforesd Ship friends adventure at the time afforesd. Henry Lingart theire servant to work out his passage by day wages & then to be free.

John Brock neare Stockport in the County of Chester yeoman Came in the afforesd Ship and arrived at the afforesd time. [Servants] Job Houle, Ellizabeth Eaton – To Serve each of them 4 yeares for passage meat drink & apparel dureing the Said term & land accustomed to be free the 29th day of the 7 mo 1686. Willm morton to serve sd Jon Brock Came in the Ship freeman m[ast]er John Southern to serve 4 yeares wages is passage meate drink & apparel & [to be free 6th 6th mo 1686.]

William venables & Ellizabeth his wife Came in the aforesd Ship friends adventure at the afforesd time of arrival being ye 28th of the 7th month 1682 – he Came from Chatkil in Eccleshill parish in the County of Staford husbandman – with theire Children Joyce, ffrances venables.

John Heycock of Slin in the parish of Eccleshill in the County of Staford husband[man] Came in the aforesd Ship friends adventure at the time afforesd – James morris To serve 4 yeares – Wages is passage meate drink & apparel dureing the term & land accustomed. Loose the 29th of the 7th month 1686.

Ann milcome of Armagh in Ireland widow Came in the Ship Antilop ye master Edward Cooke – arived in Delaware River the [10th of 10th mo 1682] – with her Children Jane greaves, mary milcome – ffrancis Sanders to serve

4 yeares wages is passage meate drink apparel dureing sd terme & to have
Land accustomed.

Henry marjerum & Ellizabeth his wife of Cheveral in the County of
wilts husband man arived in the Bristol marchant the master William Smith
the twelfth month 1682.

William Beakes of the parish of Backwill* in the county of Sumerset
yeoman Came in ye sd Ship Bristol merchant arived in this River the 12th
month 1682 [with] his Son Abraham Beake.

[Andrew Ellet] seller of Smal wares and Ann his wife of ye parish of
fifed** in the County of Sumerset arrived in Delaware River in the Ship ye
factor of Bristol the m[ast]er Roger Drew [with] Servants John Rob[er]ts
& mary Sanders.

John Wood of Atterclife in the parish of Sheafeild & County of york
husbandman arived in Delaware River in the Shild the master Daniel Toes
in the 10th month 1678 - with his Children John, Joseph, ester, mary, Sarah
wood.

John Purslone of Dublin in Ireland - husband man arived in Delaware
River in the phenix the master mathew Sheare in the 6th month 1677.

John Rowland of Billinghurst in the County of Sussex husbandman Came
in the Ship welcome - arived in this River the 8th month 1682 with his wife
pricilla - the masters name Robt greeneway. [Servant] Hannah mogridge
to have fifty Shillings per annum - Loose in the 3 month 1684.

Thomas Rowland Came from Billinghurst aforesd in the Ship welcome
the 6th day 6th month***.

Josuah Boare of Drainefeild in Darby Shire husbandman arived in Delaware River in the martha of Hull the master Thomas Wildcup - the 7th
month 1677 - margret his now wife of Norton Bavent in wilt Shire arived in
the River Delaware in the Ship Ellizabeth & Sarah the master Richard ffriend
the 29th day of the 3 month 1679.

William Buckman of the parish of Billinghurst in the County of Sussex
Carpenter arrived in Delaware River in the Ship Welcom the m[ast]er Robt
greenaway with his Wife Sarah in the 8th month 1682 - with theire Children
Sarah, mary Buckman.

gideon gambel of the vises****[Devizes] in the County of wilts Slator
arived in Delaware River in the Bristol factor the m[ast]er R[og]er Drew
in the 10th month 1681.

William Biles of Dorcester in the County of Dorcet fell monger & Johannah his wife arrived in Delaware River in the Ellizabeth & Sarah of
waymouth the 4th day of 4th month 1679. [Children] William born 12: 11 mo
'71. george 4: 7 mo '73. John 31: 1 mo '78. Ellizabeth 3: 4 mo '70. Johannah 1: 1 mo '75. Rebecka 29: 10 mo '80. Mary 1: 11 mo '82. Edward
Hancock his Servant to Serve 8 yeares to have meate drink apparel dureing
the term & passage & land accustomed - free the last day of the 3 month
1687. Ellizabeth Petty to Serve 7 yeares to have passage meat drink & apparrel dureing ye term & land accustomed - Loose the last day of the 3
month 1686.

---

 * Blackwell is a parish in Somerset
 ** Fifehead is a parish in Dorset.
 *** date obviously in error.
 **** Probably intended to be Devises.

Charles Biles brother of the Said William Biles Came with his brother in the said Ship at the time afforesaid.

gilbert Wheeler fruiterer & martha his wife Came from London in the Ship Jacob & mary the master Richard Moore arived the 12th of the 7th mo 1679 - theire Children William, Briant, martha wheeler. Charles Thomas, Robt Benson, Katherine knight Servants.

James Harrison of Bolton in the County of Lancaster Shoomaker aged about 54 yeares & Ann his wife aged about 61 yeares Sailed away from Liverpoole towne Side the 5th day of the 7th month 1682 in the Ship Submission of liverpoole the master James Settle - arrived att Choptank in mary land the 2nd day of the 9th month 1682 & at Apoquimene in this Province the 15th day of the 11th month following. Phebe his daughter - wife to Phinehas Pemberton. Joseph Steward his [Harrison's] servant or apprentice to Serve according to agreemt with his parents. Allis Dickerson & Jane Lyon to serve each of them 4 yeares wages is passage meate drink apparrel & land accustomed - free from the time of theire arival after the expiration of foure yeares.

Agnes Harrison ye mother of the sd James Harrison aged about 81 yeares Came at the aforesd time & arrived in mary land at the aforesd time & in this Province the 9th of the 3 month 1683.

Phinehas Pemberton of Botlon aforesaid grocer aged about 33 yeares & his wife Phebe aged about 23 yeares both Came in the Ship Submission & arrived in mary land the 2nd day of ye 9th month 1682 as afforesaid. Theire Children Abigal about 3 yeares of age, Joseph not one yeare of age. William Smith Servant to the Sd Phinehas Pemberton Came in the Ship friends adventure arived the 28th day of the 7th month 1682 to serve 4 yeares - wages is passage meat drink apparrel dureing the term & land accustomed - free ye 28 of the 7th month 1686.

Ralph Pemberton father of the Said Phinehas Pemberton aged 72 yeares arrived in maryland in the Ship & at the time aforesaid. Ralph Pemberton, Phebe Pemberton, Joseph & Abigall Pemberton arived in this River from maryland the 9th day of the 3 month 1683. Joseph mather & Ellizabeth Bradbury Servants to [Ralph & ?] Phines Pemberton to Serve dureing 4 yeares wages is passage meat drink apparrel dureing the terme & land accustomed - free at the expiration of 4 yeares from the time of theire arrival. Ellizabeth [blank]

Robt Bond Son of Thomas Bond of Waddicar hall neare garstang aged about 15 or 16 yeares Came with James Harrison in the afforesd Ship Submission being left his father to the tuition of sd James Harrison.

Lydia Wharmby of Bolton afforesd Came in the Ship afforesd at the time aforesd.

Ellis Jones & Jane his Wife Came from Wales in the Ship Submission at the time aforesd with theire Children Rebecka, Dorothy, mary, Isaac Jones - all of them Servants to govener Penn.

Jane & marjery mode - daughters to Thomas Winn Came in the Ship Submission at the time aforesd. ffarclif Hedges apprentice to Thomas winn.

James Clayton of Middlewitch in the County of Chester black Smith & Jane his wife Came in ye Said Ship Submission at the time aforesd - with theire Children James, Sarah, John, mary, Josuah, Lydia Clayton.

Thomas Janney of Stial in the County of Chester yeoman & marjery his wife Came in the Ship Endeavor of London the masters name george Thorp

- arived in this River the 29th of ye 7th month 1683 - with theire Children Jacob, Thomas, Abel, Joseph Janney - theire Servants John Neild to serve 5 yeares. Hannah ffalkner to serve 4 yeares to be free after the expiration of the sd term from the time of theire arival - wages is passage meat drink apparrel dureing the term & land accustomed.

John Clows the elder of goesworth in the County of Chester - yeoman & his wife marjery Came in ye afforesaid Ship the Endeavor of London at the afforesaid time - with theire Children marjery, Rebecka, William Clows. Joseph Chorley to serve 2 yeares & to have Land accustomed - free the 29th of the 7th month 1685. Samuel Hough & John Richardson to Serve 4 yeares apeice to have passage meat drink apparrel dureing the term & land accustomed.

Richard Hough of macclesfeild of the County of Chester Chapman arrived in the aforesd Ship Endeavor the 29 day of the 7th month 1683. ffrancis Hough to Serve 2 yeares. Thomas Wood to serve 5 yeares. mary wood to serve 4 yeares. James Sutton to serve 4 yeares & to have 3£:15s. to be ended from the day of theire arrival - to have passage dyet dureing the term & land accustomed.

george Stone of ffrog moore in the parish of Charlton in the County of Devon weavor arived in maryland in the Daniel & Elizabeth of plimouth the m[ast]er Willm ginney in the 9th month 1683 - from thence to this River in the 10 mo 1683. Thomas Dyer to serve 4 yeares to have land accustomed & Loose the 9th month 1687.

Randle Blackshaw of Hollingee in the County of Chester yeoman & Allis his wife arived in mary land the 2nd day of the 9th month 1682 in ye Ship the Submission of Liver poole the masters name James Settle and Randle arrived in this Province att Apoquimene the 15th day of the 11th month 1683 & parte of his Servants & Allis his wife arrived at sd place apoquimene the 9th day of the 3 month & most of theire Children & Some of the servants 1683. Children arived with Randle Phebe, Sarah, mary, Jacob, Nehemiah, martha Blackshaw with Allis his wife. William Bewsie, Ralph Nuttall & Ralph Cowgill Servants to Randle to Serve each of them 4 yeares & to be provided for dureing the term & to have land accustomed. These 3 servants Came in the Ship friends adventure the m[ast]er Tho: Wall & arrived here the 28 of the 7th month 1682 & to be free from the time of arrival. Roger Bradbury & Ellenor Bradbury & Sarah, Roger, Jacob, Joseph, martha Bradbury theire Children Came in the Ship Submission at the time aforesd to serve 4 yeares apeice except Sarah to serve 8 yeares to have nessessarys dureing the term & land accustomed. Ellenor, Rogr, Jacob, Joseph, martha Bradbury gott sold in mary land by Randle Blackshaw.

John Chapman aged about 58 yeares and Jane his wife about 42 yeares Came from Stangnah in the parish of Skelton in the County of York yeoman Came in the Ship the Sheild of Stockton the master Daniel Toes arived in mary land in the begining of the 8th month 1684 & from thence in this River the latter end of the Same month - Children: marah born the 12th 2 mo 1671. Ann born the 18th 3 mo 1676. John born ye 9th of the 11th mo 16--. Jane his daughter Came at Same time & dyed at Sea.

Ellin pearson of kirk lydam in the County of york spinster aged about 54 yeares Came at the above Said time in ye above mentioned Ship.

Ann peacock of kill deale in the County of York Came at the Same time in the sd Ship Sheild.

Henry Paxson of Bycot house in the parish of Stow in the County of oxford aged about 37 yeares Came in ye Ship Samuel of London the m[ast]er John Adee - arived in the midle of the 7th month 1682. Ellizabeth his daughter born about the 5th of the 9th month 1675. His Wife Came at Same time & dyed at Sea about the last week of the 5th month 1672 [sic]. His Son Henry Paxson dyed at Sea the day before his mother. John paxson dyed about the midle of the 5th month aforesaid. Thomas Paxson brother of the said Henry Paxson Came in the Said Ship & dyed at Sea about the begining of the 7th month in the sd yeare.

Richard Ridgway & Elizabeth his wife of Woll ford in the County of Bark Taylor - arived in this River in the Ship Jacob & mary of London in ye 7th month 1679. Thomas Ridgway theire Son born ye 25th of 5th month 1677.

Samuel Dark of London Calenderer arived in the Ship the Content of London the master william Jonson in the 8th month 1680. Ann knight now wife of Samuel Dark - arived in this River in the Ship Society of Bristol the master Thomas Jordan in the 6th month 1682. [Servants] James Craft to serve 4 [years] from the 2nd day of the 12th month 1682 - wages pd in hand 10 bushels of Corn & at the expiration of the term to have one Cow & Calf & 50 ackers of land accustomed. mary Craft to serve one yeare loose the 10th day of the 8th month 1683 to have 4£ wages.

John Palmer of Cleiveland in york Shire husbandman & Christian his wife arived in this River in the Ship the providence of Scarborough the master Robt Hopper the 10th of the 9th month 1683.

Josuah Hoops of Skelton in Cleiveland aforesd (& Iseabel his wife) yeoman Came in the above mentioned Ship at the time aforesaid. Their Children Daniel, Margret, Christian Hoops.

William Bennet of Hammonds worth in ye County of midlesex - yeoman & Rebecka his wife arived in this River in the 9th month 1683 in the Ship Jeffery of London Thomas Arnold master. Rebecka, Ann & Sarah Bennet his Children.

Lyonel Britan of Alny in the County of Bucks black Smith & Ellizabeth his wife Arived in this River in the owners advice of Barmoodoes the master georg Bond in the 4th month 1680. Ellizabeth theire daughter dyed as they Came up the bay & was buryed Burlington.

Thomas ffitzwater of Hanworth in the County of midlesex Husbandman Arived in this River in the welcom of London the master Robt greenaway the 28 day of the 8th month 1682. mary his wife and Josiah & mary his Children dyed Coming over Sea. Thomas & george his Children. [Servant] John ottey to serve 6 yeares from his arrival to be found with necessarys dureing the term & Land accustomed.

Robt Lucas of Deveral Long Bridg in the County of wilts yeoman arived in this River the 4th of the 4th month 1679 in the Ellizabeth & mary of waymouth. Ellizabeth his wife arived in the Ship Content of London the master Willm Jonson in the 7th month 1680. Children John Lucas born the 11th day of the 11th month 1654. Edward, Robt, Ellizabeth, Rebecka, mary, Sarah Lucas.

Daniel Brinson of membury parish in ye County of Devon - arived in this River the 28 day of the 7th month 1677 in the Willing mind of London the m[ast]er Lucome. maryed to ffrances green land of East Jersey the 8th day of the 8th month 1681.

John Hough of Hough in the County of Chester yeoman & Hannah his wife - arived in this River in the 9th month 1683 in the frendship of Liver poole the m[ast]er Robt Crosman. John Hough theire Son. [Servants] george gleave and Iseabel his wife to Serve 4 yeares from theire arival & george glave theire son to serve to the age of 21 yeares. Nathaniel Watmough, Thomas Hough to Serve 4 yeares from theire arival all to have necessarys dureing the term & land accustomed.

William Dark of Chipping Cambden in the County of gloster glover - arived in this River about the midle of the 4th month 1680 in the Content of London the m[ast]er wm: Jonson - aged about 58 yeares. Allis his wife Came in the Ship the Charles of London the master Edward paine arived in this River the latter end of the 6th month 1684 - aged about 63 yeares. John Dark theire Son born the 4th day of the 3 month 1667 arived with his mother.

James Dilworth of Thornley in Lancashire husbandman Came in ye Ship the lamb of Liver poole the master John Tench arived in this River the 8th month 1682 with his wife Ann. William their Son. [Servant] Stephen Sands to Serve one yeare to have necessarys during the term - free the 22 day of the 8th month 1683.

Jacob Hall of maxfeild in the County of Chester Shoomaker & mary his wife arived in mary land the 3 day of the 12th month 1684 in the frendship of Liver poole the master Edmund Croston and afterwards transported to this River where his family arived the 28 day of the 3 month 1685. Children Jacob theire Son born the 8th day of the 12th month 1679. Sarah theire daughter born the 23 day of the 5th month 168-. Joseph theire Son born the 11th day of the 12th month 1686. Sarah Charlesworth Sister in law to the sd Jacob Hall Came in ye sd Ship & at the said time with her Said brother in law. [Servants] Epharim Jackson to Serve 4 yeares free the 24th of the 12th month 1688 - wages is meate drink washing & lodging & 6Ł per annum. John Raynolds to Serve 4 yeares free the 25 of the first month 1689 - wages is meat drink washing Lodging and 2Ł:10s per annum. Joseph Hollinghead to Serve 4 yeares free the 30 day of the 10th month 1688 - wages to have Necessarys as above and 6Ł per annum. John Evans to serve 2 yeares free the 24th day of the 12th month 1686 - wages he is to have Necessarys as above & 4Ł per annum. William ffowler to serve Jacob Hall 4 yeares free the 22 day of the 12th month 1688 - wages he is to have necessarys as before to other Servants and for 3 of the last yeares 5Ł:6s 8d per annum. Isaac Hill to serve 4 yeares free the 25 of the first month 1689 - to have necessarys dureing ye term. John Jackson to serve 7 yeares free the 25 day of the first month 1691 - wages to have necessarys dureing the terme. Jane gibbons to serve 4 yeares free the 25 day of first month 1689 - wages to have meate drink washing and Lodging & 35s per Annum.

Servants to Jacob Hall & Thomas Hudson of maclesfeild in the County of Chester in old England: John Bolshaw to Serve 4 yeares dyed & was buryed at oxford in mary land the 2nd month 1685. Thomas Rylands to serve 4 yeares dyed & was buryed at oxford afforesaid in the first month 1685.

Servants to the sd Thomas Hudson & Jacob Hall as ffoloweth arived in the amity of London the master Richard Dyamond in this River the 28 day of the 3 month 1685: Joseph Hull to Serve 2 yeares - free the 28 of ye 3 month 1687 - wages to have one new suite of apparel & other necessarys dureing the Said term & at the expiration thereof to have one new Suit of apparrel & on hundred acres of Land. William Hasselhurst to serve 3 yeares - free the 28 day of the 3 month 1688 - wages is apparrel & other necessarys dureing the term & land allowed by ye governer. Randle Smalwood to serve 3 yeares free the 28 day of the 3 month 1688 - Wages to have necessarys dureing the term & land as above allowed by the governer.

Servants to the afforesaid Thomas Hudson & Jacob Hall Came in the Ship the Richard & micheal of Boston & arrived in this River the 24th day of July 1685: William Thomas to serve 4 yeares - free the 24th day of ye 5th month 1689 - wages is passage necessarys dureing the term & land accustomed. Daniel Danielson van Beck & his wife Ellenor to serve three yeares & a half a peice - free the 24th day of the 12th month 1688 - wages is passage & necessarys dureing the term & land accustomed.

Servants to the afforesaid Thomas Hudson & Jacob Hall Came in the francis & dorothy of London the 10th day of the 7th month 1685: Policarpus Rose to Serve 4 yeares - free the 10th day of the 7th month 1689 - Wages is to have passage & necessarys dureing the terme & land accustomed.

Richard Lundy of axmenster in the County of Devon Son of Silvester Lundy of the Said Towne in old England Came in a Catch from Bristol the m[ast]er William Browne for Boston in new England in ye 6th month 1676 & from thence Came for this River the 19th day of the 3 month 1682.

Ellizabeth Bennet Daughter of william Bennet late of this County of Bucks & now wife to ye abovesaid Richard Lundy Came from Long ford in the County of middlesex in the Ship the Concord of London the master William Jeffferys arived in this River the 8th month 1683.

Edmund Cuttler of Slate bourn in bowland in york Shire - Webster Came in the Ship the Rebecka of Liver poole the master James Skinner arived with his wife Iseabel Cuttler in this River the 31st day of the 8th month 1685. theire Children: Ellizabeth born the 14th day of the 3 month 1680. Thomas theire Son born the 16 day of the 9th month 1681. William theire Son born the 16th of the 10th month 1682. Servants to Edmund Cuttler Came in the same Ship & at the same time with him: Corneiliis Netherwood to serve the Said Edmund Cuttler one yeare - Loose the 31 day of the 8th month 1686 - wages is necessarys dureing ye term. Richard mather to serve 2 yeares - Loose the 31 day of the 8th month 1689 - wages is half passage & necessarys dureing the term. Ellin wingreen to Serve 4 yeares - free the 31 day of the 8th month 1689 - wages is passage & necessarys dureing the term & at the expiration to have 16s.

John Cuttler brother to the Said Edmund Came at the time above said in the Ship & from the place aforementioned. [Servants] Willm Wardle to serve 4 yeares - free the 30 day of the 2 month [1689] necessarys dureing the term & passag. James mollinex Son to James mollinex late of liver poole about 3 yeares of age is to se[rve to] age of 22 yeares.

David Davies Son of Richard Davies of welch poole in the County of mountgomery Chirurgeon Came in the Ship the morning Star of Liverpoole arived in this River the 14th day of the 9th month 1683 the m[ast]ers name [blank]

Richard Amor of Bucklebury in Barkshire - husbandman Came in the Ship Samuel of London John Adee master arived in this River the 22 day of the 7th month 1682.

Edward the Son of george Stanton of Woster Joyner Came in the Ship the ffrancis & dorothy of london the master Richard Bridgman arived in this River the 10 day of the 8th month 1685.

Peter Worral & mary his Wife of northwitch in the County of Chester wheele wright Came in the Ship the Ann & Ellizabeth of Liver poole the master Thomas gotter arrived in this River the 7th day of the 8th month 1687.

Robt Hudson Son to Thomas Hudson of macles feild in the County of Chester in old England & his Wife Sarah Came in the Ship prosperous the master – Conway who Carryed them to Barmoodoes from thence Came in a Sloope & arived at philadelphia the 23 day of the 2nd month 1686. John Shippey Servant to the Said Thomas Hudson Came in the Ship Amity of London the master Richard Dyamond arived in this River the 11th of the 4th month 1686 to serve 4 [?] yeares free at ... from his ariv[al ...] necessarys dure[ing the] term passage ... [land] accustomed.

Thomas Tunneclife of Haughton in the County of Staford Tannor & Sussannah his Wife arived in this River in the unicorn of Bristol the master Thomas Cooper the 20 day of 10th month 1685. [Servant] Willm Tayl[or ... to] Serve ye ... Loose the ... 1689 – wages is ... the ter[m ...]. ffrancis ... [to serve] 5 yeares & to ... dureing the [term]. Ann Silvester [to serve] as they agree.

John Turner of Crookby bank in Shrop Shire Came in the said Ship at the Same time.

PASSENGERS ON THE FRIENDS' ADVENTURE AND THE ENDEAVOR

From J. H. Battle, History of Bucks County, Pennsylvania (1887) pp. 440-441

Passengers on the Friends' Adventure, arrived 28, 7 month 1682.
John Brock, Stockport, Cheshire, with servants: Job Houle, William Morton*, Eliza Eaton.
George Pownall, Laycock, Cheshire, wife Eleanor, children: Reuben, Elizabeth, Sarah, Rachel, Abigail; servants: John Brearly, Robert Saylor**, Martha Worral.
William Yardley, Ranscleugh near Leeke, Staffordshire, wife Jane; children: Enoch, Thomas, William; servant: Andrew Heath (Phineas Pemberton was his nephew).

Passengers on the Endeavor of London, arrived 29, 9 month 1683.
Richard Hough, Macclesfield, Cheshire, and family***; servants: Francis Hough, John Sutton****, Thomas Wood and wife Mary.
Thomas Janney, Shioll, Cheshire, wife Margery; children: Jacob, Thomas, Abel, and Joseph; servants: John Neald, Hannah Faulkner.
John Clows*****, Gosworth, Cheshire, wife Margery; children: Sarah, Margery (married Richard Hough just before departure), William; servants: Joseph Chorley, Samuel Hough, John Richardson.

---

* The Book of Arrivals (see foreword) states that Morton came on the Freeman.
** Saylor is a misreading. The indentured servant was Robert Laylor.
*** The Book of Arrivals shows no family in his listing.
**** Sutton is named James in the Book of Arrivals.
***** The Book of Arrivals shows him as John Clows Jr., came with his brother Joseph and Sarah his sister. There is no mention there of a wife and children. As to servants, the Book of Arrivals names Harry Lingart as his only servant, not shown in Battle.

THE NAMES OF THE EARLY SETTLERS OF DARBY TOWNSHIP, CHESTER COUNTY, PENNSYLVANIA.

CONTRIBUTED BY MORGAN BUNTING.

[The recent recovery of the "Darby Township Book" has enabled Mr. Bunting to extract from it the names of the early settlers of the township. For the copy of the map of 1683, by Charles Ashcom, surveyor, we are indebted to Mrs. William B. Middleton.—ED. PENNA. MAG.]

The Originall Record of the Township of Darby in the County of Chester and province of Pensilvania as it was setteled by The English under William Penn Esquire Proprioter and Governor in Cheif of the said Province in the Year of our Lord one Thousand Six hundred and Eighty Two ; Giving an Account when Each Settlement was begun, ffor the better Regulating the Inhabitants in Serving the Respective offices of the said Township as Constables Supervisors overseers of the poor Veiwers of fences &c.

Samuel Bradshaw and
Thomas Worth came from Oxton in the County of Nottingham
John Blunston and
Michael Blunston from Littel Hallam in the County of Darby
George Wood from Bonsall in ye County of Darby
Joshua ffearne from Darley in ye County of Darby
Henry Gibbins from Parwidge in ye County of Darby
Samuel Sellers from Belper in ye County of Darby
These came in the year 1682.

Richard Bonsall from Mouldrige in ye County of Darby
Edmund Cartlidge from Ridings in ye County of Darby
Thomas Hood from Brason in the County of Darby
John Hallowel from Hucknall in ye County of Nottingham
John Bartram from Ashburn in ye County of Darby
William Wood from Nottingham.

NOTE: The present whereabouts of the Darby Township Book is unknown to us, and therefore we have been unable to compare the text of this article with the original material.   W. L. S.

A drauft of some part of
the county of Chester in pensilvaria
wherein is showed how the people
are setled and what distance other
from other and what part of the
land they dwell upon and who
lives nearest to other Also what
quantety of acres every one hath.
    by Charles Ashcom surveiour
        for the county of Chester
            1683

randall maison 250
allin robbinet 250
peter taylor 350
350
wm taylor
thomas taylor 400
richard crausby 380
robert vernon 330
iohn martin 350
iohn marsh
thomas couborn 300
thomas vernon 300
randall vernon 300
richard fou 230
ioshua haistens 300
churchman 100
Sharples 50
thomas bragoy 500
iohn Sharples 200
lib busby 100
50 townsend
nosston 200
nixson 76
iohn Simcock 100

thomas spowell 130
randall croxson 150
thomas menshall 300
iaseph spowell 125
iohn Sharples 330
thomas spowell 170
iohn ogg 125
150
rebeca Candiwell
henry mattock
iames Kenerly 800
iohn Simcock 1100

georg gloaver
peter loster

Chester Creek
Raggy Creek
Crum Creek

330
ashcoms
refudg
antony
henry
henrock 200
sproist
henrick
thorton
iohn
henrickson
iohn c

A scale of one mile

Delaware river

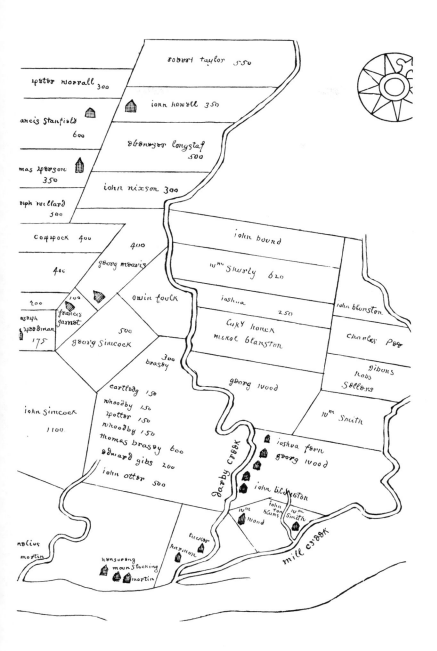

robert taylor 550

peter worrall 300

ancis Stanfield 600

iohn howell 350

ebenezer longstaf 500

mas peerson 350

iohn nixson 300

siph millard 300

compock 400   400

georg meavis   400

400

200   100

france garnet   owin foulk

josiph   500
goodman
175   georg Simcock

300
brasey

iohn Simcock
1100

cartledg 150
whoodby 150
potter 150
whoodby 150
thomas brasey 600
edward gibs 200
iohn otter 500

nelius
mortin

hansureng
mounStocking
mortin

iohn bound

wm Sherly 620

ioshua   250   iohn blunston

Cuky honer   charles pee
mikol blanston

gibons
Robs
Sollens

georg wood

wm Smith

ioshua forn
georg wood

iohn blunston

john   wm
blun   Smith
ton
wm
wood

tuckey

harmon

darby creek

mill creek

Thomas Bradshaw from Oxton in ye County of Nottingham
Robert Naylor from Manniash in the County of Darby
Richard Tucker from Warinister in ye County of Wilts
These came in the year 1683.

Robert Scorthorne from Oxton in ye County of Nottingham
James Cooper from Bolton in the County of Lancaster in [   ]
   and from Mayfeild in the County of Stafford in ye ye[ar ——]
John Hood from Casteldunington in ye County of Leic[ester]
William Garratt from harby in the County of Leices[ter]
Samuel Levis from harby in ye County of Leices[ter]
John Smith from harby in The County of Leicest[er]
William Smith from Croxton in ye County of Leiceste[r]
Robert Cliffe from harby in the County of Leicester
Thomas Smith from Croxton in The County of Leiceste[r]
Richard Parker from upper broughton in ye County of Nottingham
Adam Roades from Codnor in The County of Darby
Thomas ffox from Sutton uppon Trent in ye County of Nottingham
These came in the year 1684.

Thomas Coates from Sprixton in the County of Leicester
William Gabitas from East Markham in ye County of Nottingham
Joseph Need from Arnold in The County of Nottingham
These came in the year 1686

Edward Peirson from Wimslow in ye County of Chester
John Kirke from Allfreetown in The County of Darby
John Marshall from Elton in The County of Darby
These settled in the year 1687.

Thomas Collier from Nottingham
John Ball from Darley in the County Darby
John Wood from Nottingham
Nicholas Ireland from Laxton in the County of Nottingham
These settled in the year 1689.

Note that Calconhook was added to Darby in ye year 1686
Containing Six Settlement viz.

Morton Mortonson	Peter Peterson
Hance Urine	Swan Boone
Hance Boone	Mathias Natsilas

Anthony Morgan from Cardife in Clamorganshire
John Hood, Junr from Casteldunington in ye County of Leicester
Robert Smith from Sawley in the County of Darby
Lewis David }
Ralph Lewis }

These settled in the year 1691.

John Bethell Setteled in the year	1694
James Cooper Setteled in the year	1695
William Bartram Setteled in the year	1696
Samuel Garret Setteled in the year	1696
Josiah Hibbard Setteled in the year	1697
John Dawson Setteled in The year	1697
Christopher Spray Setteled in the year	1698
Obadiah Bonsall Setteled in the year	1698
Josiah ffearne Setteled in The year	1700
Peter Petersons new Settlement in the year	1698
Anthony Morgans new Settlement in the year	1700
Samuel Hood Setteled in the year	1700
John Bethell Junr Setteled in the year	1704
John Bown Setteled in the year	1706
Job Harvey Setteled in the year	1707
John Blunston, Junr Setteled in the year	1707
Lawrance Morton Setteled in the year	1708
John Broom Setteled in the year	1708
John Test Setteled in the year	1711
Thomas Paschall Setteled in the year	1711
Joshua Calvert Setteled in the year	1712
Samuel Bradshaw Setteled in the year	1712
Mathias Morton Setteled in the year	1712
David Thomas Setteled in the year	1714
James Whitacer Setteled in the year	1715
George Wood Setteled in the year	1715
Job Harvey's new Settlement in the year	1715
Joshua Johnson Setteled in the year	1715
John Marshall Setteled in the year	1716
Thomas Broom Setteled in The year	1716
William Preist Setteled in the year	1716
William Wood Setteled in the year	1719
Joseph Hibbard Setteled in the year	1725
Charles Justis Setteled in the year	1725
Samuel Bunting Setteled in the year	1725
Thomas (Medwier)? Setteled in the year	1725
Awbray Wood Setteled in the year	1726

Benjamin Lobb Settled in the year	1726
Enoch Eliot Settled in the year	1727
Isaac Lea Settled in the year	1728
John Marshall Junr Settled in the year	1727
John Wallis Settled in the year	1729
Everard Ellis Settled in the year	1729
Benjamin Peirson Junr Settled in ye year	1729
Th : Tatnalls new Settlement in ye year	1730
John Marshalls new Settlement in ye year	1730
Andrew Boons new Settlement in ye year	1730
Benjamin Bonsall's new Settlement in ye year	1731
Josiah ffearn's Settlement made in Lower Darby in The year	1732
Thomas Peirson Settled in the year	1733
David Mortons new Settlement made in ye year	1733
Joseph Bonsalls Settlement made in ye year	1733
Benjamin Lobbs Settlement in Lower Darby —— in ye year ——	1734
William Kirks Settlement made in ye year	1734
ffrancis Pullin Setteled in the year	1734
James Hunts Settelment made in Lower Darby In the year	1735
John Ball Settled in the year	1735
Benjamin Bonsall's settilment in Lower Darby	1736
John Roades settelment in the year	1737
Isaac Leas settlement in the year	1738
Samuell Garratts new Settlement in ye year	1738
Joseph Bonsalls new Settlement in water street in ye year	1734
John Paschalls new settlement in front street in ye year	1739
Elizabeth Hibberds Settlement in front street in ye year	1739
Evered Ellis's new Settlement in upper Darby in ye year	1739
Swan Boons Settlement in upper Darby in ye year	1739
Soloman Humphry settled in Lower Darby in ye year	1740
Edward Waldron settled in Lower Darby in ye year	1740
Isaac Pearson settled in Lower Darby in the year	1741
Edward Waldron settled in Lower Darby in ye year	1749
Jacob Webber settled in Lower Darby in ye year	1742
Stephen Paschall settlement in Upper Darby in ye year	1743
Matthew Ash settled in Upper Darby in ye year	1744
Enoch Bonsall's new settlement in Lower Darby	1744
Thomas Tatnel's new settlement in Upper Darby in ye year	1744
Ambrose Wilkcocks settled in Lower Darby in year	1745
John Davis's new Settlement in Upper Darby in ye year	1745
Cunrod Nethermark's new settlement in Calconhook in ye year	1745
Andrew Urin new Settlement in Calconhook in the year	1746
Abraham Lewis Jun'r settled in Upper Darby in ye year	1750
Samuel Kirk Settled in Upper Darby in ye year	1751

William Garret settled in Upper Darby in ye year   1751
Abraham Johnson Settled in Upper Darby in ye year   1751
Swan Boons new Settlement in Lower Darby   1752
Tobias Mortens new Settlement in Lower Darby   1752
Enoch Bonsalls new Settlement in Lower Darby   1755
William Parker new Settlement in Lower Darby   1760
Abraham Bonsalls new Settlement in Upper Darby   1760
Abraham Johnson's new settlement in Upper Darby   1760
Benjamin Lobbs new Settlement in Upper Darby   1760
John Kirk's new settlement in upper Darby   1760

THE SAILING OF THE SHIP "SUBMISSION" IN THE YEAR 1682, WITH A TRUE COPY OF THE VESSEL'S LOG.

L. TAYLOR DICKSON.

THE log of the ship "Submission," of which the following is a copy, commences the fourth day of the week, sixth day of the seventh month (September) and ends on the seventh day of the week, the twenty-first day of the eighth month, 1682. The vessel at this day being near the mouth of the Chesapeake Bay, which appears by the entry made on the nineteenth day of October, at which time the odor from the pines was noticed, "supposing ourselves not to be within 80 leagues." Phineas Pemberton in his record states that they arrived in the Choptank, Maryland, on the second day of ninth month, 1682, thus making the voyage in fifty-eight days from port to port, the last days of the passage not being recorded in the log.

As Captain Settle was bound for another port, and the weather being overcast, it is highly probable that upon the twenty-first day of the seventh month he did not know where he was, and therefore did not complete the log.

Many of the passengers remained in Maryland for a considerable time (some of them married there), and then walked to Appoquinimink, the lowest section of New Castle County, about forty miles from the place of landing, and twenty miles south of the established town of New Castle.

The most important colonists on the "Submission," judging from their respective positions in after-life, were: Phineas Pemberton and Randle (or Randolph) Blackshaw. Pemberton states in his record that the Blackshaws arrived in Appoquinimink on the fifteenth day of eleventh month, 1683. And as James Harrison, Phineas Pemberton, James Clayton, Randle Blackshaw and Ellis Jones with their families were residents of Bucks County in 1684, it is evident that they did not remain in the lower county long. The voyage across the Atlantic had been a most trying one to the passengers, due principally to the severe exactions of the Master, James Settle, but partly from the fact that many of them had over-invested in that commodity of the time known as "servants," [1] so much so that their funds became exhausted and Randle Blackshaw was compelled to sell in Maryland Eleonore, the wife of Roger Bradbury, [2] together with her three sons, so as to liquidate his indebtedness to the Captain and enable him to reach the Quaker province on the Delaware. Much information can be obtained of these people and of their lives and form of transportation from the Choptank to Bucks County. Of the passengers other than those settled in Bucks County possibly the most interesting to the genealogist are the daughter and

[1] Many of those registered as servants appear to be closely related to and quite the equal of their masters, and had been influenced to emigrate on account of the liberal inducements offered by the Proprietor; for even before this time we find in the Upland court records the sale of William Still, tailor, for four years to Captain Edmund Cantwell. And a short time after this the clergyman at New Castle in a letter states that they have lost their schoolmaster, but that he can be replaced, as he learns that a vessel is shortly to arrive, when he will go to the dock and buy one. And it is also stated that no less a person than a distinguished signer of the Declaration of Independence was sold in his youth as a servant and after the expiration of his time taught school.

[2] As the name of Bradbury does not appear among the residents of Bucks County it is to be presumed that the entire family remained in Maryland.

step-daughters of Dr. Thomas Wynne, Rebecca Winn and Marjory and Jane Mede. Hannah Logan Smith commits an error when she states that Elizabeth, the second wife of Thomas Wynne, came in this ship with their children, for as her name does not appear in the list of passengers, it is fair to presume she came with her husband in the "Welcome." This mistake could be easily made when we consider that the vessels made the voyage at the same time. Rebecca, daughter of Thomas Wynne, married first Solomon Thomas, and secondly John Dickinson. Marjory Mede, his step-daughter, married Thomas Fisher (whose descendants are numerous), and Jane Mede married and died probably without surviving children. From the Bucks County Friends Record it would appear that Robert Bond died seventh month, sixteenth, 1684; that Jane Lyon married Richard Lundy fourth month, twenty-fourth, 1691, and that Phœbe Blackshaw became the wife of Joseph Kirkbride on the thirteenth day of first month, 1688. Neither of the company's servants appear on the records, and the name of Jane-clif Hodges in Pemberton's list looks more like Farclif Hodges, although it may be Francis, but not Harriet as printed in the *Pennsylvania Magazine*, Vol. IX. There are a number of books and manuscripts in the library of the Pennsylvania Historical Society[1] that throw much light on the lives of these early emigrants, from which much genealogical information could be obtained.

The Log of the "Submission."
Voyage of the
Submission
from Liverpool to
Pennsylvania
1682.

An acct of our passage towards Pens[ylvania —— the passengers Subscribers, went Abord the vessel Submission from

[1] The most interesting are the records of Phineas Pemberton, printed in Volume IX of the *Pennsylvania Magazine*, and his book of ear-marks of the cattle and horses made in 1684.

the port of Liverpoole 5$\frac{\text{th } 7}{\text{mo}}$ 1682.   The master's name
James Settle, the mate Samuel Rigg — Brian ffleetwood the
Carpenter, Anthony Busshell the cooper, Ellijah Cobham,
Thomas Bullock, Peter Travis, John Royle, Thomas Hate-
ley, servants.   Henry ~~Blivin~~, Michael C**ə**lon, apprentices.
Heads ii.   *Blevin,*

The Passengers names & ages & number as — near as
cold be well taken.

				Passengers
ffree Passengers.				
James Harrison	54 years	Annâ Harrison	58 years	2 — 0
Agnes Harrison	80 —	Richard Radclif	21 —	2 — 0
Robert Bond	14 —	Joseph Steward	14½ —	2 — 0
~~Phineas~~ Pemberton	32½ —	Phebe Pemberton	22½ —	2 — 0
~~Abigail~~ Pemberton	2½ —	Ralph Pemberton	70 —	1 — 0
Joseph Mather	18 —	Joseph Pemberton (16 weeks Age) — 0		
Lydia Wharmby		Elizabeth Bradbury	16 —	2 — 0
Allis Dickinson		Jane Lyon	16½ —	2 — 0
James Clayton	50	Jane Clayton	48 —	2 — 0
James Clayton	16	Sarab Clayton	14 —	2 — 0
John Clayton	11	Mary Clayton	8 —	1 — 0
~~Joseph~~ Clayton	5	Lydia Cleaton	5 —	1 — 0
Randulph Blackshaw	60	Allis Blackshaw	43 —	2 — 0
Phebe Blackshaw	16	Sarah Blackshaw	14 —	2 — 0
Abraham Blackshaw	10	Jacob Blackshaw	8 —	1 — 0
Mary Blackshaw	6	Nehemiah Blackshaw	3 —	1 — 0
Martha Blackshaw	1	freight tree		
His servants.				
Roger Bradbury	49	Ellenor Bradbury	46 —	2 — 0
Jacob Bradbury	18	Martha Bradbury	14 —	2 — 0
Joseph Bradbury	10	Sarah Bradbury	8 —	1 — 0
Roger Bradbury	2			
Ellis Jones	45	Jane Jones	40 —	1 — 0
Barbary Jones	13	Dorothy Jones	10 —	1 — 0
Mary Jones	12½	Isaac Jones (4 months)	0 —	i
Rebeckah Winn	20	Jane ~~Mode~~ *Mode*	15 —	2 — i
Marjory ~~Mode~~ *Mode*	11½			

Of Lancashire.

hinenas Abigal

Of Cheshire.

Josua

From Wales.

whole passengers 37

heads 49
hed the owners servants for sale
~~Jameslif~~ Hodges & Ellen Holland.

Parclife

1682 about 4 afternoon set sails & came to an anker black Rock about 6 from whence & sent 3 letters by boat one Roger Longworth one for Henry Haydock one for Thomas Jonjois

for

4— 6. about one in the morning I sail & came that night to an anker about 7 betwixt Hollyhead and Beaumorris

5— 7. about 12 in the morning set sails & the wind came south & put us a little to the north till about 10 in the morning then it came no-west & we came about Hollyhead & left sight of it yt night

6— 8. that night over agt Waterford fair wether

7— 9. A misty day Becalmed   *over agt*

1—10. A clear day the wind easterly in the morning ~~on east~~ Waterford

2—11. A fair day wind easterly at 10 in ye morning ~~on east~~ Kingssale   *over agt*

3—12. in the forenoon left sight of Cape Cleare

4—13. the wind south-westerly.

5—14. Wind S W that day we spoke with A ship from East India bound for London, that we ~~went~~ *were* about 75 leagues from the Capes

6—15. becalmed

7—16. A high wind much westerly that day we saw at A distance A whale

1—17. A high wind westerly in the afternoon A whale came neare us & appeared fair to us & followed us some time

2—18. The wind much westerly about 12 in the night there arose A great storm that day were forced to take of the main top & to lay the ship by for about 10 hours the sea was exceedingly high ye waves ran as high as the main yards but we received little damage.

3—19. in the afternoon the wind S west

4—20. about four in the morning the wind n west the day fair

5—21. Wind N W day cold

6—22. Wind N W very cold & stormy

7—23. Wind N W very cold & stormy

1—24. Wind N W a calm day & cleare

2—25. A calm day & cleare

3—26. becalmed most of the day in the afternoon wind S W in 48 degrees 31 minutes no latitude

4—27. The wind westerly at night wind high in 48 degrees & 20 minutes about 15 degrees in longitude from the Cape

5—28. The wind westerly till evening no-east

6—29. Westerly and cold

7—30. about 11 in the forenoon we saw a ship about 12 we saw 14——? one company about 3 in the afternoon we saw a ship all supposed to be a ffrench ship

1— 1.$\frac{8}{n10}$ the wind N W at night was high & the sea very [——?]

2— 2. the sea very rough the wind high about 4 in the [——?] dyed Abraham the son of Randulph Blackshaw about 6 in the morning A great head sea broke over the ship & staved the boat & took the most part of it away, broke up the main hatches that were both nailed & corked & took them away that they were not seen where they went, broke the boat's mast & ~~hyst~~ that were lashed in the midship, broke of the gunnell head in the midship & broke the forre shet & took severall things of the decks & severall things that were in the boat it cast betwix decks. At 9 in the morning the boy was put overboard, about 4 in the afternoon A ~~great~~ sea fell on our Rudder & broke it about 1 yard or Something more from the head, was again pieced as well as it cold that night—not being discovered until about 10 at night & was made pretty firm the next day.

a yard

3— 3. The Sea rough.

4— 4. The Sea indeferent high the wind calme

5— 5. The wind No-E.

6— 6. The day faire wind easterly

7— 7. day faire wind N E.

1— 8. A fresh gale N, we Saw a ~~whale~~ turtle.

2— 9. faire wether and wind, hundreds of porpoises about the ship some leaped high out of the water and followed the ship about an hour.

3—10. faire wether and wind, this morning we saw another great school of porpoises in ~~30~~ 38 degrees 57 minutes no latitude.

4—11. The day faire, the wind East this day we spoke with a New England ship bound for Lisborne.

5—12. The wind Southerly extraordinary hot.

6—13. in the morning the wind S. E. with raine from 8 in morning to 4 in the afternoon that day was seene in the great raine at the ship's side blood the half compas of the ship.

7—14. at twelve in the morning it began to raine and continued showering all day, the sea rough, the wind northerly and N.N.E.

1—15. the wind easterly the day faire.

2—16. winds and wether good in 37 : 46 minutes latitude and 31 de 48 minutes Longitude.

3—17. day and wind faire.   At evening it began to lighten & continued.

4—18. lightened all day & night but little raine to us

5—19. faire this morning the wind being nor west we smelled the pines, supposing ourselves not to be within 80 leagues.

6—20. this day faire till evening it begun to blow wind S W.

7—21. raine some pte of the day.

THE FIRST PURCHASERS
OF PENNSYLVANIA

by

Hannah Benner Roach

On the fourth day of March, 1681, William Penn, Founder and first Proprietor of Pennsylvania, received his charter for the province from Charles the Second. Within a month Penn's initial plans for settling the land were in print in Some Account of the Province of Pennsilvania ... for the Information of such as are or may be disposed to Transport themselves or Servants into those Parts. In this first promotional tract, he proposed offering for sale shares of 5000 acres at Ł100 per share, and for those unable to buy, the opportunity to take up land upon a nominal quitrent.

In consultation with prospective buyers during the next three months, these initial offers were refined and outlined in greater detail, and incorporated as Certain Conditions or Concessions agreed upon by William Penn, Proprietary and Governor of the Province of Pennsylvania, and those who are the Adventurers and Purchasers in the same Province. As an attraction toward investment in the province, these included a provision which entitled each of those who bought the first 100 shares for a total of 500,000 acres, to a lot, proportionate to the size of each individual purchase, in the first settlement to be laid out in the province.

The first sales were consummated in mid-July, 1681, and by the following October, sixty-four of the one hundred shares had been sold. The names of these first purchasers and the acreage each had bought were entered in a "catalogue" as purchaser-groups numbered from one to thirty-two, inclusive. Apparently in order to simplify the computation of the amount of land sold, the acreage of each purchaser-group in the catalogue was intended to total 10,000 acres, or two shares. The acreage of several, however, was either over or under that amount.

In view of the alacrity with which some sixty percent of the land reserved for the first purchasers had been purchased in less than three months, Penn decided not to wait until all 500,000 acres had been sold, but to send off this first catalogue of purchasers with the first shipload of settlers to set out for the new land. Appointing commissioners to supervise their settlement, he entrusted them with the catalogue. They sailed from Bristol in October on the Bristol Factor, and reached New Castle on the Delaware December 15, 1681.

Between October, 1681, and the end of April, 1682, all of the 500,000 acres were sold, and Penn closed his list of first purchasers the end of the month. Eighteen new purchaser-groups were entered in a second catalogue, were numbered from 33 to 50, inclusive. This second catalogue, probably sent on the Samuel which left London toward the end of May or early in June, 1682, reached Philadelphia by mid-September. The names in it and in the first catalogue represented all of the original purchasers who were entitled to proportionate lots in the first settlement.

But during the summer and up to the end of August, 1682, when

Penn himself sailed, he found that some of those on the first and second lists had changed their minds or failed to complete their bargain with him. There were also several large purchasers in Ireland and elsewhere whose money was not received in time to have their names entered on the second catalogue. To compensate for the deficiencies of his original purchasers, and to satisfy those who had bought under the impression they would be considered first purchasers, their names appear to have been included on a third list, compiled at an unknown later date. Neither the original of the second or third list appear to have ever been recorded, and if extant, their present whereabouts are unknown.

The first list, on two skins of parchment, however, was extant in 1763, when it was copied into and recorded in the books of the Land Office, now in Harrisburg. The following "Accompt of the Land in Pennsylvania Granted ... to several Purchasors within the Kingdom of England," is transcribed from photostats of that copy, and here published for the first time. It is not to be confused with what have purported to be lists of first purchasers which have appeared in print from time to time.

The earliest of these was published by John Reed in 1774 as part of his An Explanation of the Map of the City and Liberties. He apparently used the original or the 1763 recorded list as a basis, but arranged the names on his list alphabetically, and added to it subsequent purchasers. That alphabetical list was again published in 1894 in The Pennsylvania Archives, Third Series, III, 327-344. Reed also included on his Map of the City and Liberties of Philadelphia, appended to the Explanation, the names listed in the first catalogue or "Accompt" and their acreage, but omitted the places of residence and occupations. To this list he added the names in the "Second Catalogue" of purchaser-groups thirty-three to fifty, and a third but undated alphabetical list of names. The latter, on examination, appear to be a medley of under-purchasers (those who bought from original purchasers and so acquired proportionate rights in the city and liberties), later purchasers, and first purchasers who bought additional land.

In 1850, Samuel Hazard, in his Annals of Pennsylvania from the Discovery of the Delaware, 1609-1682, 637-642, published a "List of Purchasers" taken from a list he said was then in the Land Office in Harrisburg, and which he believed was the second list. But this list, subsequently reprinted in 1852 in Volume I of The Pennsylvania Archives [First Series], 40-46, contained fifty-seven purchaser-groups, and obviously could not have been the second catalogue. It may have been the third catalogue, revised to eliminate those who had failed to complete their sales and to include the new sales made during the summer of 1682. In it, names of some original purchasers found on the first two lists have been shuffled from their original group to a different group, and the number of acres assigned to several purchasers has been altered. Significantly, it was headed "An Account of the lands in Pennsylvania granted by William Penn, Esq. chief proprietary and governor of that province, to several purchasers within the kingdom of England, Ireland and Scotland, &c." Its present whereabouts has not been located.

The names of purchasers in the "Second Catalogue," printed hereinafter, are taken from the list appearing on John Reed's Map of the City and Liberties of Philadelphia, inserted at the end of Volume IV of The Pennsylvania Archives, Third Series. In group XXXIV of this list, the Christian names Mathew, Thomas and Thomas appear with no last names indicated, and no acreage entered. These names have been omitted in the present transcript. In the same group, below the 125 acres of Philip Alford (Oxford), an additional 1000 acres is listed, with no name assigned. As no evidence has been found that Alford acquired additional acreage so early, this, too, has been omitted. Otherwise the list is as Reed presented it, with the addition, wherever possible, of place of residence and occupation and, as occasion indicated, a corrected version of the purchaser's name, all inserted within brackets.

The sources for such information are varied. Some come from original deeds of lease and release in the collections of the Historical Society of Pennsylvania, or from data supplied by Dr. Gary B. Nash, who examined the original deeds now deposited in the Wynne Collection, Penn Papers, Bedfordshire County Record Office, England. An examination of the recorded grants in the Land Office in Harrisburg, and of the exemplification of others in the Department of Records, City Hall, Philadelphia, revealed further information. The Philadelphia and Bucks County registers of arrivals, transcripts of which are included in this present work, were consulted. The digested copies of English Friends' Records in the collections of the Genealogical Society of Pennsylvania in Philadelphia, were examined. George Smith's History of Delaware County, Pennsylvania .... (1862); W.W.H. Davis's History of Bucks County ..., (1876); and Futhey and Cope's History of Chester County ..., (1881), each supplied information on places of residence and occupations not found elsewhere. The most useful source was the "Minutes of the Board of Property," in The Pennsylvania Archives, Second Series, XIX, and Third Series, I.

An Accompt of the Land in Pennsylvania Granted by William Penn Esq[r] Sole Proprietary & Governour of that Province To several Purchasors within the Kingdom of England, Viz[t] To

I
	Acres
Philip Ford of London Merchant	5000
Thomas Rudyard of London Gent	2000
The same	2000
Herbert Springet of London Gent	1000

II
Samuel Jobson of St. Mary Magdalens Bermondsey...	
James Claypoole of London Merchant	5000
John Moore and Joseph Moore of Lond. Merchants	1000
Sabian Coles of London Merchant	1000
Thomas Barker of London Wine Cooper	1000
Humphrey South of London Merchant	1000
Samuel Jobson of St. Mary Magdalens Bermondsey in the County of Surrey Fellmonger	1000

III
	Acres
Edward Jefferson of Ashwell in the County of Hertford Maulster	1500
Thomas Scott of London Taylor	500
John Goodson of London Chirurgeon	500
John Beckley of London Perfumer	250
Daniel Quare of London Clockmaker	250

	Acres
John Stringfellow of London Taylor	500
Richard Townsend of London Carpenter	250
Caleb Pusey of London Glassmaker	250
John Hicks of London Cheesemonger	250
Henry Murey of London Taylor	250
Edward Blake of London Turner	250
William Moore of London Plaisterer	500
Henry Sleighton of London Turner	250
John Pusey of London Dyer	250
Thomas Virgoe of London Clockmaker	500
Thomas Burbary of London Shoemaker	250
John Allington of London Salter	250
Richard Jordain of London Shoemaker	250
Samuel Bennett of London Flaxdresser	250
Thomas Cobb of London Shoemaker	250
Thomas [John] Tibbye of London Joyner	250
Elizabeth Shorter of London Glover	250
Amos Nichols of London Distiller	250
John Barber of London Brewer	250
Jonathan Stanmore of London Shoemaker	250
John Spencer of London Taylor	125
Mark Keynton of London Carpenter	125
John Jones of the Parish of St. Andrews Holbourne London Glover	500
William Boswell of Southwark in the County of Surrey Poulterer	500
Edward Simkins of the same Place Feltmaker	250

IV

| Thomas Farmborrough of London Chairmaker | 5000 |
| Arent Sonmans of Walliford in the County of Midlothian in the Kingdom of Scotland Gent | 5000 |

V

| Nicholas Moore of London Gent | 10000 |

VI

| William Bowman the Elder of Wansworth in the County of Surrey Glazier | 5000 |
| Griffith Jones of the Parish called Mary Magdalens Bermondsey in ye County of Surrey Glover | 5000 |

VII

Benjamin East of Brookswharf London Sugar Baker	1250
Charles Bathurst Citizen and Salter of London	1250
William Kent Citizen and Merchant Taylor of London	1250
John Tovey of London Grocer	1250
William Philips of London Wine Cooper and Joseph Philips Son of ye said Wm Philips	1250
John Barnes of Chiltington in the County of Sussex Taylor for his Daughter	1000
Nathaniel Harding of London Basket maker	500
William Carter of Wapping in the County of Middx Turner	500

	Acres
Francis Harrison of London Poulterer	250
John Carver of Hedly in ye County of South'on Maulster	500
John Swift of ye Town of South'on in ye County of Glazier	500
William Lawrence of Axbridge in the County of Somersett Woolen draper	500

VIII

	Acres
Robert Dimsdale of Edmenton in the County of Middx Chirurgeon	5000
Hugh Lamb of the Parish of St. Martins in the Fields in the County of Middx Hosier	2500
Thomas Rudyard of London Gent	1000
Herbert Springet of London Gent	500
William Russel of London Phisitian	1000

IX

	Acres
William Markham of London Gent	5000
Henry Waddy of the Parish of St. Andrews Holbourn in the County of Middx Millener	750
John Day of London Carpenter	1250
Francis Plumstead of the Minorites London Iron Monger	2500
William Haige of London Merchant	500

X

	Acres
George Fox of London Gent	1250
Allexander Parker of London Haberdasher	1000
Robt. Lodge in the County of York Yeoman	500
John Burnyeat, Tho: Zachary & Cuthbert Hurst	1250
James Park, Thomas Langhorn & Thomas Lawson	1000
Ambrose Rigge, William Piggot, Nathanl Owen	5000

XI

	Acres
William Bacon of ye Middle Temple London Gent	10000

XII

	Acres
Nathaniel Allen of the City of Bristoll Cooper	2000
John Hort of the City of Bristoll Curryer	1000
Henry Comby [Comly] of the City of Bristoll Weaver	500
William Smith of the City of Bristoll Brass founder	500
James Wallis of the City of Bristoll Merchant	1000
Richard Crosllet of the City of Bristoll Goldsmith	1000
Edmund Bennet of the City of Bristoll Tobacco cutter	1000
William Smith of Bristol Mariner	1000
Margarett Martindale Wife of Edward Martindale of ye City of Bristol Merchant	1000
John Love of ye City of Bristoll Grocer	1000

XIII

	Acres
Charles Marshall of the City of Bristol Phisitian	1000
Charles Jones Senr of the City of Bristoll Sope boyler and Charles Jones Junr of the same Place Merchant	2000
Robert Vickris of Chew in ye County of Somersett Merchant and Richard Vickris of Bristoll Merchant	2000
John Moon of the City of Bristoll Linnendraper	500

	Acres
William Brown of the City of Bristoll Merchant	1000
Charles Harfford of the City of Bristoll Sopeboyler	1000
Richard Snead of ye City of Bristoll Mercer	1500
John Jones of the City of Bristoll Linnen Draper and Michael Jones of the same Place Grocer	1000

XIV

Richard Marsh of the City of Bristoll Merchant	5000
The same	5000

XV

Thomas Callowhill of the City of Bristoll Mercer	5000
The same	500
Nathaniel Evans of [blank]	500
Thomas Paget of the City of Bristoll Mealman	500
Thomas Paschall of the City of Bristoll Pewterer	500
Jone Dixon of the City of Bristoll Widdow	500
James Pebre [Petre]	500
John Jennett of the City of Bristoll Silkweaver	500
Roger Drew [Mariner]	500
Edward Erberry of the City of Bristoll Sope boiler	500
William Lane of the City of Bristoll Grocer..................	500

XVI

Edward Martindale of the City of Bristoll Merchant	1000
Philip Theodore Leman [Lehnman] of the City of Bristoll Gent .	1000
Arnold Brown and William Cole of ye Custom and two more ...	5000
Peter Young of the City of Bristoll Sope-boiler...............	500
Thomas Bailey of the City of Bristoll Bodies Maker	250
Joel Jelson [of Barton Regis, Gloster, Haberdasher]	250
John Bristo of the City of Bristoll	500
Thomas Briggs of Hedelston in the Parish of Acton in the County Palatine of Chester Yeoman	500
George Keith of Edenburgh in the Kingdom of Scotland Gent....	500

XVII

George Powell of the Parish of Bucklam in ye County of Somersett Butcher	500
John Clare of Froms Elwood in ye County of Sussex [Somerset] Butcher	500
John Hill of Berbington in the County of Somersett Shoemaker .	500
Christopher Forford of Froom in ye County of Somersett Wire drawer	500
William Beabes [Beakes] of Backwell in ye County of Somersett Yeoman	1000
Samuel Allen of Chew Magna in the County of Somersett Shoemaker	2000
Walter King of Haveyard	1000
John Passons [Parsons] of Middlezey in the County of Somersett Carpenter & Abraham Hoope of Bridgewater in ye same County Joiner	500
Thomas Pleas of Edenton in the same County Serge maker	250
Richard Mills of Bridgewater in ye County of Somersett Taylor.	250

	Acres
William Salloway of Taunton Deane in the County of Somersett Sergemaker	250
Francis Harfford of the same Place Sergemaker	250
John Wall of Moorelinch in the County of Somersett Husbandman and John Wallis of the same Place Husbandman	250
John Coles of Catrott in the Parish of Moorelinch in the County of Somersett Sergemaker	1000
Richard Collins of Bath	1250

XVIII

	Acres
George White of Buckleberry in the County of Berks Yeoman	2500
John Sansom of Chevels in the County of Berks Woodmonger and John May of Bucklebury in the Same County Button maker	500
George Green of Farringtdon in ye County of Berks Roper	2000
Francis Smith of Great Illford in the County of Essex Yeoman	5000

XIX

	Acres
John Barber of Shipley in the County of Sussex Yeoman	2500
Thomas Roland of Billingshurst in ye County of Sussex Yeoman	2500
Thomas Adams of Alfreston in the County of Sussex Yeoman	1250
John Songhurst of Chiltington in the County of Sussex Carpenter and John Baines [Barnes] of the same Taylor	1250
Thomas Bankes of Alfreston in the County of Sussex Maulster	1250
William Wade of Westham in ye County of Sussex Yeoman	1250

XX

	Acres
George Willard of Warre in the County of Sussex Yeoman	1250
Priscilla Sheppard of Worminghurst in ye County of Sussex Spinster	500
Sarah Hersent of the same Place Spinster	500
Israel Brench of the same Place Husbandman	500
Elizabeth Symmes of Steyning in the County of Sussex Spinster	500
Thomas Bourne of Crawley in the County of Sussex Mercer	1250
Walter Martin of Westminston in the County of Sussex Husbandman	500
Thomas Herriott of Hurst Perpoint in the County of Sussex Yeoman	2500
Thomas Herriott of Hurst Perpoint in the County of Sussex Yeoman	2500

XXI

	Acres
Thomas Dell of Upton in the County of Bucks Yeoman	500
John Pennington of Woodside in the Parish of Agmondisham in ye County of Bucks Gent	1250
William Pennington the Younger of the same Place Druggster	1250
Edward Pennington of the same Place	1250
Mary Pennington the Younger of the same place Spinster	1250
Thomas Elwood of Hungerhill in the same County Gent	500
Thomas Couborne of Lambern Woodlands in the County of Berks Carpenter	500
Alexander Beardsley of the County of Worcester Glover	500

	Acres
John Price of the same City Taylor	500
William Pardoe of the City of Worcester Merchant	1250
Francis Fincher of the City of Worcester Glover	1250

XXII

Charles Lloyd Gent., Richard Davis Gent., Margarett Davis Widdow, John Humphreys Gent., Edward Thomas Yeoman All of the County of Mountgomery. Robert Owen Gent., Lewis Owen Gent. & Rowland Ellis of Merienethshire Gent...	10000
William Powel of Southwark in the County of Surrey	1250

XXIII

William Bingley of the City of Oxford Maulster	500
Anne Oliffe of the City of Oxford Widdow....................	500
John Hart of Witney in the County of Oxon Yeom.............	1000
Joseph Richards of Newgate in the County of Oxon Yeom.......	500
Joshua Hastings of Swarford in the County of Oxon Yeom.......	1000
Richard Ward of the same place Yeom......................	1000
Richard Hand of the same Place Husbandman	1000
John March of Neather Hayford in the County of Oxon Carpenter	1000
Sylvester Jourden of the same Place Carpenter	500
William Cecill of Longcomb in the County of Oxon Carpenter ..	500
Thomas Cerey of the City of Oxford Farrier	500
Edward Bettris of the City of Oxford Chirurgeon	2000

XXIV

John ap John of the Parish of Ruabon in the County of Denby Yeoman and Thomas Wynne of Cajerwit in the County of Flint Chirurgeon	5000
John Thomas of Llaitheum in the County of Merioneth Yeoman & Edward Jones of Bala in the same County Chirurgeon ...	5000

XXV

Ralph Withers of Bishops Canning in the County of Wilts Yeoman	500
John Bezer of the same Place Maulster	500
The same	500
John Clark Junr of the Devizes in the County of Wilts Baker ...	500
Isaac Selfe of Market Levington in the County of Wilts and Edward Guy of the same Place Maulsters	500
Edward Luffe of Market Levington in the County of Wilts Shoemaker and John Luffe Son of the said Edward Luffe ...	500
Richard Fue Senr of the same Place Shoemaker & Richard Fue Junr of Weadhampton in the County of Wilts Son of Richard the Elder	500
John Brothers of Markett Levington in the County of Wilts and Robert Serghell of Weadhampton in the same County Yeoman	500
Edward Bezar of Rowde in the County of Wilts Mason	500
Anthony Elton of Yatesbury in the County of Wilts Yeoman	500
Edward Brown of Marleborrough in the County of Wilts Yeoman	500

	Acres
Daniel Smith of the same Place Distiller	500
John Harding of the same Place Maulster	500
John Gibbon of Warmnester in the County of Wilts Shoemaker..	500
William Smith of Broomhamhouse in the County of Wilts Yeoman	1250
Samuel Noyes of ye Devizes in the County of Wilts Sergemaker.	500
Thomas Sagar of Foxham in the Parish of Christian Melford in the County of Wilts Yeoman and Susannah Bayley of Catcomb in the Parish of Hill Marton in the same County Widdow	500
John Buckley Junr of Melkysham in the County of Wilts Husbandman	250
William Withers of Bishops Canning in the County of Wilts Yeoman	500

XXVI

	Acres
George Andrews Junr of Rowde in the County of Wilts Sergemaker	250
William Shute of Segre in the County of Wilts Yeoman	500
Francis Smith of the Devizes in the County of Wilts Gent	500
Anne Crawley of Rowde in the County of Wilts Spinster	500
Robert Somer of the same Place Yeoman	500
Robert Stevens of the same Place Yeoman	250
Thomas Gerrish of Bromham in the County of Wilts Clothier ..	500
William Clowde of Seene in the County of Wilts Yeoman	500
Oliver Cope of Awbury in the County of Wilts Taylor	250
Enoch Flower of Corsham in the County of Wilts Barber	2000
John Rebye [Retye] of Marllborrough in the County of Wilts Maulster	250
John Bunce of the same Place Maulster	250
John Kinsman of Fifel in the County of Wilts Yeoman	500
William Hitchcock of Marlborrow in the County of Wilts Maulster	500
William Bezer of the Parish of Bishops Canning ye County of Wilts Husbandman	250
Thomas Hatt of Goatacre in the County of Wilts Cordwinder ...	500
Thomas Haywood [of Charlecott, Wilts, Sergemaker]	250
James Hill [of Beckington, Somerset, Shoemaker]	500

XXVII

	Acres
John Boy of Luckington in the County of Wilts Mercer	1000
Jane May of the Devizes in ye County of Wilts Widdow	250
Edward Edwards of Brinkworth in the County of Wilts Yeoman .	250
Robert Frame [Freame]	250
Philip Runing als Rackings [of Lyneham, Wilts, Shoemaker] ...	250
William Bayly [of Gottacre, Wilts, Yeoman]	500
Henry Barnard [Bernard]	250
John Collett	500
Thomas Minchin	500
Edward Jeffryes of Cirencester in ye County of Glocester	500
Hugh Chamberlain of the City of London Doctor of Phisick	5000

Acres

XXVIII

William Lowther Margaret Lowther Junr. and Anne Charlotte
Lowther Children of Anthony Lowther of Malke in the
County of York Esquire 10000

XXIX

William Crispin & Silas Crispin of Kingsale in ye Kingdom
of Ireland Gents..................................... 5000
Benjamin Chambers [of Bearsted, Kent, Turner] 5000

XXX

Laurence Growdon of Trevore in the County of Cornwall Gent.. 5000
Joseph Growdon of Austle in ye County of Cornwall Gent....... 5000

XXXI

William Penn the Younger and Laetitia Penn the Children of
William Penn Propr. & Govr............................ 10000

XXXII

Joseph Martin of London Merchant 5000
James Lyel of London Merchant 5000

The present Duty of the Commissioners is to lay out Ten Thousand Acres for a Town in which the Purchaser or Purchasors of every five Thousand Acres shall have one hundred Acres. And that the Town Shares be laid out Together according to this Catalogue and the Contiguousness of the Counties the Purchasors belong to. And I do farther Order that the last part of this Town be laid out for the present Purchasors and for the Rest I refer to my Instructions dated ye Fourteenth of October 1681. /s/ Wm Penn

William Penn Proprietary and Governour of Penn-sylvania Greeting To his Trusty and well beloved Friends William Crispin William Haige John Bezer and Nathaniel Allen:

These are to Authorize and Appoint you my Commissioners in my name fully and Effectually to Act whatever may be Requisite for settling the Present Colony Embarqut this Autumn at London and Bristoll for Pennsylvania and all other Adventurers with respect to the Survey and Allottment of every Man his Share according to the Cataloge of Purchasors and the Instructions that are herewith given to you. For all which this shall be Your sufficient Warrant and Authority. Given under my Hand and Seal at London in the Kingdom of England this five and twentieth day of October in ye Year of our Lord according to the English Accompt One thousand six hundred Eighty and One. /s/ Wm Penn (seal)

N. B. The Original in three pieces of Parchment Connected together by a Label on which Label was the Seal at Arms of William Penn ye late Proprietary of Pennsylvania &ca. The two first Pieces of Parchment were each of them divided into four Columns and Numbered as above in ye Margin over against [opposite] ye Beginning of each Paragraph of ye Column next ye Margin. And where ye Columns were not next the Margin over the Top of each Paragraph in Roman Figures as above Beginning with One and Ending with thirty two. The Paragraph or Clause beginning with ye Words: The Present Duty, signed Wm Penn, was in the fourth Column of the Second piece of Parchment And the Rest in the third Piece of Parchment as above.

The whole Recorded the 21st Day of July 1763 [in Patent Book AA-5, 130-139, Land Office, Harrisburg, Pa.]

The Second Catalogue

of Purchasors

	Acres
XXXIII	
George Whitehead	500
William Low	500
Richard Webb [of Kingston on Thames, linen draper]	1000
Leonard Fell [of Beakley in Furnis, Lancaster]	250
Richard Richardson	250
Robert Knight [of Godmersham, Kent]	2500
William Tanner [of Uxbridge, Middlesex, Tanner]	500
John Tanner [of Lovelane, London, Distiller]	500
Joseph Tanner	500
Robert Greenway [of London, Mariner]	1500
Francis Borrough [of London, Milliner]	1000
Isaac Martin [of London, Feltmaker]	500
Nathaniel Paske	250
William Neil [Neale of the Parish of St. Olave, Surrey, Wool stapler]	250
A. B.	500
XXXIV	
Thomas Powell [of the Lordship of Rudheath, Cheshire]	250
Ralph Ward [Shoemaker]	125
Philip Alford [Oxford, Cordwainer]	125
Nehemiah Mitchell [of Redwith Middlesex, Cooper]	500
Nathaniel Mitchell	250
Francis Dove [of London, Tallow Chandler]	500
Edward Samways [of London, Cook]	500
William Wiggan [of Westminster, Perfumer]	500
Richard Glutton [Gunton]	1000
Barzilion Foster	1000
Daniel Gammell	1650
John West [Parish of St. Sepulchre, London, Citizen and Girdler]	1250
Ralph Kinsey [of London]	125
William and Peter Tailor [Taylor of Sutton, Cheshire]	1250
John Reynolds	1000
Randle Croxton	250
Thomas Vernon [of Stanthorne, County Palatine of Chester]	500
Robert Vernon [of Stoke, Cheshire]	500
Randle Vernon [of Sandyway, Cheshire]	500
Randle Malin [of Great Barrum, Cheshire]	250
Allen Robinett	250
Henry Maddock & James Kennerly [both of Hoomhall, Cheshire]	1500
John Sharpless [of Hadderton, Cheshire]	1000
Richard Kirkman	250

206

	Acres

XXXV
The Society of Traders 10000
The Same 10000

XXXVI
Thomas Ellwood [of Hunger Hill, Bucks] and Mary Ellwood
    his wife 500
Henry Child [of Coleshill, Herts.] 500
Amy Child [of Herts. Spinster] 500
Henry Child & Wife 500
Thomas Saunders [Sanders of Illmore, Bucks] 500
John Kirkton [Kirton of Kensington] 500
Richard Kemming [Heming of Middlesex, malster] 250
Robert Jones [of Cholesbury, Bucks, malster] 500
John Greary [Geary, Jr. of Dunsley, Parish of Tring,
    Herts. Yeoman] 500
Henry Greary [Geary of Chesham, Bucks.] 500
John King [of Hadbury, Bucks.] 1000
Henry Paxton [Paxson of Bycot House, Parish of Slow,
    County of Oxford] 500
Henry Pawlin 1000
John Martin [of Parish of Millbrook, South'n, Malster] 500
Richard Baker [Barker (?) of Siddleston Abbey, Berks.] 1000
William Ashby [of Hayes, County of Northampton] 500
Robert Dunton 500
William Baker 1000
Thomas Wolff [of "Hartford County"] 250

XXXVII
Richard Amor [of Bucklebury, Berks.] and William Amor 250
Richard Worrell [of Bottomstead, Parish of Hamstead Norris,
    Berks. Maulster] 500
William Bryant and John Wisdom [both of Bucklebury in the
    County of Berks.] 500
Samuel Carpenter [of Bridgetown, Barbados] 5000
Abraham Pascoe [of Cornwall] 1250
William Champin [Campion] 500
Richard Adams [of Upper Hayford, Northamptonshire] 500
Robert Carter 500
A.B. 250

XXXVIII
Thomas Rowland [of Acton, Cheshire] 1000
Vide No. 35 [sic]

XXXIX
Joseph Powell [of Charleton, Cheshire, Husbandman] 250
Jane Lownes 150
John Worrell [of Ore, Berks.] 250
Thomas Cross [of Kingsley, Cheshire, Yeoman] 250
George Pownall [of Lostock in the County of Chester, Yeoman]. 1000
Bartholomew Coppock [of Northwood, Cheshire] 250
Peter Luister [Leicester] 125

	Acres
George Glem [Glen ?]	125
Shadrick Walley [of Bickley, Cheshire, Innholder]	250
John Nixon [Nickson of Pownall, Cheshire]	500
Shadrick Welsh	500
John Clowes [of Gosworth, Cheshire, Yeoman]	1000
William Charley [Chorley]	500
John Peirce	250
William Bostock	500
Joseph Hall	500
James Dicks	250
John Hodgkinson [Hodskin, Hoskins of Frodsham, Cheshire]	250
Thomas Lindsay [Lewsly, Livezey of Norton, Cheshire]	250
John Brooks [Brock of Bramhall, Cheshire]	1000
Charles Pickering [of Holton, Cheshire]	1000
John Brown [of Kingsley, Cheshire]	250
Peter Worrell	125
Thomas Bulkley [of Rumford, Cheshire] & Samuel Bulkley [of Plumbley, Cheshire]	500

XL
Thomas Brassey [of London, Grocer]	5000
John Simcock [of Cheshire, Yeoman]	5000

XLI
John Alsop [of Inquestry, Staffordshire, Yeoman] and Thomas Woolrich [of Shalford, Staffordshire]	3125
William Yardley [of Rushton Spencer, Staffordshire]	500
John Huccok [Heycock in the Parish of Slin, Staffordshire] and Thomas Barrett [of Staffordshire]	875
Joseph Milnor [of Poonall, Cheshire, Blacksmith] and Daniel Milnor [of the same Place]	250
Richard Crosbey [of the Parish of Runcorn, hundred of Bucklow, Northern Division of Cheshire]	1000

XLII
Robert Turner [of Dublin, Ireland, Linen draper]	5000
Joseph Fisher [of Dublin, Yeoman]	5000

XLIII
Samuel Claridge [of Dublin, Merchant]	5000
George Rodgers [Rogers of Cork, Ireland, Merchant]	2500
Francis Rodgers [Rogers of Cork, Merchant]	2500

XLIV
Thomas Holme [of Waterford, Ireland]	5000
George Shore [of Athlone, Ireland, Merchant]	5000

XLV
Solomon Richards Aurthur Perrin John Napper & John Dennison	5000
Thomas Philsher	5000

XLVI
William Sharlow [Shardlow of London, Merchant]	5000

208

	Acres
John Blunston [of Little Hallam, Parish of Ilstone in the County of Derby]	1500
Luke Hanks	500
Michael Blunston [of the County of Derby]	500
Joshua Fenn [Fearne of Ashoner, Derbyshire]	500
Thomas Whitley [Whitbey of Sawle in the County of Derby, Cloath worker]	500
Edmund Cartlidge [of Riddings, Derbyshire]	250
Joseph Potter	250
George Wood	1000
Thomas Worth [of Oxton, Notts.]	250
John Oldham	250
Samuel Bradshaw [of Oxton, Notts.]	500

XLVII

Sarah Fuller	1000
Elizabeth Lovett	250
John Rowland [of Billinghurst, Sussex]	1250
Edward Buckman [of Sussex]	300
Henry Killinbert [Humphrey Killinbeck]	1000
John Bish	1000
A. B.	5500

XLVIII

William Isaac	500
Daniel Smith [of Marlborow, Wilts.]	2000
John Jones [of London, Glover]	500
Daniel Midlescott [Meddlecott of Rattleinghope Salop, Husbandman]	400
Rodger Bork	500
Richard Hunt [of Bramyard, Herts. Chirurgeon]	500
John Sumbers [Sommers]	500
Robert Coomer [Toomer of Worcester, Phisitian]	1000
[The same ?]	2100
William Lloyd [and Abraham Lloyd of Bristol, Merchants]	2000

XLIX

Sir William Petty	5000
Sir Henry Ingoldsby [of Dublin, Ireland]	5000

L

George Evans	5000
The Same	5000

William Penn Proprietary & Governour of Pennsylvania to his trusty & well beloved Friends Thomas Holme, Willm Haige, John Bezer & Nathaniel Allen. These are to authorize you to See the Lotts of Land laid out by Order of my Surveyor General According to the Affixed Catalogue & the first second and third Instructions he has Recev'd to that purpose for which this shall be your sufficient Warrant. Given under my Hand and Seal at Gravesend in the Kingdom of England this one & thirtieth day of the second month [April] in the year one thousand six Hundred Eighty and Two.
/s/ William Penn

APPENDIX

A FINAL NOTE ON DELAWARE SHIPPING

In an effort to identify more passengers to the east bank of the Delaware, during the summer of 1969 Mrs. Balderston examined the port books for Hull for 1678 and '79; for Liverpool for 1680; London for 1675, '77, '79, and '80; and Bristol for 1678, '79, '80, and '81. It should be noted that none of these years are complete, and many whole years are missing. The wool books were sometimes the only extant ones, and these while they identify the master, do not name the ship.

A probable passenger seen shipping effects to New Jersey was: Nathaniel Roper, who went through customs at London 9 August, 1676, on the St. John Nicholas.

Mrs. Balderston was never completely satisfied with the identification of a New England vessel as one of William Penn's 23 ships. She now thinks that the real 23rd was the Grayhound, with Samuel Groome, then later Joseph Wasey, shown as master, which sailed first for New York. Samuel Groome the elder settled in New Jersey. Robert Lawrence loaded for New Jersey on the Grayhound, Jos. Wasey master, on 23 Sept. 1682. Others on this trip were: Joseph Marcy, loaded 11 Sept., and William Dingley who loaded 30 Sept. Francis Plumstead loaded goods on this ship, but did not sail. (The items on the Grayhound will be found in port book E 190/109/1).

Mrs. Balderston notes that Samuel Groome had taken the Globe to Virginia in 1676, and another Samuel Groome, perhaps his father, had sailed to Russia many years earlier.

Albert Cook Myers' Immigration of the Irish Quakers Into Pennsylvania, which contains excerpts from the removal certificates of many Friend's Meetings provides some further data on shipping to the east bank.

Joseph White [son of Samuel] "took ship at Dublin in Ireland for West Jersey in Amerika who after eight weeks, two days Arrived to Elsinburgh" West Jersey 9 Mo. 17, 1681 together with servants as followeth.

"Hugh Middleton whose father was of Lestershire and his mother of Glocestershire.

"Allsoo Mathias bellore (?) his father and mother weere English people.

"31y Hannah Asbury her father an Englishman her mother borne in Ireland".

(From Salem Monthly Meeting records. Note that the time of arrival is only one day different from that of the following Ye Owner's Choice. It seems likely White was on the same ship.)

19 Sept. 1681 from Dublin, the pink Ye Owner's Choice, Thomas Lurting of London, master fell ill and ship taken to the Delaware by the mate John Dagger, arrived the Capes of Delaware 18 Nov. 1681. The passengers were:

Mark Newby, "tallow chandler", Dublin, prob. with wife and children.

William Bates, "carpenter", co. Wicklow, with wife and children.

Thomas Thackara, "stuff maker", Dublin, prob. with wife and children.

George Goldsmith, said to be of "Ballinakill, Queen's Co., Ireland."

Thomas Sharp, "woolstead comber", Dublin.

(Statement written 1718 by Thomas Sharp, in Liber A, Gloucester Co. (N. J.) deeds, p. 98.)

Robert Zane of Dublin, "sergemaker", probably came with Fenwick's party since in 1675 he was a member of the Salem Monthly Meeting. No date of arrival seen.

INDEX OF VESSELS

INDEX OF NAMES

NOTE: All names with the Welsh patronymic "ap" (ab) have been grouped together under "Welsh names"

BERRY (Bury), William, 48, 61
BERWICK, Hannah, 83
BESTITRASER, Richard, 166
BETHELL, John, 183
BETTRIS, Edward, 202
BEVAN, Barbara (—), 94
  John, 94, 99
BEWSIE, William, 171
BEZER (Beazer), Ann (—), 93
  Edward, 93, 202
  Edward, Jr., 93
  Elizabeth, 32
  Elizabeth (Whitehead), 85
  Frances, 32
  John, 32, 33, 60, 63, 93, 202,
    204, 208
  John, Jr., 85
  Richard, 32
  Sarah (Coole), 93
  Susanna, 32
  Susanna (—), 32
  William, 93, 203
BICKERSTAFF, Sarah, 56
BIDDLE, William, 146
BIDDULPH, William, 144
BILES, Charles, 145, 170
  Elizabeth, 145, 169
  George, 145, 169
  Joanna, 112
  Johannah, 145, 169
  Johannah (—), 145, 169
  John, 145, 169
  Mary, 169
  Rebecka, 169
  William, 145, 169, 170
  William, Jr., 145
BILLINGE, Edward, 36
BINGLEY, William, 202
BINKE, Sarah, 165
BISH, John, 208
BLACK, William, 142, 143
BLACKSHAW, Abraham, 65, 190,
  192
  Alice (Allis)(Burgis), 65, 110,
    171, 190
  Jacob, 65, 171, 190
  Martha, 65, 171, 190
  Mary, 65, 171, 190
  Nehemiah, 65, 171, 190
  Phoebe, 65, 171, 189, 190

BLACKSHAW, Randle (Randolph or
  Randulph), 46, 64, 65, 110, 171,
  188, 190, 192
  Sarah, 46, 65, 171, 190
BLAKE, Edward, 97, 198
  Hannah (—), 97
  Sarah (—), 97
BLAKER, Catherine, 53
BLANCHARD, Jane, 80
BLEASE (Bliss), Joseph, 114
BLEVIN, Henry, 190
BLIJKERS (Bleickers), Johannes, 96
BLINSTON, Isaac, 35
  Mary, 35
BLISS (see Blease)
BLOMERSE, Marieke, 84
BLUN(S)TON, John, 37, 48, 56, 179,
  183, 208
  Katherine, 56
  Michael, 179, 208
  Sarah, 56
  Sarah (Bickerstaff), 56
BOARE, Joshua(h), 142, 145, 169
  Margaret (—), 145, 169
BOLSHAW, John, 173
BOLTON (see Boulton)
BOM, Abraham, 84
  Agnes (—), 84
  Christian, 84
  Cornelius, 84
BOND, George, 146, 172
  Robert, 64, 170, 189, 190
  Thomas, 64, 170
BONIFOYE, David, 166
BONSALL, Abigail, 117
  Abraham, 185
  Ann, 117
  Benjamin, 184
  Elizabeth, 117
  Enoch, 184, 185
  Joseph, 184
  Mary (Wood), 117
  Obadiah, 117, 183
  Rachel, 117
  Richard, 117, 179
BOOME, Ralph, 97
BOON(E), Andrew, 184
  Hance, 182
  Swan, 182, 184, 185
BOOTH, Deborah, 118, 163

FISHER (ffisher), Margaret (—),
    7, 11, 23
  Margery (Maude), 156, 157
  Martha, 99, 164
  Mary, 99, 164
  Moses, 99, 164
  Thomas, 156, 157, 163, 189
  William, 92
FITZWATER (ffitzwater), George,
    5, 7, 11, 23, 58, 172
  Josiah, 7, 11, 23, 58, 172
  Mary, 7, 11, 23, 58, 172
  Mary (—), 7, 11, 23, 58, 172
  Thomas, 4, 5, 7, 11, 12, 23, 50,
    58, 172
  Thomas, Jr., 7, 11, 23, 58, 172
FLEETWOOD (ffleetwood), Brian,
    190
  William, 35
FLETCHER, James, 89
  John, 36
FLOWER (fflower), Ann (—), 92
  Daniel, 166
  Elizabeth (—), 92
  Enoch, 92, 203
  Henry, 92
  Seth, 92
FORD (fford), Henry, 165
  Philip, 4, 5, 30, 33, 34, 35, 37, 38,
    39, 49, 58, 59, 103, 197
  Reuben, 93
  Richard, 165
FORDHAM, John, 60
FORFORD, Christopher, 200
FORT, —, 100
FOSTER, Barzilion, 205
  Joseph, 156, 157, 158
FOULKE (Fowke), Ann, 72
  Ellenor, 72
  Ellenor (—), 72
  Henry, 72
  Owen, 72
  Sarah, 72
  Stephen, 72
  Thomas, 140
FOWLER (ffowler), William, 173
FOX (ffox), Elizabeth, 166
  Elizabeth (—), 166
  Francis, 120
  George, 4, 9, 44, 166, 199
  James, 86, 166

FOX (ffox), John, 83, 91, 165, 166
  Justinian, 166
  Richard, 166
  Sarah, 166
  Thomas, 182
FRAME (Freame), Robert, 203
  Thomas, 43, 44
FREELAND, Esther (Willcox), 95
  William, 95
FREEMAN, James, 6, 44
FRENCH (see Tench)
FRETWELL, John, 143
  Peter, 144
FRIEND (ffriend), Richard, 145, 169
FRY, Henry, 166
FUE, Richard, Jr., 202
  Richard, Sr., 202
FULLER, Sarah, 24, 45, 208
FURLEY, Benjamin, 90
FURNACE (Furniss), Daniel, 98, 164
  Henry, 98, 164
  John, 98, 164
  Joseph, 98, 164
  Kath., 98, 164
  Samuel (?), 98
FUTHEY, J. Smith, vii, 90, 91, 93,
    100, 106, 118, 159, 197

G

GABITAS, William, 182
GAMBEL (Gamble), Gideon, 32, 169
GAMMELL, Daniel, 205
GANO, Jane, 72
GARDINER (Gardner), Edward Cary,
    151
  Elizabeth (Walter), 120
  John, 96, 97, 120
  Joseph Ransted, 161
  Salathiel, 150
GARNIER, Isaac, 166
GARRATT (Garret), Samuel (1),
    183, 184
  William, 182, 185
GARRELL, John, 165
GASPER, Thomas, 84
GEDDES, William, 101
GEERE, Elinor, 137
  Ruth, 137
  Zacharia, 137
GERRISH, Thomas, 203
GIBBINS, Henry, 179

HOOD, Thomas, 116, 117, 179
HOOPE(S), Abraham, 200
  Carpenter, 200
  Christian, 100, 162, 172
  Daniel, 100, 162, 172
  Isabell (Iseabel)(—), 100, 162, 172
  Jane (Worrilow), 100
  Joshua (Josuah), 100, 162, 172
  Marg. (Margret), 162, 172
  Mary, 100
HOOPER (Hopper), Robert, 49, 67, 100, 116, 122, 124, 162, 163, 172
HOOTEN (Hooton, Hotten), Thomas, 46, 143
HOPES, John, 166
  Tho., 166
HOPKINS (see Hodgkins)
HOPPER (see Hooper)
HORSMAN, Marmaduke, 143
HORT, John, 199
HOTTEN, John Camden, 66, 101
HOUGH, Francis (ffrancis), 87, 162, 171, 177
  Hannah (—), 109, 172
  John, 47, 87, 109, 111, 172, 173
  Margery (Clowe), 88, 177
  Oliver, 35
  Richard, 87, 88, 109, 162, 171, 177
  Samuel, 88, 162, 171, 177
  Thomas, 109, 173
HOULD (see Howell)
HOULE (Howell), Job, 47, 168, 177
HOULSTON, John, 57
  Martha, 57
HOWELL (see also Houle), Ann, 42
  Hannah, 89, 162
  Jane (Luffe), 93
  John, 89, 162
  Mary (Williamson), 89, 162
  Philip, 93, 97, 105
  Thomas, 47
HUCCOK (see Heycock)
HUDSON, Robt., 175
  Sarah (—), 175
  Thomas, 16, 50, 67, 122, 165, 173, 174, 175
HUES, Charles, 162
HUFF, Peter, 138
HUGHES (Hughs, Hewes), John, 112
  Mary, 106

HULL, —, 96
  Joseph, 173
  William I., 81
HUMPHREY, Anne, 119
  Benjamin, 119
  Daniel, 119
  Elizabeth (—), 119
  Gobeitha, 119
  Humphrey, 119
  Joan (—), 119
  John, 119
  Lidia, 119
  Richard, 119
  Samuel, 119
HUMPHREYS, Daniel, 155
  John, 202
HUMPHRIES, Janet, 100
HUMPHRY, Soloman, 184
HUNT, James, 184
  Richard, 208
HUNTSMAN, Esther, 95
HURST (see Hayhurst), Jon, 163
HUTCHESON, George, 118
HUTCHINGS (Hutchins), Esther, 138
  Roger, 138
  Sarah, 137, 138
HUTCHINSON, George, 142
  Thomas, 49
HUTSON (see Hudson)
HYNCK (see Heycock)

I

INGELO (Ingels), Richard, 7, 12, 23, 57
INGOLDSBY, Henry, Sir, 208
INGRAM, Isaac, 7, 8, 12, 13, 18, 20, 23, 58
IRELAND, Nicholas, 182
IRONMONGER, John, 166
IRVINE, William, 108
ISAAC, William, 208

J

JACKMAN, George, 102
JACKSON, Epharim, 173
  John, 173
  Joseph, 144
  Samuel, 144
  Thomas, 154
JACOBS, James, 104
JACQUES, Thomas, 95

Q

QUARE, Daniel, 197
QUINN, David, 165

R

RADCLIFF(E), James, 64
Richard, 64, 190
RANDALL, Marmaduke, 144
RANSOM(E), James, 79
RAPPE, Gabriel, 84
RATCLIF(F)E, Edward, 165
James, 165
Mary, 165
Rachell, 165
Rebecca, 165
Richard, 165
RAWDEN (Rowden), Elizabeth, 47,
155, 156, 157
John, 157
RAWLE, ffrancis, Jr., 166
ffrancis, Sr., 166
RAYNOLDS, John, 173
READ (Reade), Edward, 41, 44, 67,
122
John (Capt.), 43, 90, 116, 122, 163
REBYE (Retye), John, 203
REED, H. Clay, 35, 86
John, viii, 10, 16, 18, 22, 196, 197
Joseph, 30
REES, ap Edward, 39
Edward, 39
Gwen, 55
Jane, 110
REEVE, Mark, 137, 138
REEVES (Reave), Anne (—), 42
John, 98, 164
Walter, 42
RENNELL, Samuell, 166
REVEL, Thomas, 144
REVELL, Elizabeth, 63
Thomas, 36, 39
REYNOLD (Renault), Ann, 105
REYNOLDS, John, 205
RHYDDERCH, John, 119
RICHARDS, Bridget, 162
Hannah, 162
Jane (—), 36, 43
John, 94, 162
Joseph, 36, 43, 202
Nathaniel, 43

RICHARDS, Philip, 82
Solomon, 207
Susan (—), 162
ap Thomas, 106
RICHARDSON, Francis, 81, 87
John, 30, 37, 52, 88, 145, 162, 171,
177
Joyce (Venables), 88
Richard, 205
Samuel, 91
RIDG(E)WAY, Elizabeth (—), 146,
172
Richard, 146, 172
Thomas, 146, 172
RIGG, Jane, 79
Robert, 79
Samuel, 190
RIGGE, Ambrose, 199
ROACH, Hannah Benner (Mrs. F.
Spencer), vii, viii, 80, 159, 195
ROADES, Adam, 182
John, 184
ROBERT, John, 106
ROBERTS, Charles, 159
Clarence V., 37, 56, 117
Edward, 100, 105
Ellin, 105
Gainor (Gaynor), 105, 107
Hugh, 100, 104, 105, 106, 107
Jane (—), 105
John, 105, 107, 119, 166, 169
Jonathan, 105
Katherine, 107
Owen, 105
Robert, 105
Susanna (Painter), 100
William, 105
ROBERTSON, William, 99, 164
ROBINET(T), Allen, 205
Samuel, 40
ROBINSON, Catherine (Hollingsworth),
62
George, 62
John, 100, 165
Katherine, 165
Patrick, 102
ROBOTHAM (Robothan), Anne, 87,
162
ROCHFORD, Dennis, 4, 5, 7, 12, 13,
15, 16, 23, 24, 57, 59, 164
Grace, 7, 16, 57, 164

Made in the USA
Middletown, DE
18 July 2017

Passengers and Ships Prior to 1684

Volume 1
of
Penn's Colony

Genealogical and Historical Materials
Relating to the Settlement of Pennsylvania

Walter Lee Sheppard, Jr.

This is the definitive work on early passenger lists to the Delaware River. The volume contains reprints, reprints with corrections and additions, and original articles pertaining to shipping and passengers arriving during the first years of the founding of Pennsylvania. While the bulk of the material is concerned with immigrants to the western (Pennsylvania) shore, several articles deal with immigrants to the eastern (New Jersey) shore. Two maps show landowners in Dalby Township in 1683 and lot owners in Philadelphia in 1684. Separate indices to ships and people add to the value of this work.

U.S.A. $26.00
S0664

ISBN 1-55613-664-1

52600>

9 781556 136641

www.HeritageBooks.com